Shanghai

Bradley Mayhew

LONELY PLANET PUBLICATIONS
Melbourne • Oakland • London • Paris

Shanghai
1st edition – January 2001

Published by
Lonely Planet Publications Pty Ltd ABN 36 005 607 983
90 Maribyrnong St, Footscray, Victoria 3011, Australia

Lonely Planet Offices
Australia Locked Bag 1, Footscray, Victoria 3011
USA 150 Linden St, Oakland, CA 94607
UK 10a Spring Place, London NW5 3BH
France 1 rue du Dahomey, 75011 Paris

Photographs
All of the images in this guide are available for licensing from
Lonely Planet Images.
email: lpi@lonelyplanet.com.au

Front cover photograph
Cleaning windows has become an increasingly dangerous profession
in high-rise Pudong (Bradley Mayhew)

Map section title photograph
Nanjing Dong Lu or Nanjing Road as seen at night with hordes of
shoppers (Chris Mellor)

ISBN 0 86442 507 4

text & maps © Lonely Planet 2001
photos © photographers as indicated 2001

Printed by Colorcraft Ltd, Hong Kong

Although the authors
and Lonely Planet try
to make the informa‐
tion as accurate as
possible, we accept
no responsibility for
any loss, injury or
inconvenience sus‐
tained by anyone
using this book.

Contents – Text

Contents – Maps

THE BUND

EXCURSIONS

COLOUR MAPS   see back pages

MAP LEGEND   back page

The Author

Bradley Mayhew

Bradley started travelling in South-West China, Tibet and northern Pakistan while studying Chinese at Oxford University. Upon graduation he fled to Central America for six months to forget his Chinese and now regularly travels to China's borderlands in a futile attempt to get it back. He is also the co-author of LP's *Pakistan*, *Karakorum Highway*, *Tibet*, *South-West China*, *Mongolia* and *Central Asia* guides.

Bradley is also the co-author and photographer of the Odyssey Guide to Uzbekistan, and has lectured on Central Asia at the Royal Geographical Society. He splits his time between Sevenoaks in south-east England and obscure parts of Montana, USA.

FROM THE AUTHOR

Many thanks to Mark, Arthur and Shelly of *That's* (Shanghai) for providing leads and laughs. Best wishes to you all. Tess Johnston was generous with her time, knowledge and her extensive collection of books. Thanks also to Marie Cambon for a great apartment and to Dan Fox of Research International for lots of great restaurant leads. The Shanghai Municipal Tourism department kindly helped out with reference materials.

The following are readers letters we found most useful: Luis Moreton Achsel, Sam Andrew, Alessandro Arduino, Jens Behrens, Asbjorn Berge, Phil Billingsly, Peter Boers, David Boyall, Rudiger Breuer, Joerund Buen, Tony Burgess, Yiqun Chen, Michelle Chow, Adrian Coppel, Andrew Correia, Robin Deal, Cordelia Dickinson, Simon Evans, Gerard Ferlin, Paul Gaylard, Ep Heuvelink, Tasneem Hussain, Llion Iwan, Tricia Jacobson, Jeremy Keays, Jo-Ann Lim, Fabrice Mathieu, Rob Minnee, Viveca Moritz, Captain Brian Naomi, Deirde O'Neill, Blanca Oplatek, Wilma O'Sullivan, Justin Reed, Alison Rigby, Dr Jerry Schwartz, Antoine Seillan, Tang Meng Shen, M D Tinker, Cate Turk, Carla Van Diest, Rolf Walther, Kristyn Wilson, Chad Yoneda, Anson Yu.

This Book

From the Publisher

This first edition of Shanghai was produced in Melbourne by Lucy Williams (editorial) and Corie Waddell (mapping and design). Kim Hutchins proofed the text and Tim Uden guided us through layout. Maria Vallianos designed the cover; Quentin Frayne wrote the language chapter; and Kelli Hamblett Mick Weldon executed the wonderful illustrations and Martin Harris drew the great chapter end.

Thankyou to Tim Fitzgerald, Martin Heng and Jocelyn Harewood for their advice and assistance and to Tim F and Jocelyn for the artwork check; to Kusnandar for the climate chart; to Leonie Mugavin for her help with travel info; and to Charles Qin for his Chinese-language expertise.

Foreword

ABOUT LONELY PLANET GUIDEBOOKS

The story begins with a classic travel adventure: Tony and Maureen Wheeler's 1972 journey across Europe and Asia to Australia. Useful information about the overland trail did not exist at that time, so Tony and Maureen published the first Lonely Planet guidebook to meet a growing need.

From a kitchen table, then from a tiny office in Melbourne (Australia), Lonely Planet has become the largest independent travel publisher in the world, an international company with offices in Melbourne, Oakland (USA), London (UK) and Paris (France).

Today Lonely Planet guidebooks cover the globe. There is an ever-growing list of books and there's information in a variety of forms and media. Some things haven't changed. The main aim is still to help make it possible for adventurous travellers to get out there – to explore and better understand the world.

At Lonely Planet we believe travellers can make a positive contribution to the countries they visit – if they respect their host communities and spend their money wisely. Since 1986 a percentage of the income from each book has been donated to aid projects and human rights campaigns.

Updates Lonely Planet thoroughly updates each guidebook as often as possible. This usually means there are around two years between editions, although for more unusual or more stable destinations the gap can be longer. Check the imprint page (following the colour map at the beginning of the book) for publication dates.

Between editions up-to-date information is available in two free newsletters – the paper *Planet Talk* and email *Comet* (to subscribe, contact any Lonely Planet office) – and on our Web site at www.lonelyplanet.com. The *Upgrades* section of the Web site covers a number of important and volatile destinations and is regularly updated by Lonely Planet authors. *Scoop* covers news and current affairs relevant to travellers. And, lastly, the *Thorn Tree* bulletin board and *Postcards* section of the site carry unverified, but fascinating, reports from travellers.

Correspondence The process of creating new editions begins with the letters, postcards and emails received from travellers. This correspondence often includes suggestions, criticisms and comments about the current editions. Interesting excerpts are immediately passed on via newsletters and the Web site, and everything goes to our authors to be verified when they're researching on the road. We're keen to get more feedback from organisations or individuals who represent communities visited by travellers.

Lonely Planet gathers information for everyone who's curious about the planet – and especially for those who explore it first-hand. Through guidebooks, phrasebooks, activity guides, maps, literature, newsletters, image library, TV series and Web site we act as an information exchange for a worldwide community of travellers.

Research Authors aim to gather sufficient practical information to enable travellers to make informed choices and to make the mechanics of a journey run smoothly. They also research historical and cultural background to help enrich the travel experience and allow travellers to understand and respond appropriately to cultural and environmental issues.

Authors don't stay in every hotel because that would mean spending a couple of months in each medium-sized city and, no, they don't eat at every restaurant because that would mean stretching belts beyond capacity. They do visit hotels and restaurants to check standards and prices, but feedback based on readers' direct experiences can be very helpful.

Many of our authors work undercover, others aren't so secretive. None of them accept freebies in exchange for positive write-ups. And none of our guidebooks contain any advertising.

Production Authors submit their raw manuscripts and maps to offices in Australia, USA, UK or France. Editors and cartographers – all experienced travellers themselves – then begin the process of assembling the pieces. When the book finally hits the shops, some things are already out of date, we start getting feedback from readers and the process begins again …

WARNING & REQUEST

Things change – prices go up, schedules change, good places go bad and bad places go bankrupt – nothing stays the same. So, if you find things better or worse, recently opened or long since closed, please tell us and help make the next edition even more accurate and useful. We genuinely value all the feedback we receive. Julie Young coordinates a well travelled team that reads and acknowledges every letter, postcard and email and ensures that every morsel of information finds its way to the appropriate authors, editors and cartographers for verification.

Everyone who writes to us will find their name in the next edition of the appropriate guidebook. They will also receive the latest issue of *Planet Talk*, our quarterly printed newsletter, or *Comet*, our monthly email newsletter. Subscriptions to both newsletters are free. The very best contributions will be rewarded with a free guidebook.

Excerpts from your correspondence may appear in new editions of Lonely Planet guidebooks, the Lonely Planet Web site, *Planet Talk* or *Comet*, so please let us know if you *don't* want your letter published or your name acknowledged.

Send all correspondence to the Lonely Planet office closest to you:

Australia: Locked Bag 1, Footscray, Victoria 3011
USA: 150 Linden St, Oakland, CA 94607
UK: 10A Spring Place, London NW5 3BH
France: 1 rue du Dahomey, 75011 Paris

Or email us at: talk2us@lonelyplanet.com.au.

For news, views and updates see our Web site: www.lonelyplanet.com

HOW TO USE A LONELY PLANET GUIDEBOOK

The best way to use a Lonely Planet guidebook is any way you choose. At Lonely Planet we believe the most memorable travel experiences are often those that are unexpected, and the finest discoveries are those you make yourself. Guidebooks are not intended to be used as if they provide a detailed set of infallible instructions!

Contents All Lonely Planet guidebooks follow roughly the same format. The Facts about the Destination chapters or sections give background information ranging from history to weather. Facts for the Visitor gives practical information on issues like visas and health. Getting There & Away gives a brief starting point for researching travel to and from the destination. Getting Around gives an overview of the transport options when you arrive.

The peculiar demands of each destination determine how subsequent chapters are broken up, but some things remain constant. We always start with background, then proceed to sights, places to stay, places to eat, entertainment, getting there and away, and getting around information – in that order.

Heading Hierarchy Lonely Planet headings are used in a strict hierarchical structure that can be visualised as a set of Russian dolls. Each heading (and its following text) is encompassed by any preceding heading that is higher on the hierarchical ladder.

Entry Points We do not assume guidebooks will be read from beginning to end, but that people will dip into them. The traditional entry points are the list of contents and the index. In addition, however, some books have a complete list of maps and an index map illustrating map coverage.

There may also be a colour map that shows highlights. These highlights are dealt with in greater detail in the Facts for the Visitor chapter, along with planning questions and suggested itineraries. Each chapter covering a geographical region usually begins with a locator map and another list of highlights. Once you find something of interest in a list of highlights, turn to the index.

Maps Maps play a crucial role in Lonely Planet guidebooks and include a huge amount of information. A legend is printed on the back page. We seek to have complete consistency between maps and text, and to have every important place in the text captured on a map. Map key numbers usually start in the top left corner.

Although inclusion in a guidebook usually implies a recommendation we cannot list every good place. Exclusion does not necessarily imply criticism. In fact there are a number of reasons why we might exclude a place – sometimes it is simply inappropriate to encourage an influx of travellers.

Introduction

Whore of the Orient and Paris of the East; city of quick riches, ill-gotten gains and fortunes lost; the domain of socialites and swindlers, adventurers and drug runners, missionaries, gangsters and pimps, owing more to Marlene Dietrich than Mao Zedong – Shanghai has a history so impregnated with myth that it's hard to decide whether it was once a paradise or an all-encompassing evil.

The foreign powers crashed the party in 1842 and in less than 100 years, Shanghai had swelled beyond its sensibilities and was cut short just as quickly by the communist revolution. It is this short century of Shanghai's history that makes the city appealing and appalling, that has left monuments to ponder, and which the Chinese would rather forget.

Shanghai put away its dancing shoes in 1949. The masses began shuffling to a different tune – the dour strains of Marxist-Leninism and the wail of the factory siren. All through these years of oblivion, the architects of this social experiment firmly wedged one foot against the door on Shanghai's past; until the effort started to

tell. Regarded with suspicion by the communists as a hotbed of Western imperialist influence, the city has for decades played second fiddle to Beijing.

Today the city of Shanghai has reawakened and the government is catching up with a vengeance, heaping millions into the Pudong economic zone and creating a glass-and-steel skyline that rivals the Bund in a face-off between past and future. Shanghai is now the world's largest construction site, evolving at a pace so unmatched by any other Chinese city that even the morning ritual of flinging open one's hotel curtains reveals new facets to the skyline and new sounds on the streets. As with much of China these days, see the city's historical charms while you still can – slabs of old Shanghai are vanishing almost overnight.

As the past is levelled, the future, it seems, is already here. The world's tallest building is on the cards, Shanghai's stylish hotels offer aromatherapy and Web TV, the latest fashion trends hang in minimalist window displays, and entrepreneurs check share prices on the Internet through their mobile phones. This is Shanghai for the 21st century. It's a century that will be dominated by China, and Shanghai is at the driving edge. There's no better place than Shanghai to get a taste of what the world, and indeed the rest of China, can expect from the resurgent People's Republic.

For the visitor, Shanghai is China at its most recognisable and convenient. All the luxuries of China and all the comforts of home can be bought with a credit card. Hotel rooms, guides and train tickets can be booked in advance, restaurants serve up everything from Indian curry to Tex-Mex.

Shanghai is foremost a business city but there is still much of interest to capture the traveller's imagination: the old-world architecture; the excellent shopping; and the excitement and energy of China's most economically, ideologically and socially open city. Moreover, Shanghai is beginning to rival Beijing as China's cultural capital. The Shanghai Museum, Art Museum and Grand Theatre rank among the best in Asia. If the synthetic delights of Shanghai start to pale, Suzhou and Hangzhou are just two of the many places accessible within an hour or two of the city.

As the pulse of this metropolis quickens, its steps are firmer, and at this point we make an apology. A lot of what you read here will have changed by the time you have this book in your hands. But that's the fascination with Shanghai – it is constantly evolving and continually surprising. Each visit yields a unique snapshot of the city; every time you go back it will be different.

Whatever your politics, it's hard not to be impressed by Shanghai. The city has been given a unique opportunity, and the savvy with which locals have grabbed it has many nodding their heads knowingly. Shanghai, it seems, is back – with a vengeance.

Facts about Shanghai

HISTORY
Pre-Shanghai

Though the earliest imperial records date from the Warring States period (453–221 BC) when the western suburbs of Shanghai belonged to the state of Chu, Neolithic discoveries in Songze, Qingpu County, point to the existence of human settlement in the region 5900 years ago.

Up until the 7th century AD Shanghai itself, then known as Shen or Hu Tu, after the local bamboo fishing traps, was an underdeveloped marshland. In fact, most of eastern modern Shanghai didn't exist until the 17th century, when a complex web of canals was built to drain the region. The early settlement of Shanghai grew up at the confluence of the Shanghai River (long since disappeared) and the Huangpu River.

The migration of Chinese fleeing the Mongols from the north during the Sung dynasty (AD 960–1126) boosted the region's population. This, combined with the silting of the Wusong River, brought about the shift of the regional administrative centre from Qinglong to Shanghai, and in 1291 raised the town up to the status of county seat as part of Jiangsu. In 1553 a wall was erected around Shanghai to defend it against Japanese pirates, and in 1685 a customs house was built, reflecting the growth of local trade. By the late 17th century a population of approximately 50,000 was sustained by cotton production, fishing ports, and, due to the city's excellent location at the head of the Yangzi River and its tributaries, trade in silk and tea.

It All Started With a Little Bit of Opium

During the early years of the Qing dynasty (1644–1911) the British East India Company and its later incarnations were quietly trading in the only open port to the west, Canton (now Guangzhou), south of Shanghai. British purchases of tea, silk and porcelain far outweighed Chinese purchases of wool and spices, so in the late 18th century the British decided to balance the books by slipping into India for opium to swap for silver to purchase (with a profit) Chinese goods. As the British passion for tea increased so did China's craving for opium. By 1823 the British were swapping roughly 7000 chests of opium annually – with about 140 pounds of opium per chest, enough to supply one million addicts – compared with 1000 chests in 1773.

In 1825 Emperor Daoguang's census revealed the amount of silver going to the West for Indian opium and, fearing a crippling economy, he appointed Lin Zexu (Commissioner Lin, as he was known to the English) to stop the opium trade. As tensions came to a head in 1839, British merchants were arrested and forced to watch as three million pounds of raw opium were flushed out to sea. Merchants began demanding compensation from the British government. After much negotiation the British gained modified rights to Hong Kong, as well as US$6 million in reparations, but both China and Britain were unhappy with the agreement. In June 1842 the British fleet sailed into the mouth of the Yangzi and took the Wusong Fort, at the mouth of the Huangpu, in a day. Scaling the walls of Shanghai's Old Town, they met with little resistance, and went on to take the greater prize of Nanjing. On August 29 1842 Sir Henry Pottinger signed the Treaty of Nanjing aboard the *Cornwallis* upon the Yangzi River, and China's doors were prised open.

The Illegitimate Birth of Shanghai

The Treaty of Nanjing stipulated, among other things: peace between China and Britain; security and protection of British persons and property; the opening of Canton, Fuzhou, Xiamen, Ningbo and Shanghai; as well as permission of residence for foreigners and consulates in those cities (for the purpose of trade); fair import and export tariffs; the possession of Hong Kong, and an indemnity of US$18 million. Strangely enough, the trade of opium, legal or otherwise, never entered into the treaty.

Other countries soon followed suit. In July 1844 the Americans adopted the Treaty of Wanghia, which gained them much the same rights as the British and gave US missionaries the right to construct hospitals, churches and cemeteries. Two months later the French took advantage of the existing community of French Jesuits to draw up a similar treaty. In 1843 the first British consul moved into a local house in the old town, marking a foreign presence in the city that would last for the next 100 years.

Of the five port cities, Shanghai was the most prosperous due to its superb geographical location, low interference from the Chinese government, and a capitalistic edge. Trade and businesses boomed in Shanghai and by 1850 the foreign settlements housed more than 100 merchants, missionaries and physicians, three quarters of them British. In 1844, 44 foreign ships made regular trade with China. By 1849, 133 ships lined her shores and by 1855, 437 foreign ships clogged her ports.

Foreigners were divided into three concessions. The original British Concession more than tripled its size between 1846 and 1848. Bishop William Boone set up a mission in Hangkou a few years later, which founded the city's American Concession, and the French set up their own settlement, known as the French Concession, in 1849. In 1863 the British and Americans merged into a cosy enclave still known as the International Settlement.

The Municipal Council, the members of which were voted on by the business elite, was set up in 1854 to control the British Concession and later the International Settlement, while the French Consul-General ran the French *Conseil d'Administration Municipale*. From regulation to sanitation, everything in Shanghai was vested in these foreign oligarchies, a pattern that was to last as long as the settlements. It was not until the early 1920s that Chinese and Japanese (eventually the two largest groups in the settlements) were allowed limited representation on the council.

From the start Shanghai's *raison d'être* was trade. Still sailing to the West were silks, tea and porcelain, and 30,000 chests of opium were being delivered into China annually. Soon great Hong Kong trading houses like Butterfield & Swire and Jardine Matheson & Co set up shop, and trade in opium, silk and tea gradually shifted to textiles, real estate, banking, insurance and shipping. Banks in particular boomed; soon all of China's loans, debts and indemnity payments were funnelled through Shanghai. Buying and selling was handled by Chinese middlemen known as compradors (from the Portuguese) from Canton and Ningbo who formed a rare link between the Chinese and foreign worlds. The city attracted immigrants and entrepreneurs from China, and overseas capital and expertise pooled in the burgeoning metropolis.

Gradually sedan chairs and single-wheeled carts gave way to rickshaws and carriages, the former imported from Japan in 1874. Shanghai lurched into the modern age with gaslights (1865), electricity (1882), motorcars (1895) and the electric tram (1908).

The Manchu gave only cursory glances to the development in Shanghai as all eyes focused on the continued survival of the Qing dynasty.

Shanghai's Rebellious Youth

Drenched in opium, sucked dry by local militia, crippled by taxes, and bullied by foreign interests, Shanghai's population was stirring and rebellions began to erupt of an anti-Manchu nature. The first major rebellion to affect Shanghai was the Taiping, led by Hong Xiuquan. Hong Xiuquan was a failed scholar who claimed to have ascended to heaven and been given a new set of internal organs by a golden-bearded Jehova, which he used to battle the evil spirits of the world with his elder brother Jesus Christ. The rebels burst out of Jintian village in 1851, swept through Guizhou and ended up taking Nanjing three years later.

An offshoot of the Taipings, the Small Swords Society (Xiǎodāo Huì) entered the Chinese section of Shanghai in 1853 and held it for 18 months before being besieged in the Old Town and then expelled by Manchu and French forces. Fearing the seizure of Shanghai, the foreign residents organised the Shanghai Volunteer Corps, a force that would repeatedly protect the interests of foreigners in Shanghai.

The Taipings threatened again in 1860 but were beaten back from Shanghai by the mercenary armies of Frederick Townsend Ward, an American adventurer hired by the Qing government who was eventually killed in Songjiang in 1862. The British joined with Qing forces to defeat the rebels, the Europeans preferring to deal with a corrupt and weak Qing government than with a powerful, united China governed by the Taipings.

As rebellions ravaged the countryside hundreds of thousands of refugees poured into the safety of Shanghai's concessions, setting up home alongside the foreigners, sparking a real-estate boom that spurred on Shanghai's rapid urbanisation and made the fortunes of many of Shanghai's entrepreneurs.

As imperial control loosened, the encroaching Western powers moved in to pick off China's colonial 'possessions' in Indo-China and Korea. National humiliation led to the Boxer Rebellion, which was eventually quelled in 1898 by a combined British, US, French, Japanese and Russian force of 20,000 troops. As a result massive indemnities were strapped on the Qing government. The weakened state of the country, the death of the empress dowager, and the legion of conspiring secret societies marked the end of the tottering Qing dynasty. In 1911 representatives from 17 provinces throughout China gathered in Nanjing to establish the Provisional Republican Government of China.

Insular Shanghai carried out business as usual, unaffected by the fall of the Qing or by WWI. In 1912 the modernising republicans pulled down Shanghai's ancient city walls. As the rest of China fragmented and plunged into darkness, Shanghai emerged as a modern industrial city.

The Big City

By the first decade of the 20th century Shanghai's population had swelled to one million. As the elite and most cosmopolitan of China's cities, Shanghai attracted capitalists and intellectuals alike, and literature and cinema thrived in the ferment as intellectuals began to ponder the fate of a modern China.

The foreigners had effectively plucked out prime locations and, using their ever-increasing wealth, the result of cheap labour, established exclusive communities designed after their own countries and desirable to their needs.

Exploited in workhouse conditions, crippled by hunger and poverty, sold into slavery, and excluded from the city's high life created by the foreigners, the poor of Shanghai had a voracious appetite for radical opinion. Intellectuals and students, provoked by the startling inequalities between rich and poor, were perfect receptacles for the many outside influences circulating in the concessions. The Communist Manifesto was translated into Chinese and swiftly became a hot topic in secret societies. In light of the intense dislike that many Chinese felt for foreigners it seems ironic that fundamental ideals stemmed from overseas inspirations. The first meeting of the Chinese Communist Party (CCP), formed by Marxist groups advised by the Soviet Comintern, took place in Shanghai in 1921. Shanghai, with its large proletariat (30,000 textile

Shanghai'ed

If New York is so good they named it twice, then Shanghai was so bad they made it a verb. To Shanghai, or 'render insensible by drugs or opium, and ship on a vessel wanting hands', dates from the habit of press-ganging sailors. Men, many of whom were found drunk in 'Blood Alley' (off modern-day Jinling Lu), were forced onto ships, which then set sail, leaving the comatose sailors no choice but to make up the deficient crew numbers when they sobered up.

Shanghai's Russians

In the 1920s and '30s, as China's youth looked to revolutionary Russia for their future, 25,000 White Russians fled for their lives, travelling first to Siberia or Central Asia and then along the railroads to China. Many congregated in Manchuria before being pushed on to Shanghai by the Sino-Japanese War. By 1935 they formed the city's second-largest foreign community after the Japanese.

The refugees scraped the highest rungs of Tsarist society, from generals and aristocrats to poets and princesses. All had to find a way to survive. The wealthy sold off their jewellery piece by piece. Moscow's musicians played in Shanghai's hotel bands, and ballerinas from St Petersburg quickly learned how to charge by the dance. The men took whatever jobs they could find: as riding instructors or, more commonly, bodyguards, guarding the wealthy against rival gangs and kidnapping.

Huaihai Lu became the heart of the White Russian community, and was lined with Cyrillic signs and cafes serving Shanghai borscht and black bread. There were Russian cinemas, printing presses and even rival revolutionary and Tsarist newspapers.

Yet beneath the glamour was deep despair and poverty. White Russians were stateless and so, unlike other foreigners in Shanghai, were subject to Chinese laws and prisons. Those without money or skills took the city's lowest jobs, or resorted to begging for alms from the Chinese. Others became prostitutes or ended up as drunks lying in street corners. The British looked down on the Russians, believing they 'lowered the tone', but used the men ('real tough nuts') in the Volunteer Corps.

In 1949 the Russians were forced to flee their second communist revolution in 22 years. There are few signs of Mother Russia in Shanghai these days, save for the original Russian embassy, a couple of empty Russian churches, and the odd Russian cabaret act flirting with the ghosts of the past.

workers alone) and student population, had become the communists' hope for revolution, but elsewhere political violence was growing.

In May 1925 resentment spilled over when a Chinese worker was killed in a clash with a Japanese mill manager. In the ensuing demonstrations the British opened fire and nine Chinese were killed. In protest, 150,000 workers went on strike in what later became known as the May movement /massacre, later seen as a defining moment marking the decline of Western prestige and power.

In 1927 Chiang Kaishek launched his Northern Expedition in an attempt to unite various warlords under a Kuomintang-communist alliance. As the Kuomintang marched on Shanghai 20,000 Volunteer Corps troops surrounded the settlements with barbed wire. Strikes and a curfew paralysed the city as the Kuomintang (with the help of communist supporters under Zhou Enlai) wrested Shanghai from the Chinese warlord Sun Chaofang.

Kaishek's aim was not focused on the settlements or even the warlords, but rather his erstwhile allies, the communists, who he then betrayed in an act of breathtaking perfidy. Backed by Shanghai bankers and armed by Shanghai's top gangster Du Yuesheng, Chiang Kaishek armed gangsters, suited them up in Kuomintang uniforms and launched a surprise attack on the striking workers' militia. Du's machine guns were turned on 100,000 workers taking to the streets, killing as many as 5000. In the ensuing period, known as the White Terror, 12,000 communists were executed in three weeks. Zhou Enlai and other communists fled to Wuhan, leaving Shanghai in the hands of the warlords, the wealthy and the Kuomintang.

Nestled safely in a world of selectively structured law and unadulterated capitalism, by the 1930s Shanghai had slammed to the top and was soon to begin its fatal downwards slide. Shanghai had become a modern city equipped with Art-Deco cinemas and apartment blocks, the hottest bands, and the latest fashions – a place of

Green Gang Gangsters

In Shanghai's climate of hedonist freedoms, political ambiguities and capitalist free-for-all, it was perhaps inevitable that Shanghai should raise China's most powerful mobsters. Ironically, in 1930s Shanghai the most binding laws were those of the underworld, with their blood oaths, secret signals and strict code of honour. China's modern-day triads and Snakeheads owe much of their form to their Shanghainese predecessors.

One of Shanghai's early gangsters was Huang Jinrong, or 'Pockmarked' Huang, who had the enviable position of being the most powerful gangster in Shanghai, while at the same time holding the highest rank in the French Concession police force.

Another famous underworld figure was Cassia Ma, the Night Soil Queen, who founded a huge empire on the collection of human waste, which was ferried upriver to be sold as fertiliser at a large profit.

The real godfather of the Shanghai underworld, however, was Du Yuesheng, or 'Big-Eared' Du as he was known to anyone brave enough to say it to his face. Born in Pudong, Du soon moved across the river and was recruited into the Green Gang *(qīngpāng)*, where he worked for Huang Jinrong. He gained fame by setting up an early opium cartel with the rival Red Gang and rose through the ranks. By 1927 Du was the head of the Green Gang and in control of the city's prostitution, drug running, protection and labour rackets. Du's special genius was to kidnap the rich and then to negotiate their release, taking half of the ransom money as commission. With an estimated 20,000 men at his beck and call, Du travelled everywhere in a bulletproof sedan like a Chinese Al Capone, protected by armed bodyguards crouched on the running boards.

His control of the labour rackets led to contacts with warlords and politicians. In 1927 Du played a major part in Chiang Kaishek's anti-communist massacre and later became adviser to the Kuomintang. A fervent nationalist, his money supplied the anti-Japanese resistance movement.

Yet Du always seemed to crave respectability. In 1931 he was elected to the Municipal Council and was known for years as the unofficial mayor of Shanghai. He became a Christian halfway through his life and somehow ended up best known as a philanthropist. When the British poet WH Auden visited Shanghai in 1937 Du was head of the Chinese Red Cross!

During the Japanese invasion of Shanghai Du fled to the city of Chongqing (Chungking). After the war he settled in Hong Kong, where he died, a multi-millionaire, in 1951.

great energy where 'two cultures met and neither prevailed'. Chinese magazines carried ads for Quaker Oats, Colgate and Kodak, while Chinese girls, dressed in traditional *qipaos* (Chinese-style dresses), advertised American cigarettes. Shanghai's modernity was symbolised by the Bund, Shanghai's Wall Street, a place of feverish trading and an unabashed playground for Western business sophisticates. To this day it remains the city's most eloquent reminder that Shanghai is a very foreign invention.

Earning such labels as 'Paris of the East' and 'Whore of the Orient', the city became an exotic port of call. Flush with foreign cash and requiring neither visa nor passport for entrance, Shanghai became home to the movers and the shakers, the down-and-out and on-the-run. It offered a place of refuge and a fresh start; everyone who came to Shanghai, it was said, had something to hide.

By 1934 the world's fifth-largest city was home to the tallest buildings in Asia, boasting more cars in one city than the whole of China put together, and providing a haven for more than 70,000 foreigners among a population of three million. The city had become three times as crowded as London and the cosmopolitan mix of people was unequalled anywhere in the world. Between 1931 and 1941 20,000 Jews took refuge in Shanghai, only to be forced into Japanese war ghettos, and to flee again in 1949. By 1935, 25,000 White Russians had flocked to Shanghai, turning the French Concession into Little Moscow. In 1895 the Japanese had gained treaty rights and by 1915 had become Shanghai's largest non-Chinese group, turning Hongkou into a de facto Japanese Concession.

The Death of Old Shanghai

In 1931 the Japanese invaded Manchuria and Shanghai's Chinese reacted with a boycott of Japanese goods. Two Japanese were killed in scuffles as anti-Japanese sentiment grew and the Japanese seized the opportunity to protect their interests. Warships brought 20,000 Japanese troops, who proceeded to take on the ragtag Chinese 19th Route army. As Japanese bombers razed Zhapei to the ground 600,000 Chinese refugees fled into the protected International Settlement. After a month of fighting, Zhapei was in ruins and 14,000 lay dead.

By 1937 Sino-Japanese tensions had grown into a full-scale war. Chiang Kaishek took a rare stand in Shanghai and the city bled for it. The Japanese lost 40,000 men, the Chinese anywhere from 100,000 to 250,000. On 14 August, a date that became known as Bloody Saturday, bombs fell onto the foreign concessions for the first time, killing more than 2000 in separate explosions at the Bund, the Palace Hotel, Great World and Nanjing Lu. Even today it is unclear whether the bombings were a tragic mistake by short-sighted Chinese pilots or a cynical ploy by Chiang Kaishek to drag Western powers into the war. Either way, most foreign residents reacted not by fighting, as they would have done for a colony, but by evacuation. Four million Chinese refugees were not so lucky.

Under Japanese rule the easy glamour of Shanghai's heyday was replaced by a dark cloud of political assassinations, abduction, gun running and fear. Espionage by the Japanese, the nationalists, the British and the Americans for wartime information was rife. The rich were abducted and fleeced. Japanese racketeers set up opium halls in the so-called Badlands in the western outskirts of the city, and violent gangs ran rabid. The Kuomintang had long since fled to Chongqing, pulling as much of Shanghai's industry with them down the Yangzi as possible.

By December 1941 the hostilities between Japan and the allied powers had intensified abroad, giving the Japanese incentive to take over the foreign settlements in Shanghai. Suspect foreigners were taken off for interrogation and torture in notorious prisons such as the Bridge House. In early 1943 the Japanese rounded up 7600 allied nationals into eight internment camps. The British and American troops had abandoned Shanghai in 1942 to con-

Swinging Shanghai

While the rest of China suffered warlords and famine, the Shanghai elite sipped wine and gin at the Shanghai Club and gambled at the racecourse, all the while surrounded by jazz musicians and Siberian acrobats. If these elite moved in the right circles then life was an endless line of parties, balls and functions, of dinners at the club and tea dances at the Astor. It was a life of imported Oxford marmalade, flannel suits and freshly ironed newspapers, mixed with liberal amounts of blinkered arrogance and open racism.

As word of the good life spread, Shanghai quickly became a place of celebrity, and soon cruise liners began to dock next to foreign gunboats. Noel Coward arrived with 27 pieces of luggage and a gramophone, caught the flu and wrote *Private Lives* at the Cathay (Peace) Hotel. Wallis Simpson lived here with her naval officer husband (George V would later abdicate the throne of England in order to marry the divorcee). Bertrand Russell, Bernard Shaw and Charlie Chaplin tripped the light fantastic; Mary Pickford and Douglas Fairbanks created a social stir; Eugene O'Neill had a nervous breakdown; and Josef Von Sternberg toured the city's sleazy side for inspiration before directing *Shanghai Express,* starring Marlene Dietrich.

As Shanghai slid into seediness, the socialites were replaced by arms dealers, hit men, spies, drug runners, gangsters, con men, warlords, revolutionaries, Filippino musicians, metered 'taxi dancing'

girls (prostitutes), 'sing song' hostesses (prostitutes) and prostitutes (reportedly about one in every dozen Chinese women were prostitutes). Shanghai became a byword for exploitation and vice; the home of adventurers and con men, addicts and artists, of all nationalities and occupations, all fleecing each other for goods and services and living on a mixture of credit and bluff. By the late 1930s the party was over and darker days loomed on the horizon.

centrate their energies elsewhere and the British and American governments, unable to overtake the Japanese, signed over their rights of the foreign settlements to Chiang Kaishek in Chongqing in 1943, bringing to a close a century of foreign influence.

In 1945, following the surrender of the Japanese, the Kuomintang took back the city, fusing the International Settlement and French Concession along with the rest of Shanghai into the Nationalist Administration, closing treaty ports and revoking for-

eign trading and self-governing rights. Once released from their internment a few foreigners tried to sweep out their Tudor homes and carry on, but priorities and politics had shifted. The gangs, con men, dignitaries, merchants, and anyone who could, had already made their escape to Hong Kong. Those who remained had to cope with biting inflation of 1100%.

The Kuomintang-communist alliance, temporarily united against the Japanese, had collapsed by 1941 and as the two returned to

Shanghai Vice

Underneath the glitz and glamour of 1930s Shanghai lay a pool of sweat, blood and desperate poverty. In the words of a British resident, Shanghai was violent, disreputable, snobbish, mercenary and corrupt – 'a discredit to all concerned'. 'If God allowed Shanghai to endure', said the missionaries, 'He owed Sodom and Gomorrah an apology'. Others agreed: 'Shanghai is a city of 48-storey skyscrapers built upon 24 layers of hell.'

The city was often a place of horrific cruelty and brutal violence. After the Small Sword Rebellion, 66 heads, even those of elderly women and children, were stuck up on the city walls. In 1927 striking workers were beheaded and their heads put in cages. Up to 80,000 rickshaw pullers worked the littered streets until they dropped while overcrowded factory workers routinely died of lead and mercury poisoning. In 1934 life expectancy of the Chinese in Shanghai stood at 27. In 1937 municipal refuse workers picked up 20,000 corpses off the streets.

Shanghai offered the purely synthetic pleasures of civilisation. Prostitution ran the gamut from the high-class escorts in the clubs of the International Settlement and 'flowers' of the Fuzhou Lu teahouses, to the *yějī*, or 'wild chickens', of Hongkou, who prowled the streets and back alleys. The 'saltwater sisters' from Guangdong specialised in foreigners fresh off the boats. Lists of the city's 100 top-ranking prostitutes were drawn up annually and listed next to the names of 668 brothels, which went by such names as the 'Alley of Concentrated Happiness'.

Prostitution was not the exclusive domain of the Chinese. The traditional roles were reversed when White Russians turned to prostitution and Chinese men could be seen flaunting Western women. An American madam ran The Line, the most famous foreign brothel in town, at 52 Jiangsu Lu.

Linked to prostitution was opium. At the turn of the century Shanghai boasted 1500 opium dens (known locally as 'swallow's nests') and 80 shops openly selling opium. Even some hotels, it is said, supplied heroin on room service, 'served on a tray like afternoon tea'. Opium financed the early British trading houses and most of the buildings on the Bund. Later it funded Chinese gangsters, warlord armies and Kuomintang military expeditions. It was true that the police in the French Concession kept a close eye on the drug trade, but only to ensure that they got a reasonable slice of the profits. Not that there was much they could do even if they had wanted to; it was said that a wanted man in 1930s Shanghai need only pop into the neighbouring concession to avoid a warrant for his arrest.

internal antagonism, China was in the grip of an all-out civil war. By 1948 the Kuomintang was on the edge of defeat and hundreds of thousands of Kuomintang troops joined sides with the communists. In May 1949 Chen Yi led the Red Army troops into Shanghai and by October all the major cities in southern China had fallen to the communists.

In Beijing on 1 October 1949, Mao Zedong stood atop Tiananmen Gate, announced that the Chinese people had stood up, and proclaimed the foundation of the People's Republic of China (PRC). Chiang Kaishek then fled to the island of Formosa (Taiwan), taking with him the entire gold reserves of the country and what was left of his air force and navy, to set up the Republic of China (ROC), naming his new capital Taipei.

The world has lost old Shanghai. No one should think that its passing should be the cause of lamentations. Its presence for a century or more was evidence of oppression, of cruelty and unforgivable discrimination. The foreigners have left the scene of their debauches. Their spirits, I am sure, in ghostly forays must be seeking out the scenes of their earthbound joys – alas, in vain, as the Leninist-Marxist thoughts of Chairman Mao have swept away the last lingering whispers of a hundred years of sensuality.

Ralph Shaw, 1949

The People's Republic

The birth of the PRC marked the end of 105 years of 'the paradise for adventurers'. The PRC dried up 200,000 opium addicts, shut down Shanghai's infamous brothels and re-educated 30,000 prostitutes, eradicated the slums, slowed inflation and eliminated child labour – no easy task. In February 1952, 160,000 workers attended every one of the 3000 meetings held in Shanghai that were designed to denounce the bourgeoisie, with which Shanghai was particularly imbued. The state took over Shanghai's faltering businesses, the racecourse became the obligatory People's Park and Shanghai fell uniformly into the rest of China's modern history. Under Beijing's stern hand, the decadence and splendour faded.

Yet the communists, essentially a peasant regime, remained suspicious of Shanghai. The group lacked the experience necessary to head a big city and they resented Shanghai's former leadership, which they always regarded as a den of foreign imperialist-inspired iniquity, a constant reminder of national humiliation and the former headquarters of Kuomintang.

Perhaps because of this, Shanghai, in its determination to prove communist loyalty, became a hotbed of political extremism and played a major role in the Cultural Revolution, the decade of political turmoil that lasted from 1966 to 1976. Sidelined in Beijing, it was to Shanghai that Mao turned in an attempt to reinvigorate the revolution and claw his way back into power. For most of a decade the city was the power base of the prime movers of the Cultural Revolution, the Gang of Four: Wang Hongwen; Yao Wenyuan (editor of *Shanghai Liberation Army Daily*); Zhang Chunqiao (Shanghai's Director of Propaganda); and Jiang Qing, wife of Mao (and one-time failed Shanghai movie actress known as Lan Ping, who used her position to exact revenge on former colleagues at Shanghai Film Studios). In 1969 the city was also the launch pad for the campaign to criticise Confucius and Mengzi (Mencius), before the campaign spread nationwide in 1973 and was linked to Lin Biao, Mao's former offsider.

Encouraged by Mao, a rally of a million red guards marched through Renmin Square, a force of anarchy that resulted in the ousting of the mayor. Competing Red Guards tried to outdo each other in revolutionary fervour, Shanghainese who had any contacts with foreigners (and who didn't?) were criticised, forced to wear dunce caps, denounced and sometimes killed.

Most extraordinarily, in 1966 a People's Commune, modelled on the Paris Commune of the 19th century, was set up in Shanghai. (The Paris Commune was set up in 1871 and controlled Paris for two months. It planned to introduce socialist reforms such as turning over management of factories to workers' associations.) The Shanghai Commune, headed by Zhang Chunqiao from headquarters in the Peace Hotel, lasted just three weeks before Mao, sensing that the anarchy had gone too far, ordered the army to put an end to it.

As the Cultural Revolution unfolded, between 1966 and 1970, one million of Shanghai's youth were sent to the countryside. Shanghai's industries closed. The Bund was renamed Revolution Boulevard and the road opposite the closed Soviet consulate became Anti-Revisionist St. In the revolutionary chaos and a bid to destroy the 'four olds' (old customs, old habits, old culture and old thinking), the Jing'an Temple was destroyed and the Xujiahui Cathedral desecrated. At one point there was even a plan to change the revolutionary red of the city's traffic lights to mean 'go'.

In 1976, after the death of Mao, the Gang of Four was overthrown and imprisoned. Accused of everything from forging Mao's statements to hindering earthquake relief efforts, the gang's members were arrested on 6 October 1976 and tried in 1980. Jiang Qing remained unrepentant, hurling abuse at her judges and holding famously to the line that she 'was Chairman Mao's dog – whoever he told me to bite, I bit'. Jiang Qing's death sentence was commuted and she lived under house arrest until 1991, when she committed suicide by hanging.

When the Cultural Revolution lost steam, pragmatists like Zhou Enlai began to look for ways to restore normalcy. In 1972 US President Richard Nixon signed the Shanghai Communique at the Jinjiang Hotel. The agreement provided a foundation for increased trade between the USA and China and marked a turning point in China's foreign relations. With the doors of China reopened to the West, and with Deng at the helm, China set a course of pragmatic reforms towards economic reconstruction, resulting in an annual growth of 9% over the next 15 years.

In communist China, however, the rush of economic reform has generated very little in the way of political reform. Corruption and inflation have between them led to widespread social unrest, which in 1989 resulted in the demonstrations in Tiananmen Square.

The demonstrations overtaking Beijing's Tiananmen Square spread to Shanghai. While students and workers demonstrated, students based at Fudan University constructed their own 'statue of liberty'. The city was threatened with martial law and four days after the massacre in Beijing on 4 June, tanks arrived in Shanghai's Renmin Square. Mayor Zhu Rongji handled the situation adeptly and the momentum petered out after a week or so. Recriminations were swift and several demonstrators were publicly shot.

Shanghai Reincarnate

In 1990 the central government began pouring money into Shanghai. By the mid-1990s more than a quarter (some sources say half) of the world's high-rise cranes could be found looming over Shanghai. As the 20th century drew to a close the city had built two metro lines, a light railway system, a US$2-billion airport at Pudong, a US$2-billion elevated highway, several convention centres, two giant bridges, several underground tunnels and a whole new city in Pudong.

The government has declared its aim to make Shanghai the financial centre of Asia. Nothing would satisfy the central government more than for Shanghai to replace Hong Kong as China's frontier of the future,

swinging the spotlight of attention from the ex-colony on to a home-grown success story. The city is still 20 (officially 10) years behind its southern rival but is catching up so fast that it sometimes appears out of breath.

And yet, as fast as Shanghai strides into the future, its past remains oddly familiar. Joint-venture companies are cautiously returning to claim their former offices; foreign-run bars, restaurants and sporting clubs are back; and Westerners are filing back into expat-centric communities in the International Settlement and French Concession. To the Shanghainese, the Shanghai of the 1930s is dead history, but ghostly images of the past continue to haunt the city as it strives to become a financial, cultural and intellectual hotspot and a major city of the 21st century.

GEOGRAPHY

Shanghai owes its life to its port, and its port to its geography. Even the name *shànghǎi*, or 'on the sea', comes from its location. Shanghai is positioned at the confluence of the Wusong and Huangpu Rivers, 20km from the Yangzi River, China's premier waterway and linked to the Grand Canal.

Shanghai municipality covers more than 6340 sq km. This includes the 748 sq km city of Shanghai as well as the surrounding counties and 30 islands of the Yangzi. One of these, Chongming Island, is China's second-largest island (or third-largest, if you recognise Taiwan as part of China). The city consists of 15 districts, ten of which comprise the city centre, and four counties (Nanhui, Qingpu, Fengxiang and Chongming Island), plus the Pudong New Area. The municipality includes the satellite towns of Songjiang, Jiading, Jinshan and Baoshan.

Shanghai is bordered by the province of Jiangsu to the north-west and Zhejiang to the south-west. To the east is the East China Sea and to the south is Hangzhou Bay. The city of Shanghai rests on a delta plain with a dizzying average elevation of 4m above sea level.

CLIMATE

Climate-wise the best times to visit Shanghai are March and April (during spring) and October and November (during autumn). In winter, temperatures can drop well below freezing, with a blanket of chilling drizzle. The coldest month is January. If you are staying in local accommodation prepare to wrap up; Shanghai is designated as *jiāngnán*, or south of the Yangzi (even if it's only 25km south of the Yangzi!), and so buildings are not entitled to central heating. All hotels, of course, have heating.

Summers are hot and humid, with temperatures sometimes as high as 40°C (104°F) in July and August, the two hottest months. Many buses and most hotels have air-con but outside the humidity makes things very uncomfortable.

Shanghai gets 1200mm of rain per year, 60% of which falls between May and September. Mild typhoons (from the Cantonese *tai feng*, meaning 'big wind') occasionally hit Shanghai.

In short, you'll need silk long johns and down jackets for winter, an ice block for each armpit in summer and an umbrella wouldn't go astray in either of these seasons.

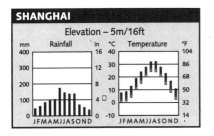

ECOLOGY & ENVIRONMENT

In its grab for wealth, Shanghai thinks it can get rich and clean up later. Conspicuous and unsustainable consumption is the city's major environmental ill.

Shanghai consumes the largest amount of energy per square kilometre in China. Drains carry more than five million tons of industrial waste and untreated sewage into the mouth of the Yangzi each day. Until the 1920s Shanghai got its tap water direct from the Suzhou Creek. Now the river is a fetid cesspool. In fact, all of Shanghai's water as far as the East China Sea is categorised as 'seriously polluted'.

Over-fishing in Dianshan Lake has resulted in a drop in species of fish from 250 to 35. Several chemical works and breweries that pour their effluent straight into the lake worsen the situation. It is feared that the lake could be devoid of life within 10 years.

Shanghai creates 30,000 tons of construction waste each day and finding a place to put it all is a problem. Some goes via a 23.5km pipeline to land reclamation projects in the East China Sea but most simply gets dumped into the suburbs.

Shanghai has one of the worst air qualities in China, after Chongqing, Xining, Xian and Chengdu. Coal briquettes, used by most homes and noodle stalls over the winter, are a major pollutant. Shanghai's restaurants throw away 673 million polystyrene boxes and 1300 million bamboo chopsticks a year.

The government has started to address some problems. A US$6-billion, 15-year environmental plan was unveiled in 1999. A second sewage plant, the largest environmental project ever undertaken, was part of the package. In 1999 the first stage of a US$1-billion cleanup began in Suzhou Creek. The government plans to increase per capita green area from the current 3 sq m to 6 sq m by 2002 and up to 10 sq m by 2020. There have even been early experiments with wind and solar energy in Shanghai.

Shanghai's main parks include the 333-hectare Dongping National Forest Park on Chongming Island. The city limits also hold the Daxiao Jinshan Nature Reserve and Chongming Dongtan Reserve for migratory birds.

FLORA & FAUNA

Shanghai's metropolitan sprawl and the Chinese habit of throwing anything that moves into a wok have meant that there is little flora or fauna left in Shanghai outside of the zoo and the livestock markets.

A preservation zone has been set up at the east end of Chongming Island to protect the Chinese sturgeon, thought to be on the brink of extinction. The Yangzi alligator, one of only two species of freshwater crocodiles in the world, has already disappeared from the Shanghai region, though animals remain upriver in Anhui. Other protected animals in the municipality include the wild duck. It is joked that the most common bird in the city is the crane.

Shanghai's streets are lined with plane trees, and some areas hold pockets of cypress trees. The city flower is the magnolia, which blooms in late March.

GOVERNMENT & POLITICS

Shanghai has always courted extremism in politics and has been a barometer for the mood of the nation. The Chinese Communist Party (CCP) was formed here back in 1921. Mao Zedong cast the first stone of the Cultural Revolution in Shanghai, by publishing in the city's newspapers a piece of political rhetoric he had been unable to get published in Beijing. The Gang of Four had its power base in Shanghai.

The city's influence now ripples through the whole of the Party apparatus to the upper echelons of what has become known as the 'Shanghai Clique': President Jiang Zemin is Shanghai's ex-Party chief and premier Zhu Rongji was the Mayor of Shanghai during the Tiananmen Massacre. Zeng Qinghong was the deputy Party chief of Shanghai under Jiang Zemin and is widely tipped to be the president's eventual successor. Furthermore, Hong Kong's new chief executive, Tung Chee-hwa, is a Shanghai man. Shanghai's current mayor is Xu Kuangdi.

In the 1990s, a little-noticed reform permitted small villages with a population under 10,000 to elect their own leaders. In 1999 two million people in 2900 of Shanghai's surrounding townships cast their votes to elect their village committees in a step which some have hailed as a fledgling movement towards democracy.

Shanghai is one of China's four municipalities (the others being Beijing, Tianjin and Chongqing).

ECONOMY

Making money is in the blood of most Shanghainese. The city is the largest in the world's most populous country, and the economic and trading heart of the world's fastest-growing economy. Shanghai's burgeoning economy, its leadership and intrinsic self-confidence have put it miles ahead of other cities in China. Neither Beijing nor Guangzhou can match the superficial, gilt-edged feel of modernity that covers the city.

Shanghai was left out of China's first round of economic reforms in the 1980s and its economic renaissance dates from 1990, when Shanghai became an autonomous municipality and Pudong was established as a special economic zone. In 1992 Deng Xiaoping gave the seal of approval to Shanghai's redevelopment during his 'southern tour'. Until then 80% of Shanghai's revenue went straight into Beijing's pockets. Economic reforms and restructuring have since boosted Shanghai's GDP, and there has been an increase in foreign investments – the city is now a madhouse of free-market activity. In the mid-1990s an average of five new businesses were set up every hour in Shanghai. From 1992 to 1997 Shanghai experienced an annual growth rate of 13%.

Shanghai owes its economy to its position as a clearing house for the Yangzi River. Chinese like to compare the river to a dragon, with its head at Shanghai and its body coiling through half of China, draining a potential market of 400 million people (10% of the world's population).

Shanghai further enjoys a unique position at the meeting point of both interior and coastal economic development areas. As China's economic spotlight turns increasingly westward, Shanghai is seen as the key to unlocking the hinterland. Economic boosters imagine waves of economic energy shooting up the river into the Yangzi River delta economic zone and the huge cities of Wuhan and Chongqing.

It comes as no surprise, then, that Shanghai is one of the world's ten busiest ports and that Shanghai's Jiangnan shipyard is the largest in China. The focus has shifted from the Huangpu to the Yangzi, specifically

Waigaoqiao, which is being upgraded into a major container port. Yet even this is vulnerable to the silting of the Yangzi and a new deep-water container port is planned in the Yangshan Islands, to be linked to the mainland at Luchaogang by the 30km-long Luyang Bridge, destined to become the longest bridge in the world.

Shanghai is investing heavily in the future. Massive freeway projects, metro lines, light rail systems and the US\$2-billion Pudong airport are testament to the fact that infrastructure investment in Shanghai between 1994 and 1999 was more than triple the total for the previous 35 years! Indications are that this forward planning will circumvent the infrastructure problems that face other Asian cities such as Bangkok, Jakarta and Taipei.

Industry

'Made in Shanghai' has long been a symbol of quality: ranging from Forever bicycles, Hero pens and Seagull cameras to White Rabbit sweets and even Long March space rockets. Recent restructuring has seen the demise of several venerable brands as Shanghai's smaller, loss-making, State-owned industries are sold off or merged to improve efficiency. Shanghai's two largest companies are the giant Baoshan iron and steel works and the Shanghai Automobile Corporation. Perhaps Shanghai's greatest resource is its highly skilled, well-educated and innovative workforce.

The 1999 Fortune 500 summit and the upcoming (October 2001) Asia-Pacific Economic Cooperation (APEC) summit has put Shanghai squarely on the global industrial map. By 2000, 254 Fortune 500 companies had set up offices in Shanghai and there were 17,600 foreign enterprises in operation. Foreign investment peaked at US\$10 billion per year between 1994 to 1996 but levels have since fallen back considerably. Foreign-funded businesses now make up 60% of total imports and exports and the government, keen to keep the cash flowing in, is offering all kinds of incentives. So far the city has collected US\$40 billion, the largest amount of direct foreign investment of any city in the world. Shanghai is consistently voted the best place to invest in China.

Volkswagen is the largest joint-venture operation in Shanghai and also the whole of China. Its plant in Pudong produces more than 50% of all the cars sold in China, including Shanghai's ubiquitous Santana taxis. Buick also has a plant in Shanghai. Both are eyeing Shanghai's burgeoning middle class, 70% of whom state that they would like to buy a car in the next decade.

Tourism, especially domestic, is important to Shanghai. More than 1.6 million overseas tourists (compared with Beijing's 2.4 million) and 79 million domestic tourists net the city around US\$1.15 billion annually. Shanghai authorities know that tourism makes money, so it spends a little bringing the tourists in; a simple logic that is apparently lost on the rest of the country. The travel sector is still tightly state-owned. The massive Jinjiang group owns dozens of Shanghai's top hotels, plus several taxi companies, travel agencies and more.

An important change looming on the city's economic horizon is China's imminent entry into the World Trade Organization (WTO). Entry into the organisation signifies the end of trade restrictions (both China and other countries – so no more favoured-nation status dependent on human

Shanghai's Economic Stats

- **Shanghai's GDP:** US\$45 billion (1998)
- **Per capita GDP:** Y28,253 (US\$3400), the highest in China
- **GDP growth:** around 9.5% (1999) in Shanghai, and more like 16% in Pudong
- **Foreign investment:** US\$5.85 billion in 1999, headed by Hong Kong and the USA, down on the year before
- **Annual exports:** US\$15.64 billion (1999)
- **Average annual salary:** around Y12,000 (US\$1500), ranked third in China after Guangzhou and Shenzhen
- **Inflation:** 4.9% (ie, deflation)

rights) and will open up China's telecommunications, banking and insurance industries, making Shanghai the insurance capital of Asia once again. It also means a rush of foreign goods into China (such as cars; current import tariffs of more than 80% will be slashed) and a flood of Chinese products abroad. China's WTO status will also undermine the kind of economic incentives offered by the government in areas like Pudong. The impact of the agreement will be gradual but will probably sound the death knell for many of China's state companies, which in turn could lead to a surge in China's unemployment rate, already as high as 15% in Shanghai.

Pudong

Shanghai's long economic malaise came to an abrupt end in 1990, with the announcement of plans to develop Pudong on the eastern side of the Huangpu River. Designed by architect Richard Rodgers, Pudong is an economic zone eight times larger than London's Canary Wharf, stretching from the Bund to the East China Sea. It has been variously described as a window, a bridge and a launch pad for companies wishing to get into the near-mythical Chinese market. And it worked. By the end of 1999, US$30 billion had been contractually invested in Pudong and the zone was accounting for 20% of the city's GDP; not bad for a marshland that had nothing but fields and pig farms a decade ago.

The most visible part of Pudong is the skyscraper-filled Liujiazui Financial District, home to China's stock market and the headquarters of most foreign banks. Shanghai's goal is to regain its position as a major financial centre and it plans Liujiazui to be a future Asian Wall Street. Other major investment areas in Pudong include Waigaoqiao, a tax-free foreign trade zone for distribution and processing in the north-east corner; the Zhangjiang hi-tech zone, the centre of China's fledgling biomedicine industry; and the Jinqiao Export and Processing Zone, which houses General Motors, Kodak and Coca-Cola among others.

Shanghai.com

Shanghai is one of China's most wired cities. Add to that a willingness to accept outside ideas and new technologies and a long-proven ability to make money out of anything and it's not hard to see why the city is riding the crest of China's current Internet wave.

China has around 10 million Internet users, and this figure is doubling every six months. By 2005 China will have the largest number of Web surfers, after the US. Already, more than 50,000 Chinese domain names have been registered, advertisements for which are plastered over most of Shanghai's public buses.

Even the government is getting in on the act, announcing a drive to make Shanghai an 'infoport' and pushing e-commerce, while at the same time remaining deeply distrustful of the Internet. China has already tried to control news content on Chinese Web sites: The government requires Web journalists to earn State accreditation and continues to block foreign news sites like the BBC (though not CNN). However, the nebulous nature of the Internet makes it almost impossible to control; close down one site and a parallel one opens within the hour.

As foreign money pours into Chinese Web sites like Netease, Soho and Eachnet (an electronic auction house set up in Shanghai), local entrepreneurs are increasingly seeing the Internet as a way to leapfrog the economic and technological gap between China and the West, to catch up in one electronic 'great leap forward'. Though most housing in Shanghai still has no central heating in winter, several million Shanghainese will soon be able to access the Internet through their mobile phones. It's an information revolution – one that will bring great economic, social and ultimately political change to China – and there's little the government can do about it.

Shanghai's other major hi-tech park is in Caohejing, across the river in Puxi. Other important trade zones are in Minhang, south of the city, and Songjiang, to the north.

Economic Problems

Seen from the river, towering above their couchant guardian warships, the semi-skyscrapers of the Bund present, impressively, the facade of a great city. But it is only a facade.

Christopher Isherwood, 1937

For all the hype about its 'potential market of 1.2 billion', China's economy faces several problems, foremost of which is a growing inequality in what is supposed to be an egalitarian country. Shanghai is now reckoned to be ten times wealthier than the province of Guizhou. Its average annual income of around US$1500 per year is double the national average.

Corruption is a chronic problem; the government itself admits that US$15 billion was embezzled from state coffers in 1999. Moreover, China's banks are loaded with massive bad debts and are technically insolvent. Even China's impressive economic statistics are often exaggerated by up to 30%. For all its capitalist trappings, the state retains a tight control of the economy.

Fuelled by the gushing enthusiasm of both foreign and local propaganda, Shanghai is at times gripped in a hyped-up vision that is in danger of crumpling against the sheer reality of managing a city of this size and complexity. Moreover, the visionaries seem to forget that there is more to a great city than gleaming buildings and metro systems. Public discourse and critique of the economy and its relationship to culture and politics is as lacking in Shanghai today as private telephones were two decades ago.

China's Party chiefs realise that Shanghai's economy is central to China's economy, and that a thriving economy is central to their continued control of the country. When the people question the Party's economic model, it can only be a matter of time before they perhaps also question its political model.

POPULATION & PEOPLE

Shanghai has a population of around 13.4 million people, but that figure is deceptive since it takes into account the whole municipal area of 6340 sq km. Nevertheless, the central core of some 220 sq km has more than 7.5 million people, which must rate as one of the highest population densities in China, if not the world.

Shanghai's target is a population of 16 million people by 2020, with a population of 8 million in the city centre. Shanghai has a very low fertility rate (0.96 births per woman) but this requires a population redistribution out of the city centre and it's already happening at a breathtaking rate. In the late 1990s old housing was being bulldozed at the rate of one million sq m per year and more than 200,000 families were being moved into suburban tower blocks annually.

Shanghai has several noticeable minority populations. Of the city's 50,000 Muslims, the majority are ethnic Chinese Hui Muslims from Gansu, Ningxia and Shaanxi provinces, though there is a small but visible number of Central Asian Uyghurs from Xinjiang. There are also around 40,000 expats (compared with around 70,000 in 1934), though unofficial estimates range between 20,000 and 100,000.

Shanghai also has a huge floating population of rural migrant workers, totalling between two and four million. Most are lured from the surrounding provinces of Jiangsu, Anhui or Sichuan by higher wages but, without local *hùkǒu* (residency permits), they end up living on the fringes of Shanghai society without access to certain jobs, health and housing benefits or even permission to marry.

The Shanghainese have a distinct and stereotyped persona in China. They are generally thought to be brash, uncultured, in love with money, arrogant, shrewd, stylish, motivated, smart, faddish, trendsetting, open to new ideas and quick to catch on. If Beijingers can talk about anything and the Cantonese can eat anything, then, so the saying goes, the Shanghainese can do anything.

EDUCATION

Shanghai has a compulsory nine-year education system and was the first city in China to introduce schooling for ages one to six. The government professes to lay extra

Future Shanghai

Shanghai is Asia's, if not the world's fastest-changing city, which makes it a singularly difficult place about which to write a guidebook. With this in mind, here's our look into Shanghai's crystal ball, taking a wild guess at some of the things that might happen during the lifetime of this book.

Transport will be one of the big changes. The next 20 years will see 11 metro routes and seven light railway lines linking the city centre and Pudong with 11 new satellite cities, all within an hour's commute of Shanghai. Pudong's 22.5km Yanggao Expressway, which currently links up with the elevated inner ring road, will eventually be joined by a light railway line which will swing over the Huangpu River to form a ring around the city. A high-speed rail link to Beijing will cut the trip down to six hours by around 2007. There are also big plans to develop Chongming Island, connecting it to the city via a series of underground tunnels and railway lines.

There is no end in sight to Shanghai's building frenzy. The 280m-high Plaza 66, near the Shanghai Centre on Nanjing Xilu, is due to open at the end of 2002, by which time the adjacent CITIC Square should be well established. Concord Plaza is a new shopping and entertainment complex planned for the junction of Yan'an Xilu and Nanjing Xilu. Raffles Plaza is a huge complex being built opposite the Renmin Square metro station. If all goes well the city will also host the world's tallest building, the World Finance Centre, next to the Jinmao Tower.

stress on life management, teamwork and personality development, as most children are from single-child homes.

Shanghai has some of China's best universities and competition for places is very tight. The largest specialised program in Shanghai is engineering. More than 150,000 students are currently enrolled in university. Masters of Business Administration (MBA) are currently all the rage, though high rollers and people with good connections still prefer to study abroad. The Western-managed China Europe Business School in Pudong was the first of its kind in China.

Jobs for graduates are no longer government-assigned and competition has become intense. In 1996 government financial aid was introduced and unsecured bank loans have been available since 1997. The average tuition for four years of study varies from the equivalent of US$1200 to US$2000.

Shanghai's literacy rate for residents at age 15 stands at 98%. This doesn't, of course, include workers from outside the city limits, though Shanghai has introduced a 'Spark Plan' to encourage adult education.

ARTS
Chinese Opera

Contemporary Chinese theatre, of which the most famous is Beijing opera, has a continuous history of some 900 years, having evolved from a convergence of comic and balladic traditions in the Northern Song period. From this beginning, Chinese opera has been the meeting ground for a disparate range of forms: acrobatics; martial arts; poetic arias; and stylised dance.

There are more than 100 varieties of opera in China today and many are performed in Shanghai. Huju or Shenju is Shanghainese opera: It is performed in the local dialect and has its origins in the folk songs of Pudong. Yueju opera was born in Shaoxing and Shengxian counties of neighbouring Zhejiang (the ancient state of Yue) in the early 20th century. Yueju roles are normally played by women. Kunju opera originates from Kunshan, near Suzhou in nearby Jiangsu.

Operas were usually performed by travelling troupes whose social status was very low in traditional Chinese society. Chinese law forbade mixed-sex performances, forcing actors to act out roles of the opposite sex. Opera troupes were frequently associated with homosexuality in the public imagination, contributing further to their 'untouchable' social status.

Despite this, opera remained a popular form of entertainment, though it was considered unworthy of the attention of the scholar class. Performances were considered an obligatory adjunct to New Year celebrations, local festivals and marriages, and sometimes to funerals and ancestral ceremonies.

Formerly, opera was performed mostly on open-air stages in markets, streets, teahouses or temple courtyards. Described by American writer PJ O'Rourke 'as if a truck full of wind chimes collided with a stack of empty drums during a birdcall contest', the shrill singing and loud percussion were designed to be heard over the public throng.

Opera performances usually take place on a bare stage, with the actors taking on stylised stock characters that are instantly recognisable to the audience. Most stories are derived from classical literature and Chinese mythology and tell of disasters, natural calamities, intrigues or rebellions. The musicians usually sit on the stage in plain clothes and play without written scores.

China's most famous 20th-century opera star was Mei Lanfang, who allegedly performed privately for several of Shanghai's gangland bosses in the 1930s.

Other Theatre

The lower Yangzi region has a long tradition of storytelling, farce, comic talk and mimicking, all of which were traditionally performed in teahouses. Yangzhou, Hanghou and Suzhou all have their own variants. Pingtan balladry is a mix of *pínghuà* (Suzhou-style storytelling) and *táncí* (ballad singing), accompanied by the *pípā* (lute) and *sānxián* (banjo).

Literature

In the 1920s and '30s Shanghai was a publishing industry hub and home to a vibrant literary scene. Protected from Nationalist and warlord censorship by the foreign settlements and invigorated (and appalled) by the city's modernity and foreign influences, Shanghai was host to a golden era in modern Chinese literature.

Mao Dun, an active leftist writer in the 1930s, wrote *Midnight (Ziye)*, one of the most famous novels about Shanghai. Lu Xun, China's greatest modern writer, also lived in Shanghai for a while (for more on Lu Xun see the boxed text 'Lu Xun' in the Things to See & Do chapter). Ding Ling, whose most famous work was *The Diary of Miss Sophie*, also lived in Shanghai, as, for a time, did the writers Yu Dafu and Ba Jin. Writers were not immune to political dangers; Lu Xun's friend Rou Shi was murdered by the Kuomintang in February 1931.

Eileen Chang (Zhang Ailing, 1920 –1995) is one of the writers most closely connected to Shanghai. Born in Shanghai, she only lived in the city from 1942 to 1948, before moving to Hong Kong and then the USA. Her books are inspired by and capture the essence of Shanghai and are full of the city's details and moods. One of her favourites spots to socialise is what is now the Always Café on Nanjing Xilu (see the Places to Eat chapter). She died a recluse in California, having attained a cult-like status among overseas Chinese. Chang's most famous books include: *The Rouge of the North; The Faded Flower; Red Rose and White Rose; The Golden Lock;* and *Love in a Fallen City.*

Modern Shanghai is given a literary voice by writers such as Mianmian, a former drug addict who writes about complicated sexual affairs, suicide and drug addiction in modern Shanghai.

Cinema

Films are the sharpest ideological weapon of the class struggle, and the enemy would certainly not let us grasp this weapon easily.

Chiang Kaishek

The first cinema opened up in Shanghai in 1906, but before it reached its glamorous peak, filmmakers had to convince the distrustful Shanghainese that it was worth their hard-earned dosh. The first cinema owners would therefore run a few minutes of film, cut the reel and go around collecting money from patrons who wanted to see the rest. The Shanghainese soon became hooked and by 1930 the city boasted more than 35 cinemas and 141 film companies. Stars like

Marlene Dietrich, Katharine Hepburn, Claudette Colbert and Greta Garbo were household faces in 1930s Shanghai.

For decades Shanghai was China's Hollywood and big studios like Mingxing (Star) and Lianhua churned out copies of Western films adapted with Chinese flair.

The genre changed in 1932 with the Japanese bombing of Hongkou. As film studios were destroyed and companies lost money they began showing film coverage of the bombing as a last resort; hence, the patriotic film was born. Filmmakers turned to social issues for inspiration and suddenly prostitutes, beggars and factory workers saw themselves on the big screen. Themes reflected collective action and fear of poverty as left-wing writers began writing the scripts.

This era produced its own adored movie stars like Ruan Lingyu, Zhou Xuan, Zhao Dan and Shi Hui, who became national celebrities as the 'mosquito press' churned out stories of film-star scandal and gossip. The powerful popularity of film hit home when the wedding of Butterfly Wu, revered actress and film icon, eclipsed the wedding of Song Mailing to Chiang Kaishek.

One of the greatest of the movie icons of the 1930s was Ruan Lingyu, who gained fame playing a virtuous prostitute in the silent film *Shennu (Goddess)* (1934). Ruan became an even greater icon when, like a Chinese Marilyn Monroe, she committed suicide at age 24 at the peak of her career, much like the novelist she portrayed in her 1935 film *New Woman*.

Zhou Xuan was another of the top actresses and singers from the 1930s and 1940s; her most famous film was *Street Angel* (1934). Zhou died, insane, at the age of 38. *Street Angel* was directed by Yuan Muzhi, who later became the head of the film bureau under the communist regime.

The film industry continued as a mechanism of propaganda for both the nationalists and the communists, each vying for the audience of the people.

These days more innovative film studios like Xi'an have captured much of the international glory of the so-called fifth genera-

tion of directors such as Chen Kaige and Zhang Yimou (the latter produced *Shanghai Triad* in 1995). Co-production films with Hong Kong money have been the most successful. One recent critical success was *The Red Violin*, a co-production between Canada and the Shanghai Film Studio. It is possible to get a tour of the Shanghai Film Studio (Map 8), which is on Caoxi Beilu, south of Xujiahui, but you will have to arrange it in advance with the studio or via a travel agency like the China International Travel Service (CITS; Zhōngguó Guójì Lǚxíngshè).

Western cinema has been so fixated with Shanghai that Shanghai films are almost a genre. For information on foreign films about Shanghai see the Facts for the Visitor chapter.

Music

The *èrhú* is a two-stringed fiddle that is tuned to a low register, providing a soft, melancholy tone. The *húqín* is a higher pitched two-stringed viola. The *yuèqín*, a sort of moon-shaped four-stringed guitar, has a soft tone and is used to support the èrhú. Other instruments are the *shēng* (reed flute), *pípā* (lute), *gǔzhēng* (seven-stringed zither), *xiāo* (vertical flute) and *xūn*, a wind instrument shaped like an egg which sounds a bit like an Andean panpipe. There's a whole host of drums, bells and cymbals and the *bǎn*, a time-clapper that is used in opera to beat time and give the actors their cues.

Art

Shanghai Fine Arts Academy is one of the most important centres of art in the country. One of China's most commercially successful artists is Shanghai's Chen Yifei. One of his paintings sold for more than US$500,000 in the USA, the highest price then paid for any living Chinese artist's work. Chen has recently branched into fashion and film, producing several documentaries on Shanghai.

Modern Shanghainese artists include Pu Jie, with his colourful pop-art depictions of Shanghai; Ding Yi, with his weaving-like designs; and Wu Yiming, who creates calmer, more Impressionistic works. In general, Beijing is an easier place for an artist. Shanghai artists are said to be stylistically more daring and modern, focusing on abstract and avant-garde styles, and thematically less political than their Beijing counterparts.

The southern suburb of Jinshan has its own school of 'peasant' painters, whose untrained painters have been turning out colourful and vibrant paintings for years. The designs have their roots in local embroidery designs and have no perspective. The themes are mostly rural and domestic scenes full of detail of everyday life. You can see a selection of paintings from the Jinshan srea in several shops in Yuyuan's Old Street, or you can head out to Jinshan itself.

Another form of Shanghai art is the calendar posters of the 1920s and 30s, started as advertisements by Western tobacco companies and now collected as nostalgia.

Embroidery

Shanghai's finest embroidery can be traced back to the Ming-dynasty family of Gu Mingshi, a wealthy official in the imperial court. The finest work, termed Gu embroidery, came from Gu's eldest son's concubine. As the Gu family declined, the women went commercial and embroidery became a livelihood. At the beginning of the Qing dynasty Gu's great-granddaughter opened a school to teach the art of embroidery.

Suzhou also has its own style of double-sided sū embroidery. Other styles local to Shanghai include embroidered 'paintings' and embroidery using human hair.

Architecture

For information on Shanghai's architecture see the special section 'Architecture of Shanghai'.

Chinese Temples Temple architecture in China tends to follow a certain uniformity. There is little external difference between Buddhist, Confucian and Taoist temples, all of which are groups of buildings, arranged in courtyards, aligned on a north-south orientation.

The main entrance complex normally consists of two stone guardian lions, an impressive main gate adorned with calligraphy and two painted celestial guardians. A spirit wall blocks the passage of evil spirits, who can only travel in straight lines.

Inside is a small courtyard with a large bronze basin in which incense and paper offerings are burnt. There is no set time for prayer and no communal services except for funerals. Worshippers enter the temple whenever they want to make offerings, pray for help or give thanks.

Statues include the Four Heavenly Kings, holding between them the flag of Buddhist truth, a lute, a sword and the pearl of perfection; the guardian general Wei Tuo; Sakyamuni (historical buddha) with four disciples; Dipamkara (buddha of the past); and Maitreya (future buddha). Maitreya is often portrayed as fat and smiling, with long ear lobes that symbolise wisdom, and bushy eyebrows, which indicate happiness and wisdom. Sakyamuni has set hand positions to symbolise pursuits such as meditation and teaching. Buddhas are often seated on a lotus, a symbol of purity.

Other religious beings include Bodhisatvas, such as the 1000-armed Avalokiteshvara, who, though they have reached buddhahood, forego the path to nirvana in order to help people remaining on earth. Another popular deity is Guanyin, the Goddess of Mercy. You will also see statues of the 18 Luohan or *arhats*, men who have achieved their own salvation through meditation but who are selfishly concerned only with their own salvation.

Taoist temples have statues of the three immortals, the Eight Immortals, the Yellow Emperor and other historical characters.

The most striking feature of the Buddhist temple is the pagoda. It was probably introduced from India along with Buddhism in the 1st century CE. They were originally built to house relics of the Buddha and later to hold religious artefacts and documents, to commemorate important events, or to store the ashes of the deceased.

Art Galleries in Shanghai

As well as the excellent Shanghai Art Museum (see the Things to See and Do chapter) several galleries have changing exhibitions for display.

The **Liu Haisu Art Gallery** (Map 9; Liú Hǎisù Měishùguǎn; ☎ 6270 1018), on the 2nd floor at 1660 Hongqiao Lu in Hongqiao, exhibits works of the eponymous painter, as well as impressive visiting exhibitions.

The **Shanghai Chinese Painting Institute** (Map 6; Shànghǎi Zhōngguó Huàyuàn; ☎ 6474 9977), at 197 Yueyang Lu, also has major exhibitions. Check the local press for details.

Old China Hand Reading Room (Map 6; Hànyuán Shūdiàn; ☎ 6473 2526), at 27 Shaoxing Lu, holds interesting regular exhibitions of folk art and photographs.

The **Shanghai Art Fair** is an annual event held in November to bring traditional and modern Western and Chinese art, artists and galleries together. It's open to the public and offers an interesting insight into the current art scene.

Most other galleries are in the business of selling paintings but welcome people to have a look:

AA Gallery (Map 4; ☎ 6279 8600) 4th floor, Shanghai Centre, 1376 Nanjing Xilu
Babisong Gallery (Map 5; ☎ 6473 1202) 644 Fuxing Zhonglu
Black Apple Gallery (Map 6; ☎ 5403 6960) 777 Julu Lu
Duoyunxuan (Map 6; ☎ 6466 2805) 422 Nanjing Donglu. Several galleries reside in this famous art supplies shop, including the Sun Moon Mountain (SMM) Gallery on the 2nd floor.
Eastlink Gallery (Map 6; ☎ 6437 1255) 70 Fuxing Xilu. This gallery houses modern Chinese art.
Fanguzi Art Gallery (Map 9; ☎ 6229 6307) 127 Xianxia Lu, Hongqiao
Gang of One Photographs (☎ 6259 9716) 3rd floor, Lane 461, Tianshan Lu. This gallery displays works by excellent photographer Gang Feng Wang.
Grand Theatre Gallery (Map 5; ☎ 6386 9696) 286 Huangpi Beilu. This gallery includes a permanent exhibition by Ting Shaokuang, who also created the mural at the entrance of the adjacent Grand Theatre.
J Gallery (Map 6; ☎ 6554 0181) 191 Changle Lu, with a branch in the Shanghai Centre, 1376 Nanjing Xilu
ShanghART (Map 6; ☎ 6359 3923) 2A Gaolan Lu, next to Park 97 at the western edge of Fuxing Park. This is the first stop for contemporary Chinese art; open daily from 10 am to 7 pm, Thursdays until 10 pm.
  Web site: www.shanghart.com
Stanney Gallery (Map 6; ☎ 6473 5291), 615–617 Changle Lu
Yibo Gallery (Map 5; ☎ 5888 0111) 198 Huayuan Shiqiao Lu, Pudong
  Web site: www.yibo-art.com

There are several galleries far away in Gubei, catering mainly to the expat population:

Elegant Art Gallery (Map 9; ☎ 6208 1688) 89 Shuicheng Lu
Hoke Gallery (☎ 6219 7602) 8B Golden Deer Mansion, Lane 39, Ronghua Xidao, Gubei
Hwa's Gallery (☎ 6270 7181) Ronghua Dongdao, Gubei
Longrun Gallery (☎ 6219 9767) 2nd floor, Suite E, Roma Garden, Lane 8, Ronghua Dongdao
  Web site: www.longrungallery.com

Shanghai has a virtual gallery at www.artscenechina.com, which sells Chinese art over the Internet.

Gǔ lóu (drum towers) and *zhōng lóu* (bell towers) are normally two-storey pavilions whose function is to mark prayer time. The most famous examples of these are at the Longhua Temple (see the Things to See & Do chapter).

SOCIETY & CONDUCT
Traditional Culture

Fengshui The ancient Chinese world-views included the belief that the earth, like a human body, has 'channels' or veins, along which benevolent and evil influences flow. This belief, known as *fēngshuǐ* (geomancy) plays an important role in the choice of sites for buildings or tombs. A fengshui grand master was called in to bless the Jinmao Building before its opening in 1999.

T'ai Chi Previously spelled *tàijíquán* and usually just called *t'ai chi* (or *tàijí*), this art form has been popular in China for centuries. It's translated into English as 'slow-motion shadow-boxing'. It's basically a martial art aimed at improving and maintaining health.

T'ai chi is traditionally performed early in the morning. If you want to see it, visit any major park in Shanghai at around 6 am.

Chinese Symbols Chinese culture is suffused with a great number of symbols, partly because of the large number of homonyms, or multiple meanings for a single word or sound. For example, one commonly stylised character is *fù*, meaning happiness; as the sound 'fu' can also mean a bat, this animal has in turn become a symbol of happiness. Other common stylised symbols include the character *shòu* (longevity) and the double happiness symbol found pasted on many doorways.

Colours carry great symbolic meaning. Red signifies happiness and is worn during weddings or used on New Year cards. White symbolises death and mourning, green signifies harmony, while yellow is the colour of the emperor (and also pornography – blue movies are 'yellow movies' in China!).

Numbers are often symbolic rather than literal. Department stores or *bǎihuòlou* are 'buildings of 100 goods'; the masses are referred to as the *laǒbǎixìng* or 'old 100 names'. As Mao once said: 'Let one hundred flowers bloom and a hundred schools of thought contend'. The character *wàn* (ten thousand) is also used as a set phrase to signify a large number, as seen in the numerous '10,000 Buddha' caves.

Dos & Don'ts

Don't set anything on the ground or floor. This has nothing to do with culture, but it will save you from landing your bag on a big wad of phlegm. Even restaurateurs know this and will pull up an extra chair upon which to heap your belongings.

Don't write in red ink. If giving someone your address or telephone number, write in any colour but red. Red ink conveys unfriendliness. If you're teaching, it's OK to use red to correct papers, but if you write extensive comments on the back, use some other colour.

Greater China The notion of territorial integrity is important to China. Taiwan is an integral part of the country, even if the Taiwanese don't happen to agree. Ditto for Tibet, the Spratly Islands and perhaps Chinatown in San Francisco. In fact, Han nationalism is perhaps the fastest-growing ideology in modern China. In short, if you have any pro-independence sentiments about Tibet and Taiwan, you'd best keep them to yourself.

Public Etiquette The Chinese are not nearly as innocent as they pretend to be when it comes to sexual matters, especially in Shanghai. However, the communist regime is one of the most prudish in the world. Few people get passionate in public; refrain from it yourself. It goes without saying that topless sunbathing and so on is asking for big trouble.

In China there is no shame in public bodily functions, even highly vocal displays of burping, spitting, farting, chomping or yawning.

RELIGION

While religions such as Islam and Christianity enjoy considerable popularity in Shanghai, Confucianism, Taoism and Buddhism (and sometimes all three) are dominant among most Shanghainese. Ancestor worship is also widely practised. At the turn of the 20th century there were more than 100 practising temples in the Shanghai region.

The three main religions have gradually combined over the centuries. Confucianism, in effect state policy for the last two millennia, advocated loyalty to the emperor and to the patriarchal structure below him as its main tenets. Confucius originally set these out in the 5th century BC.

Taoism has existed in two forms: firstly in the philosophical outlook advocated by the semi-mythical Laotzu (6th century BC) which stresses acceptance of the 'way', of 'going with the flow'; and secondly in a popular form, having many gods and devils in its pantheon. Taoism has also been a strong influence in the Chinese tradition.

Mahayana Buddhism, imported from India during the Han dynasty (206 BC–AD 24) has had fluctuating fortunes, but by the 10th century was as entrenched as the other two religions.

Cultural Concepts

Diūliǎn (Losing Face)
Face can be loosely described as 'status', 'ego' or 'self-respect', and is by no means alien to foreigners. Essentially it's about avoiding being made to look stupid or being forced to back down in front of others. In the West it's important; in China, it's critical. Circumvent a problem with smiling persistence rather than tackle it straight on and always give your adversary a way out. Avoid direct criticisms of people. Venting your rage in public and trying to make someone lose face will cause the Chinese to dig in their heels and only worsen your situation. Business travellers should take note here – a lot of Westerners really blow it on this point.

Kèqi (Politeness)
Linked to face are displays of politeness and respect. Always offer gifts, cigarettes and food several times, and expect them to be refused several times before finally being accepted. It's good to refer to elders with the appellation *lǎo*, which means 'old'; for example, lǎo Wang means old Mr Wang. You may find the old chestnut 'my English is no good' – 'no, it is very good' – 'no, my English is no good' repeated ad nauseam. One good way of conveying respect is to hand things (such as business cards) with both hands. Another way of showing respect to a prospective partner is to show them to the door of your office and even the entry of your building when they leave.

Guānxi (Connections)
Those who have *guānxi* rule the roost in China. Party cadres are well placed for this; foreigners will have to resort to some sort of gift-giving (bribery?) to achieve the same result. Businesspeople donate endless hours to cultivating and massaging their guānxi, normally through business dinners and banquets. Proposals that were 'impossible' a few hours earlier can suddenly become highly possible when discussed over a plate of Beijing duck and a bottle of Johnny Walker.

Rènào (Hot & Noisy)
Rènào means hot and noisy, and this is how the Chinese like it, whether it be an evening meal out or a day at the park. Often the first thing Chinese tourists do when arriving in a new hotel room is turn the TV on full volume and open the door to get rid of the oppressively quiet atmosphere. Enormous banquets featuring eardrum-blowing drinking games and top-volume karaoke sessions are about as hot and noisy, and therefore desirable, as you can get.

Linked to this is a cultural preference for the group over the individual (especially group travel), a preference that may be part communism, part Confucianism. People who travel alone are generally to be pitied.

oung dancers in Shanghai celebrate the handover of Macau to China.

traditional lantern .... advertising Coca-Cola.

Early-morning sword exercises on the Bund.

CHRIS MELLOR

Laundry-lined longtang, French Concession.

ERIC L WHEATER

Curious Shanghai youngsters.

CHRIS MELLOR

Teapots for sale at the Flower & Bird Market.

BRADLEY MAYHEW

Washing day in Shanghai.

HILARY ADELE SMITH

Travellers on the Shanghai–Beijing train.

There are around 50,000 Muslims in Shanghai, and there has been a mosque in nearby Songjiang since the 13th century. Today the city's main mosques are the Xiaotaoyuan and Fuzhou Lu mosques in the Old Town. Muslim culture is most visible in its restaurants, with their green pendants, Arabic calligraphy and sizzling kebabs.

The Cultural Revolution devastated Chinese religion – it's yet to recover fully. Temples were destroyed, priests were conscripted to make umbrellas, monks were sent to labour in the countryside where they often perished, and believers were prohibited from worship. Posters of Chairman Mao were posted over the doors of the Jing'an Temple to stop Red Guards bursting in (and ripping the icon), and an image of Mao was even painted on the Russian Orthodox Church on Gaolan Lu and remains there to this day.

Christianity

Christians are estimated to comprise about 1% of China's total population and this is slightly higher in Shanghai, with its early Jesuit communities and history of foreign influence. Christianity is still officially frowned upon by the government as a form of 'spiritual pollution'.

Shanghai has at least 140,000 Catholics. Xujiahui Cathedral is the largest in the city, though Sheshan Cathedral is the seat of the Bishop of Shanghai, and at both locations you'll see Chinese kneeling at confessionals and praying to statues of the Virgin Mary. There is much friction between the government and the Chinese Catholic Church because the church refuses to disown the Pope as its leader. China's one-child policy doesn't sit well with the Catholic stand on abortion. (In 1973 a nationwide birth-control program was instituted, with each couple permitted to have just one child in order to limit population growth.) For this reason, the Vatican maintains diplomatic relations with Taiwan, much to China's consternation.

Churches are placed under the control of the government: The Three-Self Patriotic Movement was set up as an umbrella organisation for the Protestant churches, and the Catholic Patriotic Association was set up to replace Rome as the leader of the Catholic churches.

Proselytising is forbidden and Western missionaries who are caught preaching on the sly are unceremoniously booted out.

To see or take part in prayer, Catholics can visit the Christ the King Church (Map 6), on the corner of Julu and Maoming Lu, or the Xujiahui Cathedral. Protestants can visit the Community Church on Hengshan Lu.

LANGUAGE

Shanghai dialect is largely unintelligible to Mandarin speakers, but don't fear – almost all Shanghainese also speak Mandarin. Shanghainese say *nong ho* instead of *nǐ hǎo*, say goodbye with *ze wei* instead of *zài jiàn*, and say thank you with *sha ya nong* instead of *xièxie*.

Pidgin

In the 1920s and '30s few foreigners ever thought of trying to learn Chinese; if the natives did not speak English then that was their tragedy. Most communicated with their head servant (known as the 'number one boy') using pidgin, a mix of English words twisted up with Chinese grammar. Interestingly, many of the words eventually entered English, like 'can do', 'savvy', 'chop chop', 'look-see' and 'chow'. Many of the phrases are a riot: a live fish is a 'walkee walkee fish'; a brain is a 'savvy box'.

Facts for the Visitor

WHEN TO GO

April to mid-May, and late September to mid-November (during spring and autumn respectively) provide the best weather for a visit to Shanghai. Summer is the peak travel season, though in many ways this is the worst time to come. Winter can be surprisingly cold, though there are few tourists and most hotels are heavily discounted.

The times to avoid are during major trade fairs and Chinese New Year, when the city grinds to a halt and local transport gets swamped with domestic travellers. See Public Holidays & Special Events later in this chapter for upcoming dates of major holidays.

ORIENTATION

Shanghai municipality covers a substantial area (see Geography in Facts about Shanghai), but the city proper is a more modest size and not too confusing.

Broadly, central Shanghai is divided into two areas: Pudong (east of the Huangpu River) and Puxi (west of the Huangpu River). The first ring road (Zongshan Lu) does a long, elliptical loop around the city centre proper; a second ring road provides access to Pudong and the suburbs. The city centre has two main overpasses: Yan'an Lu running east-west and Chengdu/Chongqing Lu running north-south.

Shanghai has no single focus and the feel of the city still owes much to the original concessions. The Bund is the tourist centre-piece, though not the physical centre of town.

West of the Bund is the former International Settlement (Shànghǎi Zūjiè), which extends from the intersection of Yan'an Xilu and Nanjing Xilu north to Suzhou Creek and east to the Huangpu River. Nanjing Lu is one of Shanghai's main shopping streets. The west end is known as the Jing'an district and is the location of the Shanghai Centre, home to many airline companies and foreign offices.

South of the Bund is the Chinese city, a maze of narrow lanes, lined with closely packed houses and laundry hanging from windows. It lies on the south-western bank of the Huangpu, bounded to the north by Jinling Donglu and to the south by Zhonghua Lu. The Yuyuan Gardens are in this part of town and are well worth a visit (see the Things to See & Do chapter).

West of the old town and hidden in the backstreets north and south of Huaihai Lu, is the former French Concession (Fǎguó Zūjiè), with tree-lined streets, 1930s architecture, and cafes and bars. Huaihai Lu itself is Shanghai's premier shopping street and is lined with huge department stores. At the west end of the French Concession is Hengshan Lu, where you'll find a major collection of Western restaurants and bars. Just north of here, on Huaihai Zonglu, is the largest concentration of foreign consulates.

As you continue south-east you come to the massive shopping intersection of Xujiahui. Farther south is the Shanghai Stadium.

Western Shanghai is dominated by Hongqiao, an economic zone that is home to several top-end hotels, conference centres and office towers. Farther west is Gubei, a Legoland residential area home to many expats, and the supermarkets, restaurants and services that cater to them.

North-eastern Shanghai encompasses the Hongkou district, the former American and later Japanese-controlled concession, which has a more industrial feel and is home to several universities. Farther northwest is Zhapei and Shanghai train station; farther north-east is the suburban area of Yangpu.

On the east side of the Huangpu is Pudong, a special economic zone of banks, skyscrapers, building sites and new residential complexes, eventually petering out into farmland. Pudong is the future of Shanghai. It is made up of various zones such as Liujiazui, which you can see from

Map Terms

Street names in Shanghai are posted in pinyin, which makes navigating easy. Longer roads are split by compass points (see below), thus you will see Huaihai Xilu (west), Huaihai Zhonglu (middle) and Huailu Donglu (east). Some of the monstrously long roads are split by sectors, such as Zhongshan Dong Erlu and Zhongshan Dong Yilu, which mean Zhongshan East 2nd Rd and Zhongshan East 1st Rd, respectively.

In the central district the provincial road (eg Xizang, or Tibet) names run north-south, and the city road (eg Nanjing) names run east-west.

road	lù	路
street	jiē	街
avenue	dàjiē	大街
boulevard	dàdào	大道
alley	lòng	弄
gate	mén	门
north	běi	北
south	nán	南
east	dōng	东
west	xī	西
first	yī	一
second	èr	二

the Bund, Jinqiao, home to a small expat community, and other industrial zones. In the far south-east of Pudong is Pudong international airport.

A second (outer) ring road links Hongqiao international airport (in the west of town) with the new Gaoqiao Free Trade Zone, a port on the Yangzi River in Pudong.

MAPS

The best maps of Shanghai are published abroad, though you can normally get them in Shanghai at the Foreign Languages Bookstore (see the 'Bookstores' boxed text later in this chapter) and most top-end hotels.

Geocenter's *Shanghai* has a detailed map of central Shanghai, with a street index on the back; the index is particularly useful if you are searching for an address. Periplus is another good choice, with a clear, bilingual 1:15,000 map of Shanghai and an additional 1:85,000 map of Pudong and inserts of Suzhou, Hangzhou and the surrounding provinces.

Locally made English maps of Shanghai are available from most bookshops and occasionally from street hawkers. Watch out for the map sellers on the Bund who squawk 'English map' (the only English they know); these maps are usually just a maze of characters. The best two are the *Shanghai Tourist Map*, and the *Shanghai Official Tourist Map* (which has details of Shanghai's main shopping streets). Both are produced by the Shanghai Municipal Tourism Administration and are available for a fee at the Foreign Languages Bookstore or the Tourist Information Centres listed later in this chapter under Local Tourist Offices.

There is an infinite variety of Chinese-language maps covering every district of Shanghai municipality. Xinhua bookshops and the 2nd floor of the Duoyunxuan art supplies shop are the best places to track down these maps (see the 'Bookstores' boxed text later in this chapter).

TOURIST OFFICES
Local Tourist Offices

Shanghai operates a Tourist Information Centre in the metro station at the Shanghai train station, another at the metro station in Renmin Square (☎ 6438 1693) and a third in the international arrivals hall of Hongqiao airport (☎ 6268 8899 ext 56750). The staff at these centres are professional and polite, and sell maps of Shanghai published in a wide array of languages.

In addition to this, another dozen or so Tourist Information and Service Centres (Lǚyóu Zīxún Fúwù Zhōngxīn) were set up around Shanghai in 1999. The level of information and standard of English varies from good to non-existent. All are due to have touch-screen computerised information. Locations include:

Luwan (Map 6; ☎ 6372 8330, 6318 1882) 127 Chengdu Nanlu (just off Huaihai Zhonglu)

Yuyuan Gardens (Map 5; ☎ 6355 5032) 149 Jiujiaochang Lu (just north of Yuyuan Gardens)

Shanghai train station (Map 4; ☎ 5623 4880)

Jing'an (Map 6; ☎ 6253 4058) 1612 Nanjing Xilu

Pudong (Map 3; ☎ 6475 0593) 541 Dongfang Lu

Huangpu (Map 5; ☎ 5353 1117) Century Square, 561 Nanjing Donglu

The Tourist Hotline (☎ 6253 4058) has a useful English-language service from 10 am to 9 pm. A tourist information Web site has also been established at www.tourinfo. sh.cn. For other useful Web sites see the Internet Resources section in this chapter.

China International Travel Service (CITS; Zhōngguó Guójì Lǚxíngshè) can help with travel-related information and tickets; see the Travel Agencies section in the Getting There & Away chapter.

In general, the best sources of information on Shanghai are a few superb Web sites and magazines offering up-to-date travel and entertainment information. For information see the Internet Resources and Newspapers & Magazines sections later in this chapter.

If you are heading on to Hong Kong, the Hong Kong Tourist Association has an information line in Shanghai (☎ 6385 1242).

Travel Agencies Abroad

China National Tourist Offices (CNTO) and China National Tourist Administration (CNTA) offer brochures, maps and information. Their offices abroad include the following:

Australia (☎ 02-9299 4057, fax 9290 1958) CNTO, 19th floor, 44 Market St, Sydney NSW 2000

Canada (☎ 416-599 6636, fax 599 6382) CNTO, Suite 806, 480 University Ave, Toronto 28013

France (☎ 01 56 59 10 10, fax 01 53 75 32 88) Office du Tourisme de Chine, 15 rue Berri, 75008, Paris

Germany (☎ 069-520 135, fax 528 490) CNTO, Ilkenhans Strasse 6, D 60433 Frankfurt am Main

Israel (☎ 03-522 6272, fax 522 6281) CNTO, 19 Frishman St, PO Box 3281, Tel Aviv 61030

Japan
Tokyo: (☎ 03-3433 1461, fax 3433 8653) CNTA, 6th floor, Hamamatsu cho Building, 1-27-13 Hamamatsu cho, Minato ku, Tokyo
Osaka: (☎ 06-635 3280, fax 635 3281) CNTA, 4th floor, OCAT Building, 1-4-1 Minatomachi, Naniwa-ku, Osaka

Singapore (☎ 221 8681, fax 221 9267) CNTO, 1 Shenton Way, No 17-05 Robina House, Singapore 0106

Spain (☎ 01-548 0011, fax 548 0597) CNTO, Gran Via 88, Grupo 2, Planta 16, 28013 Madrid

UK (☎ 020-7935 9787, fax 7487 5842) CNTO, 4 Glenworth St, London NW1

USA
Los Angeles: (☎ 818-545 7505, fax 545 7506) CNTO, 333 West Broadway, Suite 201, Glendale CA 91204
New York: (☎ 212 760 9700, fax 760 8809) CNTO, 350 Fifth Avenue, Suite 6413, Empire State Building, New York, NY 10118

DOCUMENTS
Passports

The Chinese government requires that your passport remain valid for at least six months after the expiry date of your visa. If you will be staying in Shanghai for longer than a couple of weeks it's worth registering your passport with your local embassy.

Visas

Visas are easily obtainable from Chinese embassies and consulates in most Western countries (see Embassies & Consulates later in this chapter). Most tourists are issued with a single-entry visa, valid for entry within three months of the date of issue, for a 30-day stay. The easiest place to get a visa is probably Hong Kong (see Getting a Visa in Hong Kong later in this section).

Processing times and fees depend on where you're applying, but normally visas take three working days. Express services cost twice the normal fee. Fees are normally paid in cash at the time of application and you'll need two passport photos.

On the visa application you must identify an itinerary and entry/exit dates and points, though nobody will hold you to them once you're in the country. To avoid snags, don't mention Tibet or bicycles and don't give your occupation as journalist or writer. The visa you end up with is the same regardless.

Chinese embassies abroad have been known to stop issuing visas to independent travellers during the height of summer or in the run up to sensitive political events or conferences, in an attempt to control the numbers of tourists entering China at peak times.

Visas valid for longer than 30 days are often difficult to obtain anywhere other than in Hong Kong, though some embassies abroad (for example, in the UK) may give you a 60-day visa out of high tourist season if you ask nicely.

If you request it, you can also receive a double-entry or multiple-entry travel visa (each entry valid for 30 days) or, sometimes, a single-entry three-month visa. These visas cost more than the standard 30-day visa, but may be worth it, depending on your itinerary. Note that if your itinerary takes you to China, Hong Kong and then back to Shanghai you will need a double-entry visa to get 'back' into China, even though Hong Kong returned to Chinese rule in 1997. If you have trouble getting more than 30 days or a multiple-entry visa, head to a visa or travel agency in Hong Kong.

Note that a 30-day visa is activated on the date you enter China, and must be used within three months of the date of issue. Longer-stay visas often start from the day they are issued, not the day you enter the country, so you should double-check this.

Officials in China are sometimes confused over the validity of the visa and look at the 'valid until' date. On most 30-day visas, however, this is actually the date by which you must have *entered* the country, not left.

Business visas are multiple-entry and valid for three to six months from the date of issue, depending on how much you paid for it. Until recently these visas only allowed stays of 30 days each visit but now they allow you to stay for the full six months. These visas are easy to get – you do

not need to prove that you will be doing business. Business visas are hard to extend. Even so, you'd be surprised how many businesspeople are in Shanghai on a tourist visa!

When you check into a hotel, there is usually a question on the registration form asking what type of visa you have. The letter specifying your visa category is usually stamped on the visa itself. There are seven categories of visas, as follows:

type	description	Chinese name
L	Travel	*lǚxíng*
F	Business or student (less than 6 months)	*fǎngwèn*
D	Resident	*dìngjū*
G	Transit	*guòjìng*
X	Long-term student	*liúxué*
Z	Working	*rènzhí*
C	Flight attendant	*chéngwù*

Getting a Visa in Hong Kong Hong Kong is a favourite place for Shanghai residents and businesspeople to renew a visa and pick up some imported goodies like coffee and books at the same time.

Chinese visas are most cheaply processed at the Visa Office (☎ 2585 1794, 2585 1700) of the Ministry of Foreign Affairs of the People's Republic of China, 5th floor, Low Block, China Resources Bldg, 26 Harbour Rd, Wanchai. Fees are HK$100 (single entry), HK$150 (double entry) or HK$200 (multiple entry). US passport holders face an additional surcharge. Visas are issued within two or three working days; 24-hour and same-day service are more than double the price. The office is open Monday to Friday 9 am to 12.30 pm and 2 to 5 pm, and on Saturday from 9 am to 12.30 pm.

The easiest place to get a visa is through CITS (☎ 2315 7188) at 27–33 Nathan Rd in Kowloon's Tsim Sha Tsui. There's a branch office at the Hung Hom train station and the head office (☎ 2853 3533) is on the 4th floor of CTS House, 78–83 Connaught Rd C, Hong Kong Island. Single-entry 90-day tourist visas cost HK$160 for processing within three working days, or HK$210 for two working days (which means next-day pick-up if you hand the visa in before 3 pm). The office can get you six-month multiple-entry business visas for HK$850/1050 in three/two working days, though you need to supply the business card of someone in China and have a stamp in you passport proving that you have been to China before. US passport holders face an additional HK$160 surcharge.

Visa-Free Transit In January 2000 Shanghai announced that all overseas travellers who are connecting to an onward flight are allowed 24 hours visa-free transit through Shanghai. The regulation is primarily aimed at travellers transferring between Hongqiao and Pudong airports, but it applies to anyone. Travellers from the US, Canada, Australia, New Zealand, Japan, Korea and most European countries (but not the UK) are allowed a longer transit of 48 hours, and other countries may follow. There is no charge for transit.

Visa Extensions Extensions of 30 days are given for any tourist visa, though you may have to present proof of registration, either at a hotel, or if you are staying in a flat, with your local Public Security Bureau (PSB; Gōngānjú) office. You may be able to wangle more, especially with cogent reasons such as illness (except AIDS) or transport delays, but second extensions are usually only granted for one week, on the understanding that you are on your way out of China.

To extend a business visa, you need a letter from a Chinese work unit willing to sponsor you. If you're studying in China, your school can of course sponsor you for a visa extension.

Visa extensions are available at the PSB office (Map 5; ☎ 6321 1997), at 333 Wusong Lu, near the intersection with Kunshan Lu. The office is open Monday to Saturday from 9 to 11.30 am and 1.30 to 4.30 pm. Visa extensions take three days to be issued.

The cost of a visa extension varies according to nationality: Y100 for Australians; Y160 for British and French; and Y125 for Americans. The penalty for overstaying your visa is a fine of up to Y300 per day.

Registration
If you are staying in a hotel you will automatically be registered by reception. If staying in a private apartment you are supposed to register with the local PSB office.

Residence Permit
The 'green card' is a residence permit issued to English teachers, businesspeople, students and other foreigners who are authorised to live in the PRC. It's such a valuable document that you'd better not lose it if you have one, or the PSB will be all over you. Green cards are issued for a period of six months to one year, depending on the status of your employer.

To get a residence permit you first need to arrange a work permit (normally obtained by your employer), health certificate (see the Health section in this chapter) and temporary 'Z' visa. If your employer is switched on you can arrange all of this before you arrive in Shanghai.

You then need to go to the PSB office with your passport, health certificate, work permit, your employer's business registration licence or representative office permit, your employment certificate (from the Shanghai Labour Bureau), the temporary residence permit of the hotel or local PSB where you are registered, a handful of passport photos and a letter of application from your employer. You must pay a fee of around Y400 in RMB.

In all, the process usually takes from two to four weeks. Expect to make multiple visits and always carry multiple copies of every document you can think of. Each member of your family needs a residence permit and visa. In most cases your employer will take care of most of the process for you.

Student Cards
A very common but not-too-useful document is the so-called 'white card'. This is a simple student ID card with a pasted-on photo that is usually kept in a red plastic

holder (some call it a 'red card' for this reason). A white card is easily forged – they can be reproduced with a photocopy machine – and the red plastic holders are on sale everywhere.

Student cards can get you cheaper entrance to sites like the Shanghai Museum and free entry and cheap beers at several clubs in Shanghai. You might be able to bluff similar discounts with an International Student Identity Card (ISIC).

Copies

If you are married and travelling with your spouse, a copy of your marriage certificate can save some grief if you become involved with the police or other bureaucratic institutions, especially if either husband or wife is ethnic Chinese. If you're thinking about working or studying in Shanghai, photocopies of college or university diplomas, transcripts and letters of recommendation could prove helpful.

It might be useful to have a photocopy of your passport and air ticket in the unfortunate event that your real one gets lost or stolen. Even better is to bring along an expired passport if you have one – it can be used as proof of your identity so that your embassy can issue you with a replacement passport.

Name Cards

Business name cards are essential, even if you don't do business – exchanging name cards with someone you've just met goes down well. It's particularly good if you can get your name translated into Chinese and have that printed just next to your English name. You can get name cards made cheaply in Shanghai at local printers, but it's better to have some in advance of your arrival.

Travel Insurance

It's very likely that a health insurance policy that you contribute to in your home country will *not* cover you in China – if unsure, ask your insurance company. If you're not covered, it would be prudent to purchase travel insurance.

The best policies will reimburse you for a variety of mishaps such as accidents, illness, theft and even the purchase of an emergency ticket home. The policies are usually available from travel agencies, including student travel services. Read the small print: Some policies specifically exclude 'dangerous activities', which may include motorcycling, scuba diving and even hiking.

Some backpacker policies offer a cheaper option, which covers only medical cover and not baggage loss, which might be worthwhile if you are not carrying any valuables in your grotty, 10-year-old suitcase. Many policies require you to pay the first US$100 or so anyway and only cover valuables up to a set limit, so if you lose a US$1000 camera you might find yourself only covered for US$350 and having to pay the first US$100!

Paying for your air ticket with a credit card often provides limited travel accident insurance. Ask your credit card company exactly what it covers.

To make a claim for compensation, you will need proper documentation (hopefully in English). This can include medical reports, police reports, baggage receipts from airlines etc.

You may prefer a policy that pays hospitals directly rather than you having to pay on the spot (often before you receive treatment) and claiming later. Check that the policy covers repatriation and an emergency flight home.

Insurance policies can normally be extended once you are in Shanghai by a phone call or fax (and a credit card). Make sure you do this *before* the policy expires or you may have to pay a more expensive premium.

Driving Licence

Foreign tourists are not permitted to drive in China without special permission, and getting such permission will cost you dearly. In other words, it's highly unlikely that you'll get any use out of either your home country's licence or an International Driving Permit.

It's a different story if you plan to take up residence in Shanghai. If you have a Chinese residence certificate, you can obtain a Chinese driver's licence, after some complex bureaucratic wrangling. The process will be much less complicated if you bring a valid licence from your home country – otherwise you'll have to take a driving course and a driving test in China, which is a major hassle and best avoided. The procedure is basically that the Chinese authorities exchange your original driver's licence for a Chinese licence. They will keep your original licence until you depart China, at which time it will be returned to you in exchange for the Chinese one.

Dog Licence

Foreign residents can own a legally licensed dog in Shanghai provided it isn't taller than 35cm. The licence has to be applied for at the PSB office (Map 5; ☎ 6321 1997) at 333 Wusong Lu, near the intersection with Kunshan Lu. The dog will need to get a physical examination at a veterinary clinic. Try English-speaking Dr Chen at the Peng Feng Animal Clinic (☎ 6438 9433), Room 10, 18 Cao Donglu (Caobao Lu metro station).

EMBASSIES & CONSULATES
Chinese Embassies & Consulates

Diplomatic representation abroad includes:

Australia
Embassy: (☎ 02-6273 4780, 6273 4781) 15 Coronation Dr, Yarralumla, ACT 2600
Consulate: (☎ 02-699 2216) 539 Elizabeth Street, Surry Hills, Sydney, NSW 2010
Consulate: (☎ 03-9804 3683) 75–79 Irving Rd, Toorak Vic 3142
Consulate: Level 3, Australia Place, 15–17 William St, Perth, WA 6000
Web site: www.chinaembassy.org.au
Austria
Embassy: (☎ 06-753 149, fax 713 6816) Metternichgasse 4, 1030 Wien
Belgium
Embassy: (☎ 2-779 4333) Ave de Tervueren 445, 1150 Woluwe-Saint-Pierre, Bruxelles
Canada
Embassy: (☎ 613-789 3509) 515 St Patrick St, Ottawa, Ontario K1N 5H3

Consulate-General: (☎ 416-964 7260) 240 St George St, Toronto, Ontario M5R 2P4
Consulate-General: (☎ 604-736 3910) 3380 Granville St, Vancouver, BC V6H 3K3
Consulate-General: (☎ 403-264 3322, fax 264 6656), Suite 100, 1011 6th Avenue SW, Calgary, Alberta T2P 0W1
Web site: www.chinaembassycanada.org
Denmark
Embassy: (☎ 039-625 806, fax 625 484) Oregards Alle 25, 2900 Hellerup, Copenhagen
France
Embassy: (☎ 01 47 36 02 58, fax 01 47 36 34 46) 9 Ave Victor Cresson, 92130 Issy Les Mounlineaux, Paris
Web site: www.amb-chine.fr
Germany
Embassy: (☎ 0228-361 095) Kurfislrstenallee 125-300 Bonn 2
Consulate: Hamburg
Italy
Embassy: (☎ 06-3630 8534) Via Della Camilluccia 613, Rome 00135
Consulate: Milan
Japan
Embassy: (☎ 03-3403 3380, 3403 3065) 3-4-33 Moto-Azabu, Minato-ku, Tokyo 106
Consulates: Fukuoka, Osaka and Sapporo
Malaysia
Embassy: (☎ 03-242 8495) 229 Jalan Ampang, Kuala Lumpur
Consulate: Kuchong
Netherlands
Embassy: (☎ 070-355 1515) Adriaan Goekooplaan 7, 2517 JX, The Hague
New Zealand
Embassy: (☎ 04-587 0407) 104A Korokoro Rd, Petone, Wellington
Consulate: Auckland
Pakistan
Embassy: (☎ 051-821 114) Diplomatic Enclave, Islamabad
Russia
Embassy: (☎ 095-143 1540, for visa inquiries ☎ 143 1543, fax 938 2132) Ulitsa Druzhby 6, 101000 Moscow
Consulate: (☎ 812-114 6230) Naberezhnaya Kanala Griboedova 134
Singapore
Embassy: (☎ 734 3361) 70 Dalvey Rd
South Korea
Embassy: (☎ 743 1491, fax 743 1494) 1 10 Ka Hye Dong, Joungro ku, Seoul
Spain
Embassy: (☎ 341-519 4242) Arturo Soria 111, 28043, Madrid
Consulate: (☎ 455 6060, fax 433 1070) Travesera de Gracia 342, 08025 Barcelona

Thailand
Embassy: (☎ 02-245 7032/49) 57 Th Ratchadaphisek, Bangkok
UK
Embassy: (☎ 020-7636 8845, 7631 1430, 24-hour premium-rate visa information ☎ 0891-880 808, fax 020-7436 9178) 31 Portland Place, W1N 5AG, London. Visas cost £25 and are issued in three days.
Consulate-General: (☎ 0161-224 7480) Denison House, 49 Denison Rd, Victoria Park, Rusholme, Manchester M14 5RX
Consulate-General: (☎ 0131-316 4789) 43 Station Rd, Edinburgh EH12 7AF
Web site: www.chinese-embassy.org.uk
USA
Embassy: (☎ 202-338 6688, fax 588 9760, faxback 265 9809, ☎ visa@china embassy.org) Room 110, 2201 Wisconsin Ave, NW Washington DC, 20007. Single-entry visas cost US$30; double-entry visas cost US$40.
Consulate: (☎ 312-803 0098, fax 803 0122) 100 West Erie St, Chicago, IL 60610
Consulate: (☎ 713-524 4311, fax 524 8466) 3417 Montrose Blvd, Houston, TX 77006
Consulate: (☎ 213-380 2508, fax 380 0372) 443 Shatto Place, Los Angeles, CA 90020
Consulate: (☎ 212-330 7410, fax 502 0245) 520 12th Ave, New York, NY 10036
Consulate: (☎ 415-563 9232, fax 563 4861) 1450 Laguna St, San Francisco, CA 94115
Web site www.china-embassy.org
Vietnam
Embassy: (☎ 04-845 3736) 46 Hoang Dieu St, Hanoi
Consulate: Ho Chi Minh City

Consulates in Shanghai

There is a growing band of consulates in Shanghai, some located in the choicest 1930s-style real estate in the city. Your own country's consulate is worth a visit – not just if you've lost your passport, but also for up-to-date newspapers from home and to register if you are staying for a while.

If you are planning a trip to South-East Asia you'll have to go to Beijing or Hong Kong for a visa for Vietnam, Laos or Myanmar. There is also a Vietnamese consulate in Guangzhou and Thai, Lao and Myanmar embassies in Kunming.

If you're embarking on the Trans-Siberian journey and have booked a definite departure date, and a flight out of Russia, it's better to get your Russian visa here than face the horrible queues at the Russian embassy in Beijing.

Australia (Map 6; ☎ 6433 4604, fax 6437 6669) 17 Fuxing Xilu. A visa office is also located in the Shanghai Centre, open weekday mornings.
Austria (Map 6; ☎ 6474 0268, fax 6471 1554) 3rd floor, Qihua Tower, 1375 Huaihai Zhonglu
Cambodia (Map 5; ☎ 6361 9646, fax 6361 1437) Room 901–902, Huasheng Bldg, 400 Hankou Lu
Canada (Map 4; ☎ 6279 8400, fax 6279 8401) Suite 604, Shanghai Centre, 1376 Nanjing Xilu
Czech Republic (Map 6; ☎ 6471 2420, fax 6474 1159) 12th floor, Qihua Tower, 1375 Huaihai Zhonglu
Denmark (Map 9; ☎ 6209 0500, fax 6209 0504) Room 701, Shanghai International Trade Centre, 2200 Yan'an Xilu
Finland (Map 6; ☎ 6474 0068, fax 6471 3604) 7th floor, Qihua Tower, 1375 Huaihai Zhonglu
France (Map 6; ☎ 6437 7414, fax 6433 9437) 23rd floor, Qihua Tower, 1375 Huaihai Zhonglu
Germany (Map 6; ☎ 6433 6951, fax 6471 4448) 181 Yongfu Lu
India (Map 9; ☎ 6275 8885, fax 6275 8881) Room 1008, Shanghai International Trade Centre, 2200 Yan'an Xilu
Israel (☎ 6209 8008, fax 6209 8010) Room 703, New Town Mansion, 55 Loushanguan Lu, Changning
Italy (Map 6; ☎ 6471 6980, fax 6471 6977) 11th floor, Qihua Tower, 1375 Huaihai Zhonglu
Japan (Map 9; ☎ 6278 0788, fax 6278 8988) 8 Wanshan Lu, Hongqiao
Netherlands (Map 9; ☎ 6209 9076, fax 6209 9079) 4th floor, East Tower, Sun Plaza, 88 Xianxia Lu
New Zealand (Map 6; ☎ 6471 1108, fax 6431 0226) 15th floor, Qihua Tower, 1375 Huaihai Zhonglu
Norway (Map 5; ☎ 6323 9988, fax 6323 3938) 3rd floor, 12 Zhongshan Dong Yilu (Bund)
Russia (Map 5; ☎ 6324 8383, fax 6306 9982) 20 Huangpu Lu. Open Monday, Wednesday and Friday, 9.30 am to noon. Transit and tourist visas both cost US$50, available in one week. For a transit visa you need to show train or air tickets into and out of the country. A tourist visa requires visa support from a travel agency.

Singapore (Map 6; ☎ 6437 0776, fax 6433 4150) 400 Wulumuqi Zhonglu
South Korea (Map 9; ☎ 6219 6417, fax 6219 6918) 4th floor, Shanghai International Trade Centre, 2200 Yan'an Xilu
Sweden (Map 6; ☎ 6474 1311, fax 6471 6343) 6A, Qihua Tower, 1375 Huaihai Zhonglu
Switzerland (Map 9; ☎ 6270 0519, fax 6370 0522) Room 302, West Tower, Sun Plaza, 88 Xianxia Lu
Thailand (Map 5; ☎ 6323 4095, 6323 4140) 3rd floor, 7 Zhongshan Dong Yilu (Bund). Visa section open Monday to Friday, 9.30 to 11.30 am.
UK (Map 4; ☎ 6279 7650, fax 6279 7651, ✉ shangbcg@uninet.com.cn) Room 301, Shanghai Centre, 1376 Nanjing Xilu
USA (Map 6; ☎ 6433 6880, fax 6433 4122) 1469 Huaihai Zhonglu (entrance on Wulumuqi Lu)
  Web site: www.usembassy-china.org.cn

YOUR OWN EMBASSY

It's important to realise what your own embassy – the embassy of the country of which you are a citizen – can and can't do to help you if you get into trouble.

Generally speaking, it won't be much help in emergencies if the trouble you're in is remotely your own fault. Remember that you are bound by the laws of the country you are in. Your embassy will not be sympathetic if you end up in jail after committing a crime locally, even if such actions are legal in your own country.

In genuine emergencies you might get some assistance, but only in cases where other channels have been exhausted. For example, if you need to get home urgently, a free ticket home is exceedingly unlikely – the embassy would expect you to have travel insurance. If you have all your money and documents stolen, it might assist with getting a new passport, but a loan for onward travel is out of the question. Most consulates defer to their embassies in Beijing. The UK consulate, for example, can only issue emergency passports, while the embassy in Beijing can issue new passports.

Most of Shanghai's consulates recommend that you register with them if staying more than a week or so. Most embassies have useful information packs for long-term residents, with information on things like estate agents, lawyers, hospitals etc. The US Embassy produces a brochure entitled *Tips for Travellers to the People's Republic of China*, which you can get before you travel.

CUSTOMS

Customs formalities are so streamlined in Shanghai that you won't need to fill in a customs form, even if you are carrying a laptop computer, video camera etc. There are clearly marked 'green channels' and 'red channels'; take the red channel only if you have something to declare.

Duty free, you're allowed to import up to: 400 cigarettes or the equivalent in tobacco products; two litres of alcoholic drink; 72 rolls of still film; and 50g of gold or silver. Importation of fresh fruit is prohibited. You can legally only bring in or take out Y6000 in Chinese currency. There are no restrictions on foreign currency, however you should declare any cash that exceeds US$5000 (or its equivalent in another currency).

It's illegal to import into China printed material, film, tapes etc that are 'detrimental to China's politics, economy, culture and ethics'. But don't be too concerned about what you take to read. As you leave China, any tapes, manuscripts, books etc 'which contain state secrets or are otherwise prohibited for export' can be seized. Mainly, the authorities are interested in things written in Chinese – they don't usually pay much attention to English publications.

Pirated VCDs (video CDs) and CDs are illegal going out of China as well as going into most other countries. If they are found they will be confiscated.

A very peculiar restriction is the Y300 limit (Y150 if going to Hong Kong or Macau) on taking herbal medicines out of the country. One would think that China would like to encourage the export of Chinese medicine, a profitable (and mostly state-run) industry. Our favourite Chinese regulation is the one that strictly forbids anyone bringing more than 20 pieces of underwear into the PRC.

Antiques

The Chinese government takes the export of Chinese antiques very seriously. The general rule in China is that if it is over 200 years old it may be prohibited from export. Until recently, cultural relics, handicrafts, gold and silver ornaments and jewellery purchased in China had to be shown to customs on leaving. If these items were deemed to be 'cultural treasures', they would be confiscated. Nowadays customs are much looser, rarely checking hand baggage, presumably because the items in question are worthless fakes. To be on the safe side make sure that you have a receipt and business card from the dealer for anything that you purchase. See the Shopping chapter for more details.

MONEY
Currency

The Chinese currency is known as Renminbi (RMB), or 'People's Money'. Formally the basic unit of RMB is the *yuán* (Y), which is divided into ten *jiǎo,* which again is divided into ten *fēn.* In spoken Chinese the yuan is referred to as *kuài* and jiao as *máo.* The fen has so little value these days that it is rarely used.

The Bank of China issues RMB bills in denominations of two, five, 10, 50 and 100 yuan. Coins are in denominations of one yuan, five jiao and one, two and five fen. There are still a lot of paper versions of the coins floating around, but these will gradually disappear in favour of the coins.

A new red Y100 bill featuring Chairman Mao on one side and Beijing's Great Hall of the People on the other was introduced in 1999. Older bills feature the communist pantheon of Mao Zedong, Zhou Enlai, Zhu De and Liu Shaoqi. Both bills are legal tender.

Exchange Rates

There are continual rumours that China might devalue its currency. The following rates were current at the time of going to press.

country	unit		yuan
Australia	A$1	=	Y4.88
Canada	C$1	=	Y5.55
France	FF1	=	Y1.20
Germany	DM1	=	Y4.03
Hong Kong	HK$1	=	Y1.06
Japan	¥1	=	Y0.07
Netherlands	f1	=	Y3.85
New Zealand	NZ$1	=	Y3.81
Singapore	S$1	=	Y4.76
Switzerland	SFr1	=	Y5.09
UK	UK£1	=	Y12.49
USA	US$1	=	Y8.27
euro	€1	=	Y7.88

Exchanging Money

You can change foreign currency and travellers cheques at money-changing counters at almost every hotel, even cheapies like the Pujiang, and at many shops and department stores. Some top-end hotels will only exchange money with their guests. Exchange rates in China are uniform, wherever you change money, so there's little need to shop around. The Bank of China charges a 0.75% commission to change cash and travellers cheques.

Hong Kong dollars, Japanese yen, Australian dollars and most Western European currencies can be exchanged at major banks, but US dollars are still the easiest to change.

Whenever you change foreign currency into Chinese currency you will be given a money-exchange voucher recording the transaction. You need to show this to change yuan back into foreign currency. Changing Chinese currency outside China is a problem, though it's easily done in Hong Kong.

Cash In Shanghai you can change cash at almost any bank or major department store (as long as you have your passport), and travellers cheques at any Bank of China. The enormous main branch of the Bank of China, right next to the Peace Hotel, tends to get crowded, but is the best place to come for tricky things like transfers (and it's worth a peek for its grand interior).

American Express (Map 4; ☎ 6279 8082) has an office and an ATM at Room 206,

Shanghai Centre, 1376 Nanjing Xilu. The office is open weekdays 9 am to 5.30 pm, and 9 am to noon on Saturday. AmEx cardholders can cash personal cheques with their card at branches of the Bank of China, China International Trust & Investment Corporation (CITIC), Industrial Bank or the Bank of Communications.

Useful Bank of China branches with 24-hour ATMs include: Nanjing Donglu, next to the Peace Hotel (Map 5); Huaihai Lu, at the corner of Huangpi Nanlu (Map 7); 698 Huaihai Zhonglu (Map 6); 1207 Huaihai Zhonglu, near Huating Market (Map 6); Fuzhou Lu, next to the Wugong Hotel (Map 5); and the south-west corner of the Grand Gateway, Xujiahui (Map 8).

Most Bank of China branches are open on weekdays from 9.30 to 11.30 am and 1 to 4 pm.

Black Market Forget it – with relatively easy local access to dollars, there's little to gain and much to lose from the black market. Moneychangers on the street are mostly tricksters and should be avoided.

Travellers Cheques Besides the advantage of security, travellers cheques are useful to carry in China because the exchange rate is actually more favourable than what you get for cash. You can even cash US$ travellers cheques into US$ cash for the standard 0.75% commission.

Cheques from most of the world's leading banks and issuing agencies are now acceptable in China – stick to the major companies such as Thomas Cook, American Express and Citibank and you'll be OK. You can buy US$- or RMB-currency travellers cheques from the Bank of China at a commission of 4%.

ATMs & Debit Cards Most of Shanghai's ATMs now accept foreign credit and debit cards, but the system is not foolproof; save receipts and compare them later with your bank statements. Bank of China branches scattered throughout the city have 24-hour ATMs that take international cards such as Cirrus, Plus, Visa etc.

The Industrial and Commercial Bank of China (ICBC) and the China Construction Bank also have ATMs that take MasterCard and Cirrus, and often other cards. Many of the large department stores have ATMs inside. Look on the back of your card to see which systems are compatible. ATM screens show messages in English and Chinese. Only yuan is dispensed.

There's a 'branch' of Citibank next door to the Peace Hotel on the Bund that is open 24 hours for ATM withdrawal. You can get up to Y2000 with a single transaction. The Shanghai Centre has Hong Kong and Shanghai Bank, Bank of China and ICBC ATMs.

Credit Cards Credit cards are more readily accepted in Shanghai than in other parts of China. Most tourist hotels will accept major credit cards such as Visa, AmEx, MasterCard, Diners and JCB, as will banks, upper-end restaurants, friendship stores and tourist-related shops, airlines and most travel agencies.

Credit card cash advances are commonplace at Bank of China branches. A 3% commission is deducted and you can get the money within minutes in US dollars or Chinese yuan.

Credit hasn't caught on among most Chinese and most local credit cards are in fact debit cards.

The following are emergency contact numbers in case you lose your card:

American Express (☎ 6279 8082) 9 am to 5:30 pm; out of business hours call the 24-hour refund line in Hong Kong (☎ 852-2885 9331/9332)
Diners Club (☎ 5879 1200 ext 6753)
MasterCard (☎ 00-852-2544 2222 in Hong Kong)
Visa (☎ 108-00-110 2911)

Opening an Account Foreigners can open both RMB and US$ bank accounts in China. You do not need to have resident status – a tourist visa is sufficient. Take your passport to a branch of the Bank of China or CITIC to open the account. You can then access the account at any Bank of China branch in Shanghai but not branches outside Shanghai.

International Transfers You can have money wired to and from a Bank of China account (see Opening an Account earlier) but the process is still vulnerable to hitches. You may need to find out the details of the clearing bank used by your bank to send money to China. If US$ are wired you can withdraw US currency.

Western Union operates through its Chinese partner China Courier Service Corp (CCSC; ☎ 6356 6666). There is a service fee of 0.5% and you can pick up the money (in US$ or RMB only) on presentation of your passport at any of their offices, including the international post office on Sichuan Beilu.

Foreign Banks

At present foreign banks are limited in the services they offer. China's impending entry into the WTO should give them more power to offer banking services to customers, though the process is likely to be gradual.

Contact details for the main foreign banks in Shanghai are:

ABN AMRO Bank (☎ 6329 9303) 20 Zhongshan Dongyi Lu (The Bund)
Bank of America (☎ 6881 8686) 18th floor, 528 Pudong Nanlu, Pudong
Banque National de Paris (☎ 6472 8762) Room 101, 58 Maoming Nanlu
Chase Manhattan Bank (☎ 6279 7288) Suite 700A, Shanghai Centre, 1376 Nanjing Xilu
Citibank (☎ 5879 1200) 1 Pudong Lu, Pudong
Credit Lyonnais (☎ 6355 0070) 6th floor, Central Place, 16 Henan Nanlu
Credit Suisse (☎ 6219 0808) 11F Shartex Plaza, 88 Zunyi Lu
Hang Seng Bank (☎ 6472 8781) Room 1301, Ruijin Bldg, 205 Maoming Nanlu
Hongkong & Shanghai Bank (☎ 6321 8383) 6th floor, 185 Yuanmingyuan Lu
National Westminster Bank (☎ 6279 8820) Suite 708, Shanghai Centre, 1376 Nanjing Xilu
Société Générale (☎ 6249 7500) 8th floor, 172 Yuguan Lu
Standard Chartered Bank (☎ 6279 7337) 66 Zhaoshang Bldg, 66 Lujiazui Lu, Pudong

Security

A moneybelt or pockets sewn inside your clothes are the safest ways to carry money.

Waist bags are popular but just advertise all your goodies. Be particularly careful of pickpockets in crowded markets, buses and the train station.

It pays not to keep all your money in one place. Keep an emergency stash of money (say US$100) buried deep in your luggage or in your hotel safe etc, with a record of the serial numbers of your travellers cheques, and your passport number.

See also Copies and Dangers & Annoyances elsewhere in this chapter.

Costs

Shanghai is one of China's most expensive cities and if you frequent foreign restaurants and supermarkets you'll end up paying much the same as in the West, if not more.

Local Chinese restaurants offer excellent value, with most dishes from Y10 to Y20, if you can navigate the Chinese menu. Western food, on the other hand, is even more expensive than it is in the West and it's easy to blow US$20 on a meal. Other major budget-busters are cafes, which charge up to Y40 (US$5) for a coffee, and bars, where the smallest of beers costs Y30. You can get a decent meal for the same price elsewhere.

Accommodation is generally expensive in Shanghai. The Pujiang Hotel still offers dorm beds for around US$7, though Shanghai's cheapest private room generally costs at least Y250 (US$30). Discounts are common so always try to knock down the price – hardly any of Shanghai's hotels actually charge their rack rates.

There is little formal overcharging in Shanghai, as was once so common in China. Fruit sellers and antiques sellers are the worst culprits, plus the occasional restaurant.

A bare-bones daily budget in Shanghai would be US$15, which involves staying in a dormitory, eating basic snacks and not doing much else. If you stay in a decent hotel, eat in mid-range places, see a few sights, take a few taxis and maybe go see the acrobats then figure on anything from US$50 up. And that's without shopping, for which you should budget more than you think.

Tipping & Bargaining

China is one of those wonderful countries where tipping is generally not expected and is even discouraged by the authorities. However Shanghai has always been open to Western ideas and keen to make a buck, so staff are becoming used to it in fancy restaurants, where most people round up the bill. In general there is no need to tip if a service charge has already been added.

Bargaining is something else. The government has only recently stopped its official policy of charging foreigners at least double for everything, and many private businesses still show their patriotism by charging three or four times the Chinese rate; this leaves considerable room for negotiation.

See the Shopping chapter for information on bargaining tactics and etiquette.

Taxes

Big hotels and fancy restaurants normally add a tax or 'service charge' of 10% or 15%, which extends to the room and food; all other consumer taxes are included in the price tag.

POST & COMMUNICATIONS

China has a very efficient postal system and telecommunications are generally excellent.

Post

The larger tourist hotels and foreign business towers have post offices from where you can mail letters and small packages, and this is by far the most convenient option.

Shanghai's international post office (Map 5) is at the corner of Sichuan Beilu and Bei Suzhou Lu. The section for poste restante is in the same building, but in a separate room. Parcels and customs are at counter No 11, packing materials are at No 9, international express mail is at No 6, and poste restante is at No 12. The international mail counters are open daily from 9 am to 5 pm.

Letters take about a week to reach most overseas destinations; Express Mail Service (EMS) cuts this down to three or four days. Courier companies can take as little as two days.

The international post office is the easiest place from which to send parcels. Bear in mind that most countries impose a maximum weight limitation (10kg is typical) on packages received. If you have a receipt for the goods, then put it in the box when you're mailing it, since it may be opened again by customs further down the line.

Postal Rates

Like elsewhere, registered mail costs extra in China, but cheaper postal rates are available for printed matter, small packets, parcels, bulk mailings and so on.

Letters Up to 20g: domestic Y0.50; Hong Kong, Macau and Taiwan airmail Y2.50; Asia-Pacific Y4.70; other countries Y5.40. Above 20g is Y6.40 to most foreign countries.

Postcards Domestic Y0.30; Hong Kong, Macau, Taiwan airmail Y2.0; Asia-Pacific Y3.70; other countries Y4.20.

Aerograms Hong Kong, Macau and Taiwan Y1.80; Asia-Pacific Y4.50; other countries Y5.20.

Parcels Albert Einstein may have developed the theory of relativity but he woul not have stood a chance against China Post's system of pricing international parcels. All we can say is that the system works well but that it's not all that cheap. Prices vary from Y153 to Y174 to send a 1kg parcel airmail to Australia, the UK or USA. After this, for every extra 500g add on Y54 to Australia, Y90 to the US and Y84 to the UK, and then expect the final amount due to be completely different!

EMS Domestic EMS parcels up to 200g cost Y15; each additional 200g costs Y5. International EMS charges vary according to country. Some sample minimal rates (up to 500g parcels) are:

Australia Y195; Eastern Europe Y382; Hong Kong and Macau Y105; Japan and Korea Y135; Middle East Y375; North America Y217; South America Y262; South Asia Y255; South-East Asia Y150; Western Europe Y234.

Courier Companies

Several foreign courier companies operate in China, in joint ventures. Prices seem fairly standard. An express document of 500g costs Y200/210 to the USA/UK, plus Y80 per additional 500g. Australia is slightly cheaper at Y180, plus Y55 per additional 500g. Packages are a little pricier at Y300/320 to the USA/Europe, plus Y80 per additional 500g. Australia is Y260, plus Y55. Express documents can take as little as two days to arrive.

The following companies offer door-to-door pick-up and delivery:

DHL (☎ 6536 2900, 800-810 8000) 303 Jinian Lu; Shanghai International Trade Centre, 2200 Yan'an Xilu, Hongqiao; Shanghai Centre, 1376 Nanjing Xilu. Offices also in Hangzhou and Suzhou.
TNT Skypak (☎ 6421 1111) near Hongqiao airport
UPS (☎ 6391 55555) Room 1318, Central Plaza, 381 Huaihai Zhonglu

Telephone

China's phone system is generally excellent and in Shanghai you are never far from an international dialing phone of some description. Shanghai's main telecommunications building is at the corner of Yan'an Zhonglu and Huangpi Lu (Map 5).

Long-distance phone calls can be placed from hotel rooms and don't take long to get through, though you pay for this with a surcharge of up to 30% and sometimes a three-minute minimum. You may have to ask the hotel staff for the dial-out code for a direct line. The usual procedure is that you make the call and someone comes to your room five or 10 minutes later to collect the cash. Local calls are normally free.

If you are expecting a call to your hotel room, try to advise the caller beforehand of your room number as operators frequently have trouble with Western names. Otherwise, inform the receptionist that you are expecting a call and write down your name and room number.

Telephone (IC) cards, available from the telecommunications office on Yan'an Zhonglu, are useful as they can be used in public phones along the main streets, in telecom offices and most hotels. Cards come in denominations of Y20, Y50, Y100 and Y200, and there are two kinds: one for use only in Shanghai, the other nationwide. If you are just using a phonecard for international calls you may find yourself left with up to US$2 of unusable credits on the card, as this is less than the minimum one-minute charge for an international call.

A recent innovation is the Internet phonecard (IP), which works like a prepaid phonecard but connects via the Internet. You can use any public phone to dial a special telephone number and then a password (there are English and Chinese instructions). The main advantage here is the cost, currently Y4.8 per minute to most countries and a third of the cost of a traditional phone call. Cards can be bought in a growing number of shops around Shanghai as well as the main telecommunications building on Yan'an Zhonglu. Cards come in denominations of Y50, Y100, Y200 and Y500. Again, some cards are valid for most major cities in China, while others can only be used in Shanghai, so make sure you buy the right one.

The other major form of public phone is just a phone attached to a magazine booth or small shop. Just pick up the phone, make your call, and then pay the attendant (usually five mao for a local call).

A variant of this, found in many bars and hotels, is an oversized white phone with a slot for coins on top. Local calls from these phones cost Y1.

Long-distance calls and faxes can also be made from any telecom office. A useful 24-hour telecom office is conveniently located next to the Peace Hotel at 30 Nanjing Donglu.

Most international calls cost Y15 per minute, though you pay Y12 per minute for calls to Japan, Korea and other neighbouring countries, and Y5 to Hong Kong. Rates drop by 40% between midnight and 7 am. A one-page fax to most countries costs a pricey Y54.70. You are required to leave a Y300 deposit for international calls.

City Telephone Codes in China

These codes are valid if dialling from within China. From abroad you must omit the first 0.

city	code
Shanghai	021
Beijing	010
Chengdu	028
Chongqing	023
Fuzhou	0591
Guangzhou	020
Guilin	0773
Hangzhou	0571
Hong Kong	0852
Kunming	0871
Nanjing	025
Ningbo	0574
Qingdao	0532
Shenzhen	0755
Suzhou	0512
Tianjin	022
Wuhan	027
Xiamen	0592
Xian	029
Zhuhai	0756

An English-language Yellow Pages is available at most business centres.

To telephone into Shanghai, dial your country's international access code (normally 00) + 86 + 21 + the local number.

To telephone out of Shanghai to another country, dial international access code (00) + your country code + the local area code (omitting the first 0) + the number you want to reach.

Home Country Direct Another option is to dial the home country direct dial number (☎ 108), and then your country code, which puts you straight through to a local operator in that country. You can then make a reverse-charge (collect) call or a credit-card call with a telephone credit card valid in the destination country. Several top-end hotels like the Westin Taipingyang and the Garden Hotel have home country direct phones in the lobby, putting you through to

an operator in Canada, the UK, Japan, Hong Kong or the USA at the touch of a button.

Dialling codes include:

country	direct dial	home country direct
Australia	☎ 00-61	☎ 108-610
Canada	☎ 00-1	☎ 108-1
France	☎ 00-33	☎ 108-330
Hong Kong	☎ 00-852	☎ 108-852
Japan	☎ 00-81	☎ 108-810
Netherlands	☎ 00-31	☎ 108-310
New Zealand	☎ 00-64	☎ 108-640
UK	☎ 00-44	☎ 108-440
USA	☎ 00-1	☎ 108-1*

* For the USA you can dial ☎ 108-11 (AT&T), ☎ 108-12 (MCI) or ☎ 108-13 (Sprint)

Other Options There's a wide range of local and international phonecards. Lonely Planet's eKno Communication Card is aimed specifically at independent travellers and provides budget international calls, a range of messaging services, free email and travel information – for local calls, you're usually better off with a local card.

You can join online at www.ekno.lonely planet.com or by phone from Shanghai by dialling 108-00-180 0073. Once you have joined, to use eKno from Shanghai, dial 108-00-180 0072.

Check the eKno Web site for joining and access numbers from other countries and updates on super budget local access numbers and new features.

If you will be staying in China for more than a few months and make frequent overseas calls, it's worthwhile to sign up with a

Essential Telephone Numbers

International Directory Assistance:	☎ 114
Police:	☎ 110
Ambulance:	☎ 120
Fire:	☎ 119
Weather:	☎ 121
Tourist Hotline:	☎ 6439 0630

emple candles, Putuoshan.

burning good-luck joss stick.

The peaceful tranquility of a Zen-style garden.

he man himself, looking suitably philosophical, at the Confucian Temple, Old Town.

Shanghai Buddhist monks deep in conversation.

The intricate carvings of a Buddhist temple statue.

callback service. Virtually all such services are based in the USA (to take advantage of America's cheap phone rates). Some of the choices available include:

Justice Technology (☎ 310-526 2000, fax 526 2100)
Web site: www.justicecorp.com
Kallback (☎ 206-599 1992, fax 599 1982)
Web site: www.kallback.com
Kallmart (☎ 407-676 1717, fax 676 5289)
Web site: www.kallmart.com
New World (☎ 201-488 5811)
Web site: www.newworldtele.com

The cheapest (if not the most convenient) way to make overseas calls is through the Internet. Getting this to work requires making prior arrangements with the person you wish to call, having the proper software, a fast modem connection and a bit of luck. There are various publications that explain how to do it, but it's beyond the scope of this travel guide. One company that can help set this up is Net2Phone (www .net2phone.com).

Pagers Those living on a budget, such as foreign students, may well find pagers a more realistic option than having a phone installed. Though considered a luxury in other countries, pagers are far more common in China than telephones (there are more than three million alone in Shanghai). China is the world's second-largest pager market after the USA and will probably soon be the largest.

Pagers for use in Shanghai cost around Y300 to buy and then Y30 a month for line rental, though it is thought that the latter will drop to Y15 before long. For a pager usable throughout China, expect to pay around three times this. There are now about 1700 paging firms in China so it's difficult to say which company is best. The leading manufacturers of cellular phones and pagers are the USA's Motorola and Sweden's Ericsson.

If you want to page somebody, you may have to negotiate the Chinese-speaking operators. They will ask first for the number you are paging, the name of the party

(guìxìng), the return number *(huídiàn)*, and possibly the extension *(fēnjī)*.

Email & Internet Access
Shanghai is easily the most wired city in China and most businesses and individuals have an email address. A major stumbling block is that the government monopolises telecommunications, so only state-run companies offer email services.

Foreign companies such as CompuServe have tried to set up local nodes in Shanghai, but the government gives them so little bandwidth that their systems soon overload. As a result, you'll have much difficulty getting online in Shanghai if you want to use a foreign-based Internet Service Provider (ISP). If you're travelling with a portable computer and want to access your email, your only alternative may be to make an expensive call to Hong Kong or abroad.

Probably the cheapest way to keep in touch while on the road is to sign up for a free account with Hotmail (www.hotmail .com), Rocketmail (www.rocketmail.com) or eKno (see Other Options earlier in this chapter) and access your account from an Internet cafe.

Laptop Connections If you're travelling with a portable computer and modem, all you need is an IDD line with an RJ-11 phone jack to call to your favourite email service abroad. However, it's risky to attach your modem to the phone in your hotel room and dial out through the switchboard – if the switchboard is digital (as opposed to analog) you risk frying your modem. Ironically, this is a bigger problem at newer hotels – old hotels usually have analog equipment.

One of the few companies to come up with a solution to the tricky connection problem is Konexx (www.konexx.com), which sells a device called a 'mobile konnector' which protects the modem and allows you to hook up to the phone's handset cord.

Internet Providers Things are a lot easier if you're a legal foreign resident of

China and wish to set up a local Internet account. Chinese ISPs are all government-run, but the service is gradually improving and costs have come down. You do have to put up with some censorship – the Chinese government has blocked access to sites that offer pornography or balanced news reporting (it's uncertain which of the two is the lesser evil). Nevertheless, you can get quite a lot of useful work done on the Internet. Some companies in Shanghai offering Internet service are as follows:

ChinaNet (☎ 6327 0333) Room 1204, Shanghai Telecommunications Office, 333 Wusheng Lu
Shanghai Online (☎ 6353 4319) 2nd floor, Bldg 2, 100 Changan Lu
  Web site: www.online.sh.cn
Uninet (☎ 6217 1229, 6218 4895, ✉ uninet@uninet.com.cn) Room 5B-3, Central City Mansion, 8 Ruijin Yilu (near Yan'an Zhonglu)

Email Centres & Internet Cafes There's a small but growing number of Internet cafes in Shanghai. President Clinton even visited a cybercafe on his visit to Shanghai (though it has since closed).

Shanghai Library has terminals in the basement and is the cheapest and most pleasant place in the city for Internet use at Y6 per hour (minimum one hour). It's open from 9 am to 6 pm daily. Bring your passport or ID if you have no library card. Connections range from lightening fast to maddeningly slow.

A recent arrival on the Shanghai scene is icafe (Map 7; ☎ 6391 5582), Shanghai's only Internet cafe with real coffee (Y15), at 381 Huaihai Zhonglu in Central Plaza. Without a membership the charge is Y22 per hour, or you can pay a Y100 membership fee and go online for Y15 an hour.

The British Council (Map 6), at 88–90 Changshu Lu, offers free Internet use, though you may have to queue for the one computer.

The massive Book City (Map 5), at 465 Fuzhou Lu, has an Internet cafe on the 2nd floor, charging Y7 per half-hour (minimum). It's open daily from 9.30 am to 6.45 pm and Friday to Sunday until 9 pm.

Net 2000 (Map 5; Wǎngluò Kāfēibā), on Henan Lu just south of the crossing with Fuzhou Lu, offers Internet access and a host of other computer and email services, though it's pricier than most at Y20 per hour. It's tricky to find as it's on the 2nd floor, accessed through a restaurant; look for the sign on Henan Lu.

Most hotel business centres offer Internet access, but at high prices of around Y32 per hour.

There are several Public Internet Clubs (PIC; Gōngzhòng Diànnǎo Shì) recognisable by their signs. They are mostly dingy places full of kids playing computer games, but you can get Web access for Y12 to Y15 per hour, though connections can be slow. Internet cafes are constantly in flux, though there seems to be a concentration around Xujiahui.

INTERNET RESOURCES

The World Wide Web is a rich resource for travellers. You can research your trip, hunt down bargain air fares, book hotels, check on weather conditions or chat with locals and other travellers about the best places to visit (or avoid!).

There's no better place to start your Web explorations than the Lonely Planet Web site (www.lonelyplanet.com). Here you'll find succinct summaries on Shanghai and other regions of China, postcards from other travellers, and the Thorn Tree bulletin board, where you can ask questions before you travel or dispense advice when you get back. You can also find travel news and updates to many of our most popular guidebooks, and the subWWWay section links you to the most useful travel resources elsewhere on the Web.

Other Shanghai-related sites include:

Shanghai Edition This site covers almost everything from hot bars to business news and has online text of several hard-to-find books on Shanghai.
  www.shanghai-ed.com
That's Shanghai An excellent guide to what's happening in Shanghai entertainment. www.thatsshanghai.com
Shanghai Municipal Government Lots of statistics and official news.
  www.shanghai.gov.cn

Shanghai Business Connection Offering plenty of tips if you are coming to Shanghai to stay, including a searchable database of apartments, classifieds and a five-day weather forecast.
www.shanghhabc.cn
China Now Includes travel information on Shanghai, and surrounding excursions.
www.chinanow.com
Shanghai Guide A good general guide, with an emphasis on expats, and listings for kids and local schools.
www.shanghaiguide.com
Time Out A general introduction to the city's entertainment scene.
www.timeout.com/shanghai/index.html
China Guides A general tourist guide to Shanghai's sights.
www.chinaguides.net

BOOKS

Most books are published in different editions by different publishers in different countries. As a result, a book might be a hardcover rarity in one country while it's readily available in paperback in another. Fortunately, bookshops and libraries search by title or author, so your local bookshop or library is best placed to advise you on the availability of the following/earlier recommendations.

You can get most of the books below in Shanghai. Costs are generally much the same as in Hong Kong, which is generally more expensive than other countries.

Lonely Planet

Lonely Planet produces the comprehensive country guide *China,* and the more detailed guide *South-West China* (covering Yunnan, Sichuan, Guizhou and Guangxi provinces), as well as *Tibet, Beijing, Hong Kong* and *Hong Kong, Macau and Guangzhou.* Also published by LP are *Healthy Travel Asia & India,* and *Read This First: Asia & India.*

Guidebooks

Odyssey produces a good general *Shanghai* guide (7th edition 1999). It also publishes *The Western Food Lovers Guide to Shanghai.* This 1997 edition is getting a bit out of date now so hopefully they'll produce a new edition.

Fodors (in association with AA guides) publish a colourful but lightweight Shanghai guide, which is accessible if you just have a day or two in the city. It also comes with a good fold-out map. Fodors also publish a pocket guide to Shanghai but it suffers from dull format and baffling use of pinyin.

There are several guides aimed at expats living in Shanghai, though almost everything written about Shanghai becomes out of date as soon as the ink is dry. All are most easily obtained in Shanghai and unfortunately suffer from a severe lack of decent maps.

Odyssey finish their Shanghai trilogy with *Living in Shanghai,* by Jennifer Dawson & Douglas Dawson III, a mother and son team who run a relocation company in Shanghai. The same authors also publish the rather outdated *Vigers Guide to Setting Up in Shanghai* (1998).

One of the most fascinating (and often hilariously politically incorrect) guides to Shanghai is *All About Shanghai: A Standard Guidebook.* Written in 1934, the guide was recently republished by Oxford University Press.

Photographic

Eternal Shanghai, by Jean Francois Danis and Greg Somerville, offers a photo tour of modern Shanghai.

Shanghai: A Century of Change in Photographs (1843–1949) is a hardback album of wonderful historic photographs brought alive with some interesting text and captions by famous Shanghai aficionado Lynn Pan.

Shanghai in Old Days has equally interesting photos but the Chinese-language text makes it far less accessible.

History

Pan Ling's *In Search of Old Shanghai* gives a rundown on who was who and what was what back in the bad old days. At 140 pages, it's an easy read and an excellent intro to the city's murky past.

Shanghai: Crucible of Modern China, by Betty Peh-T'I Weh, is a more detailed history of the city until 1943. *Old Shanghai,* by the same author, is a shorter, easier read.

Bookshops

Shanghai is one of the better places in China to stock up on reading fodder. Fuzhou Lu has traditionally been the bookshop (and brothel) street of Shanghai and is well worth a stroll (the brothels have gone).

The main Foreign Languages Bookstore (Map 5) is at 390 Fuzhou Lu and was undergoing a facelift at the time of writing. The 1st floor currently has a good but pricey range of cards, maps and books on Shanghai and the 4th floor has an astonishing range of imported books including Lonely Planet guides and phrasebooks, though at higher prices than you'll find abroad. The Foreign Languages Bookstore is open daily from 9 am to 6 pm. Smaller branches can be found at 71 Shuicheng Nanlu in Gubei and at 50 Hongqiao Lu in Xujiahui.

Book City (Map 5), just down the road at No 456 Fuzhou Lu, puts many Western bookshops to shame and includes a restaurant and Internet cafe. Unfortunately most of the books are in Chinese except those on the 6th floor, which are mainly art books. Other branches at 345 Nanjing Donglu and 701 Huaihai Zhonglu are smaller and of less interest.

The Shanghai Museum bookshop has an excellent range of books on Chinese art, architecture, ceramics and calligraphy and is definitely worth a visit if you are in the museum. It also has a wide selection of good-quality cards and slides.

One of the best places for heavy art books, both international and Chinese, is the 2nd floor of the Duoyunxuan art shop (Map 5) on Nanjing Donglu.

The small but well-stocked bookshop in the Friendship Shopping Centre (Map 9), at 26 Xianxia Lu in Hongqiao, has a good range of magazines, tourist books and postcards. The Friendship Store (Map 5), near the Bund, also has a good selection of books about Shanghai on the ground floor.

Also worth a visit is the Old China Hand Reading Room (Map 6), at 27 Shaoxing Lu, open late to 11 pm. See Teahouses in the Places to Eat chapter for more information.

Several of the top hotels have good bookshops, including the Equatorial, Huating and Jinjiang. One of the best is in the Hilton, where most books are, surprisingly, often 20% cheaper than at the Foreign Languages Bookstore.

The China National Publications Import & Export Co (Map 4) at 555 Wuding Lu has a good collection of art books. Both it and the Foreign Languages Bookstore will order almost any book if you give them the ISBN.

Shanghai, by Harriet Sergeant, is recommended. This portrait of the city in its heyday combines first-hand accounts with extensive research and lively reconstruction. The latest book to chronicle the good old bad old days of Shanghai is Stella Dong's *Shanghai: the Rise and Fall of a Decadent City, 1842-1940.* Released in 2000, the book is well researched and received good reviews

No Dogs and Not Many Chinese; Treaty Port Life in China 1843–1943, by Frances Woods, is another look at foreigners' experiences in Shanghai and the other treaty ports, largely pieced together through reminiscences and quotes.

A Short History of Shanghai, by FL Hawks Potts, was written in 1928 by the man who headed Shanghai's top university, St John's, for 52 years.

Secret War in Shanghai, by Bernard Wasserstein, is a dense, sometimes heavygoing look at 'Treachery, subversion and collaboration in the Second World War'. The real joy of the book is its fascinating cast of characters, such as 'abortionist, brothelowner and sexual extortionist' Dr Albert Miorini, 'monkey expert, narcotics dealer and unqualified 'Doctor'' (and friend of Errol Flynn) Hermann Erben, the British gun runner General 'One-Arm' Sutton, and 'journalist, aviator and pimp' Hilaire du Berrier.

For a scholarly look at wartime Shanghai, *Shanghai Badlands,* by Frederic Wakeman Fr, focuses on the clandestine terrorist war waged between Kuomintang agents and Japanese assassins in the Badlands area of western Shanghai between 1937 and 1941.

Economics & Business

The China Business Handbook is an annual business guide to China published by China Economic Review. It offers an excellent and up-to-date overview of doing business in China and gives an economic sketch of all China's provinces and major cities.

There are plenty of books on doing business in China. If you're headed for Shanghai on business you might want to check out *China Business Etiquette,* by Scott D Seligman; *Managing China; An Executive Survival Kit,* by Dr Stephanie Jones; *Sun Tzu and the Art of Business,* by Mark McNeilly; or *The Business Guide to China,* by Lawrence Brahm and Li Daoran.

For an academic look at the economic history of the region try *Shanghai; Transformation and Modernisation under China's Open Policy,* edited by YM Yeung and Sung Yun-Wing, or *Shanghai and the Yangzi Delta; a City Reborn* edited by Brian Hook.

Art

Ancient Chinese Bronzes in the Shanghai Museum, by Chen Peifen, gives a good rundown on the bronzes on display at the museum. It is available in the Shanghai Museum bookshop for Y150.

The Chinese Garden, by Joseph Cho Wang, is an Oxford University Press mini-hardback that gives a good introduction to the concepts behind Chinese gardens. It's especially worth a read if you are headed to the famous gardens of Suzhou.

Fiction

Shanghai '37, by Vicky Baum, is a novel set in 1930s Shanghai and climaxing at the Peace Hotel. It draws a thinly veiled depiction of Du Yuesheng.

Shanghai, by Christopher New, is an epic novel tracing several generations of Chinese and expats in Shanghai.

Shanghai: Electric and Lurid City, by Barbara Baker, is an anthology of more than 50 passages of writing about Shanghai, from its pre-treaty port days to the eve of the 21st century. It takes extracts from novels, biographies, letters, diaries, poems and short stories.

JG Ballard's *Empire of the Sun* tells of the author's internment as a child in the Longhua Camp during WWII, and was subsequently made into a film by Steven Spielberg.

Biographies & Reminiscences

Life and Death in Shanghai, by Nien Cheng, is a classic account of the Cultural Revolution and is one of the few biographies with a Shanghai angle.

Red Azaela, by Anchee Min, is a sometimes racy account of growing up in Shanghai in the 1950s and 1960s amid the turmoil of the Cultural Revolution.

Daughter of Shanghai, by Tsai Chin, has less to say about Shanghai but is still a good read. Chin left China in 1960 and later starred in the films *The World of Suzie Wong* and the *Joy Luck Club.*

The Life, Loves and Adventures of Emily Hahn, by Ken Cuthbertson, is a look at the fascinating life of Emily Hahn, who passed through Shanghai in 1935 (accompanied by her pet gibbon Mr Mills), got hooked on opium and became the concubine of a Chinese poet.

Captive in Shanghai, by Hugh Collar, is a fascinating personal account of life in the Japanese internment camps in the early 1940s. It's published by Oxford University Press, but is pretty hard to get your hands on.

WH Auden and Christopher Isherwood visited China in 1938 during an unsettled time in Shanghai. They investigated local factory conditions and met with Du Yuesheng. Only one chapter of their subsequent book *Journey to a War* covers Shanghai, but it's worth a read if you can track it down.

Architecture

A Last Look: Western Architecture in Old Shanghai, by Tess Johnston and Deke Erh, offers a fascinating photographic record of buildings in the city. Shanghai is also partly covered in their book *Western Architecture in China's Southern Treaty Ports*. Keep an eye out for their newest book on the old French Concession. These books are widely available in Shanghai, particularly at the Old China Hand Reading Room.

A Tour of Shanghai Historical Architecture is a blue paperback book, published by the Shanghai Municipal Tourism Administration. It's excellent for those in search of the remaining islands of colonial architecture.

Shanghai Architecture & the City, by Luigi Novelli, is an architect's view of Shanghai. There is an emphasis on the city's modern buildings, with the merger of Western and Chinese architecture a major theme.

Children's Books

A favourite with children and adults alike is Hergé's *The Blue Lotus*, written in 1931 as the fifth in the 'Tintin' series, and based on actual events.

The Ghost of Shanghai, written by Claude Guillot with fine illustrations by Fabienne Burckel, is a children's picture book which tells the story of a young Chinese girl who is visited by a (friendly) ghost from 1920s Shanghai.

Language

Lonely Planet produces an indispensable Mandarin phrasebook. Berlitz also offers a good Chinese phrasebook.

Making Out in Chinese, by Ray Daniels, is an outrageous language guide that gives a bilingual translation for the whole process of finding a mate, from chat-up lines in a bar to sex, arguments and the apparently inevitable acrimonious split. Perfect for Julu Lu at 4 am.

A similarly provocative language guide is *Outrageous Chinese,* by James J Wang, which teaches fluent street language, with sections on swearing, bribery and sex – all the words you never learned at school.

NEWSPAPERS & MAGAZINES

In the late 1990s life for foreigners in Shanghai improved considerably with the appearance of three entertainment publications edited and compiled by native speakers of English. There were some shaky beginnings and changeovers as the authorities tried to come to terms with these upstart foreigners creating their own broadsides – in a country that controls its media with an iron fist, this was no small feat. If you want to know what's going on in Shanghai, these are your best sources of information. They're free and available in most of the Western-style bars and restaurants and some hotels. The classified sections are a good place to find a flat, a VCD for sale, language teachers and even a job.

The most comprehensive is the glossy monthly magazine *That's Shanghai* (now known simply as *That's*), the Shanghai equivalent of London's *Time Out,* packed with cultural info and entertainment listings.

The monthly *Shanghai Talk,* put out by Ismay Publications, is another excellent insight into Shanghai's cultural life and entertainment scene.

Quo is a new glossy magazine with a more artistic feel but also with good Shanghai listings.

Shanghai Travel, produced every two months by the Shanghai Municipal Tourism Administration, has some listings, travel news and features on local sites, though it's mostly just a plug for expensive hotels. *Travel China* is the national version, published by National Tourism Administration, and has news pertaining to tourism in China, with the occasional interesting feature on little-known destinations.

Shanghai's other English-language papers and periodicals appear anaemic by comparison. Apart from the national *China Daily,* there's the more locally focused but equally insipid *Shanghai Daily,* which also has a Web site at www.shanghaidaily.com. The *Shanghai Star,* owned by *China Daily,* comes out every Tuesday and Friday, and is the best of the bunch, with listings of events, hotel buffets and airline schedules. It's Web site is at www.shanghai-star.com.cn.

A small range of foreign newspapers and magazines is available from the larger tourist hotels (eg, Park, Jinjiang, Hilton) and some shops. Publications include the *Wall Street Journal, International Herald Tribune, Asiaweek, South China Morning Post, Far Eastern Economic Review, Economist, Time* and *Newsweek.* They are relatively expensive, however, with *Newsweek* and *Time* usually costing about Y35, with *Far Eastern Economic Review* double this. The bookshop at the Hilton stocks German newspapers.

The China National Publications Import & Export Co (Map 4; ☎ 6255 4199), at 555 Wuding Lu, can arrange subscriptions to more than 400 periodicals from around the world.

FILMS

Dozens of films have been made about Shanghai. In many, Shanghai was merely a backdrop, brought in whenever the film needed an element of mystery, allure or just plain sleaze. Shanghai never even appears in Hitchcock's *East of Shanghai,* Orson Welles' *Lady from Shanghai* or Charlie Chaplin's *Shanghaied.*

Charlie Chan had a couple of inevitable adventures in a Shanghai about as Chinese as Charlie Chan. In *Charlie Chan in Shanghai,* the Chinese government invites Charlie to investigate a murder involving an opium ring. Follow-ups include *Shanghai Cobra* (1945) and *The Shanghai Chest.*

The most famous Shanghai-related movie is probably *Shanghai Express* (1932), one of the world's top-grossing films in 1932/33. It won an Oscar for best cinematography and a best director nomination for director Josef von Sternberg, though it created a strong backlash in China. It features Marlene Dietrich purring the immortal line: 'It took more than one man to change my name to Shanghai Lily'.

Other films that buffs can track down are *The Shanghai Gesture* (1941), directed by Joseph Von Sternberg and starring Gene Tierney and Victor Mature; and *West of Shanghai* (1937), starring Boris Karloff.

Steven Spielberg's *Empire of the Sun* was based on JG Ballard's autobiographical account of his internment in Shanghai as a child during WWII (see Books earlier in this chapter). For something lighter there's always Madonna's 1986 *Shanghai Surprise,* co-starring her then-husband Sean Penn.

The recent Hollywood film *Pavillion of Women,* adapted from Pearl Buck's novel and starring Willem Defoe and Luo Yan, was filmed in nearby Suzhou and tells the story of a US missionary who falls in love with the concubine of a rich Chinese family.

Shanghai's most famous recent actress is Joan Chen (Chen Chong) who started her career at the Shanghai Film Studio in the late 1970s and gained international fame in David Lynch's *Twin Peaks.* Shanghai's most famous domestic actress is Liu Xiaoqing.

The best documentary on modern Shanghai is Phil Agland and Charlotte Ashby's superb *Shanghai Vice.* The soap-opera style series offers an absorbing glimpse of the seedy underside of Shanghai and the concerns of local Shanghainese.

CD-ROM

The only CD-ROM about Shanghai we found was *Century of Shanghai,* published by the Jiangsu General Publishing House, for sale in the bookshop of the Peace Hotel (Y125). There are several China-related CD-ROMs for sale on the 2nd floor of the Duoyunxuan art shop, Nanjing Donglu, though most are in Chinese.

RADIO & TV

Expats and travellers staying in mid-range hotels can get their fix of CNN, ESPN and Star TV. For the rest of us it's slim pickings.

Record-breaking grain harvests and other encouraging news about Shanghai's development is broadcast in English on Shanghai Broadcasting Network (SBN), on weekdays at 10 pm. *Citybeat,* a truly dreadful cultural program, replaces this on Sundays. CCTV4 has a slightly better English-language news program on weekdays at 7 pm and 11.00 pm, and at noon on the weekend. It also has *China This Week,* at 2.30 pm on Sunday, and *Centre Stage,* an entertainment program, at 12.30 pm on Sunday, though broadcast times change fairly regularly.

If you simply can't do without a weekly dose of Americana then JT Video Club

(☎ 6388 3049) can provide videos of last week's American TV favourites such as *Friends, Frasier, Ally McBeal* and *ER*.

The BBC World Service can be picked up on 17760, 15278, 21660, 12010 and 9740 kHz. Voice of America (VOA) is often a little clearer at 17820, 15425, 21840, 15250, 9760, 5880 and 6125 kHz. You can find tuning information for the BBC on the Web at www.bbc.co.uk /worldservice/tuning/, for Radio Australia at www.abc.net.au/ra/, and for VOA at www.voa.gov/.

VIDEO SYSTEMS

The various countries of the world cannot agree on a single TV broadcasting standard and this creates problems. China subscribes to the PAL system, the same as Australia, New Zealand, the UK and most of Europe. Competing systems not used in China include SECAM (France, Germany and Luxembourg) and NTSC (Canada, Japan, Taiwan, Korea, Latin America and the USA).

This should become less of a problem as video yields to DVD. If you are thinking of buying a VCD (video CD) player, note that these can play both VCDs and CDs, but not DVDs.

PHOTOGRAPHY & VIDEO

Photo opportunities are a mixed bag in Shanghai. Many of the old buildings are hidden behind electricity cables and telephone lines, making it impossible to get a clear picture. Grey weather can last for weeks, especially in winter, so it's worth bringing a range of film speeds.

Photography is a common pastime among Shanghainese and most people are happy to pose for a picture, especially if you're taking a shot of their child. Nobody (except a few obnoxious stallholders at the Yuyuan Gardens) expects any payment for photos, so don't give any or you'll set a precedent.

Many Chinese will disagree with you on what constitutes good subject matter; they don't really see why anyone would want to take a street scene, a picture of a beggar or a shot of a Shanghai alley.

Film & Processing

Big-name colour print film (Kodak, Fuji etc) is available almost everywhere, but is mostly 100 ASA. Black-and-white film can be found at a few select photo shops, but it's expensive to process in Shanghai. Costs are around Y20 for 36-exposure 100ASA Kodak print film. Slide film *(fănzhuănpiàn)* is relatively easy to get in Shanghai. A roll of 36 exposures costs from Y45 for 100 ASA Elite Chrome to Y59 for 100 ASA Sensia.

Processing is available everywhere, courtesy of the Kodak franchising empire, but it's not especially cheap. Print developing costs from Y30 to Y77 for 36 exposures, depending on the size of the prints. Slide processing costs around Y45/65 for 24/36 exposures for a standard next-day service. For where to buy and process film see the Shopping chapter. There is no place in China to develop Kodachrome. Undeveloped film can be sent out of China and, going by personal experience, the dreaded X-ray machines do not appear to be a problem.

Lithium batteries can generally be found at photo shops, but you should always carry a spare.

Instant passport photo machines are located in most metro stations.

Restrictions

Some museums and temples prohibit photography, mainly to protect the postcard and colour slide industry. It prevents Westerners from publishing their own books about these sites and taking business away from the Chinese-published books. It also prevents valuable works of art from being damaged by flash photos. We have mentioned any photo restrictions in the relevant sections of the Things to See & Do chapter.

Photography from aeroplanes, and photographs of airports, military installations, harbour facilities, train terminals and bridges can be touchy subjects. Of course, these rules only get enforced if the enforcers happen to be around.

TIME

Time throughout China is set to Beijing local time, which is set eight hours ahead of

GMT/UTC. There is no daylight-savings time. When it's noon in Shanghai, it's 8 pm (the day before) in Los Angeles, 11 pm (the day before) in Montreal and New York, 4 am (the same day) in London, 5 am in Frankfurt, Paris and Rome, noon in Hong Kong, 2 pm in Melbourne, and 4 pm in Wellington.

ELECTRICITY

Electricity is 220 volts, 50 cycles AC. Plugs come in at least four designs: three-pronged angled pins (like in Australia); three-pronged round pins (like in Hong Kong); two flat pins (US-style but without the ground wire); and two narrow round pins (European-style).

Conversion plugs and voltage converters are easily found if you need to convert from a Chinese to foreign system but are a pain to track down the other way round. Bring all your converters with you.

WEIGHTS & MEASURES

The metric system is widely used in China. However, traditional Chinese weights and measures persist, especially in local markets. Fruit and vegetables are weighed by the *jīn* (500g). Smaller weights (for dumplings, tea, herbal medicine etc) are measured in *liǎng* (50g). The following equation may help:

metric	Chinese	Imperial
1m *(mǐ)*	3 *chǐ*	3.28 feet
1km *(gōnglǐ)*	2 *lǐ*	0.62 miles
1L *(gōngshēng)*	1 *shēng*	0.22 gallons
1kg *(gōngjīn)*	2 *jīn*	2.2 pounds

The other unit of measure that you might encounter is the *píng*. Píngs are used to measure area, and one píng is approximately 1.82 sq m (5.97 sq feet). When you buy cloth or carpet, the price may be determined by the number of píngs. It's the same deal for leasing or purchasing an apartment or house.

LAUNDRY

Almost all tourist hotels have a laundry service; if you hand in clothes in the morning you should get them back the same evening or the next day. If the hotel doesn't have a laundry, the staff can usually direct you to one. Hotel laundry services tend to be expensive and if you're on a tight budget you might wind up doing what many travellers do – hand washing your own clothes.

Shanghai has plenty of dry-cleaners *(gānxǐdiàn)* – you can find them in most metro stations. The cheaper, family-run places will sometimes do laundry as well.

TOILETS

Shanghai has plenty of public toilets, normally marked by English signs; they run the gamut from a communal ditch costing three mao to a flash computer-controlled portaloo for Y1. The best bet is to head for a top-end hotel, where someone will hand you a towel, pour you some aftershave and wish you a nice day.

The golden rule is: *Always* carry an emergency stash of toilet paper – you never know when you'll need it. You can often buy a piece of industrial-strength cardboard at a public toilet but this is a worst-case scenario.

Toilets are generally sitters not squatters, especially in hotels, museums etc. In all but the cheapest hotels it's safe to flush toilet paper down the toilet. If you see a small wastepaper basket in the corner of the toilet, that is where you should throw the toilet paper. Tampons always go in the basket.

Remember, the Chinese characters for men and women are:

men:　男　　women:　女

HEALTH

Shanghai is a reasonably healthy city, apart from the smog and the danger of getting knocked down crossing the road. The major dangers facing travellers are upset stomachs, dehydration in the hot summers and pneumonia or flu in winter (the latter compounded by endemic spitting). If you suffer from a respiratory problem like asthma you may find that it is aggravated by the pollution.

Immunisation

No immunisations are required for entry into China, except yellow fever if you are coming from an infected area (parts of Africa and South America – there is no risk of yellow fever in China). As a basic precaution before travelling anywhere, it's a good idea to ensure that your tetanus, diptheria and polio vaccinations are up to date (boosters are required every 10 years).

Discuss your requirements with your doctor, but other vaccinations you should consider before coming to China are hepatitis A, which is a common food- and water-borne disease, and hepatitis B, which is transmitted through sexual activity and blood (hepatitis B is highly endemic in China). Other vaccinations for a longer-term stay include Japanese B encephalitis and rabies.

Plan ahead for getting your vaccinations: Some of them require more than one injection, while some vaccinations should not be given together. Malaria is not a problem in Shanghai. If you live in Shanghai it's not a bad idea to get a vaccination every autumn against influenza, especially for seniors.

Health Insurance

It is essential that you have adequate health insurance that includes repatriation. You may want a policy that pays hospitals directly rather than requires you to pay first and then reimburses you later. See Travel Insurance under Documents earlier in this chapter for details.

Other Preparations

If you wear glasses take a spare pair and your prescription. If you require a particular medication take an adequate supply, as it may not be available locally. Take part of the packaging showing the generic name rather than the brand, which will make getting replacements easier. To avoid any problems, it's a good idea to have a legible prescription or letter from your doctor to show that you legally use the medication.

Basic Rules

Food There is an old colonial adage that says: 'If you can cook it, boil it or peel it

you can eat it ... otherwise forget it'. Vegetables and fruit should be washed with purified water or peeled where possible. Beware of ice cream that is sold in the street or anywhere it might have been melted and refrozen; if there's any doubt (eg, a power cut in the last day or two), steer well clear. Shellfish such as mussels, oysters and clams should be avoided, as should undercooked meat, particularly in the form of mince or undercooked dumplings. Steaming does not make shellfish safe for eating.

In general, Chinese dishes are cooked individually and stir-fried at such a heat that all the germs get incinerated. More worrying are the cheaper, buffet-style canteens, which cook food and then keep it (and the bugs) warm over a low flame. Avoid these places. If a place looks clean and well run then the food is probably safe.

Water Shanghai's tap water is chemically purified but one look at Suzhou Creek (once the city's main water supply) should be enough to send you heading for the bottled water. The main problem with the tap water is that it tastes so awful. Bottled water is available everywhere – just check that the seal is in place. Milk should be treated with suspicion, as it is often unpasteurised, though boiled milk is fine if it is kept hygienically. Tea or coffee should also be OK, since the water should have been boiled.

Medical Problems & Treatment

Influenza The most likely illness to befall you in Shanghai is influenza *(liúxíngxìng gǎnmào)*. China is notorious for outbreaks of nasty strains of flu and pneumonia is a possible complication. The problem is especially serious during winter, though you can catch it at any time of the year. The situation is exacerbated by the Chinese habit of spitting anywhere and everywhere, which spreads respiratory illnesses. You can protect yourself up to a limited extent with a flu vaccine, but 100% protection would require that you live in total quarantine or give up breathing. People over the age of 65 should consider a pneumonia shot.

Medical Kit Check List

Following is a list of items you should consider including in your medical kit – consult your pharmacist for brands available in your country.

☐ **Aspirin** or **paracetamol** (acetaminophen in the USA) – for pain or fever
☐ **Antihistamine** – for allergies, eg, hay fever; to ease the itch from insect bites or stings; and to prevent motion sickness
☐ **Cold and flu tablets, throat lozenges** and **nasal decongestant**
☐ **Multivitamins** – consider for long trips, when dietary vitamin intake may be inadequate
☐ **Antibiotics** – consider including these if you're travelling well off the beaten track; see your doctor, as they must be prescribed, and carry the prescription with you
☐ **Loperamide** or **diphenoxylate** –'blockers' for diarrhoea
☐ **Prochlorperazine** or **metaclopramide** – for nausea and vomiting
☐ **Rehydration mixture** – to prevent dehydration, which may occur, for example, during bouts of diarrhoea; particularly important when travelling with children
☐ **Insect repellent, sunscreen, lip balm** and **eye drops**
☐ **Calamine lotion, sting relief spray** or **aloe vera** – to ease irritation from sunburn and insect bites or stings
☐ **Antifungal cream or powder** – for fungal skin infections and thrush
☐ **Antiseptic** (such as povidone-iodine) – for cuts and grazes
☐ **Bandages, Band-Aids (plasters)** and other wound dressings
☐ **Water purification tablets or iodine**
☐ **Scissors, tweezers** and a **thermometer** – note that mercury thermometers are prohibited by airlines
☐ **Sterile kit** – in case you need injections in a country with medical hygiene problems; discuss with your doctor

Diarrhoea Simple things like a change of water, food or climate can all cause a mild bout of diarrhoea, but a few rushed toilet trips with no other symptoms is not indica-tive of a major problem. In Chinese diarrhoea is known as lā dùzi (spicy stomach).

Dehydration is the main danger with any diarrhoea, particularly in children or the elderly as dehydration can occur quite quickly. Weak black tea with a little sugar; soda water; and soft drinks allowed to go flat and diluted 50% with clean water are all good. Urine is the best guide to the adequacy of replacement – if you have small amounts of concentrated urine, you need to drink more. Keep drinking small amounts often. Stick to a bland diet as you recover.

Gut-paralysing drugs such as loperamide or diphenoxylate (examples are Lomotil or Immodium) can be used to bring relief from the symptoms, though they do not actually cure the problem. Only use these drugs if you do not have access to toilets, eg, if you *must* travel. Note that these drugs are not recommended for children under 12 years.

In certain situations antibiotics may be required: diarrhoea with blood or mucus (dysentery); any diarrhoea with fever; profuse watery diarrhoea; persistent diarrhoea not improving after 48 hours; and severe diarrhoea. These suggest a more serious cause of diarrhoea; in these situations gut-paralysing drugs should be avoided and you should seek medical help.

Sexually Transmitted Diseases & AIDS Shanghai's image as the 'Whore of the Orient' may have passed, but the sexual revolution is booming in China, and Sexually Transmitted Diseases (STDs; xìng bìng) are spreading rapidly. Therefore it pays to be cautious in sexual activity, particularly as you could be unlucky enough to catch herpes (incurable) or, worse still, acquired immune deficiency syndrome (AIDS). Apart from sexual abstinence, condoms provide the most effective protection and are available in China. The word for condom is bǎoxiǎn tào, which literally translates as 'insurance glove'.

Infection with the human immunodeficiency virus (HIV) may lead to AIDS, which is a fatal disease. Any exposure to blood, blood products or body fluids may put the individual at risk. The disease is often transmitted through sexual contact or dirty needles – vaccinations, acupuncture, tattooing and body piercing can be potentially as dangerous as intravenous drug use.

Much of the blood supply in China is *not* tested for AIDS, so if you really need a transfusion it is safest to find a healthy friend to donate blood to you rather than rely on the stocks in hospitals. You may choose to buy your own acupuncture needles, which are widely available in Shanghai, if you intend to have that form of treatment. Medical clinics which cater to foreigners all use disposable needles and syringes, which you can ask to see unwrapped in front of you. Fear of HIV/AIDS should never preclude treatment for serious medical conditions.

Medical Facilities

Shanghai is credited with the best medical facilities and most advanced medical knowledge in China. The main foreign embassies keep lists of the English-speaking doctors, dentists and hospitals that accept foreigners.

Hospital treatment and out-patient consultations are available at the 19th-floor foreigner's clinic of the Huashan Hospital (Map 6; Huáshān Yīyuàn, ☎ 6248 9999, ext 1921) at 12 Wulumuqi Zhonglu, which has a Hong Kong joint-venture section; and at the International Medical Care Centre (IMCC) of Shanghai First People's Hospital (Map 5; Dìyī Rénmín Yīyuàn, ☎ 6306 9480, 6324 0090 ext 2101) at 585 Jiulong Lu in north-east Shanghai.

The New Pioneer International Medical Centre (NPIMC; Map 8; Xīnfēng Yīliáo Zhōngxīn, ☎ 6469 3898, fax 6469 3897), 2nd floor, Geru Bldg, 910 Hengshan Lu, just north of Xujiahui, provides comprehensive private medical care by expat doctors as well as dentists and specialists. It is affiliated with BUPA International (Britain's largest private medical plan) and accepts RMB, US$ and credit cards. It can provide individual and corporate health-care plans, home visits, ambulances and evacuation services; the centre is open 24 hours. For non-members, expect a doctor's consultation fee of US$70 and an ambulance charge of US$100.

World Link (Ruìxīn Guójì Yīliáo Zhōngxīn) offers similar medical and dental services to NPIMC and also provides family and corporate health plans, as well as Chinese traditional medicine and health-education classes. There is a clinic located at Suite 203 in the Shanghai Centre, 1376 Nanjing Xilu, (Map 4; ☎ 6279 7688, 6466 1614, fax 6279 7698), open Monday to Friday 8 am to 5 pm and Saturday 9 am to 4 pm; and in Hongqiao (Map 9; ☎ 6405 5788, fax 6405 3587), which is at 788 Hongxu Lu, is open Monday to Friday 9 am to 5 pm, and also offers dental work. The consultation fee is US$70. After-hours services and an emergency hotline are provided for members. The clinic has a Web site at www.worldlink-shanghai.com.

Contacts for medical assistance include:

Dr Anderson & Partners (☎ 6270 3263, fax 6209 6099) Room 1001, New Century Plaza, 48 Xingyi Lu, Hongqiao. This private clinic welcomes walk-in patients.

Australian Clinic (Map 6; ☎ 6433 4604) 17 Fuxing Xilu (in the Australian Consulate). Open 9 am to 4.30 pm Monday and 9 am to 1 pm Thursday and Friday for Australian passport holders, though other passport holders can phone for advice on other facilities.

Huadong Hospital (Map 6; ☎ 6248 3180 ext 3106) 221 Yan'an Xilu, 2nd floor, Foreigners Clinic

International Peace Maternity Hospital (Map 8; ☎ 6438 2434) 910 Hengshan Lu

Ruijin Hospital (Map 6; ☎ 6437 0045, fax 6431 2610) 197 Ruijin Erlu

Shanghai Medical University Children's Hospital (Map 6; ☎ 6403 7371) 183 Fenglin Lu. Staff will make house calls.

Dental services include:

Shanghai Dental Medical Centre (Map 7; ☎ 6313 3174 fax 6313 9156) 7th floor, 9th People's Hospital, 639 Zhizaoju Lu.

Shanghai Ko Sei Dental Clinic (Map 6; ☎ 6247 6748) 666 Changle Lu. This clinic is a Sino-Japanese joint venture.

Shenda Dental Clinic (Map 6; ☎ 6437 7987 fax 6466 1798) 1, Lane 83, Taiyuan Lu

World Link (Map 9; ☎ 6405 5788, fax 6405 3587) 788 Hongxu Lu, Hongqiao

Traditional Chinese Medicine Hospitals specialising in traditional Chinese medicine include the Longhua Hospital (Map 3; ☎ 6438 5700) at 132 Lingling Lu, 1km east of Shanghai Stadium, and Shuguang Hospital (Map 7; ☎ 6326 1650) at 185 Pu'an Lu, just next to Huaihai Park.

One of Shanghai's most famous Chinese herbal medicine stores is Cai Tong De (Map 5), at 450 Nanjing Donglu, with a branch at 396 Jinling Donglu.

Pharmacies
The Hong Kong store Watson's sells imported toiletries and over-the-counter pharmaceuticals. There are many branches in Shanghai – see the Toiletries section of the Shopping chapter for a few. For harder-to-find foreign medicines try the Shanghai No 1 Dispensary at 616 Nanjing Donglu or the 24-hour pharmacy (Huáshān Yàofáng) outside the Huashan Hospital on Wulumuqi Zhonglu.

Medical Testing
Chinese health authorities seem convinced that the entire population of certain countries is infected with or at risk of HIV. Foreigners planning to live in Shanghai for a period of six months or more are required to undergo an AIDS test. You can do the test outside China and present the results (on an official Chinese form, stamped by your doctor or hospital) to obtain the required certificate but there is a chance that you may still have to take a local test. Inquiries can be made and tests done at the following centres:

Shanghai Health & Quarantine Bureau
   (☎ 6286 6171) 1701 Hami Lu
Pujiang Health & Quarantine Bureau
   (☎ 6323 1752) 13 Zhongshan Dong Yilu

Emergencies
For an ambulance call ☎ 120, though the person answering may not always speak English. Even ambulance workers admit that unless it is a life-or-death situation, or you are immobile, you are better off taking a taxi.

International SOS Assistance/Asia Emergency Assistance (AEA) International

(☎ admin 6295 9951, alarm centre 6295 0099) has an office at No 2606, Shartex Plaza, 88 Zunyi Nanlu. It has a Web site at www.internationalsos.com.

WOMEN TRAVELLERS
In general, foreign women are unlikely to suffer serious sexual harassment in Shanghai. There have been reports of foreign women being harassed by Chinese men in parks or while cycling alone at night, but rape cases involving foreign women are not common and most Chinese rapists appear to target Chinese women.

Police tend to investigate crimes against foreigners more closely than they do crimes against locals, and more severe penalties (like execution) are often imposed. This provides non-Chinese women with a small but important aura of protection.

It's always a good idea to dress modestly in a foreign country, though most young Shanghainese women dress somewhat provocatively.

GAY & LESBIAN TRAVELLERS
Local law is ambiguous on this issue, but generally the authorities take a dim view of gays and lesbians. Certainly a scene exists in Shanghai and has done for a while (WH Auden and Christopher Isherwood investigated gay Shanghai together in 1938) but few dare say so too loudly. While the police tend not to care what foreigners do, things can get heavy when Chinese nationals are involved. Chinese men sometimes hold hands; this carries no sexual overtones in China.

For excellent and up-to-date information on the latest gay and lesbian hot spots in Shanghai and elsewhere throughout China, have a look at the Web site at www.utopia asia.com/tipschin.htm.

DISABLED TRAVELLERS
Shanghai's traffic and the city's many over- and underpasses pose the greatest challenges to disabled travellers. The metro system currently isn't wheelchair friendly, though there are plans to change this.

That said, Shanghai is placing increasing emphasis on accessibility, especially in the wake of the 2000 National Games for the Disabled, which were held in Shanghai. Deng Pufang, eldest son of Deng Xiaoping (and himself a paraplegic), is the director of the Chinese Federation for the Disabled and has used his influence to push through many proposals. An increasing number of modern buildings, museums, stadiums and most new hotels display the white symbol of a wheelchair, showing that they are wheelchair accessible. Bashi Taxi has a number of wheelchair-accessible minivan taxis (☎ 6431 2788). It is advised that disabled travellers bring at least one able-bodied companion; it's best not to rely on the kindness of the Shanghainese.

Shanghai's blind community has an informal centre at the braille reading room of Xujiahui District Library, 80 Nandan Donglu, open 1 to 5 pm daily.

China's sign language has regional variations, as well as some elements of American Sign Language (ASL), so foreign signers may have problems communicating in sign language.

SENIOR TRAVELLERS
As already noted in the Health section, China is one vast reservoir of the influenza virus. The elderly are particularly prone, and pneumonia can be a fatal complication. Older travellers should be sure that their influenza vaccines are up to date and should not hesitate to seek medical care or leave the country if problems arise.

Aside from this, Shanghai poses no particular problems for seniors.

SHANGHAI FOR CHILDREN
China's one-child policy has created a generation of spoiled, demanding and, more often than not, overweight 'Little Emperors'. Fortunately for visitors with children Shanghai's entrepreneurs have devised plenty of ways of keeping kids occupied.

Amusement and water parks like Ocean World, Dino Beach, Aquaria 21 and Jinjiang Amusement Park (see the Entertainment chapter) are favourites and a blessing in summer when temperatures can be uncomfortably high.

Shanghai's parks can be a bit tame for kids, though Fundazzle in Zhongshan Park is a favourite, especially as McDonald's, Pizza Hut and KFC are all nearby. Several McDonald's restaurants offer play areas for young children. The Botanical Gardens have a nice children's park. The zoo and circus are other favourite standbys, and children often enjoy activities like paintball, karting etc (see the Things to See & Do chapter).

In general 1.4m is the cut-off height for children's cheaper fares or entry tickets.

For shops catering to children see the Shopping chapter. Ikea has play tables for shoppers' kids. All department stores and malls have entertainment complexes on the top or basement floors.

A good source for children's sports leagues, classes, toy stores and schools is www.shanghaiguide.com/shanghai/kids.

For advice on travelling with children pick up *Travel with Children*, by Maureen Wheeler, published by Lonely Planet.

Schools
Schooling is usually part of an expat job package, which is good, as most of the schooling options in Shanghai range from US$6000 to US$14,000 per year. The following is a contact list:

Shanghai American School (SAS)
   West Campus: (☎ 6221 1445, fax 6221 1269, ℮ info@saschina.org) 50 Jidi Lu
   East Campus: (☎ 5837 6173, fax 5837 4898) 2700 Huaxia Lu, Pudong
   Web site: www.saschina.org
Concordia International School Shanghai (CISS) (☎ 5899 0380, fax 5899 1685) 52 Huangyang Lu (PO Box 206 005) Jinqiao, Pudong. An American school.
   Web site: www.ciss.com.cn
Shanghai Changning International School (☎ 6252 3688, fax 6212 2330, ℮ scis@uninet.com.cn) 155 Jiangsu Lu. An American-based school.
Yew Chung Shanghai International School (SIS) (☎ 6242 3243, fax 6242 7331, ℮ enquiry@ycef.com) 11 Shuicheng Lu. Offers kindergarten, primary and secondary education with a UK-based curriculum, and campuses in Hongqiao, Gubei and Pudong.
   Web site: www.ycef.com

French/German School of Shanghai (☎ 6405 9220, fax 6405 9235, ✉ shgrsch1@ online.sh.cn) 437 Jinhui Lu
Web site: www.dss.online.sh.cn

L'ècole Française de Shanghai (☎ 5976 3431/335, fax 5976 3429) New Rainbow Asia Garden A8, 1655 Huqingping Gonglu

Shanghai Middle School (☎ 6476 5516) 400 Shangzhong Lu. The international division offers bilingual tuition.

Soong Qing Ling Kindergarten (☎ 6242 9841) 61 Hongmei Beilu

USEFUL ORGANISATIONS
Clubs

Shanghai has an incredible number of clubs, with interests ranging from French cooking to scuba diving. Most are aimed at expats but if you will be in Shanghai for a while and have a special interest they can be a good contact point. Most nationalities have their own social clubs (eg, Brits Abroad, Le Cercle Francophone etc); enquire at your embassy. Major universities also have alumni clubs. Contact details change as expats come and go so check listings magazines for details. For sporting clubs see the Things to See & Do chapter.

Organisations

The Shanghai Expatriate Association is the largest such organisation in Shanghai and is a good first contact point for new arrivals. The Expatriate Professional Women's Society (EPWS; ☎ 6279 1563, 6279 1699) holds regular meetings and social gatherings, forming a network for professional working women. The American Women's Club (☎ 6279 8316) is more social and arranges monthly lunches, with guest speakers.

For information on the countless other expat organisations in Shanghai check out the Community pages of *That's* and *Shanghai Talk*.

Charities

A couple of foreign-run charities exist in Shanghai, for those who wish to contribute something back to the city.

Friends of Hope (☎ 6384 0609) supports and raises money for Project Hope, a US program aimed at raising levels of health care in China. Projects in Shanghai include a children's medical centre. Volunteers also teach English to hospital staff.

Shanghai Sunrise arranges for expats to sponsor the education of a local underprivileged child for about Y2500 per year, and also provides education and library materials. Volunteers are needed to help find sponsors, organise libraries and visit children's homes. Contact Bonnie Guerra (☎ 5897 2233) or check local listings for contact details.

LIBRARIES

Shanghai Library is the biggest in Asia. For Y25 you can get a reading card valid for up to six months, which allows you to read but not borrow publications. The 3rd floor has a wealth of (uncensored) foreign magazines and newspapers such as *Newsweek* and *National Geographic*. For English books published within the last four years head for the 3rd floor, otherwise you have to track books down on the computer system and order them through the stacks. You can photocopy books here for five mao per A4 page.

The foreign languages section of the Shanghai Library is open weekdays from 9 am to 5 pm.

UNIVERSITIES

Shanghai has some of China's finest universities and with its international outlook, good entertainment scene and general modernity, is a fairly popular place for foreigners looking to study Chinese.

Two of the most famous universities in Shanghai are Fudan University (Fùdàn Dàxué, ☎ 6549 2222), 220 Handan Lu, the biggest and best of Shanghai's universities and Tongji University (Map 3; Tóngjì Dàxué, ☎ 6598 1057), 1239 Siping Lu; both are way out in Shanghai's north-eastern suburbs. Around here you'll find the majority of Shangai's foreign students, as well as a collection of local student bars and restaurants. Just south-west of here is Shanghai's Foreign Languages Institute (Wàiyǔ Xuéyuàn).

Other universities include Jiaotong University (Map 6; Jiāotōng Dàxué, ☎ 6281 2414)

1954 Huashan Lu, near Xujiahui (Jiang Zemin's alma mater), and Shanghai Normal University (Shànghǎi Shīdàxué) in the southwest.

Most foreign students live on campus in designated foreign-student dormitories, where they are looked after by the *wàibàn* (foreign affairs department) of the university. Note that if you have a student visa and intend to make a visit to Hong Kong or abroad you will need to arrange a re-entry visa through your *wàibàn*.

CULTURAL CENTRES

The following are useful places to keep you culturally connected to your home country and are also a good place to meet internationally minded Shanghainese:

British Council (Map 6; ☎ 6249 3412, fax 6249 3410, ✉ bc.shanghai@britishcouncil.org.cn) 3D Dongyi Bldg, 88–90 Changshu Lu. This is a typically snobbish place, of interest mainly to Chinese wishing to study in the UK, but they do have recent British newspapers and generous free Internet access. There are plans to move in the future; try the Web site for the new location. The centre is open weekdays from 8.30 am to noon and 1.30 to 5pm.
Web site: www.britishcouncil.org.cn

Alliance Française (Map 5; ☎ 6357 5388, fax 6325 1183, ✉ shanghai@alliancefrancaise .org.cn) 297 Wusong Lu. On the 5th floor of a crummy office block, this is an excellent resource for French speakers. French films are shown every Friday at 6.30 pm (while we were there great films like *Subway, Diva* and *A Bout de Souffle* were playing) as well as unedited TV5, France's version of CNN. There's a large French library with magazines, newspapers and videos and the occasional exhibition. The centre also offers French language classes and Internet access. Membership is Y120 per year but short-term visitors can just pop in.
Web site: www.alliancefrancaise.org.cn

German Centre (Map 3; ☎ 6501 5100) 1233 Siping Lu. In the middle of nowhere at Tongji University in Shanghai's north-eastern suburbs, the centre holds regular consular events and shows German films every Friday night.

US Consulate Bureau of Public Affairs (Map 4; ☎ 6279 7662) Room 532, Shanghai Centre, 1376 Nanjing Xilu. This has a reading room with American newspapers and periodicals, and Internet access.

DANGERS & ANNOYANCES

The crime rate is really quite low in Shanghai; even the taxi drivers don't try to rip you off. One of the most unsavoury parts of town lies around the train station, where many migrant workers end up scraping a living until they get proper jobs.

If you do get something stolen you need to report the crime at the district PSB office and get a police report. If you get something stolen on the metro, the Renmin Square metro station has its own PSB office.

Traffic is a major danger in Shanghai; it is essential to look in five directions at once (including above you, in case of falling construction debris) whenever you cross the street. Don't *ever* expect any vehicle to stop for you. Shanghai's most annoying traffic problem is the swarm of mopeds and bikes that weave up and down the pavements dodging pedestrians (because certain sections of Shanghai's roads are off-limits to bikes). The sheer volume of people in Shanghai can be too much on the weekend, especially visiting Yuyuan Gardens or getting on the metro at Renmin Square.

In many ways Shanghai is unlike the rest of China and it's certainly an easier place to visit as a tourist. Public transport is largely non-smoking and levels of service are far higher than other parts of China. Many people speak English and are used to foreigners. However, Chinese who have had little contact with foreigners become embarrassed by the language barrier and in defence they will giggle and shake their heads. Your own emotions in these situations may run the gamut from humiliation to frustration to outright anger. The only way for you to save face is to laugh along with them.

Spitting

China's national sport, spitting, is not as widespread in Shanghai as the rest of China. Government campaigns to stamp out the practice have been reasonably successful and spitting is prohibited in many buildings and the Nanjing Donglu pedestrian zone. But there will still be times, especially in the early morning, when you hear an ear-shattering, lung-scraping 'HOIK!'.

Most Chinese spit for health reasons – they believe that the mucus is better out than in. Some Taiwanese like to joke that the mainlanders spit because they've had a bad taste in their mouths ever since the communists took power.

Personal Space

Years of communism, communalism, Confucianism and living in the same house as your parents and grandma have resulted in the fact that personal space is generally not as highly valued a commodity in China as it is in other countries. No-one is ever going to get a lot of personal space in a country of 1.2 billion people but the reasons for this are often as much cultural as physical.

Westerners have an unspoken and sacrosanct 12-inch halo of private space around them and Chinese don't. Don't, for example, expect someone to walk out of your path if you are headed on a collision course. And don't be surprised if when you are standing a foot from a museum exhibit or notice board someone squeezes into the space between you and the plate glass and blocks out your view.

Expect people to come up and stare if you are reading or writing. Don't be surprised if someone nonchalantly takes the book out of your hands to get a better look, even while you are reading it.

Lǎowài!

Lǎo means 'old' in Chinese and is a mark of respect; *wài* means 'outside' – together they constitute the politest word the Chinese have for 'foreigner'. Get outside the centre of Shanghai and you will sometimes hear the exclamation '*lǎowài*', or alternatively 'Hello, *lǎowài*, hellaaooo'.

There is no point getting annoyed by it. If you answer by saying hello, they (the audience) will often as not break into hysterical laughter. To be fair to the urbane Shanghainese, most people who react this way are migrant workers from the countryside.

You probably won't hear the word *wàiguǐ* ('foreign devil'), a pejorative phrase dating from the end of the Qing dynasty, nor *dàbízi* (big nose), another common epithet. The Qing dynasty 'department of barbarian affairs' has also been disbanded. But even if you speak Chinese fluently, marry a Chinese and spend the rest of your life in China, you will always be a foreigner.

Noise

The Chinese are generally much more tolerant of noise than most foreigners. People watch TV at ear-shattering volumes to drown out the karaoke from a nearby restaurant, drivers habitually lean on the horn, telephone conversations are conducted in high-decibel rapid-fire screams and most of Shanghai seems to wake uncomplainingly to the sound of jackhammers and earth-moving vehicles. If it's peace and quiet you want, head for a remote part of Putuoshan or bring a good set of earplugs.

Racism

There is no racism in China because we don't have any black people.

Student, Chengdu University

I Queue

For all Shanghai's modernity, the lining-up system hasn't exactly caught on here. If there are only two or three people in the queue then you might be able to hold your own but beyond this the line quickly degenerates into a surging mass and it's every frail old man for himself. This is Darwinian theory at its most ruthless.

The metro currently offers the most breathtaking acts of rudeness. One tip is to stand in the centre of the yellow arrows; this is exactly where the door will open. But even with your toes hanging off the platform, someone will manage to slide in front of you. Be polite if your patience persists, but don't expect reciprocation. This is Shanghai – you have to accept the fact that there's nothing you can do about a city of 15 million people! Fortunately, no-one will think it rude when you finally give up and join the scrum.

FACTS FOR THE VISITOR

Racism in China is a knotty problem. Most Chinese will swear blind that neither they nor their government are racist. But then very few Chinese you meet will have thought very deeply about the issue, and the Chinese government itself would never allow lively public debate on China's racist policies and attitudes.

The Chinese are a proud people. Being Chinese links the individual to a long historical lineage, for the most part of which, Chinese believe, their country was the centre of the world (*zhōngguó* (China) literally means 'The Middle Kingdom'). Most Chinese believe it is their destiny to once again lead the world. There's nothing new here, except that being Chinese is defined by blood, not nationality. Chinese public discourse is littered with metaphors of racial purity and fulsome praise for the achievements of the great race of Chinese people, and this is the stuff that racism thrives on.

Gripes aside, foreigners in China are generally treated well. It does help, however, if you are from a predominantly white and prosperous nation. Other Asians and blacks often encounter discrimination in China. The most famous outright racist incident occurred in 1988 when Chinese students in Nanjing took to the streets to protest about black overseas students dating local Chinese women.

Beggars

Yes, beggars do exist in Shanghai's 'socialism with Chinese characteristics' and they are becoming increasingly prevalent. Some beggars squat on the pavement beside posters that detail their sad story. Almost all perk up when they see a foreigner heading their way.

The adults tend not to pounce on foreigners, but it's a different situation with children, who practically have to be removed with a crowbar once they've seized your leg. Child beggars are usually an organised operation, working under the instructions from nearby older women who supervise them and collect most of the cash. There have even been stories of children being kidnapped, taken hundreds of kilometres from their homes and forced into these begging gangs.

LEGAL MATTERS
Dual Nationality

China does not officially recognise dual nationality or the foreign citizenship of children born in China if one of the parents is a PRC national. If you have Chinese and another nationality you may in theory not be allowed to visit China on your foreign passport. In practice, Chinese authorities are not switched on enough to know if you own two passports, and will accept you on a foreign passport. Dual nationality citizens who enter China on a Chinese passport are subject to Chinese laws and are legally not allowed consular help.

Drugs

China takes a particularly dim view of opium and all its derivatives. Shanghai's foreign concessions owe their entire existence to the 1842 Opium War and many a foreign fortune (including some of Hong Kong's largest companies) was made through the opium trade. Today Shanghai has a growing drug problem, this time in heroin, much of which is blamed on the city's Uyghur population.

Foreign passport holders have been executed in China for drug offences and one US citizen convicted on drug-related charges received a 15-year prison sentence. Trafficking of more than 50g of heroin can lead to the death penalty. In 1998 another US citizen was sentenced to death, with a two-year reprieve, on a conviction of drug dealing.

Many Uyghurs deal quite openly in marijuana (hashish). It's uncertain what attitude the police would take towards a foreigner caught using marijuana – they often don't care what foreigners do behind closed doors if no Chinese are involved. Then again, Chinese authorities like to make examples of wrongdoers – 'killing the rooster to frighten the monkey' – so steer clear of all drugs if you don't want to become a surrogate rooster.

Embassies

In the unlikely case that you are arrested, Americans and most other foreign citizens have the right to phone their embassy. Consuls shall be notified within two days of your arrest and consular officials have the right to visit any US detainee within two days of requesting to do so.

BUSINESS HOURS

Banks, offices and government departments are normally open Monday to Friday from 9 am to noon and about 2 to 4.30 pm. Most major post offices open daily from 8.30 am to 6 pm, sometimes until 10 pm. Central telecom offices are open 24 hours. Local post offices are closed on the weekend. Bank of China branches are normally open weekdays from 9.30 to 11.30 am and 1 to 4.30 pm, and most now have 24-hour ATMs.

Most museums are open on the weekend; a few close on Mondays. Most stop selling tickets 30 minutes before they close. The majority of shops and department stores stay open daily to around 10 pm, especially on the weekend.

Shanghai's entertainment is 24-hour. Several Shanghainese restaurants and hotel coffee shops are open 24 hours and bars on Julu Lu stay open until dawn.

PUBLIC HOLIDAYS & SPECIAL EVENTS

New Year's Day (Yuándàn) 1 January

Spring Festival (Chūn Jié) Usually in February, this is otherwise known as Chinese New Year and starts on the first day of the first moon of the traditional lunar calendar. Although officially lasting only three days, many people take a week off work. This is a bad time for a visit – planes are booked out by overseas Chinese and foreigners fleeing the madness, trains are packed with migrant workers returning home, and hotels are booked solid. In Shanghai there is an explosion of firecrackers and fireworks at midnight to welcome the New Year and ward off bad spirits, and there are special services at the Longhua and Jing'an temples. Top Chinese restaurants are booked out well in advance for *niányèfàn* (New Year's Eve dinner). Families paste red couplets onto their doors and hand out *hóngbāo*, red envelopes stuffed with money. Another explosion of firecrackers on the fifth day of the New Year heralds the arrival of the God of Wealth. If you are in China at this time, book your room in advance, don't expect to get

much business done and sit tight until the chaos is over! The Chinese New Year will fall on the following dates: 24 January 2001; 12 February 2002; 1 February 2003.

International Working Women's Day (Fúnǚ Jié) 8 March

International Labour Day (Láodòng Jié) 1 May. This is the closest thing the communists have to a worldwide religious holiday.

Youth Day (Qīngnián Jié) 4 May. This commemorates the student demonstrations in Beijing on 4 May 1919, when the Versailles Conference decided to give Germany's 'rights' in the city of Tianjin to Japan.

Children's Day (Értóng Jié) 1 June

Anniversary of the Founding of the Chinese Communist Party (Zhōngguó Gòngchǎndǎng Qìng) 1 July. This holiday also celebrates China's resumption of sovereignty over Hong Kong.

Anniversary of the Founding of the PLA (Jiěfàng Jūn Jié) 1 August

National Day (Guóqìng Jié) 1 October. This celebrates the founding of the PRC in 1949 with fireworks over the Bund.

Special prayers are held at Buddhist and Taoist temples on days when the moon is either full or just a sliver. According to the Chinese lunar calendar, the full moon falls on the 15th and 16th days of the lunar month and on the last (30th) day of the month just ending and the first day of the new month.

Other festivals include:

The Lantern Festival (Yuánxiēo Jié) It's not a public holiday, but this is a colourful time to visit Shanghai, especially the Yuyuan Gardens. People take the time to walk the streets at night carrying coloured paper lanterns and make *yuánxiao* or *tángyuán* (sweet dumplings of glutinous rice with sweet fillings). The festival falls on the 15th day of the 1st lunar month, and will be celebrated on: 7 February 2001; 26 February 2002; and 16 February 2003.

Birthday of Guanyin (Guānshìyīn Shēngrì) Guanyin is the Goddess of Mercy and this is a good time to visit Taoist temples or Putuoshan. Guanyin's birthday is the 19th day of the 2nd moon and will fall on: 13 March 2001; 1 April 2002; and 21 March 2003.

Tomb Sweeping Day (Qīng Míng Jié) This is a day for worshipping ancestors. People visit the graves of their dearly departed relatives and clean their grave sites. They often place flowers (particularly magnolias, the city's flower) on the tomb and burn 'ghost money' (for use in the afterworld) for the departed. It falls on 5 April in the Gregorian calendar in most years, 4 April in leap years.

Dragon Boat Festival (Duānwǔ Jié) Commemorates the death of Qu Yuan, a 3rd century BC poet-statesman who drowned himself to protest against the corrupt government. It is celebrated with boat races on Lake Dianshan, Zhujiajiao and sometimes even the Huangpu, on the fifth day of the fifth lunar month, ie: 25 June 2001; 15 June 2002; and 4 June 2003.

Mid-Autumn Festival (Zhōngqiū Jié) Also known as the Moon Festival, this is the time to give and receive tasty moon cakes stuffed with bean paste, egg yolk, coconut, walnuts and the like. The Xinghuolou, Xinya and Gongdelin restaurants are Shanghai's most famous cake makers and you'll need to order from here weeks in advance. Gazing at the moon, eating duck and lighting fireworks are popular activities, and it's also a traditional holiday for lovers. The festival takes place on the 15th day of the 8th moon, and will be celebrated on: 1 October 2001; 21 September 2002; and 11 September 2003.

Cultural Events

The Longhua Temple has large New Year celebrations, with dragon and lion dances. At New Year the abbot strikes the bell 108 times while the monks beat on gongs and offer prayers for the forthcoming year.

A Temple Fair is held at Longhua Temple on the third day of the third lunar month (around April). It is eastern China's largest and oldest folk gathering, with all kinds of snacks, stalls, jugglers and stilt walkers. The fair coincides with the blossoming of the local peach trees.

The Shanghai International Tea Culture Festival is usually at the end of April. If you fancy something stronger, the Shanghai Beer Festival staggers into town around the end of July. The Shanghai Tourism Festival kicks off in late September and offers a wide variety of cultural programs. Shanghai also hosts a disappointing biannual international film festival (the next is in 2001) and an annual International Arts Festival, held in November and early December (see the Entertainment chapter for more details).

Most Western festivals are also celebrated where you'd most expect them: St Patrick's Day at O'Malleys; Oktoberfest at Paulaner Brewhouse; 4th July at any American restaurant (see the Entertainment chapter).

Of less interest to foreign visitors is the Nanhui Peach Blossom festival in mid-April, the Osmanthus festival (near Guilin Park) in September or October, and the Tangerine festival in early November.

DOING BUSINESS

Many a business deal has been lost due to social disgraces. If you are doing business in China, it is important to refer to the Society and Conduct section of the Facts about Shanghai chapter. It also helps to have patience, a sense of humour, a cultural adaptability and a tolerance for smoky rooms.

In bureaucratic China, even simple things can be made difficult. Renting property, getting a telephone installed, hiring employees, paying taxes, and so on, can generate mind-boggling quantities of red tape. Many foreign businesspeople working in Shanghai and elsewhere say that success is usually the result of dogged persistence and finding cooperative officials. One thing to make sure of is that you are meeting with the right people, ie, the people who have the power to give you the permission you seek. Knowing who holds the reins of power in Shanghai is essential.

If you have any intention of doing business in Shanghai, be it buying, selling or investing, it's worth knowing that most urban districts *(shìqū)* have a Commerce Office (Shēngyè Jú). If you approach one of these offices for assistance, the reaction you get can vary from enthusiastic welcome to bureaucratic inertia. In the case of a dispute, the Commerce Office may assist you.

Buying is simple, selling is more difficult, but setting up a business in Beijing is a whole different can of worms. If yours is a high-tech company, you can go into certain economic zones and register as a wholly foreign-owned enterprise. In that case you can hire people without going through the government, enjoy a three-year tax holiday, obtain long-term income tax advantages and import duty-free personal items for corporate and expat use (including a car!). The alternative is listing your company as a representative office, which doesn't allow you to sign any contracts in China – these must be signed by the parent company.

It's easier to register as a representative office. First find out where you want to set up (the city or a special economic zone), then go through local authorities (there are no national authorities for this). Go to the local Commerce Office, Economic Ministry, Foreign Ministry, or any ministry that deals with foreign economic trade promotion. Contact your embassy and national trade organisation first – they can advise you.

The most important thing to remember when you go to register a company is not to turn away when you run into a bureaucratic barrier. Bureaucrats will tell you that everything is 'impossible'. In fact, anything is possible – it all depends on your *guānxi* (relationships). Whatever you have in mind is negotiable, and all the rules are not necessarily rules at all. The flip side of this is that without a legal framework in China, companies often find themselves without any legal recourse in the event of a dispute, such as when your staff leaves en masse to set up an identical enterprise across the road.

Rates of taxation vary from zone to zone, authority to authority. It seems to be negotiable but 15% is fairly standard in economic zones. Every economic zone has a fairly comprehensive investment guide, which is available in English and Chinese – ask at the economic or trade section of your embassy, which might have copies of these.

Finally, don't expect to make a quick buck in Shanghai. Of the 17,622 foreign enterprises operating in Shanghai, over half of them are losing money and most don't expect investments to pay off for another decade.

Useful Organisations

Shanghai Foreign Investment Development Board, under the auspices of the Foreign Economic Relations and Trade Commission, has been set up to keep foreigners informed of the government's latest economic regulations.

Networking nights are currently held on the last Thursday of every month in Charlie's Bar in the Crown Plaza Hotel. Call the hotel for details.

US Commercial Center (Map 4; ☎ 6279 7640) Room 631, Shanghai Centre, 1376 Nanjing Xilu. This is the overseas office of the US Department of Commerce and can assist US businesses to find Chinese business partners.

American Chamber of Commerce (AmCham) (Map 4; ☎ 6279 7119) 4th floor, Shanghai Centre, 1676 Nanjing Xilu. This office helps members only.

British Chamber of Commerce (BritCham) (Map 4; ☎ 6218 5022, fax 6218 5066, ✆ british@uninet.com.cn) Room 1701–1702, Westgate Tower, 1038 Nanjing Xilu; the China Britain Business Council (☎ 6218 5183) is also here.

Exhibitions & Conventions

Apart from the monster venues listed in this section, all the top-end hotels provide conference facilities (see Places to Stay). A new conference centre is currently being built in Pudong's Central Park.

Shanghaimart (Map 9; Shànghǎi Shìmào Shāngchéng, ☎ 6236 6888, fax 6236 0181, ✆ smtexc@shangmart.com.cn) 2299 Yan'an Xilu

Shanghai Exhibition Centre (Map 6; Shànghǎi Zhǎnlǎn Zhōngxīn, ☎ 6270 0279, fax 6247 4598) 1000 Yan'an Zhonglu. This centre houses 42 exhibition halls covering 15,000 sq m, plus a theatre, restaurants and cafes.

Intex Shanghai (Map 9; Shànghǎi Guójì Zhǎnlǎn Zhōngxīn, ☎ 6275 5800, fax 6275 7210, ✆ intex@public.sta.net.cn) 88 Loushanguan Lu
Web site: www.intex-sh.com

Shanghai International Convention Centre (Map 5; Shànghǎi Guójì Huìyì Zhōngxīn, ☎ 5879 2727, fax 5887 9707) 2727 Binjiang Dadao, Pudong. Opened in 1999 for the Fortune 500 forum, this centre offers a 3000-seat ballroom, an 800-seat conference room and a hotel.

Shanghai Everbright Convention and Exhibition Centre (Map 8; Shànghǎi Guāngdà Huìzhǎn Zzhōngxīn, ☎ 6451 6345, fax 6436 0000) 40-80 Caobao Lu. Has an attached four-star hotel.

Shanghai Worldfield Convention Centre & Hotel (Map 3; Shànghǎi Shìbó Huìyì Dàjiǔdiàn, ☎ 6270 3388, fax 6270 4554, ✆ conventh@public.sta.net.cn) 2106 Hongqiao Lu
Web site: www.conventhotel.com

Printing

Alphagraphics (Map 4; ☎ 6215 3115, fax 6215 0432) Room 102, Zhongchuang Bldg, 819 Nanjing Xilu; and (Map 9; ☎ 6275 8861, fax 6275 1626) Suite 102, Shartex Plaza, 88 Zunyi Nanlu, Hongqiao. In addition to photocopying, printing, design and copying services, this company will hire out Mac computers.

Copy General (Map 6; ☎ 6279 4207, fax 6279 1563, ✉ copygsh@uninet.com.cn) 88 Tongren Lu; and (☎ 5835 8223) 1st floor, Xinlian Plaza, 721 Zhangyang Lu, Pudong

Snap Printing (Map 6; ☎ 6248 8877, fax 6248 7210, ✉ snapsha1@guomai.sh.cn) 85 Fumin Lu; and (☎ 6209 9392, fax 6209 5910) 108 New Town Mansion, 55 Loushanguan Lu, Hongqiao. Copying, design, printing, laminating, binding, IBM and Mac computer hire (Y40/80 per hour) and Internet access. It offers free pick-up/delivery for jobs over Y200. Web site: www.snapprint.com.au

Accountants

For help with with tax-related issues try:

Ernst & Young (☎/fax 6219 1219) 12th floor, Shartex Plaza, 88 Zunyi Nanlu

Deloitte Touche (☎ 6393 6292, fax 6393 6290) Room 1402, Liangyou Tower, 618 Shangcheng Lu

Price Waterhouse Coopers (☎ 6270 9989, fax 6270 9990) 7th floor, Shartex Plaza, 88 Zunyi Nanlu

Translation Services

Businesspeople should always hire their own translator, who should speak both Mandarin and Shanghainese dialect.

International Communication Concepts (☎ 5830 4990). Offers simultaneous translation over the phone, 24 hours a day.

President Translation Services (☎ 5490 0228, fax 5490 0229, ✉ sherry@public.sta.net.cn) 9E Huijia Mansion, 37 Caoxi Lu Web site: www.pts.com.tw

Insurance

AIU (☎ 6350 8180 ext 6134, fax 6350 8183, ✉ info@aiush.com.cn) 7th floor, Novel Plaza, 128 Nanjing Xilu

Office Space

There are dozens of buildings looking for office occupants and buildings keep going up, despite current occupancy rates of about 60% (40% in Pudong). If you are looking

for a temporary office the following companies offer 'instant offices' equipped with bilingual secretaries:

Bellsouth (☎ 6729 8900, 6279 8011) 4th floor, Shanghai Centre, 1376 Nanjing Xilu. Virtual offices and computer services.

Regus (☎ 6465 1308, 5047 8837, fax 6465 1240) 31st floor, Jinmao Bldg, Pudong Web site: www.regus.com

Servcorp (☎ 2890 3000, ✉ shang21 @online.sh.cn) Senmao International Bldg, Pudong Web site: www.servcorp.net

For couriers see the Post & Communications section earlier in this chapter.

MOVING TO SHANGHAI

These companies can box it up, ship it over, deal with customs officers, and deliver to your new home, though officially only if you have local residency. Prices vary from around US$275 to US$500 per cubic metre, depending on the destination and how much you have to ship.

Asia-Pacific Worldwide Movers (☎ 6209 6690, fax 6208 6774, ✉ aspac@mail.online.sh .cn) Room 1808, Block 1, 1024 Hongqiao Lu

Asian Express International Movers (☎ 6386 0606, fax 6385 0106, ✉ shanghai@aemovers .com.hk) 7th floor, Yujia Mansion, 1336 Huashan Lu

Crown Relocations (☎ 6472 8761, fax 6472 0255, ✉ general.cnshg@crownworldwide.com) 6306–7 Ruijin Business Centre, 118 Ruijin Erlu Web site: www.crownworldwide.com

Orient Pacific International Worldwide Mover (☎ 5831 8927, fax 6876 2074) 2102 Jiaxing Mansion, 877 Dongfang Lu

Schenker (☎ 5404 8067, fax 5404 8090, ✉ schsha@scenker-sha.com.cn) Room 304–306, Shanghai Taipan Business Center, 2 Donghu Lu

Sino Santa Fe (☎ 6233 9700, fax 6233 9005, ✉ santafe.ssf-sha@eac.com.sg) 3rd floor, No 8, Lane 137, Xianxia Lu, Hongqiao

Sources Far East Ltd (☎ 6268 9541, fax 6268 8004, ✉ sources@public.sta.net.cn) Longbai1 1 11B, 2461 Hongqqiao Lu

For moves within Shanghai or elsewhere in China try Linmin Home Moving Service (☎ 6377 1260), at 1470 Zhongshan Nanlu.

ARCHITECTURE
OF SHANGHAI

ARCHITECTURE OF SHANGHAI

From the Roman to the British empires, massive public monuments have been erected to express a sense of permanence and wealth. Shanghai's architecture, from the elegant edifices of the early 20th century to the hi-tech vision of the future in Pudong, is no different.

Shanghai's cosmopolitanism is most apparent in its buildings. A stroll of less than a kilometre can reveal an amazing spread of architectural designs: from Georgian to Gothic, Chicago to Neoclassical, Spanish villas to imperial Chinese courtyards. According to Tess Johnston, author of *A Last Look: Western Architecture In Old Shanghai*, 'there is no city in the world today with such a variety of architectural styles'.

For many, the greatest pleasure in Shanghai is to wander down the city's side streets, tracking down the ghosts of the past. Like giant skeletons, these buildings are all that remains of old Shanghai and each holds its own tales and history.

Concession Architecture

Early architectural construction hit some unusual snags in Shanghai. Due to the lack of qualified architects, some of the earliest Western-style buildings in Shanghai were partially built in Hong Kong, shipped to Shanghai, and then assembled on site.

Moreover, the glorious Bund was built (literally and metaphorically) on unstable foundations, due to the leeching mud of the Huangpu River. Bund buildings were first built on concrete rafts that were fixed onto wood pilings, which were allowed to sink into the mud. Thus, the bottom entrance step usually originated six feet in the air and sank to ground level with the weight of the building.

In the 1920s the British architectural firm of Palmer and Turner designed many of Shanghai's major buildings (13 buildings on the Bund alone), including the **Bank of China**, the Neoclassical **Hong Kong and Shanghai Bank**, the **Peace Hotel**, **Yokohama Specie Bank**, **Grosvenor House** and **Customs House**, the latter apparently inspired by the Parthenon. In a remarkable stroke of continuity, the company that shaped so much of 1930s Shanghai has returned to design many of the buildings of the 1990s, including the **Harbour Ring Plaza** just off Renmin Square.

Old Shanghai's other main architect was Ladislaus Hudec, a Czech who eventually made it to Shanghai after being exiled to Siberia by the Russians. Shanghai's **American Club**, **Moore Memorial Church**, **China United Apartments**, **Grand Theatre** and **Park Hotel** (the largest building in the Far East until the 1980s) all owe their creation to Hudec.

Many of Shanghai's buildings were constructed in Baroque, Neo-Grecian and Neoclassical styles to affirm ties with the homelands of the British and French. The 1920s saw the introduction of Art Deco to Shanghai, particularly in theatres, providing a cultural link with New

Title Page;
The Longtangs
(Illustration by
Kelli Hamlett)

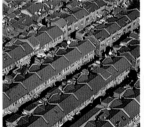

Clockwise from top:
Detail of a Shanghai
Christian church; the
1930s Chicago-style
Shanghai Mansions on
the Bund; an opulent
colmn of the Russian-
influenced Shanghai
Exhibition centre; the
Georgian-style Jinjiang
Hotel; the shikumen
housing of Shanghai that
combines the Western
terrace with the Chinese
interior courtyard.

CHRIS MELLOR

CHRIS MELLOR

BRADLEY MAYHEW

MARIE CAMBON

Top left: The magnificent former Hong Kong & Shanghai Bank on the Bund.

Top right: The facade of the Bund's Everbright Bank.

Middle right: A Russian Orthodox Church in the former French Concesiion.

Bottom: A sweeping view of the grand colonial architecture of the Bund.

CHRIS MELLOR

BRADLEY MAYHEW

MARIE CAMBON

Top left: The Peace Palace Hotel.

Top right: Customs House: a fine example of Shanghai colonial architecture.

Middle left: The legendary Peace Hotel on the Bund.

Bottom: The 1919 brief for the Hong Kong & Shanghai Bank read: 'Spare no expense but dominate the Bund'

CHRIS MELLOR

BRADLEY MAYHEW

CHRIS MELLOR

Top: The striking pink baubles of the Oriental Pearl Tower.

Bottom: The main atrium of the Shanghai Museum.

York. The buildings of the 1930s owed more to the USA Chicago style, reflecting rising American power. Fine examples include the **Metropole Hotel, Hamilton House, Grosvenor House (Jinjiang Hotel), Shanghai Mansions** and **Picardie Mansions (Hengshan Hotel)**.

These vast buildings, with their imposing presence, provided a sense of security as well as reflecting the financial optimism of the time. In the end, though, after all the expense and effort, most buildings only served their original purpose for about 15 years before their owners were booted out in 1949. Communism successfully mummified rather then transformed Shanghai, and recently the government has begun to preserve and restore these architectural giants.

Those interested in old houses and backstreet architecture might be interested in contacting the Shanghai Historic House Association. For contact details see *That's* or other local magazines.

Lòngtángs

Lòngtángs are to Shanghai what *hútòngs* are to Beijing: back alleys which form whole communities. Lòngtángs are Shanghai's major indigenous urban architectural feature.

After the Small Swords Rebellion in 1853, and subsequent civil strife, some 20,000 Chinese fled into the International Settlement. Sensing they could make a quid or two, the British decided to scrap the law forbidding foreigners owning or subletting houses, and British and French speculators built hundreds of houses in what became Shanghai's biggest real estate boom. The result was the *shíkūmén* (stone gatehouse), a unique mixture of East and West, of interior Chinese courtyard and English terraced housing, which at one stage made up 60% of Shanghai's housing. These were originally designed to house one family, but Shanghai's growth led to sublets of many families, each of which shared a kitchen and outside bathroom to complement the *matang* (chamber pot). For the Shanghainese, a single-family kitchen and separate bedrooms remained a dream until the 1990s.

One preserved, prettified example of the shíkūmén is the Xintiandi complex, south of Huiaihai Zhonglu, between Madang Lu and Huangpi Nanlu (see that entry in the Things to See & Do chapter), though there are hundreds more around town.

Modern Architecture

In a rush towards modernity Shanghai is rapidly deconstructing and reconstructing itself. There is more construction and relative investment now than there ever was in the 1920s. Much of the city resembles a huge building site of ambitious new projects, forested by cranes and fuelled by migrant workers from Sichuan and Anhui.

The results are mixed, but Shanghai has undoubtedly become a testbed of Western and Chinese architecture. Shanghai's theatres evoke some particularly interesting comparisons: Compare the **Chinese**

theatre in Yuyuan Gardens with the 1930s Art-Deco style of the **Lyceum Theatre**; and compare that with the millennial **Shanghai Grand Theatre**.

The Shanghai Grand Theatre, designed by French architect Jean-Marie Charpentier, has an interesting design, incorporating the sweeping eaves of Chinese tradition with a futuristic use of plastic and glass. This mix of East and West is nothing new to Shanghai; just look at the Chinese roofs on the otherwise foreign-inspired **YMCA** and **Bank of China** buildings.

The architecture of the **Shanghai Urban Planning Exhibition Hall** echoes that of the Grand Theatre. Its distinguishable roof has four 'florets' to symbolise four budding magnolias, the city's flower.

The buildings in Renmin Square have an interesting layout. The three main buildings lie on an axis cutting through a circle formed on the north by Renmin Park and the south by Renmin Square, to form what some say is the character *zhōng* (China). All the main buildings orientate south, in line with Chinese imperial tradition and the tenets of *fēngshuǐ*, which are to create harmony, order and a positive flow of energy. You can find more symbolism at the **Shanghai Centre**, which was built in the shape of the Chinese character *shān* (mountain).

The Bladerunner-style Pudong skyline forms a modern, ostentatious, hi-tech counterpart to the historic Bund. The gaudy flamboyance of the **Shanghai International Convention Centre**, with its Neoclassical lines and giant glass globes, is rivalled only by the shocking pink baubles of the **Oriental Pearl TV Tower**. Only the graceful **Jinmao Tower** can stand tall with the fine buildings of the Bund, tied as it is to their collective past with its own modern Art-Deco twist.

If things go according to plan, Shanghai may well soon have the tallest building in the world. The **Shanghai World Finance Building**, whose plot stands next to the Jinmao, will total 90 storeys and 460m (1518 feet), topping Malaysia's Petronas Tower (the current highest building) by 35 feet. A giant vertical hole cored through the top floors will house an open-air observatory. Construction is due to start in mid-2000, at an estimated cost of US$750 million, and is racing other planned building projects in Hong Kong, India, Sao Paolo, Melbourne and Chicago to become the

Left: Jinmao Tower (Illustration by Kelli Hamblett)

tallest building in the world. Success may be short-lived though; the Shanghai Urban Exhibition Hall has a model of an even taller building planned for next door.

Jinmao Tower

Towering above Pudong like a 21st-century pagoda, the US$540-million Jinmao Tower is the tallest building in China and, at 420.5m, the third tallest in the world. Designed by the same team that built the Sears Tower in Chicago, the building is highly symbolic. Its 88 floors are auspicious (8 is a lucky number in Chinese) and its 13 bands are linked to Buddhist imagery. Furthermore, the segmented tower is supposed to symbolise bamboo, and also a pen, acting as a counterpoint to the open book–shaped podium. The name Jinmao, meaning 'economy' and 'trade', also carries the additional meanings of 'gold' and 'prosperity'.

Getting There & Away

Shanghai is easy to get to. It is already China's second-largest international air hub (third-largest if you count Hong Kong) and if you can't find a direct flight the city is only an hour's flight from Beijing or Hong Kong. With rail and air connections to places all over China, ferries travelling up the Yangzi River, many boats along the coast, and buses to destinations in adjoining provinces, you'll be hard pushed to find somewhere you can't get to. If you are so inclined you can even travel to and from Shanghai by train all the way from Europe, via Russia's Trans-Siberian Railway.

AIR

The Civil Aviation Administration of China (CAAC; Zhōngguó Mínháng Zǒngjú) has been split into more than 30 regional airline companies. Air China covers most international routes, and China Eastern Airlines, which operates out of Shanghai, has a few

Warning

The information in this chapter is particularly vulnerable to change: Prices for international travel are volatile, routes are introduced and cancelled, schedules change, special deals come and go, and rules and visa requirements are amended. Airlines and governments seem to take a perverse pleasure in making price structures and regulations as complicated as possible. You should check directly with the airline or a travel agent to make sure you understand how a fare (and ticket you may buy) works. In addition, the travel industry is highly competitive and there are many lurks and perks.

The upshot of this is that you should get opinions, quotes and advice from as many airlines and travel agents as possible before you part with your hard-earned cash. The details given in this chapter should be regarded as pointers and are not a substitute for your own careful, up-to-date research.

international services. China Eastern is China's third-largest carrier in terms of fleet. Shanghai Airlines also operates out of Shanghai but is a much smaller airline and currently only has domestic flights.

For domestic and international flights on Chinese airlines the baggage allowance for an adult passenger is 20kg in economy class and 30kg in 1st class. You are also allowed 5kg of hand luggage, though this is rarely weighed. The charge for excess baggage is 1% of the full fare for each kilogram.

Airline information in Chinese is available by phone at ☎ 6247 5953 (domestic) and ☎ 6247 2255 (international).

Departure Tax

International departure tax (known as an 'airport construction fee') is Y90. The domestic departure tax is Y50. Both taxes are paid at the airport. Children under 12 years are exempt from the tax.

Airports

Shanghai is the only city in China to have two international airports.

Up until early 2000 almost all international flights operated out of Hongqiao airport (☎ 6268 8899, 6268 8918), on Shanghai's western outskirts. By mid-2000, however, most international flights had shifted or were in the process of shifting to Pudong airport. Hongqiao will eventually be used mainly for domestic flights, though a few domestic flights also operate out of Pudong.

Pudong international airport (☎ 6834 1000; flight information in English and Chinese ☎ 3848 4500) was formally opened on 1 October 1999 and is expected to eventually handle 20 million passengers per year. The airport is inconveniently located, near the East China Sea, 30km south-east of Shanghai, making it considerably more difficult to get to than Hongqiao airport. If you are making an onward domestic connection from Pudong it is essential that you find out if the domestic flight leaves from Pudong or Hongqiao, as the latter will require *at least* an hour to cross the city. Your ticket should indicate which airport you are flying to/from; Pudong's airport code is PVG, Hongqiao's is SHA.

If you do have to transfer, airport buses and taxis connect the two airports. See the Getting Around chapter for details on how to get to/from and between the airports.

Other Parts of China

Daily (usually several times daily) domestic flights connect Shanghai to every major city in China. Minor cities are less likely to have daily flights, but chances are there will be at least one flight a week, probably more, to Shanghai.

At the time of writing there was no difference in price between Air China, Shanghai Airlines or China Eastern and the government had outlawed discounted fares. However, policies on this change like the wind so it's worth inquiring about the current state of play. You can buy tickets from hundreds of airline offices around town, though only a few take credit cards.

The airlines have Web sites that show current timetables: Shanghai Airlines is at www.shanghai-air.com; China Eastern is at www.cea.online.sh.cn; and Air China is at www.airchina.com.cn.

Business-class tickets cost 25% over economy class, and 1st-class tickets cost an extra 60%. Babies are charged 10% of the adult fare; children aged two to 12 are charged 50% of the adult fare; those over 12 are charged adult fare.

Cancellation fees depend on how long before departure you cancel. On domestic flights, if you cancel 24 to 48 hours before departure you lose 10% of the fare; if you cancel between two and 24 hours before the flight you lose 20%; and if you cancel less than two hours before the flight you lose 30%. If you don't show up for a domestic flight, you are entitled to a refund of 50%.

Airlines often ask you to check in two hours before departure but one hour before is more realistic. More important is to give yourself enough time to get through Shang-

hai's traffic, especially if you are travelling during rush hours. Few people bother to check in luggage on a domestic flight. It's quicker to just lug it on and off the plane.

Domestic air fares from Shanghai include:

destination	one-way fare
Beijing	Y900
Chengdu	Y1290
Chongqing	Y1190
Fuzhou	Y620
Guangzhou	Y1020
Guilin	Y1040
Haikou	Y1330
Huangshan	Y460
Kunming	Y1520
Nanning	Y1330
Ningbo	Y300
Shenzhen	Y1120
Tianjin	Y820
Ürümqi	Y2240
Xian	Y1010
Xiamen	Y770

For fares to Hong Kong and Macau see later in this chapter.

Australia & New Zealand

Qantas Airways, China Eastern and Air China fly direct two or three times weekly to/from Sydney. Other flights are routed via Hong Kong, Seoul, Tokyo and South-East Asian hubs on Ansett Australia or Cathay Pacific Airways.

At the time of research, Qantas fares to Shanghai ranged from A$999 to A$1139. Fares on Singapore Airlines, Cathay Pacific, Thai Airways International and Malaysia Airlines ranged from A$1119 to A$1489 in high season.

Fares from Auckland to Shanghai cost from around NZ$1645 on Malaysia Airlines via Kuala Lumpur to NZ$1985 on Qantas via Sydney.

STA Travel, Trailfinders and Flight Centre International are major dealers in cheap air fares, each with dozens of offices. STA has many offices, including: Sydney (☎ 02-9212 1255, fax 9281 4183), 855 George St, Sydney, NSW 6911; and Auckland (☎ 09-309 0458, fax 309 2059) Ground floor, 10 High St (PO Box 4156), Auckland NZ. Call

☎ 131 1776 Australia wide for the location of your nearest STA branch or try the Web site at www.statravel.com.au.

Flight Centre books tickets on the Internet or by phone (☎ 1300 362 665) and has many offices in Australia and New Zealand listed on its Web site at www.flightcentre .com.au.

Trailfinders has offices in Sydney (☎ 02-9247 7666) at 8 Spring St, Sydney, NSW 2000; in Cairns (☎ 07-4041 1199) at Hides Corner, Shields St, Cairns, Qld 4870, and in Brisbane (☎ 07-3229 0887) at 91 Elizabeth St, Brisbane, Qld 4000.

The UK

Virgin Atlantic raised the standard of travel from the UK when it opened direct flights between London Heathrow and Shanghai in 1999. Flights run four times a week to Pudong and take about 11 hours.

The cheapest discounted fares we found were with Virgin, Air France (via Paris), Lufthansa Airlines (via Frankfurt), and Air China (via Beijing). One-way fares with Virgin are around £270. The cheapest return fares were around £450 but these are only valid for return within 30 days. Tickets valid for a year are more expensive at around £590. Despite what nervous travel agents tell you, it is no problem to enter China on a one-way ticket.

If you are combining a visit to Shanghai with Beijing you can buy 'open-jaw' tickets (ie, in Shanghai, out Beijing) from Lufthansa and Air France.

London's best-known bargain-ticket agencies include:

Trailfinders (☎ 020-7938 3366, fax 7937 9294) 42–50 Earl's Court Rd, Kensington, London W8 6EJ; and (☎ 020-7938 3939) 194 Kensington High St, W8 7RG
Web site: www.trailfinders.com
STA Travel (☎ 020-361 6262) Priory House, 6 Wrights Lane, London W8 6TA
Web site: www.statravel.co.uk
Usit Campus Travel (☎ 020-7730 8111) 52 Grosvenor Gardens, London SW1W 0AG; Campus is also found in many YHA shops
Web site: www.usitcampus.com
Bridge the World (☎ 020-7911 0900) 47 Chalk Farm Rd, Camden Town, London NW1 8AH

Continental Europe

Although Air China has direct flights from Shanghai to Europe, the best fare deals are generally available with European airlines. Air France has direct return flights from Paris to Shanghai for around US$1105 and Lufthansa has direct return flights from Frankfurt for around US$1180.

In France, reliable travel agency chains include the French student travel company OTU (☎ 01 40 29 12 12; www.otu.fr), Nouvelles Frontières (☎ 08 03 33 33 33; www.nouvelles-frontieres.fr) and the Franco-Belgian company Wasteels (☎ 01 43 62 30 00; www.voyages-wasteels.fr).

In Amsterdam, agencies with cheap tickets include the NBBS subsidiary Budget Air (☎ 020-627 1251; www.nbbs.nl) at Rokin 34. In Copenhagen, STA Travel (☎ 33 141 501; www.sta-travel.com) is at Fiolstraede 18 and Kilroy Travels (☎ 33 11 00 44) is at Skindergarde 28. In Berlin, STA Travel (☎ 030-311 0950) has one of its many branches at Goethesttrasse 73 (U2 stop: Ernst-Reuter-Platz).

Recommended travel agencies in Rome include CTS Viaggi, whose many offices around Italy include one at 16 Via Genova (☎ 06-462 0431); and Passagi (☎ 06-474 0923), which is at Stazione Termini FS, Galleria Di Tesla. In Madrid, Usit Unlimited (☎ 902 25 25 75; www.unilimited.es) is at 3 Plaza de Callao; Barcelo Viajes (☎ 91 559 1819) is at Princesa 3; and Nouvelles Frontières (☎ 91 547 42 00; www.nouvelles frontieres.es) is at Plaza de España 18.

The USA

American Northwest Airlines flies direct from Los Angeles daily. United Airlines, American Airlines and American Northwest fly from San Francisco with a stop or change of planes at Tokyo's Narita. Air China flies direct from San Francisco and operates a code-sharing system with Northwest. Flying times are about 16 hours from the west coast and 22 hours from the east coast.

The cheapest fares we found from San Francisco to Shanghai were with United/ China Eastern at around US$770, rising to

US$900 on American Airlines. Fares from New York on United ran between US$913 and US$995. Fares quoted are for high season, from June to early September.

Council Travel (Web site: www.ciee.org) and STA (Web site: www.sta-travel.com) are reliable sources of cheap tickets in the USA. Each has offices across the country. Council's headquarters is at 205 East 42nd St, New York 10017-5706 (☎ 212-822 2600, or toll-free from the USA and Canada 800-226 8624, fax 822 2699, ✆ info@ciee.org). STA's main US offices are at 7202 Melrose Ave, Los Angeles 90046 (☎ 213-934 8722), and 10 Downing St, New York 10014 (☎ 212-627 3111, or toll free 800-777 0112). Also try Gateway Travel (☎ 800-441 1183).

Canada

Air China is generally the cheapest option from Vancouver and flies direct twice a week for around C$1100. Air Canada/Canadian Airlines International are a little more expensive from Vancouver but is cheaper from Toronto at around C$1400. Indirect options include via Tokyo with

---

Hong Kong & Macau SARs

Hong Kong was handed back to China in 1997 and Macau was handed back on 20 December 1999, but for most practical purposes the ex-colonies still act as independent territories. They are now referred to as Special Administrative Regions (SARs).

Flights from Shanghai to Hong Kong and Macau are considered international and so the departure tax is Y90. You will also have to go through Chinese immigration and customs when you travel between the SARs and China proper, so if Hong Kong or Macau is part of your Shanghai itinerary you'll need a double- or multiple-entry Chinese visa to enable you to return to Shanghai.

At the time of writing most nationalities did not require a visa to visit either Hong Kong or Macau.

JAL (Japan Airlines) or via Seoul with Asiana, both about C$1100 (a little more with a stopover).

The best bargain-ticket agency in Canada is Travel CUTS, with a Web site at www.travelcuts.com and around 50 offices located in all major cities. The parent office is at 187 College St, Toronto M5T 1P7 (☎ 416-979 2406, fax 979 8167).

Hong Kong & Macau

China Eastern flies daily to and from Hong Kong for Y1610/3070. Dragonair flies four times a day for about Y1910/3714. You can book Dragonair flights at Cathay Pacific offices around the world.

Air Macau flies twice a day to/from Macau and Shanghai Airlines flies four times a week to Macau, with connections on to Taiwan.

Asia

The Japanese are Shanghai's number one overseas visitors and so there are many flights daily from Shanghai to Tokyo (Narita), Osaka, Nagoya, Fukuoka and Sendai, plus a couple of flights a week to Nagasaki, Hiroshima and Nigada. Your choice of airlines includes JAL, All Nippon Airways, United, Northwest Airlines, China Eastern, Air China and China Northwest.

Getting to South-East Asia is more tricky as there are currently no direct flights from Shanghai to Vietnam, Myanmar, Cambodia, Laos or Indonesia. Thai and China Eastern Airlines fly daily to/from Bangkok, from where you'll probably have to change for connections to Indochina. Alternatively, you can fly to Kunming, where there are flights to Vientiane and Yangon, or to Guangzhou, where there are flights to Hanoi and Ho Chi Minh City. There are plenty of direct flights from Shanghai to Singapore, Kuala Lumpur and Hong Kong.

There are no direct flights to Taiwan, though travellers to/from Taiwan's Kaohsiung and Taipei can buy a single ticket with Shanghai Airlines via Macao and check their luggage all the way through.

There are up to four flights every day to Seoul.

Fares from Shanghai

Buying air tickets in China has never been a great money-saver and in general you won't find many bargains in Shanghai. A London-Shanghai return air ticket, for example, will be much cheaper than a Shanghai-London return. That said, some airlines offer discounted excursion fares and travel agencies often put together hotel and flight packages to popular destinations like Thailand. In general the cheapest available fares are with China Eastern or Air China.

Here is a sample of the best fares (one way/return) we could find in Shanghai at the time of writing:

destination	airline	fare
Bangkok	China Eastern	Y2000/3000
Bangkok	Thai Airways	Y2500/3500
Kuala Lumpur	China Eastern	Y3600/7050
London	Virgin	Y3800/6210
Los Angeles	All Nippon	Y3200/4800
Los Angeles, San Francisco & Seattle	United	Y3500/5490
Any US city	United	Y4510/7040
Paris	China Eastern	Y3500/6100
Seoul	China Eastern	Y1100/2000
Singapore	Air China	Y2700/3700
Sydney	China Eastern	Y4500/5300
Sydney	Qantas	Y5600/6900
Taipei	Air Macau/ Cathay Pacific	Y1970 to Y2160
Tokyo	China Eastern	Y2200/4350
Vancouver	Canadian	Y4000/5600

Airline Offices

China Eastern's main office (Map 6; domestic ☎ 6247 5953, international ☎ 6247 2255) is at 200 Yan'an Xilu, and is open 24 hours a day. There are many other sales offices, as well as ticket sales counters at most major hotels and at the main China International Travel Service (CITS; Zhōngguó Guójì Lǚxíngshè) office in the Guangming building, on Jingling Donglu.

Aeroflot (Map 4; ☎ 6415 6700) Suite 203A Shanghai Centre, 1376 Nanjing Xilu. Flies to/from Moscow and Seoul once a week.

Air China (Map 6; ☎ 6269 2999) 600 Huashan Lu

Air France (Map 5; ☎ 6360 6688) Room 1301, Novel Plaza, 128 Nanjing Xilu. Flies to/from Paris three times a week.

Air Macau (Map 6; ☎ 6248 1110) Room 104, Hotel Equatorial, 65 Yan'an Xilu. Flies to/from Macau twice daily.

All Nippon Airways (ANA) (Map 4; ☎ 6279 7000) Room 208, Shanghai Centre, 1376 Nanjing Xilu. Flies twice a week to Tokyo and twice daily to Osaka.

Asiana (Map 9; ☎ 6219 4000) 2nd floor, Rainbow Hotel, 2000 Yan'an Xilu. Flies twice daily to/from Seoul

Austrian Airlines (Map 5; ☎ 6375 9051) Suite 1103, Central Plaza, 227 Huangpi Beilu. Flies twice a week to/from Vienna.

Canadian Airlines International (Map 5; ☎ 6375 8899) Suite 702, Central Plaza, 227 Huangpi Beilu. Daily connections to Vancouver, Toronto, Montreal and Ontario via Beijing or Tokyo, though all flights from Shanghai are with other airlines such as China Eastern or JAL.

China Northwest (Map 4; ☎ 6267 4233) 258 Weihai Lu. Flies daily to Nagoya and three or four times weekly to Hiroshima and Nigada.

Dragonair (Map 7; ☎ 6375 6375) Suite 2103–4, Shanghai Square, 138 Huaihai Zhonglu. Flies four times daily to/from Hong Kong.

JAL (Map 6; ☎ 6472 3000) Room 201, Ruijin Bldg, 205 Maoming Nanlu. Flies daily to/from Tokyo and Osaka.

KLM (Map 4; ☎ 6279 8088) Suite 207, Shanghai Centre, 1376 Nanjing Xilu. Flies twice a week to/from Amsterdam.

Korean Air (Map 9; ☎ 6275 6000) 1st floor, Office Tower, Yangtze New World, 2099 Yan'an Xilu. Flies five times a week to Pusan.

Lufthansa (Map 6; ☎ 6248 1100) Hilton Hotel, 250 Huashan Lu. Flies five times a week to/from Frankfurt.

Malaysia Airlines (Map 4; ☎ 6279 88607) Suite 209, Shanghai Centre, 1376 Nanjing Xilu. Flies three times a week to/from Kuala Lumpur.

Northwest Airlines (Map 4; ☎ 6279 8088) Suite 207, Shanghai Centre, 1376 Nanjing Xilu. Flies four times a week to/from Los Angeles, San Francisco, Detroit and New York – all via Tokyo.

Qantas (Map 4; ☎ 6279 8660) Suite 208, Shanghai Centre, 1376 Nanjing Xilu. Flies three times a week to/from Sydney.

Royal Nepal Airlines (Map 9; ☎ 6270 8352) 2067, 1st floor, Super Ocean Finance Centre, Hongqiao

Shanghai Airlines (Map 4; ☎ 6255 0550, toll free 800-620 8888) 212 Jiangning Lu

Singapore Airlines (Map 4; ☎ 6289 1000)
Suite 606–608, Kerry Everbright Shopping
Centre, 1515 Nanjing Xilu. Flies daily to/from
Singapore.

Swissair (Map 5; ☎ 6375 8211) Suite 1104,
Central Plaza, 227 Huangpi Beilu. Flies four
times a week to/from Zurich.

Thai Airways International (Map 4; ☎ 6248
7766) 201, Shanghai Centre, 1376 Nanjing
Xilu. Flies daily to/from Bangkok.

Turkish Airlines (Map 4; ☎ 3222 0022) Room
342, Shanghai Centre, 1376 Nanjing Xilu.
Flies twice weekly to/from Istanbul via
Beijing.

United Airlines (Map 4; ☎ 6279 8009) Suite
204, Shanghai Centre, 1376 Nanjing Xilu.
Flies five times a week direct to San Francisco
and daily to New York via Tokyo.

Virgin Atlantic (Map 5; ☎ 5353 4600) Room
221, 12 Zhongshan Dong Yilu (the Bund).
Flies four times a week to/from London.

BUS

Travelling by bus is not a very useful way
to leave or enter Shanghai, though the
Shanghai-Nanjing Hwy has cut road travel
times to less than three hours to Nanjing.
China is currently building a Beijing-
Shanghai Expressway, which will eventually speed up journeys to the north.

For information on getting to/from
Suzhou, Hangzhou and Zhouzhuang see the
Excursions chapter.

There are a few long-distance bus stations in Shanghai but the most useful for
the traveller is probably the Hengfeng Lu
Bus Station (Map 4; ☎ 5663 0230), which
is just next to the Hanzhong Lu metro station. Deluxe buses leave every hour for
Nanjing (Y87, three hours), Ningbo (Y89
to Y96, four hours) and Wuxi (Y35 to Y46,
two hours). The main long-distance bus
station at Hutai Lu and Zhongshan Beilu
(Map 3; ☎ 5661 8801), north of Shanghai
train station, has buses for the above destinations and also to Shaoxing (Y70, three
hours).

The new Xujiahui bus station (Map 8;
☎ 6469 7325) at 211 Hongqiao Lu has departures to Nanjing (Y73 to Y86) at 8 and 9
am and 2 pm, and to Yangzhou at 7 and 9
am and 1 and 3 pm (Y70). There are eight
departures per day along the high-speed

highway to Ningbo (Y82 to Y95), as well as
long-distance buses to Wuhan and Hefei.

Buses to Nanjing's Jinling Hotel (Y88)
depart daily at around 7.20 and 8.20 am,
and 1.30 and 3.30 pm from the Shanghai
Stadium, calling at the Yangtze New World
Hotel in Hongqiao half an hour later. There
are also eight buses daily from the stadium
to Wuxi train station (Y43, two hours) and
Lingshan (Y53), as well as weekend-only
buses to Yangzhou (Y70, three hours) leaving at 7.30 am.

TRAIN

China's rail service is gargantuan and excellent. At any given time it is estimated that
over 10 million Chinese are travelling on a
train in China. Over a billion train tickets
will be sold in the year 2000. Chinese train
travel is a sub-culture unto itself and if you
have time to travel around China after a visit
to Shanghai you should try to incorporate at
least one train journey into your itinerary.

Buying Tickets

There are many options for buying train
tickets in Shanghai. At Shanghai train station, the easiest place is the counter in the
soft seat waiting room (ruǎnxí hòuchēshì)
for current and next-day tickets. It's open
from 7 am to 9 pm, with breaks for lunch
and dinner. Another convenient place is at
the ground floor of the Longmen Hotel, a
short walk west of the train station. You can
book sleepers up to four days in advance –
there's a Y5 service charge.

In town, CITS on Jinling Donglu can
book tickets for a Y10 service charge. You
can also book train tickets across the street
at the ferry ticket office (Y5 service
charge). China Youth Travel Service
(CYTS; Zhōngguó Qīngnián Lǚxíngshè) on
Hengshan Lu also sells advance train tickets. Train ticket outlets are also at 230 Beijing Donglu and 121 Xizang Nanlu; both
are open daily from 8 am to 5 pm. Train information is available over the phone in
Chinese (☎ 6317 1880, 6317 9090).

Buying train tickets is very difficult the
week before and after Chinese New Year,
as Shanghai's migrant workers desert the

city en masse. Try not to make any travel plans at this time. Long-distance tickets should always be bought at least 24 hours, and preferably several days, in advance.

Services

Most trains depart and arrive at the main Shanghai train station (Map 4), but some depart and arrive at the Shanghai west train station (Map 3). Be sure to find out which one you should leave from. Some trains to Hangzhou also leave from Meilong train station, behind the Hongmei Lu metro station in the south-western suburbs.

Travel times from Shanghai are: Beijing (15 to 21 hours), Fuzhou (21 hours), Guangzhou (27 hours), Guilin (27 hours), Hangzhou (two hours), Huangshan (12 hours), Kunming (56 hours), Nanjing (three hours), Qingdao (20 hours) and Xi'an (24 hours).

Special double-decker 'tourist trains' operate between Shanghai and Hangzhou, and Shanghai and Nanjing (with stops at Wuxi, Suzhou, Changzhou and Zhenjiang). They are all comfortable, soft-seat trains and smoking is forbidden; attendants bring around drinks and food and, if you're going to Hangzhou or Nanjing, it is even possible to book your hotel room aboard the train.

To/from Beijing

Trains departing daily from Shanghai train station to Beijing are:

train number	depart	arrive	duration (hours)
K14	5.50 pm	8 am	14¼
K22	7.50 pm	10.05 am	14¼
462	3.36 pm	1.18 pm	21½

From Shanghai west train station to Beijing:

train number	depart	arrive	duration (hours)
K32	11.33 pm	1.40 pm	14¼
108	9.24 pm	3.40 pm	18¼

Express trains to Beijing cost around Y340/500 hard/soft sleeper. (For an explan-ation of train classes see Classes later in this section). Slower trains cost Y180/310 for hard/soft sleeper but take an additional seven hours or so. Berths go quickly on this popular line so book at least a couple of days in advance.

To/From Hong Kong

A direct train service between Shanghai and Kowloon in Hong Kong has been intro-duced to replace the defunct ferry service. Trains run on alternate days and take 28 hours. Tickets cost Y559/571/583 for an upper/middle/lower berth in hard sleeper, Y908 in soft sleeper, or Y1143 in deluxe soft sleeper (a two-berth cabin). The train stops in Hangzhou East and stops for an hour in Guangzhou East and at Dongguan, 1¼ hours from Hong Kong, where Chinese immigration formalities take place. Note that trains and timetables list the destination as *Jiulong*, the official Mandarin Pinyin spelling for Kowloon.

Many of Shanghai's train ticket offices won't sell tickets for this service so you are better off heading to the Longmen Hotel ticket office.

From Hong Kong to Shanghai, berths cost HK$508/519/530 in hard sleeper, HK$825 in soft sleeper and HK$1039 in deluxe soft sleeper. Trains leave Hong Kong's Hung Hom KCR station in Kowloon's east Tsim Sha Tsui at 3 pm and arrive in Shanghai at 6.45 pm the next day. You should arrive at the station at least 45 minutes before departure to go through Hong Kong immigration. Tickets (includ-ing the return leg) can be bought at Hung Hom up to 30 days before departure, as well as at other KCR stations and agents such as the China Travel Service (CTS; Zhōngguó Lǚxíngshè). Facilities at Hung Hom station include ATMs of most banks, restaurants, duty free and luggage storage. For more in-formation call the inquiry hotline (☎ 852-2947 7888).

Changes to the date of travel of Shanghai–Hong Kong tickets can be made up to a day before departure. Full refunds are given 15 days before departure, 70% is refunded up to three days in advance and

50% of the ticket is refunded up to the day before departure.

It's also possible to travel by train to Guangzhou (Y400/600 for a hard/soft sleeper) and then catch either the express train to Hong Kong or a combination of the local train to Shenzhen and then the MCR metro to Hong Kong but this won't save all that much money and it's much more inconvenient.

Elsewhere in China

Trains leave daily from Shanghai train station for other cities in China. See the table 'Trains to Other Cities in China' for times and duration.

A seat to Nanjing costs Y41 to Y73, depending on the train. The double-decker KC2 is China's first bullet train. It is designed to run at 180km/h, though the track won't allow this yet.

For information on trains to Hangzhou and Suzhou see the Excursions chapter.

Classes

In socialist China there are no classes; instead you have hard seat, hard sleeper, soft seat and soft sleeper.

Hard Seat Hard seat (yìngzuò) is how most Chinese travel. Trains are packed to the gills, the lights stay on all night, passengers spit on the floor, the smoke gets so thick that you can't see out the windows and the carriage speakers endlessly drone news, weather and saccharine Canto-pop.

As bad as it is, you should try to experience hard seat at least once, and the more crowded the better. This is China as it exists for the masses, a very different world from Shanghai's glittering tourist hotels.

Soft Seat The most comfortable way to get to destinations around Shanghai is on a soft seat (ruǎnzuò). The seats are comfortable and overcrowding is not permitted. Smoking is prohibited; if you must light up, you'll have to stand in the corridor between the cars. You get free tea and sometimes even a packet of dried plums.

Hard Sleeper Hard sleepers (yìngwò) are comfortable and only a fixed number of people are allowed in the sleeper carriage. The carriage is made up of doorless compartments with half a dozen bunks in three tiers and little foldaway seats by the windows.

Trains to Other Cities in China

train number	destination	depart	arrive	duration (hours)
390	Chengdu	2.32 pm	6.30 am	40
177	Fuzhou	2.23 pm	11.30 am	21
99	Guangzhou	9.40 am	9.17 am	24
49	Guangzhou	5.17 pm	7.27 pm	26
218	Huangshan	7.46 am	7.46 pm	12
79	Kunming	1.22 pm	1.22 pm	48
K2	Nanjing	7 am	10.13 am	3¼
KC2	Nanjing	8 am	10.48 am	2¾
T4	Nanjing	8.50 am	11.48 am	3
T2	Nanjing	1.55 pm	5.30 pm	3½
Y216	Nanjing	3.50 pm	8.18 pm	4¼
K6	Nanjing	5.38 pm	8.33 pm	3
287	Ningbo	6.17 am	1.15 pm	7
T15	Ningbo	9.32 am	2.45 pm	5¼
297	Ningbo	10.49 pm	5.30 am	6¾
175	Xiamen	10.14 am	10.45 am	24½
438	Xi'an	7.30 am	6.45 am	23¼

Newer services such as the train to Hong Kong are nonsmoking (though some passengers need reminding). Sheets, pillows and blankets are provided and it does very nicely as a budget hotel.

Prices vary according to which berth you get: upper, middle or lower. Lower berth *(xiàpù)* is pricier as you get to sit and have more space but it is often invaded by all and sundry who use it as a seat during the day. The top berths *(shàngpù)* are cheapest as you get the least space and nowhere to sit if lower-berth passengers are asleep.

Competition for hard sleepers has become keen in recent years, and you'll be lucky to get one at short notice (say one or two days before you travel).

Soft Sleeper Soft sleepers *(ruǎnwò)* get the works, with four comfortable bunks in a closed, carpeted compartment – complete with straps to keep the top-bunk fatso from falling off in the middle of the night.

Soft sleepers cost around twice as much as hard sleepers and marginally less than flying.

Life on Board

Trains almost always have (overpriced) dining cars and attendants who shuttle up and down the train selling snacks, beer, basic meals and anything else they think they might be able to sell, but the food is generally pretty awful. It's a good idea to bring snacks like fruit, peanuts, instant noodles and mineral water.

Useful items to bring for a long train ride include a cup and plenty of sachets of instant hot drinks, as each group of berths gets a thermos of boiling water (a boiler for refills is located near the toilets). Slippers are useful, as are earplugs to drown out the mass snoring. Cards, books and Walkmans pass the hours and wet wipes are useful, as the air gets grimy.

Once you're on board conductors will swap your ticket for a plastic token until the end of the trip. Keep your ticket when it is returned, as there is normally a final ticket check when you leave the station.

Toilets in all classes are of the squat variety and can be pretty nasty by the end of a long trip. The toilets at the end of a 48-hour hard-seat trip are a clear human rights violation if ever there was one – this is not the place to be wearing flip-flops! Toilets cannot be used when the train is stopped at a station; conductors will lock them 10 minutes before the train arrives at a station.

Lights go off at 10 pm but berths have sidelights so you can carry on reading. Blankets, sheets and pillows are provided for overnight berths. Don't use the towels as towels, or you'll earn the wrath of the conductor – they are actually pillow covers. One thing worth noting is that you can turn off the hideous music by twisting the small button underneath the loudspeaker.

The safety record of the railway system is good. Other than getting your luggage pinched or dying from shock when you see the toilets, there isn't much danger on trains. However, the Chinese have a habit of throwing rubbish out of the windows even as the train moves through a station. Avoid standing too close to a passing train or sitting too close to an open window, lest you get hit by flying beer bottles or chicken bones.

BOAT
Other Parts of China

Boat travel is definitely one of the best ways to leave Shanghai and is also often the cheapest. For destinations on the coast or inland on the Yangzi River, boat travel may even sometimes be faster than the train, which has to take rather circuitous routes. Smaller, grottier boats handle numerous inland-shipping routes.

There are some safety concerns about Chinese passenger boats, however. In November 1999 more than 200 passengers drowned after a Yantai-Dalian ferry sank in heavy seas. Another four people were killed on New Year's Eve 1999 when two boats collided between Nanjing and Shanghai.

Boat tickets can be bought from CITS, which charges a commission, or from the ferry booking office (Map 5) at 1 Jinling Donglu so it's best to compare prices before you fork out to CITS. You can also buy boat tickets at the Shiliupu wharf (Map 5;

☎ 6326 1261) at 111 Zhongshan Dongerlu, from where all domestic sailings depart. The departure point for both domestic and international ferries is eventually to be moved out to the Yangzi near Wusongkou, though no timetable has been set for this yet.

If you are headed west and money is more important than time, boats are the way to go. For example, fares to Wuhan, over 1500km by rail from Shanghai, cost from Y105 to Y351, which makes a berth in 4th class on the boat about half the hard sleeper train fare. For a bit more than a hard sleeper ticket on a train you'd probably be able to get a bed in a two-person cabin on the boat.

The main destinations of ferries up the Yangzi River are Nantong, Nanjing, Wuhu, Guichi, Jiujiang and Wuhan. From Wuhan you can change to another ferry, which will take you to Chongqing (see Yangzi River cruises later in this chapter). If you're only going as far west as Nanjing, take the train, which is much faster than the boat. There are daily departures to all destinations.

There are also daily boats at 4 pm to Dalian (36 hours) with tickets ranging from Y131 to Y387. Boats to Qingdao leave roughly five times per week, but the service might be axed soon so check with the Jinling Donglu office. The trip takes about 26 hours and tickets cost between Y151 and Y231.

Boats to Ningbo leave daily at 8.30 pm (12 hours), with ticket prices ranging from Y46 to Y170. There is also a rapid ferry that leaves daily at 8 am (Y71, five hours).

For details of ferries to Putuoshan see the Excursions chapter.

Yangzi River Cruises

Many people travelling to Shanghai also set their sights on a Three Gorges river trip, especially now that the gorges are on their way to disappearing under dam waters. Looking at the map you might consider continuing the boat trip all the way to Shanghai. The snag is that the most interesting part of the trip is from Chongqing to Yichang or Wuhan; the trip downstream from Wuhan to Shanghai is actually quite dull as the Yangzi spreads to a width of more than 1km. You're generally better off flying the Wuhan-Shanghai leg.

If you decide to take a return trip from Shanghai the best bet is to fly to Chongqing, take the boat trip to Yichang and then fly back to Shanghai. Most travel agencies listed at the end of this chapter offer this kind of package. Note that the trip is considerably slower (but cheaper) upstream compared with downstream.

For more information on the Three Gorges trip see LP's *China* or *South-West China* guides.

Other Countries

Weekly luxury ferries run to Inch'ôn (*Rénchuān*) and Chejudo (*Jìzhōudǎo*) in South Korea. Boats leave every Tuesday at 3 pm and take 40 hours to Inch'ôn. Return sailings from Inch'ôn depart every Friday at 9 pm. Per-person fares run from Y750 in a four-berth economy room to Y1000 in a double or Y2500 for a VIP cabin. Fares to Chejudo are about 50% higher.

Around six boats per month depart to Osaka (*Dàbǎn*) and twice a month to Kobe (*Shénhù*) in Japan. Tickets to either destination cost Y1300/1600/2600 in an eight /four/two-person cabin, or Y6500 in a deluxe twin cabin; the trips take about 45 hours.

Boats for all these destinations depart from the international passenger terminal (Map 5) to the east of Shanghai Mansions at 1 Taiping Lu. Passengers are requested to be at the harbour three hours before departure. Tickets can be bought from CITS or from the 2nd floor ticket office (☎ 6326 4357 for services to Japan; ☎ 6320 0452 to Korea) at 1 Jinling Donglu. This office is open Monday to Friday from 8.30 am to noon (11 am for bookings to Korea), and 1 pm to 4 pm. Both offices give a 10% discount if you have a Chinese student card.

TRAVEL AGENCIES

The big government travel agencies are CITS, CTS and China Youth Travel Service (CYTS). Their Shanghai branches can do almost everything, from train tickets to city tours, though they often have separate offices for separate divisions. CITS and CTS are represented overseas (see Chinese Travel Agencies Abroad later in this chapter).

Other private agencies can book discounted international air tickets and put together discounted hotel packages, but they aren't really all that switched on yet. You'll do best if you know exactly what you are asking for rather than relying on them to find the best deal. Most agencies in Shanghai accept international credit cards.

The main office of CITS (Map 4; ☎ 6289 8899) is at 1277 Beijing Xilu but the most useful office for tourists is on the ground floor of the Guangming building at 2 Jinling Donglu (Map 5; ☎ 6323 8748/9). There's another CITS office on Nanjing Donglu near the Peace Hotel, but it's mostly for booking air tickets.

Train, air and boat tickets can be booked at the Jinling office, subject to availability. CITS will often need at least three days to get train tickets for destinations further than Hangzhou or Suzhou. A service charge of Y10 is added. Also try your hotel or one of the other booking options mentioned in the Train section earlier in this chapter.

As middle-class Shanghainese start to travel the world a rash of local travel agents has sprung up, offering domestic tours and overseas trips to Australia, Hong Kong, Thailand etc. These are mostly for local Chinese clients and will probably have little to offer foreign travellers.

In Shanghai the following agencies are reputable:

Shanghai China Travel Service (SCTS) (Map 6; ☎ 6247 8888, fax 6247 5878, ✉ webmaster @scts.com) 881 Yan'an Zhonglu
Shanghai China Youth Travel Service (CYTS) (Map 6; ☎ 6433 1826, fax 6445 5396, ✉ cyts@public.sta.net.cn) 2 Hengshan Lu
Shanghai China International Travel Service (CITS)
(Map 4; ☎ 6289 8899, fax 6289 4928) 1277 Beijing Xilu; (Map 7; ☎ 6387 4988) 146 Huangpi Nanlu, on the corner of Huaihai Zhonglu;
(Map 5; ☎ 6323 4067) 2nd floor, 66 Nanjing Donglu; for air tickets;
(Map 5; ☎ 6323 8770) 2 Jinling Donglu; for train and boat tickets.

Shanghai Jinjiang Tours (Map 6; ☎ 6466 2828, fax 6466 2297) 191 Changle Lu, near the Garden Hotel
Shanghai Huating Overseas Tourist Company (Map 6; ☎ 6249 1234, fax 6248 5470, ✉ httravel@guomai.sh.cn) 505 Wulumuqi Beilu
Shanghai Spring International Travel Service (Map 5; ☎ 6351 6666, fax 6351 7232, ✉ spring@china-sss.com) 347 Xizang Zhonglu
Web site: www.china-sss.com
Destinations Travel Agency (☎ 6314 8917, fax 6330 6966, ✉ irs@uninet.com.cn) Room 101, Bldg 3, Lane 39, Nanjiang Lu
Nonggongshang Air Travel Service (Map 9; ☎/fax 6275 4477, ✉ guolong@honghan. com.cn) 88 Zunyi Lu, Hongqiao; IATA bonded
FASCO Various offices, including: (Map 6; ☎ 6472 3131) in the gateway of the Jinjiang Hotel, 59 Maoming Nanlu;
(Map 4; ☎ 6218 6811) Room 609 in the Westgate Mall on Nanjing Xilu

Chinese Travel Agencies Abroad
CITS and CTS, the main Chinese state travel bureaus, will book hotels, domestic flights, train tickets and tours, at high group rates and usually with a service charge. This won't save you any money, except perhaps if you are booking top-end hotels, but it can save you time and hassle if you will be combining a visit to Shanghai with other travel in China and have a tight itinerary.

CITS This bureau has offices worldwide and a general Web site at www.cits.net.

Australia (☎ 03-9621 2198, fax 9621 2919) 99 King St, Melbourne, Vic 3000
Web site: www.travman.com.au
Canada (☎ 604-267 0033, fax 267 0032) 5635 Cambie St, Vancouver BC V5Z 3A3
Web site: www.citscanada.com
Denmark (☎ 039-3391 0400, 3312 3688) Ved Vesterport 4, DK-1612, Copenhagen V
Web site: www.cits.dk
France (☎ 01 42 86 88 66, fax 01 42 86 88 61) 30 Rue de Gramont, 75002 Paris
Hong Kong (☎ 852-2732 5888, fax 2721 7154, ✉ marketing@cits.com.hk) New Mandarin Plaza, Tower A, 12th floor, 14 Science Museum Rd, Tsim Sha Tsui East
Web site: www.cits.com.hk

GETTING THERE & AWAY

Japan (☎ 03-3499 1245, fax 3499 1243, ⓔ cits-tky@magical3.egg.or.jp) 24-2 Shu Building, 6th floor, Shibuya 1-Chome, Shibuya-Ku, Tokyo 150; (☎ 06-6910 6635, fax 6910 6640, ⓔ cits-osk@magical.egg.or.jp) 2-16 YK Bldg, 9th floor, Hinomachibashi, Chuo-Ku, Osaka; (☎ 92-441 8180, fax 441 8160, ⓔ cits-fuk@magical3.egg.or.jp) 7th floor, SS Building, 3-21-15, Hakada, Fukuoko Web site: www.citsjapan.co.jp

Korea (☎ 549-2824, fax 549-2825) CITS Shanghai Office, Seoul 203-1 Nonhyun-Dong Kangnam-Ku, Seoul

Sweden (☎ 08-702 2280, fax 702 2330, ⓔ tinaxz@swipnet.sc) Gotgatan, 41, 1tr, 11621 Stockholm

USA (☎ 718-261 7329, fax 261 7569, ⓔ citsusa@aol.com) 71-01 Austin St, Suite 204, Forest Hills, NY 11375; ☎ 626-568 8993, fax 568 9207, ⓔ citslaz@aol.com) 975 East Green St, Suite 101, Pasadena, CA 91106 Web site: www.citsusa.com

CTS Overseas representatives of CTS include the following:

Australia (☎ 02-9211 2633, fax 9281 3595) 757–759 George St, Sydney, NSW 2000

Canada (☎ 1-800-663 1126, 604-872 8787, fax 873 2823) 556 West Broadway, Vancouver, BC V5Z 1E9 (☎ 1-800-387 6622, 416-979 8993, fax 979 8220) Suite 306, 438 University Ave, Box 28, Toronto, Ontario M5G 2K8

France (☎ 01 44 51 55 66, fax 44 51 55 60) 32 rue Vignon, 75009 Paris

Germany (☎ 69-223 8522) Düsseldorfer Strasse 14, D-60329, Frankfurt-am-Main; (☎ 30-393 4068, fax 391 8085) Beusselstrasse 5, D-10553, Berlin

Hong Kong (☎ 2853 3533, fax 2541 9777, ⓔ ctsdmd@hkstar.com) 4th floor, CTS House, 78–83 Connaught Rd, Central; (☎ 2315 7188, fax 2721 7757) 1st floor, Alpha House, 27–33 Nathan Rd, Tsimshatsui

UK (☎ 020-7836 9911, 7836 3121, ⓔ cts@ctsuk.com) 7 Upper St Martin's Lane, London

USA (☎ 1-800-899 8618, 415-352-0399, ⓔ info@chinatravelservice.com) 575 Sutter St, San Francisco, CA 94102; (☎ 1-800-890 8818, fax 626-457 8955, ⓔ usctsla@aol.com) 119 S Atlantic Blvd, Suite 303, Monterey Park, CA 91754 Web site: www.chinatravelservice.com

ORGANISED TOURS

Several foreign travel companies offer tours of China that stop in Shanghai for one or two days. Most of these tours concentrate on eastern China and though it is cheaper on your own, they might be worth considering if you are nervous about travelling in China.

A good halfway option is to give yourself a skeleton itinerary by pre-booking a few hotels and train tickets through a China specialist travel agency and then make the rest up when you get to China.

Getting Around

Shanghai is not exactly a walker's paradise. There are some fascinating areas to stroll around, but new road developments, building sites and shocking traffic conditions conspire to make walking an exhausting, stressful and sometimes dangerous experience.

Travelling on buses can also be hard work; the routes, and particularly the stops, are not easy to figure out and buses are packed at rush hour. The metro system, on the other hand, works like a dream and will soon be joined by a light railway train link circling the city. Travellers with money to spare can at least hop into a taxi, relatively cheap and hassle-free, to get to places off the metro line.

The city took a big swipe at traffic congestion in 1999, investing more than a billion dollars in transport – building overpasses, a second metro line and a light railway within a year. Unfortunately there is still not enough space for everyone at rush hour and from around 7 to 9.30 am and 4 to 6.30 pm it's everyone for themselves. Getting a seat can become a brawling ordeal. Cool aggression and elusive speed, along with a friendly smile, keep things from getting ugly.

There are plans to introduce a stored-value transportation card that will be valid for metro, buses and the light railway system, though there was no timetable for this at the time of writing.

THE AIRPORTS
Pudong Airport

The new Pudong airport is easy to navigate. Departures are on the upper level and arrivals are on the lower level. The middle level is dedicated to restaurants and parking. Departure tax is paid (in RMB only) after check-in on the upper level.

Trolleys are available for free and porters cost a modest Y10; tipping is absolutely forbidden.

There is a tourist information counter on the lower level near Door 10. There are also branches of China International Travel Service (CITS; Zhōngguó Guójì Lǚxíngshè) and China Youth Travel Service (CYTS; Zhōngguó Qīngnián Lǚxíngshè) in the arrivals hall.

Currency Exchange There is a Bank of China branch at the international end of the upper level, open from 8.30 to 11.30 am and 2.30 to 10.30 pm. It is possible to change RMB back into US$ here if you have your original exchange receipts. The Shanghai Pudong Development Bank, at the international end of the lower level, will cash travellers cheques and give Visa credit card cash advances at 3% commission. There are ATMs in front of the departure tax desks on the upper level and outside the arrivals hall (Door 12).

Other Facilities The international arrivals hall houses several hotel touts, as well as an Angel Car Rental representative and a business centre with fax services and computer rental (Y100 per hour). Baggage storage is available in both arrivals halls from 7 am to 9.30 pm. Rates are between Y5 and Y20, depending on the size of your bag. Bags must be locked, a passport or ID is required and the maximum storage period is 30 days.

There are post offices in both departures halls and in the domestic arrivals hall. Most restaurants are located on the 2nd floor, though a few nice cafes are on the upper level.

The souvenir shops in the departures halls have a few interesting items to drain your last few kuai, like Bund stationery, cigarette girl sweatshirts, calligraphy pillows, and Chinese wine in elaborate jugs.

Airport Accommodation A short-stay hotel on the middle level charges Y60 per hour for passengers in transit. It is accessible only after check-in or before customs clearance on arrival.

Getting to Pudong

There's now little more than a psychological gap between Pudong and Puxi. If you are headed across the Huangpu River you can choose from the following means of transportation:

Taxi – A taxi ride will cost you around Y25 as you'll have to pay the Y15 tunnel toll heading eastwards.

Tunnel bus – Bus No 518 and tunnel bus No 3 *(sùidào sānxiàn)* leave from opposite the Shanghai Museum and run to the Jinmao Tower (Y2).

Ferry – At Y0.8 this is definitely the cheapest way to cross the Bund, though it's a 10-minute walk to the Jinmao Tower on the other side.

Pedestrian tunnel – When this opens in October 2000 it will shuttle passengers under the Huangpu in tramcars between the Bund (across from the Peace Hotel) and the Shanghai International Exhibition Centre in Pudong.

Tour bus – The red Jinjiang sightseeing bus (Y18) or the green (No 3) sightseeing bus (Y4) from Shanghai Stadium take you straight to the foot of the Oriental Pearl TV Tower.

If you have to stay the night, there is a two-star hotel, the *Jinjiang Inn (Jīnjiāng Zhìxīng, ☎ 6835 3568),* about 15 minutes' walk (or around Y10 in a taxi) away. Singles/doubles cost Y118/158; the Jinjiang Hotel group can make reservations at their hotel counter.

Hongqiao Airport

Hongqiao airport is shaped like a horseshoe. The international hall is in the centre, arrivals are on the ground floor and departures are on the 1st floor. The domestic hall is to the left as you exit the international hall. Taxis and city buses leave from the domestic hall. Minibuses to surrounding cities are across the street.

Currency Exchange A Bank of China branch, located near the baggage claim in the international arrivals hall (inside the customs gate), can change cash and travellers cheques at a standardised rate so there is no need to wait until you reach the city centre. If you miss the bank, the tourist information office can change at least enough money to get you into town. Otherwise a full-service Bank of China is about 15 minutes' walk away, next to the International Airport Hotel (see Airport Accommodation in this section). Note that currently you can't change RMB back into US$ at this airport.

Tourist Information The tourist information office is very good and can provide hotel information as well as book accommodation for you at a discounted rate. The tourist office can also provide advice on transportation into town, write the Chinese script for a taxi and even phone your party if you appear in extreme despair. Avoid the hotel jackals, who will attempt to befriend you by giving 'helpful' information.

Other Facilities The post office is located in the international departures hall. Public telephones take coins or phonecards, which are for sale for Y50 and Y100 at the tourist information office.

There are a few overpriced restaurants in both halls, and a small supermarket and an uninspiring souvenir shop to the left of the domestic hall.

Luggage storage is available in the international departures hall and also to the left of the domestic arrivals hall as you exit. Rates are between Y5 and Y20 depending on the size of your bag. Bags must be locked, a passport or ID is required and the maximum storage period is 30 days.

Airport Accommodation If you've missed your flight or need to kill some time the *Huamao Hotel (Map 9; Huámào Bīnguǎn, ☎ 6268 2266)* is about two minutes' walk to the right of the international hall as you exit. It offers half-day rooms (a block of six hours) for Y150, a coffee shop, good souvenir shops, a gymnasium and a billiards room.

A pricier option is the ***International Airport Hotel*** *(Map 3; Shànghǎi Guójì Jīchǎng Bīnguǎn,* ☎ *6268 8866),* a 10-minute walk from the terminal; rooms cost Y880.

TO/FROM THE AIRPORTS

Most top-end hotels operate a shuttle bus to their hotels at fixed times. Ask at hotel desks at the airport.

Pudong Airport

Pudong airport operates five airport bus routes. The buses are large and easy to spot. They drop off at both the domestic and international departures halls and pick up outside arrivals between Doors 7 to 15. A private luxury airport bus runs from the Regal East Asia Hotel to Pudong Airport (1½ hours, Y30), picking up passangers at the Huating and Jianguo hotels en route.

You can buy tickets for the Hongqiao airport and the Exhibition Centre buses from the ticket office in the arrivals hall (near Door 6); for other destinations buy your ticket on the bus.

The journey into Puxi takes between 60 and 90 minutes. Only bus No 5 stops in Pudong. The first bus to Pudong airport leaves at around 6 am, and then runs every 30 minutes or so until around 7 pm. The last bus back from the airport is around 9 pm.

The bus routes are as follows:

No 1 Pudong to/from Hongqiao airport (Y22)
No 2 Pudong to/from Shanghai Exhibition Centre (Y19)
No 3 Pudong to/from Xujiahui and Yangtze New World Hotel, Zunyi Lu Hongqiao (Y17 to Y20)
No 4 Pudong to/from Wujiaochang, Da Baishu and Jiangwan Donglu in north-east Shanghai (Y16 to Y18)
No 5 Pudong to/from Pudong's East Hospital, Renmin Square and Shanghai train station (Y15 to Y18)

A taxi ride into central Shanghai will cost around Y170 and will take about an hour. A taxi to Hongqiao airport costs around Y180. Most taxis in Shanghai are honest, though make sure you use the meter unless you know the approximate cost and can bargain

the fare down; tipping is uncommon in China.

Eventually the No 2 metro line will link Hongqiao and Pudong airports but this is still a few years away.

Hongqiao Airport

To/From the City Centre Hongqiao airport is 18km from the Bund and getting there takes about 30 minutes if you're lucky, and more than an hour if you're not.

Bus Nos 925 and No 505 run between the domestic hall and Renmin Square (Y4, one hour). Bus No 831 also runs between the airport and Jinling Lu, just off the Bund. Alternatively you can take No 938 from the domestic hall to the Huating Hotel (Y3) and catch the metro to anywhere else in the city. A white-and-blue airport shuttle bus leaves from the domestic hall and goes directly to the Shanghai Exhibition Centre on Yan'an Zhonglu (Y4); the bus is unmarked, so you might have to ask around. Minibus No 806 runs from the airport to Xujiahui.

A taxi to the Bund will cost from Y50 to Y60, plus Y15 in toll fees; tipping is not expected. There is a queuing system just outside and to the left of the international arrivals hall; don't go with the taxi sharks who solicit you on arrival. A taxi fare *to* the airport should not include the Y15 toll.

To/From Other Cities Minibuses leave across the street from the domestic hall to Nanjing's Grand Hotel (Y95, three hours) daily at 11 am, and 1.30, 3.30 and 6 pm. Buses also run to Suzhou (Y50, one hour) eight times daily, arriving near the Public Security Bureau (PSB; Gōngānjú) on Renmin Lu, and to Hangzhou (Y70, two hours), leaving at 10.30 am and at 1.30 and 4.30 pm and arriving at the CAAC Hotel.

To Pudong Airport Hongqiao airport is about as far away from Pudong airport as you can get without leaving Shanghai. A minimum of two hours is necessary to ensure a flight connection between the two. Airport shuttle bus No 1 leaves every half-hour from the domestic hall, arriving at Pudong airport one hour later. A taxi to Pudong will cost about Y180 with tolls and will take nearly one hour; tipping is not expected.

TOUR BUS

If you want to see Shanghai in a hurry then the best way is to jump aboard one of the red Jinjiang Shanghai Tour buses that leave every 45 minutes or so from just outside the Garden Hotel on Maoming Nanlu (see the Places to Stay chapter). They are comfortable, speedy and cheap; a one-day ticket costs Y18.

The bus stops at a number of tourist destinations, including Renmin Square, the Oriental Pearl Tower and Nextage Department Store in Pudong, Nanpu Bridge, Yuyuan Gardens and the Bund, and then returns to the Jinjiang Hotel. You can get off, go and see the sight, and wait for the next bus to come along and pick you up, using the same ticket. The first bus leaves around 9 am, the last bus leaves at around 4.15 pm.

Comfortable, green sightseeing buses also operate from the east end of Shanghai Stadium, and though they primarily serve suburban sightseeing spots (see the Excursions chapter), one or two lines pass through points of interest in the city centre. These routes are probably only of interest if you are staying near the stadium, though the Shanghai Stadium metro stop is only a five-minute walk away. Information on the bus lines is available in Chinese (☎ 6426 5555).

Two useful lines are:

No 3 This travels to Pudong; Pearl Tower (Y4), Jinmao Tower (Y4) and on to Jinqiao, Zhangjiang, Sunqiao, Chuansha and Huaxia (Y12). It runs every 30 minutes from 7 am to 5.30 pm; you can pick it up from the bus stop just south of the Shanghai Museum on Yan'an Donglu.

No 10 This goes to Huaihai Zhonglu, Nanjing Donglu, Sichuan Beilu, Hongkou Park (Y3); it leaves every 15 minutes from 6.30 am to 7.30 pm.

Most top-end hotels have a free shuttle bus to the Bund for their guests, leaving several times a day. Ask at reception for times.

BUS

The closest thing to revolutionary fervour in Shanghai today is the rush hour bus ambush. During rush hour and on the weekend buses are often packed to the hilt and, at times, impossible even to board. As you squeeze yourself on and off, and while you are on board, keep your valuables tucked away since pickpocketing is easy under such conditions.

The main problem with taking the bus (once you've found the right number and right route and managed to get on the bus) is that you can never be sure where it is going to stop. The bus route may run straight past your destination but you may find the nearest stop up to a kilometre away. In general try to get on at the terminus, thus guaranteeing you a seat, try to avoid rush hours, and stick to a few tried-and-tested routes.

Older buses have wooden seats and no air-con and cost Y1. New air-con buses cost Y2 and are a godsend in summer. Private minibuses (Y2) serve some routes on the edges of town.

Suburban and long-distance buses don't carry numbers – the destination is in characters. Buses generally operate from 5 am to 11 pm, except for 300 series buses, which operate all night.

Bus routes that serve areas not easily accessed by the metro are:

No 2 Travels all the way along Huaihai Zhonglu and Hengshan Lu as far as Xujiahui.

No 11 Circles the old town following Renmin Lu and Zhonghua Lu.

No 19 Links the Bund area to the Jade Buddha Temple area; catch it at the intersection of Tiantong Lu and Sichuan Beilu.

No 20 Goes from Jiujiang Lu, just off the Bund, to Renmin Square, Nanjing Xilu, Yuyuan Lu and Zhongshan Park.

No 37 Runs from near Jing'an Temple down Nanjing Xilu to Renmin Park and down Jiujiang Lu to near the Bund (returning to the park via Tianjin Lu).

No 42 Starts from the Bund at Guangdong Lu, passes Renmin Lu close to the Yuyuan Gardens, heads along Huaihai Lu and then Xiangyang Lu to Xujiahui, terminating at Shanghai Stadium.

GETTING AROUND

No 61 Starts from the intersection of Wusong Lu and Tiantong Lu and goes past the PSB. No 55 from the Bund also goes by the PSB.

No 64 Goes to Shangai train station from the Pujiang Hotel; catch it near the Pujiang on Beijing Donglu, close to the intersection with Sichuan Zhonglu. The ride takes 20 to 30 minutes.

No 65 Runs from north-east of Shanghai train station, passes Shanghai Mansions, crosses Waibaidu Bridge, and then heads directly south along the Bund (Zhongshan Lu) to Nanpu Bridge.

No 66 Travels along Henan Lu, connecting Nanjing Donglu to the old town.

No 71 Takes you to the CAAC office, from where you can catch the airport bus; catch it from Yan'an Donglu close to the Bund.

No 112 Zig-zags north from the south end of Renmin Square to Nanjing Xilu, down Shimen Erlu to Beijing Xilu then up Jiangning Lu to the Jade Buddha Temple.

No 518 Runs from Renmin Square under the Huangpu to Pudong Nanlu and then south.

No 831 Goes all the way from Jinling Lu, around the corner from the Bund, to Hongqiao airport via Huaihai Zhonglu.

No 903 Runs from Shanghai train station past the Portman Ritz-Carlton, the Equatorial Hotel, the Hilton Hotel and the Jianguo Hotel.

No 910 Runs from Wujiaochang in the north-east, down Siping Lu to the Bund and then continues south, past Shiliupu Wharf to Nanpu Bridge.

No 911 Leaves from Zhonghua Lu near the intersection with Fuxing Zhonglu, on the west edge of the old town, and goes up Huaihai Zhong and Xi Lu, continuing to the zoo.

No 920 Runs from Yishan Lu to Xujiahui, and then east along Huaihai Zhonglu, past Shanghai Library, to the north edge of the old city. Then makes a loop around the old city before heading back west along Huaihai.

No 926 Leaves from Shanghai Stadium to Xujiahui and then east along Huaihai Zhonglu, past Shanghai Library, to Jinling Donglu, finishing near the Bund.

No 928 Runs from Shanghai train station to Shanghai Mansions (near the Pujiang Hotel) and then south down the Bund to Shiliupu Wharf and Nanpu Bridge.

No 930 Runs from Renmin Square down Xizang Nanlu to near Dongtai Market and then along Renmin Lu around the old town for Yuyuan Gardens.

No 934 Travels from Yangpu, down Changyang Lu to the Bund, then west along Zhejiang Lu to Renmin Square.

No 938 Goes from Hongqiao airport south-east to Yishan Lu and along the ring road to Shanghai Stadium, Nanpu Bridge and then Nextage department store in Pudong.

METRO

The city's metro trains are easily the best way to get around Shanghai. They are fast, cheap, clean and easy. The No 1 metro line apparently only carries 5% of Shanghai's daily commuters but it certainly doesn't feel like this at 5.30 pm. In general it's hard to get a seat at the best of times. If you are lucky you'll witness breathtaking rudeness as people fight it out to get a seat.

There are currently two metro lines and more are planned. The No 1 line runs from the train station in the north through Renmin Square along Huaihai Zhonglu, through Xujiahui and down to Xinzhuang in the southern suburbs. The No 1 line will eventually be extended up to Baoshan in the northern suburbs.

The No 2 line runs from Zhongshan Park in the east to Longyang Lu in Pudong, passing through Nanjing Lu at several places in the centre of town. The line will eventually connect Hongqiao and Pudong airports, though it will be several years before this happens. The two lines connect at Renmin Park/Renmin Square, the busiest of all the stations.

Tickets cost Y3 for a journey of up to 13 stops. Farther than this and you'll have to buy a Y4 ticket. Keep your ticket until you exit. At the moment there are no bulk-buy savings or travel cards. You can buy pre-paid tickets of Y90, though you'll save nothing except the time it takes to queue for tickets. Eventually an integrated bus, metro and light railway smart card will be available.

Trains run from around 5 am to 11 pm – once every nine minutes at rush hours and every 12 minutes during off-peak hours. Stops are announced in English as well as Chinese. The metro is non-smoking and there are no toilets in any of the metro stations.

The metro station exits can be very complicated (Xujiahui has 14 exits!) and it's sometimes important that you get the right exit number. To recognise a metro station look for the red symbol that looks like an 'M'.

LIGHT RAILWAY

The Pearl Mass Transit light railway is due to open at the end of 2000 and so should be up and running by the time you read this. The line follows the route of the Shanghai-Hangzhou railway and currently runs 25km from Caohejing in the southern suburbs to Jiangwan in the north, passing through much of western and northern Shanghai en route. The line is mostly elevated but connects with the No 1 metro line at Shanghai train station and Shanghai Stadium. There are 19 stops in total.

The second phase of the project is slated to run from Baoshan Lu in the north to Hongqiao in the south-west, marking a giant loop through Pudong. This second line is tentatively due for opening in 2004 and will create a circular loop with the first-phase line.

TAXI

Shanghai has around 80,000 taxi drivers and 41,000 taxis. Most are Volkswagen Santanas, though these are due to be upgraded to Volkswagen Passats (Volkswagen has a factory in Shanghai).

Shanghai's taxis are reasonably cheap, hassle-free and easy to flag down, outside of rush hour. Flag fall is Y10 for the first 2km, and then Y2 per kilometre thereafter; tipping is not common. Most rides around town cost from Y14 to Y20, so the first Y10 doesn't really get you all that far. Most taxi drivers are surprisingly honest, though you should always go by the meter. A few taxis now even take credit cards! At night you can tell if a taxi is empty by the red 'for hire' sign on the dashboard of the passenger side. The driver should push this down when you get in the cab, to start the meter.

If you call to book a taxi, which is not really necessary, you pay a small surcharge. A night rate operates from 11 pm to 5 am. The flag fall in this case is Y13, and then it's Y2.6 per km. It's always worth asking for a printed receipt, as this gives not only the fare but also the driver and car number, the distance driven, waiting time and the number to call if there are any problems.

In general, taxi drivers are surprisingly bad at finding their way around. If you don't speak Chinese, bring a Chinese character map or have your destination written down in characters. It also helps if you have your own directions and sit in the front with a map. If you look particularly clueless you may literally be taken for a ride. (Drivers must earn a quota of about Y4000 a month but pocket most of the money after that.)

Shanghai's main taxi companies include Dazhong Taxi (☎ 6258 1688), Qiangsheng (☎ 6258 0000), Zhenhua (☎ 6255 0880) and Friendship Taxi (☎ 6258 4584).

The taxi companies are most easily recognisable by their colours. The best of the bunch is Dazhong, which has turquoise cars. Its staff all wear uniforms. Qiansheng are yellow, Friendship are white and Bashi are lime green. A few Red Flag limousines, once reserved for top Communist Party officials, now operate as cabs in Shanghai and cost the same as normal cabs.

If you are staying for a while and find a taxi driver that you particularly like, ask for a card. Most drivers have home phones, mobile phones or pagers (and sometimes all three) and can be hired for the day.

Motorcycle Taxi

Motorcycle taxis wait at most intersections and metro stations to whisk travellers off to nearby destinations. The advantages of these are that you save money if you are alone and the motorcycles can take many roads that normal taxis can't. The disadvantages are that you have to cling on to the motorcycle for dear life (helmets are provided and strongly recommended!) and that your travel insurance probably won't cover you if you fall off. Most trips cost less than Y5 or Y10.

CAR HIRE

It's possible to hire a car in Shanghai by the day or longer, though there are so many taxis that it doesn't make much sense unless your boss is coming into town and wants a

BMW. With Shanghai's anarchic traffic in mind it is strongly recommended that you hire a driver as well.

One of the biggest car rental agencies is Shanghai Angel Car Rental (☎ 6229 0858), at 1387 Changning Lu. Other car rental agencies include Dazhong (☎ 6318 5666), at 98 Guohuo Lu, and most of the taxi companies listed in the Taxi section earlier in this chapter. Prices start at Y320 a day for a Santana and Y540 for an Audi, without a driver.

To drive in Shanghai resident expats must first pass an examination at the Shanghai Transport Bureau, even if they have an international driver's licence. Foreigners are technically only allowed to drive in Shanghai municipality, though expats report few problems driving into neighbouring Jiangsu and Zhejiang. If you have your own car and need some spare parts, Weihai Lu (Map 4) is lined with hundreds of car accessories shops.

BICYCLE

Most Shanghainese commute by bicycle; there are some 6.5 million bikes in Shanghai. It's not a bad way to get around if you pack in with the masses, though the traffic is madness and there's always a chance that you'll get wiped out by a novice taxi driver. Officially, foreigners need to register their bikes in order to pedal around the city, but in practice no-one will question you. The problem is a lack of places to hire bikes. The YMCA Bike Shop, also known as Wolf's Bicycle Club (Map 6; ☎ 6472 9325) at Block 5, 485 Yongjia Lu, between Yueyang and Taiyuan Lu, rents mountain bikes for Y20 per day with a Y100 deposit. The best area for a casual bike ride is without doubt the French Concession.

Around 130 bikes are stolen every day in Shanghai so make sure that you have your own bicycle cable lock. Bike parks are available at most shopping areas. The cost is peanuts but it's compulsory; your bike may well be towed away if you're not careful.

Bikes are cheap to buy in Shanghai so there's not much point in bringing one from home. You can get a decent mountain bike for around Y400. See the Activities section of the Things to See & Do chapter for a couple of stores and more information on cycling in Shanghai.

FERRY

Several ferries operate between Puxi and Pudong. The most useful one operates between the south end of the Bund and Pudong. The trip costs eight mao eastbound (it's free west-bound) and departs every 15 minutes all day.

Things to See & Do

HIGHLIGHTS

The main sightseeing highlight in Shanghai is unquestionably the Bund and you should give yourself a couple of hours to stroll around the area, preferably at night or, if you are jet-lagged, early morning.

The Shanghai Museum, one of China's finest, deserves at least half a day, if possible. The other great attraction of Shanghai is the Old Town, incorporating the Yuyuan Gardens and the surrounding teahouses and bazaars.

Shanghai also shows its magic in the old back streets, where pockets of faded 1930s architecture intermingle with Chinese *shíkūmén* residences (see the 'Architecture of Shanghai' special section).

Try to have at least one big night out in Shanghai to experience the modern side of the city. Take in the acrobats or a performance at the Grand Theatre, try one of the excellent restaurants and then take your pick of the bars and clubs.

Hop aboard a boat cruise for views of the Bund or make it up to the gorgeous Jinmao Tower for the best view of the city.

Huangpu River Cruise 黄浦江游船

Jiāng Yóulǎn Chuán

The Huangpu River offers some remarkable views of the Bund and the riverfront activity. Huangpu tour boats (Map 5; ☎ 6374 4461) depart from docks on the Bund at 219–239 Zhongshan Dong Erlu.

There are several types of cruises. The one-hour cruise (Y25 and Y35) takes in the Yangpu Bridge; the two-hour cruise (Y45) encompasses Yangpu and Nanpu Bridges, and a less frequent evening service heads up to Pudong Gaoqiao Bridge. The better but more expensive choice is the 3½-hour, 60km round-trip cruise, which takes you up the Huangpu to Wusongkou, the junction with the Yangzi River, and back. Several classes are available for this service, ranging in price from Y45 to Y100. Tours on weekends cost Y53/98/118; the more expensive

The Best of Shanghai

Best Walks
Discover the treasures of the Old Town, the French Concession, the Bund, and Nanjing Donglu.

Best Shopping
Find that elusive 'original' at the Dongtai Lu Antique Market, stock up on cheap souvenirs at the Yuyuan Bazaar, reinvent your wardrobe at the Huating Market, and ogle the department stores on Huaihai Lu.

Best Sights
Marvel at the colonial decadence of the Bund, discover cultural treasures at the Shanghai Museum and Shanghai Art Museum, and visit the bustling Yuyuan Gardens.

Best Parks
Stroll amid the early-morning *t'ai chi* practitioners at Fuxing Park and Hongkou Park.

Best Temple
The Jade Buddha Temple gets our vote, though the Longhua Temple comes a close second.

Best Views
Check out the Bund and Nanjing Lu; take in the city from M on the Bund, the top floor of the Jinmao Tower or, for a completely different kind of view, the Grand Hyatt's Atrium Café.

Best Entertainment
Relax and take in the waterfront on a Huangpu River Cruise, enjoy the tunes of Shanghai's musical stalwarts – the jazz band at the Peace Hotel, and treat yourself to a performance of one of the city's famous acrobatic troupes.

Best Excursions
Take trips to Suzhou and Songjiang.

Taking a Break
Unwind with tea at the Mid-Lake Pavilion Teahouse, or indulge in a massage.

Best Splurge
Splurge on anything in the Grand Hyatt, brunch at the Portman Ritz-Carlton, or post-theatre dinner at M on the Bund.

Old Town Walking Tour (Maps 5 & 7)

Route: From Yuyuan Gardens and back, or on to Nanpu Bridge
Duration: two to three hours

The Old Town is a fascinating place to wander and though it holds its secrets well, propinquity dictates that life is often on display in the streets. It's common to see people emptying their chamber pots (few houses have flush toilets here), airing duvets, playing cards and sunning themselves in winter. At every turn you might hear the hiss of a wok, dodge a pole of drying laundry, or marvel at gutted ducks strung up for curing.

From Yuyuan Gardens head west along Fangbang Zhonglu, once a canal, past an old stage to several traditional inns (one of the nicest is the Chenyonghe Inn), selling snacks and tubes of warmed *huángjiǔ* (Shaoxing rice wine). Farther along the road is the pastel blue building of a traditional Chinese medicine clinic. From here you can explore any of the surrounding alleys like Anren Jie or Danfeng Jie, before heading back along Fangbang Zhonglu to Henan Nanlu.

From this corner head north a block to Dajing Lu, once a centre of opium dens, now a vibrant produce market. At the west end of the market is the **Dajingge** (built 1815), which contains the only preserved section of the 5km-long city walls. The walls were built in 1553 to protect the city against pirates but were torn down in 1912. Entry to the gateway and its (Chinese only) displays on the history of the Old Town is Y5. On the corner is the traditional Wulong Teahouse (Wūlóng Cháyì) if you need a break.

From here head south, then west to Xizang Nanlu, where you can take a look at **Dongtai Lu Antique Market**, Shanghai's most interesting 'antiques' market. On the eastern side of the road is the **Flower & Bird Market**, which provides a fascinating stroll through bird and cricket cages, fish aquariums and garden supplies.

Head back to Renmin Lu, where you can either take Fangbang Lu back to Yuyuan Gardens, take bus No 911 to Huaihai Zhonglu, or continue south, following the course of the former city walls. Dumpling fans can stop at the Liangyuanshen snack bar at 1610 Zhonghua Lu, which is famous for its excellent *baozi*.

At Wenmiao Lu take a five-minute diversion right to visit the **Baiyun (White Cloud) Taoist Temple** (Báiyún Guān), on Xilinhou Lu; the temple was the birthplace of the Quanzhen sect of Taoism.

---

tickets include refreshments. Depending on your enthusiasm for loading cranes, the night cruises are more scenic, though the boat traffic during the day is interesting.

Shanghai is one of the world's largest ports and has been the largest in China since 1852. Today 2000 ocean-going ships and about 15,000 river steamers load and unload here every year. The tour boat passes an enormous variety of craft – freighters, bulk carriers, roll-on roll-off ships, sculling sampans, giant praying-mantis cranes, the occasional junk, and Chinese navy vessels (which aren't supposed to be photographed).

The longer boat cruise takes in Suzhou Creek, the International Passenger Terminal, Yangshupu Power Plant, Fuxing Island (site of Chiang Kaishek's last stand), the container port area, Wusongkou (site of the battle between the British and Chinese in 1842 and where the early opium traders unloaded their cargo). You also catch glimpses of Chongming Island and the Baoshan Iron and Steel Complex, the largest in China.

Departure times vary depending on which trip you take, but there are morning, afternoon and evening departures for all three categories.

OLD TOWN (MAPS 6 & 8) 老城

Known in Chinese as Nan Shi (Southern City) and previously as Nan Tao (Southern Market), the Chinese Old Town is the most traditional area of Shanghai.

Old Town Walking Tour (Maps 5 & 7)

Built in 1873, there's not much to see except the statue by the entrance, which seems to be giving the finger to anyone who enters!

Head back to Wenmiao Lu and pop into the **Confucian Temple** (see the entry in this chapter). The streets encircling the temple offer some nice views. On the north side of the temple is a book market and on the west side is the Kōngyǐjǐ Jiǔjiā, a great traditional inn, which serves wine, food and tea until 10 pm.

Wind your way through the back streets of Menghua Jie, Zhuangjia Jie and Xicangqiao Jie to reach Henan Nanlu. At the corner you'll see a Hui Moslem restaurant, recognisable by its Arabic script and lack of pork. The city's main **mosque** is just round the corner at 52 Xiaotaoyuan Lu. If you come on Friday at lunch time you'll see the faithful streaming in to prayer. (There's another mosque in the old town at 72 Fuyou Lu.) From here you can head back to Old Street (Laǒ Jīe).

Old Town Extension

Die-hards can continue south-east to Dongjiadu Lu, to the startling Spanish Baroque–style **Dongjiadu Church** at No 185, which was built in 1853 and was the first Catholic church in China. If you ring the doorbell, the caretakers are normally happy to let you look around. Services are held every Sunday morning at 7.30 am.

Continue to Zhongshan Nanlu, turn right for five minutes and then take in views of the city and its docks from **Nanpu Bridge**. The bridge is open from 8.30 am to 5 pm; entry is Y5 and photos are permitted.

A ten-minute walk farther down Zhongshan takes you to the **Museum of Folk Art** (Mínjiān Shōuzàngpǐn Chénlièguǎn), which is housed in the former Sanshan Guild Hall (Sānshān Huìguǎn), at 1551 Zhongshan Nanyilu. This area, close to the docks, used to be full of such guilds, built to look after the interests of a particular trade or group of immigrants. Today the impressive building houses rotating exhibitions of local collections (and anything else they can find), but the real star of the show is the building and its private stage. Entry is Y4 and it's open daily from 9 am to 4 pm.

From here return to Nanpu Bridge where you can take bus No 65 back to the Bund or continue into Pudong.

Yuyuan Gardens & Bazaar (Map 5) 豫园
Yùyuán Shāngshà

At the north-eastern end of the old Chinese city, the Yuyuan Gardens & Bazaar are, while arguably slightly tacky, one of Shanghai's premier sights and well worth a visit. Try not to visit on the weekend, though, as the crowds can be overpowering. See the Places to Eat chapter for details on the bazaar's justly famous snacks.

The **Yu Yuan** (Yu Gardens) were founded by the Pan family, rich Ming dynasty officials. The gardens took 18 years (1559 to 1577) to be nurtured into existence, only to be ransacked during the Opium War in 1842, when British officers were barracked here for a few days, and again during the Taiping Rebellion, by the French in reprisal for attacks on their nearby concession. Today the gardens have been restored and are worth visiting to see a fine example of Ming garden design – if you can see through the crowds. Though the gardens are small they seem much bigger due to an ingenious use of rocks and alcoves.

Things to look out for include the **Exquisite Jade Rock**, which was destined for the imperial court in Beijing until the boat sank outside Shanghai, and the **Hall of Heralding Spring** (Diǎnchūn Táng), which in 1853 was the headquarters of the Small Swords Society (perhaps one reason why the gardens were spared revolutionary violence in the

1960s). Note also the beautiful stage, with its gilded carved ceiling and excellent acoustics. The gardens are open daily from 8.30 am to 5 pm; entry is Y15.

Next to the entrance to the Yuyuan Gardens is the **Mid-Lake Pavilion Teahouse** (Húxīntíng), once part of the gardens and now one of the most famous teahouses in China, visited by Queen Elizabeth II and Bill Clinton among others. The zig-zag causeway is there to thwart spirits (and trap tourists), who can only travel in straight lines.

Surrounding all this is the restored **bazaar** area, where more than 100 speciality shops and restaurants jostle over narrow laneways and small squares in a mock 'ye olde Cathay' setting. It's a bit of a Disneyland version of historical China but if you can handle the crowds it's a great stop for lunch and some souvenir shopping.

Just outside the bazaar is **Old Street** (Lǎo Jiē), known more prosaically as Fangbang Zhonglu, another recently restored street lined with interesting shops and teahouses. See the Places to Eat and Shopping chapters for more details.

If you can tear yourself away from the shopping frenzy, the Daoist **Temple of the Town Gods** (Chénghuáng Miào), in the south-east of the complex, commemorates an ancient General Huo Guang and has some fine carvings on the roof. Entry is Y5.

Chenxiangge Nunnery (Map 5)
沉香阁
Chénxiānggé

This pleasant complex was once the home of the Pan family and has been restored to house around 40 nuns. It's a five-minute walk north-west of the Yuyuan Gardens. Opening hours are 7 am to 4 pm; entry is Y4.

Confucian Temple (Map 7) 文庙
Wén Miào

This temple is nothing special but it's worth a quick visit if you have time to investigate the Old Town. Parts of the temple date back 700 years but most of it was rebuilt in the Qing period and renovated in 1997.

The buildings include **Zunjing (Respecting Classics) Tower**; **Dacheng (Great Achievements) Hall**; **Minglung Hall**; and a hall that was formerly both a Confucian lecture hall and another of the headquarters of the Small Swords Society. The library for holding Chinese classics doubled as the state library up to 1931, and the Kuixing Pavilion is named after the God of the Literati.

Today the halls house a dull exhibition of stones, ink slabs and 'pyrography'. Entry is Y8 and opening hours are 8.30 to 4.30 pm.

RENMIN SQUARE AREA (MAP 5) 人民公园区域
Shanghai Museum 上海博物馆
Shànghǎi Bówùguǎn

Originally built in 1952, and rebuilt in 1994, this stunning new US$700-million museum is symbolic of the many changes that are afoot in Shanghai. Gone are dry exhibits, yawning security guards and stale air – replacing these is excellent spot lighting and state-of-the-art technology. Of the 120,000 works of art, one-third have never been shown publicly before. While guiding you through the craft of millennia, the museum simultaneously draws you through the pages of Chinese history. Expect to spend half, if not a whole day here. The Shanghai Museum is one of the highlights of a trip to Shanghai.

Before you go in, take a look at the outside of the building. It was designed to recall an ancient bronze *ding* (a three-legged food vessel used for cooking and serving), and also echoes the shape of a famous bronze mirror from the Han dynasty, exhibited inside the museum. The entrance is to the south and is guarded by lions and mythological beasts such as the *pixie* and *tianlu*.

The most famous collection of the museum is the **Ancient Chinese Bronzes Gallery** (see the boxed text 'Bronzes in the Shanghai Museum').

Exhibits in the **Ancient Chinese Sculpture Gallery** range from stonework of the Qin and Han dynasties to Buddhist stucco sculpture, which was influenced by Central Asian styles that travelled along the Silk

Bronzes in the Shanghai Museum

The Shanghai Museum is famed worldwide for its bronzes, some of which date from the 21st century BC. The zenith of the production of bronzes was during the late Shang (1700–1100 BC) and early Zhou (1100–221 BC) dynasties, though the Middle Spring and Autumn (722–481 BC)and Warring States (453–221 BC) periods showed a second flowering.

The impressive range of shapes and uses of bronze is striking, showing the importance of bronze in ritual ancestor worship and, later, everyday life. Vessels range in shape from a *hu* (wine bottle), *jue* (wine pourer with spout), *gu* (goblet), *bei* (wine jar), *zun* (bowl), *yan* (steamer), *gui* (round food vessel used for rice and grain), *pan* (water vessel), *yi* (square wine vessel) and various wine pots known as *jia*, *zhi*, *zun*, *he* and *you*. The hooks visible on several pots originally held a cloth bag to filter hot wine, one reason why hot-water bowls and steamers are so common.

The most important ritual bronzes are the *dings*, three-legged food vessels used for cooking and serving. The number of dings an official was allowed depended strictly on his imperial rank. Also, three-legged dings could only be grouped together in odd numbers. Ceremonial bronzes can be huge, such as the 200kg ding on display.

The most common form of early decoration is the stylised animal motif, with dragons, lions and phoenix common. This was replaced in the 10th century BC by zig-zag (representing thunder), cloud and, later, geometric shapes. Later, decoration spread to fin-like appendages, studs and relief carvings. As bronzes lost their ritual significance, decorative scenes from daily life were introduced. Later still, stamped moulds, lost wax techniques and piece moulds enabled designs to become more complicated.

It's worth remembering that the bronzes would originally have been a bright golden colour. It is only oxidisation that has given them a green patina, with reddish additions coming from the cinnabar used in burial rites.

An especially creative use of bronze is evident in the *zhong* (bells), each of which produces two notes. Up until the Han dynasty (206 BC–AD 220), bronze bells were China's most important musical instrument; traditional bell concerts are still held in Shanghai. Other examples of bronze use include 3000-year-old weapons like *dao* (daggers), *yue* (axes), *mao* (spears and swords) forged from two metals. Also shown are bronzes collected from minority nationalities such as the Yi from southwest China, with characteristic ox motifs, the Ba from Sichuan, the Central Asian Xiongnu (Kushan), with their camel and tiger motifs, and bronze drums from Guangxi.

Road. It is interesting to note that sculptures displayed were once almost all painted; only scraps of the paint remain. Images or names of donors were often seen on carvings. The sculptures are mostly of Sakyamuni Buddha, but there are also images of Buddha's disciples (Kasyapa and Ananda), tranquil boddhisatvas and fierce *lokapalas* (protectors).

The **Ancient Chinese Ceramics Gallery** is one of the largest in the museum. Exhibits include 6000-year-old pottery from the Neolithic Songze culture excavated from just outside Shanghai, *sāncǎi* (polychrome) pottery of the Tang, and the enormous variety of porcelain, or 'China', produced by the Qing. There are many pieces from Jingdezhen, one of the most important centres of ceramics work in China, where craftsmen perfected the deep blues of the 15th Yuan dynasty. There are also displays of kilns and the firing process.

On the 3rd floor, the **Chinese Painting Gallery** leads visitors through various styles of Chinese art. The audioguide is particularly useful for this section.

The **Calligraphy Gallery** is one of the hardest for foreigners to appreciate, but anyone can enjoy the purely aesthetic quality of calligraphy. The display covers everything from inscribed bamboo strips and Shang oracle bones to the various scripts such as seal script, official script, and wild cursive script, almost impossible to read even for Chinese, as it misses out many of the strokes.

The **Ancient Chinese Jade Gallery** shows the transformation of the uses of jade from early mystical symbols such as *bi* jade discs, used to worship heaven, through to later ritual weapons and jewellery. Exhibit No 414 in particular is a remarkable totem, with an engraved phoenix carrying a human head. Bamboo drills, abrasive sand, and garnets crushed in water were used to shape some of the pieces, which date back over 5000 years.

When it comes to the **Coin Gallery** it's tempting to just keep moving. The earliest coins on display have a hole in the middle so they could be carried by string, and some older coins are shaped like keys or knives. There's an interesting collection of coins that were found along the Silk Road but unfortunately there's no English text at present.

The **Ming and Qing Furniture Gallery** features the rose and sandalwood furniture of the elegant Ming dynasty and the heavier, more ornate Qing dynasty. Several mock offices and reception rooms offer a glimpse of life in a wealthy Chinese home.

It's worth saving some energy for the **Minority Nationalities Art Gallery**, one of the most interesting rooms in the museum, as it shows the enormous breadth of China's 56 ethnic groups, totalling some 40 million people. Displays vary from the salmon fishskin suit of the Hezhen in Heilongjiang, and the furs of the Siberian Oroqen, to the embroidery and batik of Guizhou's Miao and Dong, the Middle-Eastern satin robes of the Uyghurs and the wild hairstyles of the former slave-owning Yi.

Handicrafts include Tibetan jewellery, Miao silverware, Uyghur pewter, Yi lacquerwork, Tibetan *cham* festival masks and Nuo opera masks from Guizhou.

In addition to the galleries there are also three exhibition halls for temporary displays.

The museum (☎ 6372 3500) is at 201 Renmin Dadao and is open Monday to Friday from 9 am to 5 pm (last ticket sold at 4 pm) and Saturday 9 am to 8 pm (local students free from 5 to 7 pm). Tickets cost Y20, or Y5 with a local student card.

The audioguide (available in eight languages) is well worth the extra Y40. It highlights particularly interesting exhibits and has good gallery overviews and general background information. To rent the guide you need a deposit of Y500, US$40 or your passport. Photos (without a tripod) can be taken anywhere except on the 3rd floor.

The excellent museum shop sells postcards, a series of photo books focusing on individual halls (except bronzes) for Y25 each, as well as well-made replicas of the museums exhibits. There are a few overpriced shops and teahouses inside the museum, as well as an attached snack bar and cloakroom.

Renmin Park 人民公园
Rénmín Gōngyuán

Renmin (People's) Park is not one of the city's best parks but it was undergoing a multimillion-yuan facelift at the time of research. Whatever happens, there are some nice ponds and decent views of the surrounding skyscrapers.

The park was built on the site of the old settlement racecourse (built in 1862), which later served as a holding camp during WWII. Saturday sees the place packed with proud parents treating their one child to a ride on the dodgems.

The park is open daily from 6 am to 6 pm; entry is Y2.

Renmin Square 人民公园区
Rénmín Guǎngchǎng

This is a good place to relax and watch people strolling, flying beautiful kites and even waltzing in front of the musical fountain. It's hard to imagine that in 1966 a million Red Guards marched here, all waving Mao's Little Red Book. In June 1989 the square was the focus of demonstrations that echoed those in Tiananmen Square in Beijing. Underneath the square is a shopping plaza.

The building to the north-west of the square is the **Shanghai Grand Theatre** (Shànghǎi Dà Jùyùan), Shanghai's premier venue for the arts. Dubbed the 'Crystal

Nanjing Lu Walking Tour (Map 5)

Route: From the Bund to Renmin Square
Duration: one hour, 2.5km

China's Oxford St or Fifth Ave, Nanjing Lu is the most famous shopping street in China, with a reputed 1.7 million visitors per day on the weekend. Known to the Chinese as the *da malu*, or Great Horse Road, it was famously classified in 1937 as one of the seven most interesting roads in the world. A large section was pedestrianised in 1999 so it's now a much more enjoyable place to stroll.

The eastern stretch of the road is of minor interest, though the crossing with Henan Lu was once home to Shanghai's first racecourse.

Nanjing Lu was once lined with specialist shops but only a few remain. Look out for Duoyunxuan (No 422), a painting and calligraphy supplies shop which dates from 1900, and Shaowansheng (No 414), a venerable local food store which specialises in local sweets and cured meats (even dried pig's faces) from Shanghai, Shaoxing and Ningbo.

At No 429 is Sincere, one of Shanghai's oldest stores, which got its name because it was the first store to introduce fixed prices. In 1937 a misguided Chinese or Japanese bomb fell on the store, leaving 100 dead and 600 wounded in the wreckage. Sincere recently announced that it was finally pulling out of Shanghai after a string of losses.

As you continue along Nanjing Donglu you will pass many of the great department stores of the 1930s. At No 635 is the Hualian Commercial Building, formerly Wing On.

The No 1 Provisions Store, at No 720, was formerly the Sun Sun store. Just as today, old Shanghai's department stores used whatever gimmicks to win customers, offering live bands and at one time even a dwarf to get attention. Sun Sun went as far as installing a 6th-floor radio studio where customers could watch local stars perform.

Farther on, the corner of Guizhou Lu marks the site of the notorious May 30th Massacre, when a dozen or so unarmed Chinese were killed by British police during anti-Japanese protests.

At No 800, the Number One Department Store, formerly Sun Company, opened in 1936 and was the first store on the road to boast an escalator. For years the store has been the largest in China and still is, in its most recent reincarnation in Pudong. The next mammoth store is New World, originally built in 1915 as an amusement centre.

Just off Nanjing Donglu, at the intersection of Xizang Lu and Jiujiang Lu is Mu'en Church, formerly the Moore Memorial Church. Sunday services are still held at 7.30 and 9.30 am and 2 and 7 pm.

From here Nanjing Donglu becomes Nanjing Xilu (the former Bubbling Well Road) and curves around the former racecourse, which covered what is now Renmin Square and Renmin Park. The racecourse grandstand is all that remains and is now the Shanghai Art Museum.

The Pacific Hotel, formerly the China United Apartment Building, has some lovely details in its entrance lobby. At No 150 is the grey brick former YMCA.

The dark brown building at No 170 is the Park Hotel, originally built as a bank in 1934, and, with 22 floors, was formerly the highest building in the Far East. The top-floor restaurant (whose roof once slid back so that guests could wine and dine under the stars) and dance floor are still there.

The nearby Grand Theatre isn't up to much today but was the best theatre in Shanghai at the time of opening in 1933. It had 2000 sofa-style seats equipped with earphones for simultaneous translation.

The walk finishes at the junction with Huangpi Nanlu. From here you can head south to Renmin Square, or branch off west to Jiangyin Lu Bird and Flower Market.

Palace', the building is particularly brilliant at night. You can get a tour of the building (and the current exhibition of musical instruments) for Y50 or you can get a combined Shanghai Museum–Grand Theatre ticket for Y45 from the Shanghai Museum. Either way, you are probably better off spending your money on a performance.

To the north-east is the equally impressive **Shanghai Urban Planning Exhibition Hall** (Chéngshì Guīhuà Zhǎnshìguǎn, ☎ 6372 2077). The building is pitching itself as a tourist attraction but is essentially just enjoyable hi-tech propaganda. The exhibits paint a picture of how Shanghai will develop in the next 20 years (there are plenty of elderly Shanghainese looking to see what will become of their bulldozed houses) and the highlight is an absorbing scale plan of the Shanghai of the future. There are also some interesting photos of 1930s Shanghai, lots of interactive computers (including a fun video display of Nanjing Lu and a 3-D display called the Cave) and great views from the roof. If you need a break, there's a street of mock 1930s cafes underneath the building. The hall is open Wednesday to Sunday from 9 am to 4 pm; entry costs Y20.

Sandwiched between the two is the austere building of the Shanghai Government.

At the west end of Renmin Square is the tiny but charming **Sanjiao Park** (Sānjiǎo Gōngyuàn), where elderly men congregate to admire each other's caged birds. There's also a small goldfish market here.

A block north of here is the larger **Jiangyin Lu Bird and Flower Market** (Jiāngyīn Lú Niǎohuā Shíchǎng; Map 5), which is also well worth a visit.

Shanghai Art Museum 上海美术馆
Shànghǎi Měishùguǎn

This museum, first opened in 1956, recently moved from Nanjing Lu to a stunning new location in the former racecourse club building and is well worth a visit. The city council deserves much praise for supplying a wide variety of quality Chinese art in a completely restored and wheelchair-accessible Shanghai monument. The collection ranges from modern oils and pop art to the Shanghai school of traditional Chinese art.

Note the horse-head design on the balustrades and the Art-Deco chandeliers, original to the 1933 building. Admission is Y10, and Y5 with a student card. Wheelchairs and prams are available at no charge. The museum is open daily from 9 to 11 am and 1 to 4 pm.

Great World 大世界
Dà Shìjiè

At the corner of Xizang Lu and Yan'an Donglu, Great World was opened in 1917 as a place for acrobats and nightclub stars to rival the existing New World on Nanjing Rd. It soon became a centre for the bizarre and the burlesque under the seedy control of the gangster 'Pockmarked' Huang before it was commandeered as a refugee centre during WWII. After 1949 the building became a social club (The People's Pleasure Ground), a warehouse and the Municipal Youth Palace. Great World reopened as an entertainment centre in 1987 but is a pale reflection of what it was in its heyday. Entry is Y25. See the Entertainment chapter for more details.

Shanghai Museum of Natural History 上海自然博物馆
Shànghǎi Zìrán Bówùguǎn

This museum, based on the former collection of the British Royal Asiatic Society, consists of a scary assortment of pickled and stuffed animals (including a giant panda and a Yangzi alligator), housed in a drafty old building with bad lighting. Highlights include Chinese mummies unearthed while constructing Dapu Lu, a huge dinosaur skeleton from Sichuan and a Yellow River woolly mammoth. Guides are on hand for free English tours.

The museum (☎ 6321 3548) is at 260 Yan'an Donglu, midway between the Bund and Renmin Square. It's open daily except Monday, from 9 am to 4 pm. Admission is Y5, or Y13 if you want to see the mildly interesting aquarium.

The museum's chairman, the gangster Du Yuesheng, originally built the dramatic

Lost World

The establishment had six floors to provide distraction for the milling crowd, six floors that seethed with life and all the commotion and noise that go with it, studded with every variety of entertainment Chinese ingenuity had contrived. When I entered the hot stream of humanity there was no turning back even had I wanted to.

On the first floor were gambling tables, sing-song girls, magicians, pick-pockets, slot machines, fireworks, bird cages, fans, stick incense, acrobats and ginger. One flight up were the restaurants, a dozen different groups of actors, crickets in cages, pimps, mid-wives, barbers and earwax extractors. The third floor had jugglers, herb medicines, ice cream parlours, photographers, a new bevy of girls, their high-collared gowns slit to reveal their hips, in case one had passed up the more modest ones below who merely flashed their thighs. The fourth floor was crowded with shooting galleries, fan-tan tables, revolving wheels, massage benches, acupuncture and moxa cabinets, hot towel counters, dried fish and intestines, and dance platforms serviced by a horde of music makers competing with each other to see who could drown out the others. The fifth floor featured girls whose dresses were slit to the armpits, a stuffed whale, storytellers, balloons, peep shows, a mirror maze, two love-letter booths with scribes who guaranteed results, rubber goods, and a temple filled with ferocious gods and joss sticks.

On the top floor and roof of that house of multiple joys a jumble of tightrope walkers slithered back and forth, and there were see-saws, Chinese checkers, mahjong, strings of firecrackers going off, lottery tickets, and marriage brokers. And as I tried to find my way down again an open space was pointed out to me where hundreds of Chinese, so I was told, after spending their coppers, had speeded the return to the street below by jumping off the roof.

From *Fun in a Chinese Laundry* by Joseph von Sternberg, director of the film *Shanghai Express*, who visited Great World in the mid-1930s.

red brick building across Yan'an Donglu as the Chung Wai Bank. It served for years as the Shanghai Museum and is now an office block and restaurant.

Museum of Ancient Chinese Sex Culture 中国古代性文化展览
Zhōngguó Gǔdài Xìng Wénhuà Zhǎnlǎn

This must surely be the only museum in China whose exhibits include a two-headed lesbian dildo, a pillow designed to facilitate copulation and a ring that shows that the owner (a prostitute) is authorised to perform oral sex. It just goes to show how open China has become.

Professor Liu Dalin's aim in presenting the 1200 well-displayed sexual exhibits is to trace the evolution of sex in animals, marital relationships, sexual worship, literature and art, with the emphasis on the study of tradition and development. Some of the items are quite artistically aesthetic. The foot-binding devices are a particularly ghoulish curiosity. An English-language video describing some of Dalin's finds can be viewed inside the hall.

The Museum of Ancient Chinese Sex Culture (☎ 6351 4381) is located behind the former Sincere department store, 8th floor, 479 Nanjing Donglu (next to the Sofitel); access is from the west side of the building. The museum is open daily from 10 am to 9 pm; admission is Y30 and photos are not allowed. Don't forget to buy your plastic dildos and sex tonics at the gift shop on the way out.

FRENCH CONCESSION (MAP 6) 法租界

The French Concession was once home to the bulk of Shanghai's adventurers, revolutionaries, gangsters, prostitutes and writers, though ironically not many of them were French (the majority of the residents were British, American, White Russian and Chinese). Shanghai's nickname 'Paris of the East' stems largely from the tree-lined avenues and French-influenced architecture of the concession.

Today the area is still the most graceful part of Shanghai, and the most rewarding

THINGS TO SEE & DO

French Concession Walking Tour I (Maps 6 & 7)

Route: Through the heart of the French Concession
Duration: 2½ hours

The French Concession's grand avenues and impressive architecture provide fabulous inspiration for walks. From Huangpi Lu metro station head south down Huangpi Nanlu. When you cross Taicang Lu pause to look at the old brick building at No 127, where Mao and the other communist delegates stayed (in a girls' dormitory) while attending the first Communist Party congress. Continue south past the renovated *shíkūméns* (stone gatehouses) of the **Xintiandi complex**. At Xingye Lu turn right and visit the site of the 1st National Congress of the CCP.

From here head west, across Chongqing Nanlu and along Nanchang Lu. At the cafe-lined Yandang Lu head south and pass through Fuxing Park. Exit at the west side passing the very chic cafe Park 97, and continue west along Gaolan Lu to get a look at the former Russian Orthodox **St Nicholas Church**. The church was built in 1933 in dedication to the murdered Tsar of Russia, and now houses the Ashanti Dome restaurant. Note the icon of Chairman Mao painted by a caretaker during the Cultural Revolution (when it was a washing machine cooperative) to protect the church. Outside of dining times the staff will normally let you in to see the upper floor dome and restored frescoes.

From here walk south down Sinan Lu (formerly rue Massenet) past the former residences of **Sun Yatsen** and **Zhou Enlai**. This area is lined with beautiful old residences.

If you're interested, at the corner of Fuxing Zhonglu (formerly rue Lafayette) you can walk a block east to see the apartment block on the south-east corner which was once home to US communist sympathiser and journalist **Agnes Smedley**. Otherwise, back at the corner of Fuxing and Sinan roads, head west to Ruijin Nanlu (formerly Route des Soeurs) and then south to the **Ruijin Guest House**. This is the former Morris estate, home to Mohowk Morris, the founder of the *North China Daily News*, and his sons Harry and Hayley, who were famous racehorse and dog owners. You can stroll around the complex. The beautiful but pricey Face Bar is in the compound if you are in need of refreshment.

From here head north, west and then south down Maoming Lu (formerly Rue Cardinal Mercier), currently Shanghai's premier bar strip. When the bars start to peter out take an alley west which leads into a huge **flower market** in what is Cultural Square. This was once the site of the Canidrome, the French dog track, which opened in 1928 to a capacity crowd of 50,000.

From here head north to Fuxing Zhonglu, head west and then take a left to Fenyang Lu (formerly Route Pichon). One block south of here is the wonderful building of the **Shanghai Arts and Crafts Research Institute**, formerly the residence of a high-ranking French Concession official and later home to Chen Yi, the first mayor of Shanghai.

Just south of here is the Shanghai Ear, Nose and Throat Hospital, once the beautiful **Shanghai Jewish Hospital**. History buffs can continue five minutes down Taiyuan Lu to the **Taiyuan Villa**, where General Marshall, US mediator between Mao and Chiang Kaishek, resided between 1945 and 1949.

Alternatively, head west along Fenyang past the statue of Pushkin, erected by White Russians on the centenary of Pushkin's death in 1937, smashed by Red Guards in 1966 and rebuilt in 1987. Continue along Dongping Lu to No 9, once the residence of Chiang Kaishek, and, later, Jiang Qing (Mao's wife).

You are now at Hengshan Lu (formerly Avenue Petain), Shanghai's premier strip of foreign restaurants. Here at No 53 you'll find the English-style **Community Church**, built in 1924 as the largest Christian church in Shanghai and later turned into a gym during the Cultural Revolution. Sunday services (☎ 6437 6576) are at 7.30 and 10 am and 7 pm in Chinese and at 4 pm in English. The imposing building opposite the church is the former American School.

From here you can get a meal at Yang's, Bai's or one of the Western restaurants on Hengshan Lu (see the Places to Eat chapter), or take the metro home.

district for walks and bike rides. The area also hosts the lion's share of Shanghai's nightlife, restaurants and shopping.

Fuxing Park 复兴公园
Fùxīng Gōngyuán

This leafy park, laid out by the French in 1909 and used by the Japanese as a parade ground in the late 1930s, remains one of the city's most pleasant parks. The park was renamed Fuxing (Revival) after WWII.

There is always plenty to see in the park – it's a refuge for the elderly and a practising field for itinerant musicians and t'ai chi masters. There's always at least one person walking around the park backwards (apparently it's good for your health). Entry is Y2.

Site of the 1st National Congress of the CCP (Map 7)
中共一大会址
Zhōnggòng Yīdàhuìzhǐ

On 23 July 1921 the Chinese Communist Party (CCP) was founded in this French Concession building at 76 Xingye Lu (then 106 Rue Wantz), thus rendering this unassuming building one of Chinese communism's holiest shrines.

There's plenty of Marxist spin on the commentary (full of 'never-ending heroic struggles' and 'anti-feudal democratic revolutions') – just in case you had forgotten that Shanghai is actually part of the world's largest communist country – and there's not all that much to actually see here, but historians will appreciate the site as a defining moment in modern Chinese history.

The first hall paints a fine picture of the foreign settlements before getting mired in some dull exhibits of early anti-imperial rebellions. The second hall profiles the founders of the CCP and exhibits early translations of Soviet manifestos. The second building shows the room where the whole Party started, actually the house of one of the delegates, Li Hanjun.

Of the 13 original delegates only two (one was Mao Zedong) ever worked in the Chinese government. Five were killed before the communists took power and another six either quit the Party or were expelled as traitors.

The museum (☎ 5383 2171) is open daily from 9 am to 5 pm (last ticket sold at 4 pm); entry is Y3. You must buy the ticket at the north-west corner of the building but enter from the south-east. Collectors of Marxist stamps may want to peruse the souvenir shop for its complete collection of communist leaders.

Expect a big party here on the 80th anniversary of the CCP in July 2001.

Xintiandi (Map 7) 新天地
Xīntiāndì

This ambitious new business, entertainment and cultural complex, built by Hong Kong's Shui On Group, is something to keep an eye open for in the next couple of years. The complex, just off Huangpi Nanlu, consists of several blocks of renovated traditional shíkūmén houses, brought bang up to date with a stylish modern twist.

The first phase, to open in late 2000, will see cafes, restaurants (one owned by Jackie Chan), boutiques, speciality shops, galleries and a street of bars. An entertainment complex, IMAX theatre, a lake, a residential complex, two top-end hotels, a shíkūmén museum and several office complexes will follow in the years, even decades, ahead.

Sun Yatsen's Former Residence
孙中山故居
Sūn Zhōngshān Gùjū

China is simply brimming with Sun Yatsen memorabilia, and 7 Xianshan Lu (formerly

Sun Yatsen

Rue Molière) is one of his former residences (there are several – he got around). Sun lived here for six years from 1918 to 1924, supported by overseas Chinese funds. After Sun's death, his wife, Song Qingling (1893 to 1981), continued to live here until 1937, constantly watched by the Kuomintang plain-clothes police and French police. The two-storey house is set back from the street and is furnished as it was back in Sun's days, even though it was looted by the Japanese during WWII.

The entry price of Y8 gets you a brief tour of the house in English. The museum (☎ 6437 2954) is open daily from 9 am to 4.30 pm.

Zhou Enlai's Former Residence
周恩来故居
Jí Zhōu Gōngguǎn

In 1946 Zhou Enlai, the urbane and much-loved first premier of the People's Republic of China (PRC), lived at this former French Concession Spanish villa at 107 (now 73) Sinan Lu. Zhou was then head of the Communist Party's Shanghai office, and spent much of his time giving press conferences and dodging Kuomintang agents who spied on him from across the road.

There's not much to see these days except lots of Spartan beds and stern-looking desks, but the charming neighbourhood is full of lovely old houses and it's a great place to wander around. (See the French Concession walking tour).

The museum (☎ 6473 0420) is open daily from 9 to 11.30 am and 1 to 5 pm; entry costs Y2.

Song Qingling's Former Residence 宋庆龄故居
Sòngqìnglíng Gùjū

Built in the 1920s by a Greek shipping magnate, this building became home to the wife of Dr Sun Yatsen from 1948 to 1963.

Like most former residences this building can be dull unless you are an admirer of Song or of old houses. The garden of camphor trees is particularly nice.

Highlights include the sitting room where Song met Mao Zedong, Zhou Enlai

---

The Soong Family

The Soongs probably wielded more influence and power over modern China than any other family. The father of the family, Charlie Soong, grew up in Hainan Island and after an American evangelical education he finally settled in Shanghai. He began to print Bibles and money, becoming a wealthy businessman and developing ties with secret societies, during which time he became good friends with Sun Yatsen. Charlie had three daughters and a son.

Soong Ailing married the wealthy HH Kung, a descendant of Confucius, head of the Bank of China and later China's finance minister. Soong Meiling became the third wife of Chiang Kaishek (head of the Kuomintang and future President of China) in 1928. She went to the USA during China's war with Japan and fled to Taiwan with Chiang after the communist victory. Much to the disapproval of her father, Soong Qingling (more commonly known as Song Qingling) married Sun Yatsen, 30 years her elder, studied in Moscow and was the only member of the family to live in China after 1949, until her death in 1981. TV Soong, Charlie's one son, became China's finance minister, premier and the richest man of his generation.

Thus it is said by mainlanders that of the three daughters one loved money (Ailing) and one loved power (Meiling) but only Qingling loved China. Among them, the siblings stewed a heady brew of fascism and communism.

Song Qingling died in Beijing and is buried in Shanghai's International Cemetery on Hongqiao Lu, next to her parents' tomb. Her sister Meiling declined the invitation to return to China to attend the funeral.

---

and writer Guo Moruo, the dining room where she had dinner with Kim Il Song, and the Soviet limousine presented to her by Stalin.

Song Qingling's Former Residence (☎ 6437 6288) is located at 1843 Huaihai Zhonglu and is open daily from 9 to 11 am and 1 to 4.30 pm. Entry is Y8, or Y6 for students.

French Concession Walking Tour II (Map 6)

Route: From the Garden to Hilton Hotels
Duration: two hours

From Shaanxi Nanlu metro station head north up Maoming Nanlu (formerly Rue Cardinal Mercier) to the **Garden Hotel**, originally constructed as the French Club, or Cercle Sportif Français, in 1926. The club was subsequently used by the US army in the 1940s before being converted to the People's Cultural Palace after Liberation. Mao stayed in the building in 1959. The eastern entrance of the hotel features a gold mosaic statuary niche and the original staircase leading up to the ballroom with its beautiful, stained-glass ceiling piece. On the 2nd floor, the columns are capped with nude reliefs, concealed during the Cultural Revolution and unveiled in their former splendour. The former Art-Deco pool is now the Oasis Cafe, but in summertime the 3rd-floor terrace allows lovely views of the garden and the eastern window lintel.

To the east of the Garden Hotel is the **Jinjiang Hotel**. The north block, built as the Cathay Mansions in 1929, was where Zhou Enlai and President Nixon signed the Shanghai Communique in 1972, marking China's return to the world community after the isolation of the Cultural Revolution. To the south is **Grosvenor House**, a plush 1930s apartment block.

Continue north to Changle Lu and you'll see the **Lyceum Theatre** (1931), once home to the British Amateur Dramatic Club and now an unremarkable cinema. From here you can take a detour one block east to the Jinjiang Tower and take the external lift to the 41st floor for great views of the city.

Heading back west along Changle Lu, turn right up Shanxi Nanlu (formerly Avenue Roi Albert) to **Moller House**, at No 30, one of the most fantastic buildings built in the 1930s (1938). The Swedish owner, Eric Moller, was the owner of Moller Line and was a huge racing fan. The **Shanghai Exhibition Centre** is nearby on Yan'an Zhonglu.

Head back south, go one block west at Changle Lu and then head south down Xiangyang Beilu. On the corner with Xinle Lu is the lovely blue-domed **Orthodox Russian Mission Church**, built in 1934. The church now houses an ungodly securities exchange. The Grape Restaurant, next door, is a good place to grab lunch if you are hungry.

Head down to busy Huaihai Zhonglu (formerly Avenue Joffre), past the entrance to Xiangyang Park, a haven for elderly chess players, and turn right to Donghu Lu. Here at the corner, hidden behind elegant Art-Deco gates, is the former house of the gangster **Du Yuesheng** (though he rarely stayed there), which at one time also served as an opium warehouse and movie studio.

From here, head up Donghu Lu to the junction and take Changle Lu. Hidden down lane No 637 Changle Lu, at No 24, is the **Chinese Printed Blue Nankeen Exhibition Hall**, which is worth a visit if you are a fan of Shanghai's famous blue cloth (see the Shopping chapter for details).

Head north up Fumin Lu and take a left into Julu Lu, Shanghai's late-night bar strip, and then turn right into Changshu Lu. At Lane No 303 Huashan Lu take a look at No 16, the former residence of Cai Yuanpei, an early-20th-century intellectual and reformist. The picturesque lane is full of beautiful old houses. From here you are right across from the Hilton, where you can take a taxi home or step in for a break.

Shanghai Arts & Crafts Research Institute 上海工艺美术研究

Shànghǎi Gōngyì Měishù Yánjiūsuǒ

This arts and crafts centre is located at 9 Fenyang Lu and is open to anyone interested in traditional crafts such as embroidery, paper-cuts, lacquerwork, jade cutting and lantern making.

For interested visitors, the Shanghai Arts & Crafts Research Institute is open every day except Sunday from 8.30 am to 4.30 pm.

Museum of Public Security
(Map 6) 上海公安博物馆
Shànghǎi Gōng'àn Bówùguǎn

Not quite as dull as it sounds, this museum holds a few gems among the inevitable displays on traffic control. Look out for the gold pistols of Sun Yatsen and 1930s gangster Huang Jinrong amid the fine collection of Al Capone-style machine and pen guns, as well as the collection of hand-painted business cards once used by the city's top prostitutes.

The museum (☎ 6472 0256) is at 518 Ruijin Nanlu and is open Monday to Saturday, from 9 am to 4.30 pm. Entry is Y8.

XUJIAHUI (MAP 8) 徐家汇
St Ignatius Cathedral 天主教堂
Tiānzhǔjiào Táng

The Xujiahui area os Shanghai, bordering the western end of the French Concession and known to 1930s expat residents as Ziccawei or Sicawei, was once a thriving Jesuit settlement.

St Ignatius Cathedral (1904), whose 50m Gothic spires were lopped off by Red Guards, has been restored and is open once again for Catholic services. Up to 2500 Chinese Catholics cram into the impressive church at Easter.

Xu Guangqi

Xujiahui ('the Xu family gathering') is named after Xu Guangqi (1562–1633), a 17th-century Chinese renaissance man. Xu was an early student of astronomy, agronomy and the calendar and he established a meteorological observatory that relayed its information to the tower on the Bund. He was then converted to Catholicism by Mateo Ricci and was baptised with the name Paul. He became a high official in the Ming court and bequeathed land to found a Jesuit community, which eventually led to the construction of Xujihui Cathedral. Xu's tomb can still be visited in nearby Guangqi Park (Map 8), next to the modern-day Shanghai Meteorological Department, and stands as an inspirational symbol of Shanghai's openness to accept foreign ideas.

To the south-east of the cathedral is a gallery of traditional Chinese art. The yellow building across Caoxi Beilu was once part of the Jesuit settlement. Today the bustling Xujiahui crossroads is home to some of Shanghai's biggest department stores and entertainment complexes.

The cathedral is at 158 Puxi Lu, a short walk south of the Xujiahui metro station (metro exit 1). Services are held weekdays at 6.15 and 7 am, Saturday at 6 pm and Sunday at 5.30, 6, 7 and 8 am and 6 pm.

PUDONG NEW AREA
(MAP 3 & 5) 浦东新区
Pǔdōng Xīnqū

Over 1½ times larger than urban Shanghai itself, the Pudong New Area consists of the entire eastern bank of the Huangpu River. Before 1990 – when development plans were first announced – Pudong constituted 350 sq km of boggy farmland that supplied vegetables to Shanghai's markets. Today the only thing sprouting out of the ground are skyscrapers and Pudong has become Shanghai and China's economic powerhouse. For more information on the zone see the Economics section in Facts about Shanghai.

The high-rise area directly across from the Bund is the Lujiazui Finance and Trade Zone, where the Shanghai Stock Exchange is located (but not open to visitors). From the unmistakable Oriental Pearl Tower the eight-lane wide Century Ave, modelled on the Champs Elysee in Paris, runs 4.2km to Central Park.

Pudong is largely home to high-rolling financiers and businesspeople. For the visitor, Pudong's main attractions include several huge malls, China's tallest building, the views back to the Bund and the startling architecture of the area.

For the various ways of getting across the Huangpu to Pudong see the Getting Around chapter.

Oriental Pearl Tower (Map 5)
东方明珠广播电视
Dōngfāng Míngzhū Guǎngbō Diànshì Tǎ

Love it or hate it, this tripod-shaped, shocking pink, hypodermic syringe of a building has become a symbol of Pudong and of Shanghai's renaissance. At 468m, the tower has been both literally and metaphorically eclipsed by the Jinmao Tower. The building has 11 baubles in total, though only three are currently in use (at 90m, 263m and 350m). The others are up for lease so if you're looking for apartment space with plenty of light...

The tower has a complex ticket system. You can go to the first ball (Y30), the second ball and outdoor viewing platform (Y50), or both (Y65). For Y100 you can get to all three balls and for Y150/180 you can enjoy a revolving buffet lunch/dinner in the second ball and get free access to all the other balls thrown in.

The tower (☎ 5879 8888 for reservations) is open daily except Monday, from 8 am to 10 pm. Try to get there early or you'll have to queue forever to get into the high-speed elevator.

At the time of writing the **Shanghai Municipal History Museum** (Shánghǎi Shí Líshǐ Bówùguǎn) was due to move into the lower ball of the Oriental Pearl Tower. The museum highlights include a pair of copper lions, which originally guarded the entrance to the Hong Kong and Shanghai Bank on the Bund; a gun used at Wusong against the British invasion of 1842; and copies of the settlement's land agreements. Other dubious planned attractions include something called Science Fantasy World and Space City.

Boat trips on the Huangpu also run from the Oriental Pearl Tower from the docks behind it. A 30-minute tour costs Y20 per person. If you do this you can get entry to the first ball for only Y10. Boats run daily except Monday, every 45 minutes or so from 9 am to 4 pm.

Jinmao Tower (Map 5) 金茂大厦
Jīnmào Dàshà

Shanghai's most spectacular building, visible from almost everywhere in the city, is largely an office block (owned by the Ministry of Foreign Trade and Economic Cooperation), with the Grand Hyatt renting space from the 54th to 87th floors.

Size Matters

The main reason to come to Pudong is for the views, and you're spoilt for choice.

The granddaddy of the viewing towers is the Oriental Pearl Tower, with views at 263m costing a cool Y100. Whether the tower is worth the cost is debatable. For Y50 you can go to the viewing platform at the top of the Jinmao Tower (420m). Even better, for the same fee you can get a coffee and a free view on the 87th floor of the Grand Hyatt, one floor below the observation deck (only open weekday evenings, and during the day on the weekend). There's also the 54th floor of the Grand Hyatt, which has fantastic views both outside and in, looking up at its mind-spinning atrium space.

Those with vertigo may be satisfied with the vertically challenged Shanghai International Exhibition Centre, which offers views of the Bund from its roof garden (Y50). For an extra Y50 you can get similar views while splashing in the gorgeous pool.

The cheapest fix of all comes from the Riverside Park (Bīnjiāng Dàdào), which is right on the waterfront, and a steal at Y5. The park is open from 7 am to 1 pm.

The main thing to see if you are not staying here is the stupendous view from the 88th-floor observatory, accessed from the separate building to the side of the main tower. Entry is Y50 and the platform is open daily from 8.30 am to 9 pm.

A food court and a display featuring the building's remarkable construction process are in the building next to the main tower.

Huamu Tourism Zone (Map 3) 花木旅游区
Huāmù Lǚyóu Qū

This area, anchored around Central Park, has been designated as a centre for tourism development. Planned attractions are the Montreal Centre, a huge exhibition centre, a folk village food court, and, of course, plenty of shopping. Keep an eye out for Science World, a multimedia theme park and

IMAX theatre complex, which is due to be built further out in the zone.

Nanpu Bridge (Map 7) 南浦大桥
& Yangpu Bridge (Map 3) 杨浦大桥
Nánpǔ Qiáo & Yángpǔ Qiáo

These two bridges, the world's fourth-longest and longest cable-stayed suspension bridges respectively, are worth a visit or crossing for the views of the Huangpu and design works. Both bridges have viewing areas, from where you can cross to the other side and take photos. Both are open daily to viewers from 9 am to 5 pm; entry is Y5.

SOUTH SHANGHAI (MAP 3)
上海南区
Longhua Temple & Pagoda
(Map 3) 龙华寺、龙华塔
Lónghuá Tǎ

South-west of central Shanghai, close to the Huangpu River, is the oldest and largest monastery in Shanghai. It's said to date from the 10th century, when the King of Wu built it for his mother. Built in the Song style but renovated in Guangxu's reign of the Qing, it has recently been restored for tourism.

There are five main halls, starting with the Laughing Buddha Hall. To either side of the entrance are a bell and a drum tower. The temple is famed for its 6500kg bell, which was cast in 1894. To strike the bell is auspicious, at least for the temple, which charges Y10 for three strikes. If you've got a handy Y360, 108 strikes are thought to be even more auspicious. The 'longhua' refers to the tree under which Buddha achieved enlightenment.

The adjoining Longhua Pagoda was originally built in 977 and has been reconstructed many times, most recently in 1952. The seven-storey tower is 44m high, with flying eaves. A tourism complex along the lines of the Yuyuan Bazaar has recently been built around the pagoda.

Longhua stages traditional celebrations during New Year (both Western and Chinese) and during its temple fair in April, when folk performers, dragon dances and snack sellers descend on the place en masse.

The easiest way there is to take the metro to the Caobao Lu metro station, then walk or take a taxi. Alternatively, take the metro to Xujiahui then catch bus No 44 right to the temple. The monastery is open daily from 7 am to 4 pm; entry costs Y6.

Next to the monastery is the **Martyrs Memorial** (Lièshí Língyuánn; Map 8), marking the site of an old Kuomintang prison, where 800 communists were executed between 1928 and 1937. During WWII the area was a Japanese internment camp and airfield, as depicted in the JG Ballard novel and Spielberg film *Empire of the Sun*.

The memorial is open from 9 am to 4 pm. There is a Y1 entry fee to the park, plus Y5 for the Memorial Hall.

Shanghai Botanical Gardens
(Map 3) 上海植物园
Shànghǎi Zhíwùyuán

About 2km south-west of the Longhua Pagoda are the Shanghai Botanical Gardens. Though some of the gardens are sparse and neglected, there are some beautiful green areas in which to sit and enjoy the quiet if you need to escape Shanghai's concrete jungle; the gardens on the south-west side are particularly nice, as are the bonsais of the Penjing 'potted landscape' Garden.

The northern side has a dusty memorial temple, originally built in 1728. It's dedicated to Huang Daopo, who supposedly kick-started Shanghai's cotton industry by bringing the knowledge of spinning and weaving to the region from Hainan Island.

Entrance to the garden is Y6; the bonsai garden is worth the extra Y5. Open daily 8 am to 5 pm; summer hours are longer.

Guilin Park (Map 3) 桂林公园
Guìlín Gōngyuán

This park probably isn't worth a special visit but it's a pleasant enough place. It's famous for its blossoms and because it was once home to the gangster 'Pockmarked' Huang.

NORTH SHANGHAI (MAP 3 & 6)
上海北区

The area north of Suzhou Creek was once the American settlement, until it merged into the International Settlement. Originally desirable, by the 1930s the region was one of the poorest parts of Shanghai. The region was divided into Hongkou, once known as Little Tokyo because of its 30,000 Japanese residents, and Zhapei, infamous in the 1930s for its factories and slums.

Today there's not all that much to see in this gritty part of Shanghai but its interesting backstreets offer some good walks. A remnant of the Japanese influence can be seen at the former Japanese Shinto shrine at 255 Zhapei Lu. The shrine served as a karaoke bar for a while but was empty at last check. Another interesting building is the **Jingling Church** (Jīnglíng Táng) at 135 Kunshan Lu, were Chiang Kaishek married Soong Meiling.

Hongkou Park (Map 3) 虹口公园
Hóngkǒu Gōngyuán

This is another of the city's nicest parks, full of elderly Chinese practising t'ai chi or ballroom dancing, and even the odd retired opera singer giving free performances. You can take boats out onto the small lake.

The park is also known as Lu Xun Park, largely because it holds the **Tomb of Lu Xun**, which was moved here from the international cemetery on the 20th anniversary of his death in 1956. Mao himself inscribed the memorial calligraphy.

The **Lu Xun Memorial Hall** (Lǔ Xùn Jìnìnguǎn), also dedicated to the grounds, is a state-of-the art museum on the great man. It tries hard, with plenty of videos and wax figures, but you'd have to be a hardened fan to appreciate the journals, manuscripts and old photos and their socialist spin.

The museum (☎ 6306 1181) is open 9 am to 5 pm. Entry is Y5, or Y2 for students. Bus No 21 goes here, up Sichuan Beilu from near the Bund. The museum bookshop sells collections of Lu Xun's stories in English, French and German.

Ohel Moishe Synagogue (Map 5) 摩西会堂
Móxī Huìtáng

This gutted synagogue, at 62 Changyang Lu (formerly Ward Rd), was built by the

Lu Xun

Lu Xun (1881–1936) is one of China's most famous writers, and is often regarded as the father of modern Chinese literature. Part of China's May 4 literary movement, his main achievement was to break from the classical literary traditions of the past, unintelligible to most Chinese, to create a modern vernacular literature. He was also a fierce critic of China's social ills, which led to him being canonised by the communist hierarchy even though he was never a member of the Communist Party. Lu Xun's most famous works are *A Madman's Diary*, *The True Story of Ah Q* and *Kong Yi Ji*. These are presented in two collections, *Call to Arms* and *Wandering*, both of which still make excellent reading. Lu Xun was also famed for promoting woodcuts as a form of mass art.

Apart from the tomb and memorial hall in Hongkou Park (Map 3), die-hard fans can visit the house at No 9, Lane 132, Shanying Lu (Map 3), where Lu Xun lived and worked for the last four years of his life (April 1933 to 19 October 1936). Xun had a great fondness for Shanghai and named his son Haiying ('Child of Shanghai'). The house holds a lifeless collection of photographs, letters, manuscripts, furniture and other memorabilia, but few ghosts remain. Look out for the rather morbid calendar and clock showing the date and time he died. The house is open daily from 9 am to 4 pm; entry is Y4.

MH

Russian Ashkenazi Jewish community in 1927 and lies in the heart of the 1940s Jewish ghetto (see the boxed text 'Jews of Shanghai' in this chapter).

Shanghai's Jews

Shanghai has two centuries of strong Jewish connections. Established Middle Eastern Sephardic Jewish families like the Hardoons, Ezras, Kadoories and Sassoons built their fortunes in Shanghai, establishing at least seven synagogues and many Jewish hospitals and schools. It was Victor Sassoon who famously remarked: 'There is only one race greater than the Jews and that's the Derby'.

A second group of Jews, this time Ashkenazi, arrived via Siberia, Harbin and Tianjin from Russia after anti-Jewish pogroms in 1906. The biggest influx, however, came between 1933 and 1941, when 30,000 mostly Ashkenazi Jews arrived from Nazi Europe by boat from Italy or by train via Siberia.

Shanghai was one of the few safe havens for Jews fleeing the Holocaust in Europe as it required neither passport nor visa. Gestapo agents followed the refugees and in 1942 tried to persuade the Japanese to build death camps on Chongming Island. Instead, in 1943, the Japanese forced Jews to move into a 'Designated Area for Stateless Refugees' in Hongkou.

The Jewish ghetto (stateless Russians didn't have to live here) became home to Jews from all walks of life and the ghetto grew to shelter a synagogue, schools, a local paper, hospitals and enough cafes, rooftop gardens and restaurants to gain the epithet 'Little Vienna'. Those Jews who held jobs in the French Concession had to secure passes from the Japanese, specifically the notoriously unpredictable and violent Mr Goya. Poorer refugees were forced to bunk down in cramped hostels known as *heime,* and had to rely on the generosity of others. When the wealthy Anglophile Jewish trading families left in 1941, the situation grew tighter. Still, the refugees heard of events in Europe and realised that they were the lucky ones.

Today there are a few remainders of Jewish life in Shanghai, such as the Ohel Moishe Synagogue on Changyang Lu and the former Jewish Club (1932) in the grounds of the Shanghai Music Conservatory, where concerts are still performed. A new Museum of Jewish Refugees to China is planned for the site of the former Ohel Rachel Synagogue (Map 4), at 500 Shanxi Beilu (formerly Seymour Road). The synagogue was built by Jacob Elias Sassoon in the late 19th century and was recently restored for Hilary Clinton's visit. Nearby are the remains of the school founded on the grounds by Horace Kadoorie.

For information and pricey tours of Jewish Shanghai contact the Shanghai Jewish Studies Centre (Map 6, ☎ 5306 0606 ext 2431) at Room 352, No 7 (the big building at the end), Lane 622, Huaihai Zonglu. The centre offers one-day tours of Jewish Shanghai with English- and Hebrew-speaking guides. Mr Wang of the Ohel Moishe Synagogue is a remarkable source of information on the area.

There's not much to see in the building except for a few black-and-white pictures. The real reason to come is to take a tour of the surrounding streets with the resident guide Mr Wang. Eighty-one year old Wang has lived all his life in Hongkou and can bring alive many of the surrounding sites.

Things to look out for in the surrounding streets include: the Ward Rd Jail, once Shanghai's biggest, across the road from the mosque; Zhoushan Lu, once the commercial heart of the district and lined with former Jewish residences; the memorial plaque erected in Huoshan Park in time for the visit of Yitzak Rabin; the Old Broadway Theatre (now the Shenshen Restaurant) and Vienna Cafe on Houshan Lu (Wayside Rd); and the remains of Jewish shops and a kosher delicatessen on Haimen Lu (Muirhead Rd), north of Changyang Lu, which still have faded, original painted signs from the 1940s (one says 'Horn's Imbiss Stube').

The synagogue building is open Monday to Friday 9 am to 4.30 pm. Entry and a tour cost Y30 per person.

Bus Nos 37 and 934 take you back to the Bund; No 37 continues to Nanjing Donglu.

quizzical young Shanghai boy.

Detail of the Longhua Temple.

Sporting a Mao cap at the Longhua Temple, which was bulit by King Wu for his mother.

Detail of the Longhua Temple.

Old men, Old Town.

State-of-the-art Shanghai Museum, designed to recall an ancient bronze ding (three-legged vessel)

Ancient polychrome figure, Shanghai Museum.

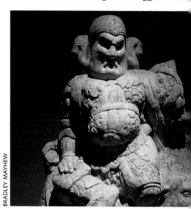

A lokpala (protective God), Shanghai Museum

10,000 Buddha stelae, Shanghai Museum.

Duolun Lu Cultural Street (Map 3) 多伦文化名人街
Duōlún Lù Wénhuà Míngrén Jiē

This recently restored street of fine old houses, just off Sichuan Beilu, is lined with art supply stores, curio shops, galleries and teahouses. The area was once home to several of China's most famous writers (as well as several Kuomintang generals) and so has been renamed the 'Duolun Street of Famous Cultural Figures'. The main appeal of the street (apart from the shopping) is its various collections. These include: the exhibition of Suzhou embroidery at No 57 (formerly the Great Virtue Church, interestingly built in a Chinese style); Wang Zaoshi's fabulous collection of 10,000 Mao badges at No 183 (Y2); the Haicitang porcelain gallery at No 185; the chopsticks collection at No 191; and the Jinquan Coin Gallery (Y10), located in an old Kuomintang officer's house down a signposted side street. With a bit of exploration you are bound to find some more.

Bus No 21 runs here, from Suzhou Creek.

Jade Buddha Temple (Map 4) 玉佛寺
Yùfó Sì

The Jade Buddha Temple is one of Shanghai's few Buddhist temples. It is active and attracts large numbers of visitors – largely local and overseas Chinese tourists.

Built between 1911 and 1918 in Song dynasty style, the centrepiece is a 2m-high white jade buddha around which the temple was built. The story goes that Hui Gen (Wei Ken), a monk from Putuoshan, travelled to Myanmar (Burma) via Tibet, lugged two jade buddhas back to China and then went off in search of alms to build a temple for them. Two of the buddhas ended up in Shanghai. This 1.9m-high seated buddha, encrusted with jewels, is said to weigh 1000kg. The other prized treasure is a complete set of the Buddhist canon printed from wood blocks in 1890 and stored on either side. No photography is allowed here.

A smaller 90cm jade buddha from the same shipment reclines on a mahogany couch, facing a much larger stone copy. The other main halls are the **Heavenly King Hall**, which features the four protector kings and a laughing buddha, the **Grand Hall**, featuring Medicine, Sakyamuni and Amithaba buddhas, with Guanyin behind, and the **Abbot Room**.

Entry is Y10, plus a cheeky Y5 extra charge to actually see the jade buddha. The temple is open daily from 8 am to noon and 1 to 4.30 pm. The temple is particularly busy during the Lunar New Year in February, when some 20,000 Chinese Buddhists throng to pray for prosperity. The surrounding shops can supply everything you might need to generate good luck, including bundles of spirit money to burn in incense pots.

The temple is in the north-west of town, near the intersection of Anyuan Lu and Jiangning Lu. One way to get there is to take the metro out to the Shanghai train station and then walk about 1km. Bus No 19 runs from around the corner from Shanghai Mansions, along Tiantong Lu and eventually past the temple.

Jing'an Temple (Map 6) 静安寺
Jìng'ān Sì

The Jing'an Temple (Temple of Tranquility) was originally built in AD 247 but was largely destroyed in 1851 and seriously renovated in 1999. Khi Vehdu, who ran the Jing'an Temple in the 1930s, was one of the most remarkable figures of the time. The nearly 2m-tall abbot had a large following and each of his seven concubines had a house and a car. At that time the temple was on Bubbling Well Rd, next to the eponymous well, but this was walled over in 1919. The temple was eventually divested of its Buddhist statues in the Cultural Revolution and turned into a plastics factory.

Today the temple is of limited interest, except at full moons when the place is packed with worshippers. Entry is Y5.

Shanghai Exhibition Centre (Map 6) 上海展览中心
Shànghǎi Zhǎnlǎn Zhōngxīn

The hulking great monolith of the Shanghai Exhibition Centre was built as the

Palace of Sino-Soviet Friendship, but the friendship turned to ideological rivalry and came to the brink of war in the 1960s. Architectural buffs will appreciate the monumentality and unsubtle, bold Bolshevik strokes – there was a time when Pudong was set to look like this.

The site of the Exhibition Centre was originally the gardens of the Jewish millionaire Silas Hardoon (for more information see the boxed text 'The Great Jewish Families' in this chapter).

WESTERN SHANGHAI (MAP 9)
上海西区

Hongqiao is mainly a centre for international commerce and trade exhibitions. There are many offices, as well as a few foreign restaurants, hotels and shopping malls. There's some striking modern architecture in the area, especially around New Century Plaza.

Gubei is a new planned community of Legoland estates. It serves as the residential area for Hongqiao so has expat-oriented

The Great Jewish Families

The Sassoon family consisted of generations of shrewd businessmen from Baghdad to Bombay, whose achievements brought them wealth, knighthoods, and far-reaching influence. Though it was David Sassoon who initiated cotton trading out of Bombay to China, and son Elias Sassoon who had the ingenuity to buy and build his own warehouses in Shanghai, it was **Sir Victor Sassoon** who finally amassed the family fortune and enjoyed his wealth during Shanghai's heyday. Victor concentrated all of his energies on buying up Shanghai's land and building offices, apartments and warehouses. Victor's affairs were plentiful but he remained a bachelor until he finally married his American nurse, when he was 70, leaving her his entire fortune. Victor left Shanghai in 1941, returning only briefly after the war to tidy up the business, and then he and his assets relocated to the Bahamas. At one time Victor Sassoon owned an estimated 1900 buildings in Shanghai. Today the Sassoon legacy lives on in the historic Peace Hotel and Sassoon House, now in the Cypress Hotel in Hongqiao, both the site of some infamously raucous Sassoon soirees.

The company of David Sassoon & Sons gave rise to several other notables in Shanghai, among them **Silas Hardoon** and Elly Kadoorie. Hardoon began his illustrious career as a night watchman and later, in 1880, as manager of David Sassoon & Sons. Two years later he set out in business on his own and promptly went bust. His second independent business venture in 1920 proved successful and Silas Hardoon made a name for himself in real estate. In his father's memory he built the Beth Aharon Synagogue near Suzhou Creek, which later served as a shelter for Polish Jews who had fled Europe. Once a well-respected member of both the French and International Councils, Hardoon's reputation turned scandalous when he took a Eurasian wife, Luo Jialing, and adopted a crowd of multinational children. He then began to study Buddhism. His estate, including the school he had erected (now the grounds of the Shanghai Exhibition Centre) went up in smoke during the Sino-Japanese war. At the time of his death in 1931, he was the richest man in Shanghai.

Like Silas Hardoon, **Elly Kadoorie** began a career with David Sassoon & Sons in 1880 and he too broke away and amassed a fortune, in real estate, banking, and rubber production. His famous mansion is the result of too much money left in the hands of an unreliable architect; after returning from three years in England, Kadoorie found a 65-foot-high ballroom aglow with 18-foot chandeliers and enough imported marble to warrant the name Marble Hall. Architecture detectives can still visit the staircases and peek at the ballroom of the former mansion, now known as the Children's Palace (Map 6), at 64 Yan'an Xilu. Kadoorie died the year the communists took power; you can visit his grave in the International Cemetery (Map 9) on Hongqiao Lu.

With their immense wealth, Jewish families were pivotal in aiding the thousands of refugees who fled to Shanghai. The Kadoorie family resides in Hong Kong and is still involved in charity work.

services like art galleries, supermarkets and restaurants.

Shanghai Zoo (Map 3) 上海动物园
Shànghǎi Dòngwùyuàn

If you don't agree with zoos then this one probably won't convert you. That said, this is still one of China's better zoos. All the major African big game is represented but the most interesting animals are probably those endemic to China, such as the red panda, the golden monkeys from Yunnan, and, of course, the pair of giant pandas. Before the first few animals arrived shivering from Yunnan's Xishuangbanna region in 1954, the grounds served as a golf club for the British.

The zoo is open daily from 7 am to 6 pm (last ticket is sold at 4.30 pm). To get there take bus No 831 from Jinling Lu off the Bund, bus No 505 from Renmin Square, or bus No 911 along Huaihai Lu. Entry is Y10, and Y25 if there are special exhibits. A few halls such as the aquarium, and the kids' rides, require additional payment.

Not far from the zoo, in the grounds of the Cypress Hotel, is the former **Sassoon Mansion**, now the residence of the Norwegian Consulate.

Zhongshan Park (Map 3) 中山公园
Zhōngshān Gōngyuán

Known as Jessfield Park to the British, this is a moderately interesting park located in the former 'Badlands' area of 1930s Shanghai. Kids will like Fundazzle (Fāndǒulè), an adventure playground with slides, mazes and tunnels, open daily from 9 am to 5 pm. Entry is Y25 to Fundazzle, and Y2 to the park.

Jingdezhen Ceramics Gallery (Map 3) 景德镇陶瓷艺术中心
Jǐngdézhèn Táocí Yìshù Zhōngxīn

This huge gallery features a display of ceramics from the five kilns of the Song dynasty. Among the displays is a huge 3.88m-high vase, said to be the largest in the world, and the giant dragons made of cups and saucers are also eye-catching.

The gallery is in the middle of nowhere, at 1258 Daduhe Lu in the north-west sub-

urbs. Sightseeing Bus No 6B goes here every 30 minutes from Shanghai Stadium, returning erratically from the opposite side of the street (flag it down). Otherwise, take the metro to Zhongshan Park and then take a taxi.

TOURS

For a unique view over Shanghai, GoFly Air Service (Map 8; ☎ 6464 6371, 6487 7882), 3rd floor, 336 Caoxi Beilu, at Jiaotong University, runs two types of helicopter tours. For Y200 you get a 15-minute flight, which takes in Nanpu Bridge, the Jinmao Tower and the Oriental Pearl Tower. The 25-minute flight (Y500) takes in Nanpu Bridge, Yangpu Bridge, Hongkou Stadium, Tianshan Park, Xujiahui and Shanghai Stadium. The helicopter used to fly oil workers out to rigs in the Bohai Sea.

Flights run every Saturday. Passports are required and photography is prohibited.

ACTIVITIES
Sports Clubs

There are many expat clubs, ranging from squash to softball, karate, darts, frisbee, basketball and even scuba diving. See local listings magazines for contact details, as these change frequently.

Badminton

There are public badminton (yǔmáo qiú) courts at Shanghai Stadium, located just east of the gymnasium. Otherwise, play Chinese-style in any street that has plenty of traffic.

Bowling

There are more than 2000 tenpin bowling (bǎolín) alleys in Shanghai, in hotels, entertainment centres (see the Entertainment chapter) and even department stores. Costs at the cheaper places range between Y6 and Y15 per person, per game, depending upon the time of day, plus shoe hire.

One of the most popular places among expats is the Buckingham Bowling Centre (Map 3; ☎ 6281 9988), at 825 Dingxi Lu, in the west of town.

Bungee Jumping

Yes, you can bungee jump in Shanghai, or to be more specific, off the roof of Shanghai Stadium. The jump is organised by the Extreme Sports Centre (☎ 6426 5535), a Sino-US joint venture. A 70m-jump costs Y180, which works out at around Y40 per second. Alternatively, you can do a reverse bungee (yanked upwards into the sky) for Y150 or try the Sky Glider (a bit like freefall hang-gliding) for Y100. Masochists can try all three jumps for Y300 and you'll even get a certificate (to prove that you are insane). If you need a witness, Y30 gets a friend in, plus a Coke and a snack.

The jump site is accessed through the lobby of the Regal East Asia Hotel. Jumps take place daily from 1.30 to 9 pm.

Cycling

Shanghai's mad traffic can make cycling the city's most stressful, if not potentially lethal activity (second to the bungee jump, of course). However, the French Concession offers some charming areas for biking and the ambitious can make longer excursions out of the city to places like Sheshan and even Suzhou.

The YMCA Bike Shop, also known as Wolf's Bicycle Club (Map 6; ☎ 6472 9325) at Block 5, 485 Yongjia Lu, between Yueyang and Taiyuan Lu, sells bikes and every kind of widget or accessory you could need (including helmets). The owner Lao Wang also rents mountain bikes for Y20 per day (with Y100 deposit) and runs popular excursions around Shanghai.

Nearby at 743 Jianguo Xulu, on the corner with Hengshan Lu, Giant Bikes (Map 6) has a good selection of their own brand mountain and other bikes for sale.

The Shanghai Bike Club is an expat organisation that organises rides every Sunday from Gubei. Check the latest *That's* magazine for contact details.

Golf

Golf in China is the reserve of businesspeople and the new elite. Add to this the fact that Shanghai's golf clubs are aimed squarely at the Japanese and it's no surprise that knocking a white ball around a piece of green is one of the city's most expensive pastimes.

The following clubs are open to non-members and charge between US$50 and US$100 for 18 holes and a caddy. On the weekend costs are generally higher, and advance reservations are required.

Hongqiao Golf Club (☎/fax 6275 2789) Room 1906, 2200 Yan'an Xilu, Hongqiao
Grand Shanghai International Golf and Holiday Resort (☎ 520-789 1999) Kunshan, Jiangsu
Sanyang Golf and Country Club (☎ 512-501 0980) Luzhi Town, Wu County, Jiangsu
Shanghai Country Club (☎ 6275 8888) Westin Taipingyang Hotel. An 18-hole golf course with club house facilities, 45 minutes by complimentary shuttle bus for guests.
Tomson Golf Club (☎ 5833 8888) Pudong. Annual membership US$5000 or 18 holes for Y550 weekdays, Y750 on the weekend. The New Asia Tomson Hotel can book for guests.

High rollers staying in the Grand Hyatt can walk out of the hotel to the Liujiazui Golf Club, an enclosed driving range just next door.

Gyms

Most top-end hotels provide gyms free for their guests and with ridiculous membership dues for everyone else. If you're not a fitness guru but just like to pop into a gym now and again, the gym at the Purple Mountain Hotel (see the Places to Stay chapter) in Pudong charges non-guests Y35 per visit. Shanghai International Convention Centre (see Exhibitions & Conventions in the Facts for the Visitor chapter), also in Pudong, charges Y50 per visit to use the gym or Y100 to use their fabulous swimming pool. The Crowne-Plaza Shanghai (see the Places to Stay chapter) offers a temporary membership, which includes three-time use of the gym, sauna, and pool for Y180, which is good value for Shanghai.

The YMCA (Map 5), on Xizang Nanlu, has a cheap gym at Y20 a visit but the equipment is worn and the place is sweaty and crowded.

The following are a few good gyms with memberships for six months or one year. Some also offer short-term rates.

Body Tech Gym (Map 6; ☎ 6281 5639) 387 Panyu Lu. A large range of muscle-toning and cardio machines, free weights, personal trainers, lots of aerobic and other classes, and sauna. The equipment is good even if the decor is tired. A six-month membership is Y2500, plus a one-time joining fee of Y300; annual memberships costs Y4500, with no joining fee. Off-peak memberships (9 am to 5 pm or 7 to 9 pm) cost Y1500 (plus joining fee) for six months and Y2600 for a year (no joining fee).

Calm Wave (Map 4; ☎ 6271 7944) 428 Jiangning Lu. A new gym with good facilities and few crowds, plus a nice pool and sauna. Annual memberships cost Y5500 for unlimited use, or Y4000 if you only visit weekdays from 2 to 6 pm. Six-month unlimited memberships cost Y3000. Open daily to 10 pm.

Citigym (Map 7; ☎ 5306 6868) 8th floor, Shui On Plaza, 333 Huaihui Zhonglu. Modern equipment, aerobics classes and sauna costs Y650 per month for a two-month trial. Membership for three/six/12 months costs Y2800/3700/5200 or Y2350/2800/3400 for off-peak times (Monday to Saturday 9 am to noon, 2.30 to 5.30 pm and 9 to 10.30 pm; aerobics not included). The branch at 317 Linping Beilu (☎ 5393 5110) can be used with the same membership.

Gold's Gym (Map 4; ☎ 6279 2000) 258 Tongren Lu. This huge US franchise is for those who take their fitness more seriously than their wallet. Annual membership is steep at Y8300, but the 24-hour facilities are the best in Shanghai and discounts are available. Body pump, yoga and kick-boxing classes cost extra. Non-members can use the gym for Y100 per visit. There are plans to open another four gyms in Gubei, Xujiahui, Renmin Square and Pudong. You may be able to transfer membership of Gold's Gym abroad.

Gubei Gym Club (Map 9; ☎ 2219 5818) 59 Ronghua Xilu, Gubei. This is only practical for local and expat residents. The sparse gym, swimming pool, tennis court, squash court, bowling alley, sauna, shooting range and aerobics classes has annual memberships ranging from Y6800 to Y10,000. The facilities can also be used for one-time fees; swimming/tennis/squash cost Y70/60/60.

Kerry Gym (Map 6; ☎ 6279 4625) 1515 Nanjing Xilu. Memberships for three/six/12 months cost Y4000/7000/13,000 or Y2500/4500/8000 at off-peak hours (weekdays 9 am to 5 pm and Saturday 9 am to 12 pm).

Physical Ladies Club (Map 5; ☎ 6329 7536) 6th floor, 311 Shandong Zhonglu, on the corner of Jiujiang Lu; and a sister gym (☎ 6486 66770) 3rd floor, 808 Hongqiao Lu, near Huaihai Xilu. These are Hong Kong-based women-only gyms, popular with young locals. Fees are Y300/800/2500 for one/three/12 months. Membership gives unlimited access to both facilities' gym, classes (aerobics, step etc), sauna and steam rooms. Off-peak memberships are a little cheaper. Open daily from 7 am to 10 pm.

Topform Health Club (Map 8; ☎ 6426 6888) 666–800 Tianyaoqiao Lu, inside the Regal East Asia Hotel. Memberships for three/six/12 months cost Y900/1600/2400 for off-peak times (Monday to Saturday 9 am to 5 pm) and get you cardio and muscle-toning machines, two aerobic classes weekly, sauna, whirlpool and very friendly staff. Unlimited memberships for three/six/12 months cost Y1500/2500/3800.

Y Wellness Club (Map 4; ☎ 6317 8789) 6th floor, 188 Hankou Lu. Owned by the YMCA, this large, clean, modern facility near the train station has free weights, cardio and strength-toning machines, aerobics, including women's self-defence and boxing, available for Y350 a month, plus a Y500 one-off joining fee. Off-peak memberships (9.30 am to 4.30 pm) cost Y200 per month plus a one-time Y200 joining fee, making this one of the best deals in town. Temporary memberships are available for Y1200, which includes 30 visits (no joining fee required).

Hash House Harriers

This eccentric expat organisation originated with British in Malaysia. The Shanghai chapter organises runs most Sunday afternoons, followed by a meal and plenty of beers. Check listing magazines for details.

Serious runners might be interested in the Shanghai Marathon, held annually around November through the streets of Shanghai, starting and ending at Shanghai Stadium.

Karting

Disc Kart (Map 4; Díshìkǎ Sàichēguǎn, ☎ 6277 5641), at 326 Aomen Lu in northern Shanghai, has the largest go-cart track. It charges Y35 for eight minutes' driving off-peak (Monday to Friday 1 to 8.30 pm and midnight to 4 am), or Y50 for other evening times. There's a bar, and credit cards are accepted. You'll have to search for it as it's hidden down a deserted alley at the junction of Aomen Lu and Jiangning Lu.

SSC Carting (Map 8; Bāwànrén Sàichē Jùlèbù, ☎ 6426 5166), at the eastern end of Shanghai Stadium, charges Y40 for eight minutes' driving. It's open 2 pm to 2 am Monday to Thursday, 1 pm to 3 am Friday and Saturday and 9.30 am to 2 am Sunday.

Martial Arts

Wushu Centre (Map 4; ☎ 6215 3599), at 595 Nanjing Xilu, runs courses in various martial arts including karate, though normally in Chinese only.

Paintball

The Weicheng Paintball Centre (Map 3; Wěichéng Cǎidàn Shèjīfáng, ☎ 5252 0278), in Zhongshan Park, is the place to get kitted up and declare war on Shanghai. The highly cathartic experience costs Y40 and is open daily from 8.30 am to 4.30 pm.

Pool & Billiards

Shooting some stick comes free at Shanghai Sally's, O'Malley's, Face and Malone's (see the Entertainment chapter) though you'll pay for it through the cost of beers. Shanghai Sally's has Thursday-night pool competitions.

Metro City, in Xujiahui, has snooker and pool tables costing Y20 to Y60 per hour, depending on the time of day.

Shanghai's biggest pool hall, at the east end of Shanghai Stadium (Map 8), is open 24 hours. Before noon a game of pool costs Y15, rising to Y25 from noon to 6 pm, or Y30 from 6 pm to 2 am. Billiards cost from Y20 to Y40, depending on the time of day.

Xinxin Snooker Club (Xīnxīn Zhuōqiu Jùlèbù) is in the same block as the Golden Cinema Haixing (Map 6). It's open 24 hours and has snooker tables for Y25 to 40, depending on the time of day.

Q's (Map 6), on Maoming Nanlu, has four pool tables for Y20 to Y30 per hour.

Rock Climbing

The Ozark Climbing Centre (Map 6; ☎ 6226 6825), at 1 Jiangsu Lu in north Shanghai, has several 12m and 15m beginner, speed and competition walls. Unlimited climbing costs Y40 Monday to Thursday and Y50 at other times, plus Y3 for shoes and Y5 for a safety belt (the best Y5 you'll ever spend). Climbs for children cost Y35, whatever the day. Opening hours are 10 am to 10 pm. Wear loose-fitting clothes.

There's a similar setup at Masterhand Climbing Club (Map 3; ☎ 5696 6657) in Hongkou Stadium, where the indoor wall costs Y40.

A pitiful, plywood climbing wall at the north entrance to Shanghai Stadium costs Y20.

Rugby

Local heroes the Shanghai Hairy Crabs take on expat rivals like Beijing's Foreign Devils. Practices are held every Saturday afternoon. Check magazines listings for contact details.

Skating & Skateboarding

The north (Lingling Lu) entrance of Shanghai Stadium has an area of ramps and jumps for skateboarding and Rollerblading. It's open 1.30 to 5 pm weekdays and 9 am to 5 pm on the weekend (Y10).

Squash

The squash (xiǎo xiàngpí qiú) courts at the Hotel Equatorial (see the Places to Stay chapter) can be rented for Y80 per hour, plus Y15 per person entrance fee, and Y30 for a racket. The JC Mandarin (see the Places to Stay chapter) charges a flat Y100 per hour for the squash court and rents rackets for Y30 per hour. If you're in town for a while, consider joining a squash league from one of the local magazine listings.

Swimming

All the top-end hotels have pools; though if swimming is your thing and you're coming in winter make sure your hotel has an indoor pool.

The Shanghai International Convention Centre in Pudong has a great circular pool enclosed in a glass dome with views of the Bund. Entry to the pool costs Y100 for non-guests.

The Shanghai Swimming Pool (or Nanatorium), near Shanghai Stadium, is open to the public on the weekend only, from 1 to 3 pm and 6.30 to 8 pm on Saturday and 3.30 to 5 pm on Sunday.

Ocean World (Map 8), in the east end of Shanghai Stadium, is an enclosed water park with waves and slides. You can't exactly swim but the kids will love it.

Tennis

There are several places to play tennis *(wǎng qiú)*, though you'll need your own rackets. Reservations are suggested for the weekend.

The Xianxia Tennis Centre (Map 9; Xianxia Wǎngqiú Zhōngxīn, ☎ 6262 8327), at 1885 Hongqiao Lu, is a premier site, though it's quite far from the centre. Weekday costs are Y40/80 per hour for daytime/evening play, or Y60/100 on weekends. Courts are a little cheaper between 6 and 8 am.

The International Tennis Centre at the Regal International East Asia Hotel (see the Places to Stay chapter) is probably the best facility in Shanghai but it's open to members only and fees are steep.

Public courts just south of Shanghai Stadium cost Y20/35 per hour from 6 to 8 am on weekdays/the weekend and Y60/80 at night.

Massage

In China, massage is traditionally performed by the blind and is closely linked to the same Chinese system of the body's pressure points that acupuncture relies on. There are over 40 massage centres in Shanghai, almost all of them legitimate. Ask locals for advice or try the centres listed in this section.

The Thumbpoint Massage Centre of Blind Person (Map 6; Dàmǔzhǐ Mángrén Bāwèi Zhǐyā Ànmó Zhōngxīn, ☎ 6473 2634), on Fuxing Zhonglu, offers 45-minute massages for Y40, or an hour-long foot massage for Y60. Discounts of around 20% are given if you buy a block of 10 hours.

The next-door Kangning Massage Centre of Blind Person (☎ 6437 8378), at 597 Fuxing Zhonglu, offers a similar deal, though it is slightly more expensive.

Markets

Shanghai doesn't have the best markets in China but a few are worth a visit. The following are ranked in order of interest:

- **Dongtai Lu Antique Market** (Map 7)
- **Flower, Bird, Fish and Insect Market** near Dongtai Lu Market (Map 7)
- **Jiangyin Lu Bird and Flower Market** just off Nanjing Donglu (Map 4)
- **Flower Market** in Cultural Square between Maoming Nanlu and Shanxi Nanlu, near Yongjia Lu. There's a smaller flower market on the east side of Maoming Nanlu with some 'antique' and gardening shops (Map 6).
- The **produce market** on Dajing Lu, in the eastern old town (Map 5).
- **Jiangning Lu market**, 1km north of Nanjing Xilu. A garden, fish and curio market, with a large fresh fish and seafood market behind (Map 4).
- **Gubei Flower and Bird Market**, 1778 Hongqiao Lu. A nice mix of flowers, birds, gardening supplies, bonsais, pet supplies and a cluster of hassle-free antique stores with more or less marked prices (Map 9).
- **New Shanghai Metropolis Flower Market**. This is not as pleasant as the Cultural Square market, but it's the biggest in town, with 350 stalls. Located behind Shanghai No 1 department store on Xizang Zhonglu (Map 5).
- **Nanjing Xilu Stones and Curios Market**. This is a new market, at 688 Nanjing Xilu (Map 4).
- The **produce market** on Yong'an Lu, just to the north of the Old Town (Map 5).
- **Wenmiao Book Market**. There's not much to buy here but it's an interesting place to visit. The market is on every Sunday in the Confucian Temple (Map 7).

Both places are open from noon to 3 am daily.

COURSES
Language

Mandarin classes are held at the Yew Wah International Education Centre (Map 4; ☎ 6215 4333, 6215 4555), 20th floor,

Cheap Thrills

Strapped for cash in Shanghai? The following are a few things that can be done for free:

• Take the exterior lift to the 42nd floor of the Jinjiang Tower or the 33rd-floor Continental Bar of the Garden Hotel for a cheap adrenalin rush and fine views of Shanghai.
• Stroll the length of the Bund.
• Take a local ferry across the Huangpu River (it's only free west-bound; heading to Pudong you'll have to spoil yourself and splash out eight mao).
• Check out the Bund Historical Museum in Huangpu Park. Inside are some fascinating photographs of old Shanghai and some interesting historical trivia.
• Hang out in Fuxing or Hongkou Park, where at any given time you may come across music, t'ai chi, mahjong, waltzing, therapeutic screaming and fishing.
• Try one of the walking tours in this chapter.

Zhongzhuang Mansions, 819 Nanjing Xilu. A seven-week evening public course costs Y50 per class; private lessons cost Y135 per hour.

MACH Mandarin Consulting (Map 5; ☎ 6364 4838, fax 6364 4839, @ machhksh @online.sh.cn), on the 22nd floor of the Shanghai Bund International Tower, 99 Huangpu Lu, offers professionally run intensive, beginner and advanced Mandarin classes, catering mostly to expat companies.

Prices range from Y100 per hour in a group class to Y500 per hour for individual tuition in your home.

The humanities department of Fudan University runs a language centre that offers evening and weekend Mandarin classes, as well as instruction in Shanghainese dialect. Contact the Mandarin Centre (Map 9; ☎ 6270 7668, fax 6270 7661, @ mandarin@online.sh.cn) at 10 Songyuan Lu, at the intersection of Hongqiao Lu. It's also possible to find a private tutor from any university who is willing to moonlight.

Several parks have English corners where locals come to practise English and are more than happy to swap some Chinese tuition for English practice. Try Fuxing or Renmin Parks on Sundays at 1 pm.

Other Courses

There are plenty of other courses in Shanghai but you may have to dig them out. Once again, the local listings magazines are the best places to look.

Occasional courses in Chinese medicine are held at Shanghai University of Traditional Chinese Medicine (☎ 6417 4600). Music courses are held at Shanghai Music Conservatory.

The informal expat association Big World (☎/fax 6530 3263) runs courses in various aspects of Chinese culture, including cooking, t'ai chi and calligraphy. Details are listed in local magazines.

The Mandarin Centre (see earlier in this chapter) also runs occasional Chinese cultural appreciation classes.

THE BUND (MAP 5)

The Bund (Wàitān in Chinese, pronounced 'bunned' in English) is the most impressive 2km in Shanghai. It is a boastful reminder of the city's cosmopolitan and decadent heyday. Originally a towpath to pull barges of rice, the Bund gets its Anglo-Indian name from the embankments built up to discourage flooding (a *band* is an embankment in Hindi). The Bund became the seat of foreign power in the early 20th century and provided a grand façade for those arriving in Shanghai by river. Today it is usually the first place to which all visitors to Shanghai head.

The Bund was once situated only a few feet from the water but in the mid-1990s the road was widened and a 771m-long flood barrier was built (the river now lies above the level of Nanjing Lu due to subsidence). The road that was once jammed with trams and traffic from riverside jetties is now known more prosaically as Zhongshan Yilu, or 'Sun Yatsen Road Section One'.

There are plenty of things to see and do around the Bund: take a boat trip, enjoy the views of Pudong and the Huangpu, visit the Bund Museum or shop at the Friendship Store. These delights will soon be easily combined with an up-close visit to Pudong, when a pedestrian tunnel across the Huangpu River is constructed.

Things to See

At the northern end of the Bund, on the north bank of Suzhou Creek, is **Shanghai Mansions**, formerly Broadway Mansions, built in 1934 as an exclusive apartment block. The Foreign Correspondents' Club occupied the 9th floor in the 1930s and used its fine views to report the Japanese bombing of the city in 1937. The building became the headquarters of the Japanese army during WWII. At one time the US military lived on the lower floors.

Just east of here, along the old Broadway is the **Russian/Soviet Consulate**, the only consulate currently occupying its original location. The building first served as the Soviet Consulate, then a seamen's club, before becoming the Soviet Consulate again in 1987, and then finally the Russian Consulate. Previously there were a string of other consulates in this area, including American, German and Japanese.

Behind the consulate is the **Pujiang Hotel**, Shanghai's backpacker favourite. The hotel opened in 1846 as Astor House, the first hotel in Shanghai, and later became the Richard Hotel. The hotel claims that it was the site of the first electric light and telephone line in Shanghai. In

No Dogs or Chinese

Huangpu Park was the site of the infamous (and legendary) sign that forbade entry to 'dogs or Chinese'. In fact there never was such a sign, though the spirit of the law certainly existed. The first of the five park regulations adopted in 1916 forbade the entry of dogs and bicycles; a separate regulation later denied entry to Chinese, except for Chinese nannies, servants and friends of foreigners. The regulation was finally rescinded in 1928 but has since become a powerful symbol of Shanghai's semi-colonial rule.

1990 China's first stock exchange was set up here in the former ballroom, until the exchange moved to Pudong in 1998.

Heading south over Suzhou Creek you will cross **Garden Bridge** (Wàibáidù Qiáo), built in 1906 in place of an earlier wooden bridge. In 1937 the bridge marked the de facto border between the International Settlement and Japanese-occupied Hongkou and Zhapei.

Huangpu Park (Huángpú Gōngyuán), the first park in Shanghai, was laid out by a Scottish gardener shipped out especially for that purpose. Today the park holds an uninspiring Monument to the People's Heroes, which offers some of the best photo opportunities of Pudong. Underneath the monument is the **Bund Historical Museum** (Wàitān Lìshǐ Jìniànguǎn), which is worth a stop for its great old photos of the Bund. Turn left at the entrance to go chronologically. The museum is open daily from 9 am to 4.15 pm; entry is free. The socialist sculpture at the entrance of Huangpu Park was built on the site of the old British bandstand.

Continuing south down the Bund you pass the former **British Consulate** (1873), the earliest building on the Bund. The imposing building is now a government department.

Farther down, at No 28, is the **Glen Line Building**, with the radio antenna on top. At No 27 is the former headquarters of early opium traders Jardine Matheson, which became one of Shanghai's great *hongs* (trading houses). According to Tess Johnston in her book *The Last Colonies,* in 1941 the British Embassy occupied the top floor and faced (presumably with a glare) the German Embassy, across the road in the Glen Line Building! The building was later taken over by the Japanese navy and after that hosted the US consulate for a while.

The imposing **Bank of China** building, at No 23, was commissioned by director HH Kung, and was built in 1937 with specific instructions that it should be higher than the adjacent Cathay Hotel. The building

is a strange architectural mish-mash, designed in a New York/Chicago style and later topped with a blue Chinese roof to make the building appear more patriotic.

Next door to the Bank of China, the famous **Peace Hotel** (1926 to 1929) was once the most luxurious hotel in the Far East and is still an Art-Deco masterpiece. The hotel was built as the Cathay by Victor Sassoon, and originally occupied only the 4th to 7th floors of the Sassoon house. The guest list included Charlie Chaplin, George Bernard Shaw and Noel Coward, who wrote *Private Lives* here in four days in 1930 when he had the flu. Sassoon himself spent weekdays in his personal suite on the top floor with its unsurpassed 360-degree views. The suite later became a bankers' club.

Even if you are not staying at the Peace Hotel you can look around the wonderful lobby (only half its original size) and visit the famous ballroom with its sprung floor. The main east entrance (next to the Citibank sign) is no longer in use but there are still some nice Art-Deco touches around it. Now, as in the 1930s, banks make up part of the lower floor. The hotel was renamed the Peace Hotel in 1956. The Gang of Four used the hotel as an operations base during the Cultural Revolution.

Opposite and part of the Peace is the older **Palace Hotel** (1906), one of the oldest buildings on the Bund. A plaque commemorates the International Opium Commission, which was held here in 1909.

Across the road from the Peace Hotel is a statue of **Chen Yi**, Shanghai's first mayor. The plinth previously held a statue of Sir Harry Parkes, British Envoy to China (1882–1885), erected in 1890 and torn down by the Japanese in 1941 to be used as scrap metal in the war effort.

Farther south, at No 17, is the former home of the **North China Daily News**. Known as the 'Old Lady of the Bund' the *News* ran from 1864 to 1951 as the main English-language newspaper in China and the mouthpiece of the municipality commission. Look above the entranceway for the paper's motto. Today the building is once again home to American Insurance International, the first of the Bund's original tenants to return to its former home after leaving en masse in 1949. Other Bund fixtures are being sold off and will no doubt be likewise dusted off and cleaned up. The current building was completed in 1923.

Three buildings down, at No 13, stands the **Customs House**, built in 1925 as one of the most important buildings on the Bund. On top of the building is a clock face and 'Big Ching', the bell that was modelled on Big Ben. The bell was dismantled in the Cultural Revolution and replaced by loudspeakers that blasted out revolutionary slogans and songs. The clockworks were restored in 1986 for the visit of Queen Elizabeth II.

Walking Tour – Beyond the Bund (Map 5)

Route: Parallel to the Bund from south to north, through the lost architecture of the International Settlement (See Map 5)
Duration: 1½ hours

From the crossing of the Yan'an overpass and the Bund (near Manabe) head south and turn right into Jinling Lu. After a short block you can see the Yong'an Market disappearing into an alley on the left; follow the market to its end, turn right and then right again into Sichuan Nanlu. Up on the left, just short of a block, you can see the spires of **St Joseph's Church** (consecrated in 1862), now surrounded by a school through which you can gain access.

From here head north on Sichuan Nanlu, under the overpass, for about two blocks. On the left you'll find the smoky old **Club de Shanghai 1920**. On the corner with Guangdong Lu look for No 93, recognisable by the letters 'Bank of Paris and Shanghai' above the door. This is the **Golden Cage**, once home to the captive concubines of a colourful Chinese entrepreneur. Peek in at the wonderful ceiling mosaics and stained-glass windows.

Continuing up Sichuan Nanlu, Alley 126 conceals a beautiful old brick *shikumen*. Look out also for the building at No 133 Sichuan Nanlu (Xinhua Bookstore offices) and its original faded sign announcing 'Imperial Chemical (China) Ltd'. At Fuzhou Lu turn right (east) and take a look at the Tudor building at No 44, the former offices of Calbeck Macgregor & Co, wine importers and agents in the 1930s for Martini & Rossi, Johnny Walker and others.

Backtrack west along Fuzhou Lu until you reach the corner of Fuzhou and Jiangxi Nanlu, where you'll find the matching architecture of the **Hamilton House** (south) and the **Metropole Hotel** (north). The former was commissioned by David Sassoon and built by Palmer and Turner as an apartment complex. Both buildings had terraced rooftop gardens. The best view is from the old Municipal Council building, the squat building on the north-west corner.

The Bund Museum has a wonderful photo of the building in the early 1950s when it was covered with a huge portrait of Mao. Government departments now occupy this whole block. Fifty metres west is the former **American Club**, at 209 Fuzhou Lu, built in 1924 in the American Georgian style with dark bricks imported

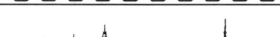

Walking Tour – Beyond the Bund (Map 5)

from the USA. It's now the People's Court; an irony considering much of Fuzhou Lu west of this point was once lined with brothels, gambling houses and opium dens.

Head back to the Metropole Hotel and turn north past the Bank of Communications, at 200 Jiangxi Zhonglu (you can go in to marvel at the marble interior), to the corner with Hankou Lu. The red brick building on the north-west corner is the Gothic church (1866), known to Chinese as the **Red Temple** (Hóng Miào). Its tall steeple has long since gone. Just in front of the church is a small park with some fading communist propaganda posters, where elderly men come to urinate. To the east is one of the former locations of the US Consulate.

Head east on Hankou Lu, once a street of publishers and presses, about one block. At the corner with Sichuan Lu lies the elegant facade of the **Guangdong Development Bank**, formerly the Joint Savings Society Bank. Across the street is an intriguing building with '1908' carved out underneath the lovely lintel. If the door is open you can see the old wooden staircase.

One block north along Sichuan Lu is Jiujiang Lu, an old banking street, where you can see the **Bank of East Asia** (formerly the Continental Bank) on the south-west corner. Continue north past the Zhongyang Market on the left and look out for the charming pale green and then blue brick buildings ahead at the junction with Nanjing Donglu. This is a good place to take a break.

Refreshed (or not), continue north on Sichuan Lu to a collection of old red brick buildings darkened by pollution and perpetually strung with enormous underpants and other laundry. Turn left onto Dianchi Lu until you hit Jiangxi Lu (there's a nice Art-Deco bank on the corner) and turn north past Ningbo Lu until you get to several impressive buildings (one is the Electric Power Co) at the junction with Beijing Donglu.

Head east past a graceful building with beautiful balconies. When you get to the Friendship Store (there are toilets on the 2nd floor if you're in need), either pop in for some shopping or turn north for, you guessed it, some nice old buildings. This is Yuanmingyuan Lu, one of the least-touched streets in Shanghai, whose buildings include the former YWCA, Rotary Club (No 133), Wenhuibao Newspaper (No 149) and Hong Kong and Shanghai Bank branch (No 185).

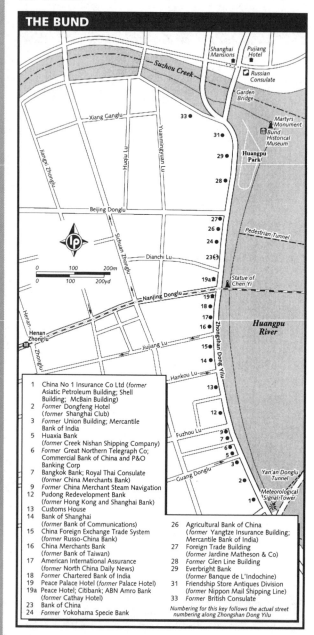

1. China No 1 Insurance Co Ltd (*former* Asiatic Petroleum Building; Shell Building; McBain Building)
2. *Former* Dongfeng Hotel (*former* Shanghai Club)
3. *Former* Union Building; Mercantile Bank of India
5. Huaxia Bank (*former* Creek Nishan Shipping Company)
6. *Former* Great Northern Telegraph Co; Commercial Bank of China and P&O Banking Corp
7. Bangkok Bank; Royal Thai Consulate (*former* China Merchants Bank)
9. *Former* China Merchant Steam Navigation
12. Pudong Redevelopment Bank (*former* Hong Kong and Shanghai Bank)
13. Customs House
14. Bank of Shanghai (*former* Bank of Communications)
15. China Foreign Exchange Trade System (*former* Russo-China Bank)
16. China Merchants Bank (*former* Bank of Taiwan)
17. American International Assurance (*former* North China Daily News)
18. *Former* Chartered Bank of India
19. Peace Palace Hotel (*former* Palace Hotel)
19a. Peace Hotel; Citibank; ABN Amro Bank (*former* Cathay Hotel)
23. Bank of China
24. *Former* Yokohama Specie Bank

26. Agricultural Bank of China (*former* Yangtze Insurance Building; Mercantile Bank of India)
27. Foreign Trade Building (*former* Jardine Matheson & Co)
28. *Former* Glen Line Building
29. Everbright Bank (*former* Banque de L'Indochine)
31. Friendship Store Antiques Division (*former* Nippon Mail Shipping Line)
33. *Former* British Consulate

Numbering for this key follows the actual street numbering along Zhongshan Dong Yilu

A statue of Robert Hart, early Inspector of Customs for the Chinese Imperial Customs Service, stood outside Customs House until the Japanese dismantled it during WWII. Born in Portadown in Northern Ireland, Hart reorganised the Chinese customs service and helped with reforms of the Qing bureaucracy. As a result he won the rare respect and friendship of Chinese and the position of the most influential foreigner in China. The previous Customs House was a Tudor mansion built on the remains of a Chinese-style building, which was itself destroyed by the Small Swords Rebellion in 1853. The original customs jetty stood across from the building, on the Huangpu River.

Next door to Customs House is the grandest building on the Bund, the former **Hong Kong and Shanghai Bank (HKSB)**. The bank was established in Hong Kong in 1864 and in Shanghai in 1865 to finance trade and it soon became one of the richest in Shanghai, arranging the indemnity paid after the Boxer Rebellion. When the current building was constructed in 1923 it was the second-largest bank in the world and 'the finest building east of Suez.' You can still see the HKSB markings on the original gates. The bronze lions that once guarded the entrance and were rubbed shiny by superstitious Chinese can now be found in the Shanghai Municipal History Museum.

Until 1995 the building held the offices of the municipal government before they moved to Renmin Park; it holds the Pudong Development Bank and several offices. Enter and marvel at the beautiful mosaic ceiling, featuring the twelve zodiac signs and the world's eight great banking centres. If you need a break, there is a nice cafe inside the building.

The **Shanghai Club** (1911), the city's best-known bastion of British snobbery, stood at No 2 on the Bund. The club had 20 rooms for residents, but its most famous accoutrement was the bar, which at 110 feet was allegedly the longest bar in the world. Businessmen would sit here according to rank (no Chinese or women were allowed in the club). The building is now empty and awaiting redevelopment after a short spell as the Dongfeng Hotel and, much to its embarrassment, a KFC. These days the modern-day variants of the club's creaking leather chairs, ironed newspapers and expensive cigars are more likely to be spotted in the Portman Ritz-Carlton or the American Club. Next door, and the last building on the Bund proper, was the **McBain Building**, or Asiatic Petroleum Building, built in 1915 in the Neoclassical style.

Just across from the overpass you can see the 49m-tall **Meteorological Signal Tower**, originally built in 1908 opposite the French Consulate and, in 1993, moved 22m north as part of the revamping of the Bund. Today there is a pleasant coffee house in the tower with a collection of old prints of the Bund and good views from the roof.

By the overpass you'll find Yan'an Donglu, once a canal and later filled in to become Avenue Edward VII, the dividing line between the International Settlement and the French Concession. South of here the Bund was known as the Quai de France. A block south, Jinling Lu is the former Rue du Consulat, where the French Embassy once stood.

Places to Stay

Shanghai boasts more than 100 star-rated hotels (including 10 five-star hotels) and more are popping up daily. Most are aimed squarely at business travellers and there is not much below around US$30 for a double room. We list standard rooms here, though deluxe and suite rooms are often available. All hotel rooms are subject to a 10% or 15% service charge, but many cheaper hotels don't bother to charge this.

The vast majority of Shanghai's hotels are identical mid-range joints, and there's little to choose between them, except location. Tourists may prefer to be based on Nanjing Donglu or the Bund, while business visitors will need to be based wherever their business takes them, often in Hongqiao or Pudong. Location near a metro station is a definite advantage for getting around the city.

Most top-end hotels list their rates in US$ but you always have to pay in RMB. Almost all hotels change money for guests and most mid-range and top-end hotels accept credit cards.

When you check into a hotel you will have to fill in a registration form, a copy of which will be sent to the local Public Security Bureau (PSB; Gōngānjú) office. You will need a copy of this registration form if you want to extend your visa.

DISCOUNTS
With so much competition around, few hotels in Shanghai actually charge the full rack rate. Outside peak times (May to September and Chinese New Year) you can normally get a discount of 30% to 40%, though it's important to ask if the discounted price includes tax, as this will eat up 10% or 15% of your discount. Newly opened hotels offer particularly good deals. You may also be able to negotiate a better rate for a longer stay, especially at top-end hotels. On the other hand there's not much discounting at the budget end of the spectrum. In this book we list the rack rate and

the best discount we were offered. Depending on when you travel, the actual price will be somewhere between the two.

It's also worth knowing that travel agencies can get you sizable discounts at the top-end hotels. See Travel Agencies in the Getting There & Away chapter.

PLACES TO STAY – BUDGET
Shanghai has some of the highest real estate values in China, and lower-end accommodation has felt the squeeze for a while now. While there are no very cheap hotels, there are a few that represent value for money.

Before you start banging on the doors of the cheapest hostel you can find it's worth knowing that foreigners can only officially stay in government-designated hotels. Many of the cheapest dives simply won't accept you, for fear of being fined by the PSB.

Budget accommodation can be swamped during summer (June to September) and at holiday times, leaving you with little choice but to upgrade to pricey doubles that cost Y300 or more. Cheap hotels are generally out in the suburbs, though this isn't a major problem if you are near a metro station.

The distinguished **Pujiang Hotel** *(Map 5; Pǔjiāng Fàndiàn;* ☎ *6324 6388, fax 6324 3179, 15 Huangpu Lu)* was originally called the Astor House Hotel and was Shanghai's first hotel. This is the place for those mindful of their mao – it's central, has loads of style and the rooms are vast. Although the galleries upstairs look like they belong in a Victorian asylum, there's a nobility about the place that makes Y55 for a dorm bed a bargain. Double rooms start at Y300; four/five-bed rooms cost Y300/350, plus a 10% service charge. From the Bund, it's a short walk across the Garden Bridge and Suzhou Creek.

The **Conservatory of Music Guest House** *(Map 6; Yīnyuè Xuéyuàn Wàibīn Zhāodàisuǒ;* ☎ *6437 2577, 20 Fenyang Lu)* is an old stand-by, with a great location off Huaihai Zhonglu. The pleasant strains of music practice waft around the courtyards, giving the surroundings a civilised air. Unfortunately, it's often fully booked in summer. Rough-and-ready doubles with a fan and access to a clean, shared bathroom are Y60, or Y80 with a broken television. Nice, carpeted doubles with private bathroom and air-con are Y200. Some floors are noisier than others; the second is probably the best. This guest house is a short walk from the Changshu Lu metro station; to find it, walk through the entrance to the conservatory, carry on about 300m and bear left.

Built in 1929, the newly renovated *YMCA Hotel (Map 5; Qīngniánhuì Bīnguǎn; ☎ 6326 1040, fax 6320 1957, 123 Xizang Nanlu)* is another option with dormitories, and it's in a great location close to Renmin Square. Bunk beds in clean four-person rooms with bathroom and air-con are US$15 per bed, but this is really only a good deal if you are travelling alone. Private rooms are pricey, starting at US$55/64 for a single/double, though these are normally discounted by around 30%.

While it is somewhat out of the way, the foreign-student dormitory at East China Normal University, known as *The International Exchange Service Centre (Map 3; Guójì Jiāoliú Fúwù Zhōngxīn; ☎ 6257 9241, fax 6257 1813)*, has reasonably priced rooms with bath and air-con for Y150. The university is located north-west of the city centre off Zhongshan Beilu. To find the foreign-student building go through the main gate, cross two bridges then turn left.

In the north-east, also a little out of the way, are a couple of good-value choices if you can spend a few dollars more. The three-star *Shizeyuan Hotel (Map 3; Shīzéyuán Bīnguǎn; ☎ 6546 6008, fax 6546 7524, 999 Changyang Lu)* has good-value and spotless doubles for Y198, rising to Y228 on the higher floors. It's popular with Chinese visitors.

The *Changyang Hotel (Map 3; Chángyáng Fàndiàn; ☎ 6543 4890, fax 6543 0986, 1800 Changyang Lu)* is even farther out. Dated but clean doubles cost Y210/250/270, depending on how much sun the room gets, but push for a discount,

which can be as high as 50%. Bus Nos 22 and 934 take you from the Bund right past both the Shizeyuan and Changyang Hotels.

The *Sports Hotel (Map 8; Tǐyùguǎn Yùndòngyuánzhijiā; ☎ 6438 5200 ext 128, 1500 Zhongshan Nanerlu)* is the tall tube next to Shanghai Stadium. It's a bit far from the centre but is close to the metro line and bustling Xujiahui crossroads. Standard two-star rooms on the 8th to 13th floors cost Y202.

Probably the most surreal accommodation choice in Shanghai is the *Zoo Guest House (Map 3; Dòngwùyuán Zhāodàisuǒ; ☎ 6269 1944)*, way out near the airport in Hongqiao. There are six clean triple rooms, which cost Y50 per bed (Y150 for the room). Bathrooms are shared but are clean, with 24-hour hot water. The guesthouse is actually in the grounds of the zoo so you get a free visit in the price of your accommodation, plus all kinds of weird jungle hoots and roars during the night. Phone ahead to check that the place hasn't been booked out by a visiting group of bearded zoologists.

PLACES TO STAY – MID-RANGE

Mid-range accommodation in Shanghai will cost between Y300 and Y400 for a double, but discounts can often bring these prices down to Y250 or so. If you're landing at the airport, try the tourist office (☎ 6268 8899 ext 56750) in the international arrivals hall. It has a list of hotels offering discounts.

Central Shanghai

The *Jingtai Hotel (Map 4; Jīngtài Dàjiǔdiàn; ☎ 6272 2222, fax 6218 4778, 178 Taixing Lu)*, just off Nanjing Xilu, has well-trained staff and clean new doubles starting at Y350. If you book at the airport information desk you can score the Y480 room for Y310, which is well worth it.

Seventh Heaven Hotel (Map 5; Qīzhòngtiān Bīnguǎn; ☎ 6322 0777 ext 701, fax 6351 7193) is right in the thick of things on Nanjing Donglu to the west of Century Square, inside the Overseas Clothing Store (look up to see the sign). The reception is on the 7th floor. It doesn't look like much from the outside but the interior was renovated in 1999. Small, clean singles/doubles start at Y280/300.

Nearby, at the corner of Zhejiang Lu, another mid-range option, the ***Chunshenjiang Hotel*** *(Map 5; Chūnshēnjiāng Bīnguǎn;* ☎ *6351 5710, 626 Nanjing Donglu)* has freshly renovated doubles for Y300 and Y330. Corner rooms have fine views of Nanjing Lu's neon glare. The entrance is set back from the road, so you'll have to look for the sign.

Another choice on Nanjing Donglu is the two-star ***Nanjing Hotel*** *(Map 5; Nánjīng Fàndiàn;* ☎ *6322 2888, 200 Shanxi Nanlu),* where newly renovated modern doubles cost Y330/400/450, which are then discounted by 20%, making this hotel quite good value.

The ***Yangtze Hotel*** *(Map 5; Yángzǐ Fàndiàn;* ☎ *6351 7880, fax 6351 6974, 740 Hankou Lu)* is right behind the Protestant church that faces Renmin Park. The hotel was built in 1934 and the exterior, including the wonderful Art-Nouveau balconies, is largely unchanged. Singles are good value at Y360 and doubles start at Y520, with a 20% discount offered at the time of research.

The ***Metropole Hotel*** *(Map 5; Xīnchéng Fàndiàn;* ☎ *6321 3030, fax 6321 7365, 180 Jiangxi Zhonglu),* near the Bund, was one of Shanghai's best 1930s hotels. Though some of the old touches remain, it's now more of a standard smoky Chinese hotel. Normal/superior rooms are Y350/450, but a 30% discount is available.

Tucked away from the fashionable districts, but still fairly close to the Bund, the two-star ***Dafang Hotel*** *(Map 5; Dàfàng Fàndiàn;* ☎ *6326 0505, fax 6311 4542, 33 Fujian Lu)* is friendly and has dark singles/doubles starting at Y308/418. Again, 30% discounts were available, which make this quite a good deal. The major problem is that rooms facing Fujian Lu are noisy (there's a bus stop just outside the hotel). Rooms facing inwards are smaller, cheaper and quieter. The hotel is just south of the Yan'an Donglu overpass.

Near the main post office in Hongkou, but also within walking distance of the Bund, the 1930s-era ***New Asia Hotel*** *(Map 5; Xīnyà Dàjiǔdiàn;* ☎ *6324 2210, 6356 6816, 422 Tiantong Lu)* has singles/doubles for around US$45/55, but discounts can also bring this price down to US$33/40. Extensive renovations inside have pushed the hotel up to three stars but have taken away some of its historical feel.

Donghu Hotel *(Map 6; Dōnghú Bīnguǎn;* ☎ *6415 8158, fax 6415 7759, 70 Donghu Lu),* just off Huaihai Zhonglu, consists of two blocks. The newer block, on the south side of the road, has singles/doubles for Y280/396. The older building has nicer doubles, starting at Y450.

The Seagull Hotel *(Map 5; Hǎi'ōu Bīnguǎn),* on Huangpu Lu, was originally built near the Pujiang Hotel as part of the Seaman's Club and was undergoing renovations at the time of research to push it up to three stars. It's due to open in May 2000 and promises great views of the Bund.

The ***Jinchen Hotel*** *(Map 6; Jīnchén Dàjiǔdiàn;* ☎ *6471 7000, 795–809 Huaihai Zhonglu)* is in the heart of Huaihai Lu's shopping strip, with singles/doubles starting at Y288/328. The ***Wugong Hotel*** *(Map 5; Wǔgōng Dàjiǔdiàn;* ☎ *6326 0303, 431 Fuzhou Lu)* is a modern two-star hotel in a good location, but has little charm. Doubles start at Y300, rising to Y500.

The ***Shanghai Railway Hotel*** *(Map 5; Shànghǎi Tiědǎo Bīnguǎn;* ☎ *6322 6633, 160 Guizhou Lu),* formerly the China Hotel, is just off Nanjing Donglu. With rooms for Y280/360/480, this isn't bad value, though some rooms have no windows. The ***Hengshan Hotel*** *(Map 6; Héngshān Bīnguǎn;* ☎ *6437 7050, fax 6433 5732, 534 Hengshan Lu)* is overpriced at US$50/98 for a single/double, but worthwhile when rooms are discounted to Y580. It used to be the Picardie Apartments in the 1930s, though little of its past charm remains.

The ***Jiangong Jinjiang Hotel*** *(Map 6; Jiàngōng Jǐnjiāng Dàjiǔdiàn;* ☎ *6415 5688, 691 Jianguo Xilu)* is a new, slightly chaotic three-star hotel in a good location just off Hengshan Lu. Doubles cost Y538 and Y588.

Train Station Area

There are several three-star hotels near the Shnaghai train station. It's not a bad place to be based as it's near the starting point of the metro line.

The **Zhao'an Hotel** (*Map 4; Zhàoān Jiǔdiàn;* ☎ *6317 2221, fax 6317 0338, 195 Hengtong Lu*) has rooms starting at Y498, discounted down to Y400, including breakfast. The **Liang'an Hotel** (*Map 4; Liáng'ān Dàjiǔdiàn;* ☎ *6353 2222, fax 6353 2558, 920 Changan Lu*) is a three-star giant located near a street full of cheap restaurants. Rooms cost Y398, and can be discounted down to Y318.

The **East China Hotel** (*Map 4; Huádōng Dàjiǔdiàn;* ☎ *6317 8000, fax 6317 6678, 111 Tianmu Xilu*) has standard/superior rooms starting at Y428/580, about 40% less than the listed price. The **Zhongya Hotel** (*Map 4; Zhōngyà Fàndiàn;* ☎ *6317 2317, fax 6317 2938, 330 Meiyuan Lu*) is a glossy place, with a bowling alley and small fitness centre. Rooms start at Y350, and can be discounted down to Y308.

Other Areas

There are several mid-range options a little out of the centre. The **Shanghai E-Best Hotel** (*Map 5; Shànghǎi Yìbǎi Jiǎrì Jiǔdiàn;* ☎ *6595 1818, 687 Dongdaming Lu*) is a new hotel in Hongkou with cheapish single/doubles at Y180/248 (listed at Y180/400). Nicer singles go for Y188 (Y300) and doubles rise to Y298 and Y368 (Y500).

Pacific Luck Hotel (*Map 5; Jīnfùyùn Dàjiǔdiàn;* ☎ *6325 9800, fax 6325 9709, 299 Wusong Lu*) has three stars and standard/superior rooms at Y476/539 (listed at Y680/770). The **West Asia Hotel** (*Map 8; Xīyà Dàjiǔdiàn;* ☎ *687 2000, 20 Tianyueqiao Lu*) has a good location on the bustling Xujiahui crossroads, with two-star singles/doubles for Y280/300.

Longhua Hotel (*Map 3; Lónghuá Yíng Bīnguǎn;* ☎ *6457 0570, fax 6457 7621, 2787 Longhua Lu*) is a modern hotel attached to, and owned by, the Longhua Temple. Rooms are clean and pleasant, though it's a shame they couldn't have incorporated more (or even any!) of the neighbouring temple architecture. Doubles run at Y580, discounted to Y304. Darker semisubterranean doubles are gloomy during the

day but are also cheaper at Y380, discounted down to Y198.

Donghong Hotel (*Map 5; Dōnghóng Dàjiǔdiàn;* ☎ *6545 5008, fax 6545 5034, 1161 Dongdaming Lu*) is part of the same building as the Ocean Hotel (see Places to Stay – Top End), but is a cheaper, two-star option. Singles cost from Y210 to Y245 and doubles start at Y300, which includes breakfast.

Olympic Hotel (*Map 8; Àolínpǐkè Jùlèbù;* ☎ *6439 1391, fax 6439 6295, 1800 Zhongshan Nanerlu*) is a three-star hotel near Shanghai Stadium. Doubles are Y650, discounted down to Y380, and give you access to the outdoor swimming pool and health club.

Huaxia Hotel (*Map 8; Huáxià Bīnguǎn;* ☎ *6436 0100, fax 6433 3724, 38 Caobao Lu*), in the Caohejing technology zone, is a bit out of the way but isn't far from the Caobao Lu metro stop. The three-star singles/doubles are good value, starting at Y260/400.

PLACES TO STAY – TOP END

Shanghai is bursting with hotels in the top-end (Y500-plus) category, though some of them have discounts that bring them into mid-range prices. Top-end hotels generally fall into two categories: the noble and aristocratic hotels of old Shanghai and the slick new towers bursting with modern amenities.

Business travellers will probably opt for modern facilities like the Portman Ritz-Carlton, Hilton or the imposing Grand Hyatt in Pudong. Those with a sense of history might want to stay at one of the more urbane options, such as the Peace Hotel, where they can wrap themselves in nostalgia.

All of the following hotels have several restaurants, a gym, business centre, Internet access and free airport shuttle. Most have executive floors that offer all sorts of perks like private meeting rooms and business services.

Central Shanghai

Interior renovations have robbed the Park, Shanghai Mansions and Jinjiang of character and history, but if there's one place left

PLACES TO STAY

in Shanghai that will give you a sense of the past, it's the old Cathay, now the *Peace Hotel* (Map 5; Hépíng Fàndiàn; ☎ 6321 6888, fax 6329 0300, 20 Nanjing Donglu, @ peacehtl@public.sta.net.cn), which rises up majestically from the Bund. The sumptuous lobby is one of the best examples of an Art-Deco interior left in Shanghai. The national deluxe suites (US$520) are laid out in 1930s Art Deco- style to represent the concessions of the time: French, British, American and Japanese, not to mention Chinese. Some travellers have rightly pointed out, however, that in terms of service, this hotel is way overpriced. Singles/doubles are US$120/160 and suites start at US$250, though discounts knock doubles down to around US$110 in summer and US$80 in winter. Only three of the standard rooms have a view of Nanjing Lu (only suites view the Bund) so book ahead. The hotel has a Web site at www.shanghaipeacehotel.com.

Across from the Peace, its annexe, the older *Peace Palace Hotel* (Map 5; Hépíng Huìzhōng Fàndiàn) has similar rates, dipping as low as Y700 for a double in winter.

Across Suzhou Creek from the Bund, *Shanghai Mansions* (Map 5; Shànghǎi Dàshà; ☎ 6324 6260, fax 6306 5147, 20 Suzhou Beilu, @ shds@public1.sta.net.cn) is another old hotel, with great views. Formerly called the Broadway Mansions, it was built as a block of apartments and was later used to house American officers after WWII. Standard double rooms (no singles) start at Y850, discounted down to Y550 in winter. Make sure you ask for a room facing the Bund.

The *Park Hotel* (Map 5; Guójì Fàndiàn; ☎ 6327 5225, fax 6327 6958, 170 Nanjing Xilu) overlooks Renmin Park. Erected in 1934, the building is one of Shanghai's best examples of Art-Deco architecture from the city's cultural peak. With recent renovations, however, the interior has lost some of its old-world charm. Singles/doubles start at US$80/150, and can be discounted to US$55/100. Rooms are comfortable and the service is efficient. Book ahead to get a view of Nanjing Lu.

A couple of doors down, the three-star *Pacific Hotel* (Map 5; Jīnmén Dàjiǔdiàn; ☎ 6327 6226, fax 6372 3634, 104 Nanjing Xilu) has a small but opulent foyer with some nice Art-Deco details and is cheaper than the Park. Singles start at US$55 and doubles cost US$70 to US$120, with discounts lowering this by 30%.

The traditional-style *Jinjiang Hotel* (Map 6; Jǐnjiāng Fàndiàn; ☎ 6258 2582, fax 6472 5588, 59 Maoming Nanlu) underwent massive renovations in 1999. The main Cathay Building has singles/doubles listed at US$155/165, both offered for Y880 in the slow season. You can find less expensive rooms for Y450 in the Jin Nan Building. The lavish *Grosvenor Villa* (Guìbīn Loú), in the southernmost part of the complex, is very luxurious, with standard rooms for US$200 (up to 30% discount offered) and suites at US$400. All rooms include access to the gym complex and indoor pool.

Adjacent to the older complex, the *Jinjiang Tower* (Map 6; Xīn Jǐnjiāng Dàjiùan; ☎ 6433 4488, fax 6415 0045, 161 Changle Lu, @ jjtrsv@public.sta.net.cn) is an ugly, five-star, glass skyscraper. Standard rooms start at US$210, but discounts can bring that down to US$98.

Another historical option is the *Ruijin Hotel* (Map 6; Ruìjīn Bīnguǎn; ☎ 6472 5222, fax 6472 2277, 118 Ruijin Erlu), which has elegant grounds and a series of old mansions converted into rooms. Building No 1 was the former Morris estate (see the French Concession Walking Tour in Things to See & Do). Singles/doubles go for Y650/950, and suites range from Y1200 to Y3200. There are some fine restaurants in the gardens.

The *Xingguo Hotel* (Map 6; Xīngguó Bīnguǎn; ☎ 6212 9070, fax 6251 2145, 72 Xingguo Lu) is a similar deal. Part of the complex was the location of the John Swire Company in the 1920s and Building No 1 was said to be one of Mao's favourites places to stay. Rooms start at Y680 and suites range from Y1100 to Y2000.

Taiyuan Villa (Map 6; Tàiyuán Biéshù; ☎ 6471 6688, fax 6471 2618, 160 Taiyan Lu) is a branch of the Ruijin, in a different location but still in the French Concession.

The peaceful complex includes the former residence of General Marshall. Doubles cost from Y300 to Y450, though rooms in the Marshall Residence hit Y1000 and Y1200. Most rooms have been modernised.

The *Portman Ritz-Carlton (Map 4; Bōtèmàn Lìsī Kǎerùn Jiǔàn;* ☎ *6279 8888, fax 6279 8887, 1376 Nanjing Xilu,* ✉ *reservation@portman.com.cn),* the cream of the crop in Puxi, was renovated in 1999 at the cost of US$30 million, and, as part of the massive Shanghai Centre, is the biggest expat hang-out since the Peace Hotel circa 1931. Rooms start at US$250 and run to US$2500. Top-notch facilities include the 7th-floor health club with swimming pools, squash courts, tennis courts and a top-of-the-line gym. Phone ahead and they'll even run a Chinese herbal bath for your arrival (for an extra US$20).

The elegant Japanese-run *Garden Hotel (Map 6; Huāyuá Fàndiàn;* ☎ *6415 1111, fax 6415 8866, 58 Maoming Nanlu)* has similar rates and nicer grounds on the site of the old French Club, across from the Jinjiang Hotel. See the French Concession Walking Tour in the Things to See & Do chapter for more on its history.

The *Regal International East Asia Hotel (Map 6; Fùháo Huánqiú Dōngyà Jiǔàn;* ☎ *6415 5588, fax 6445 8899, 516 Hengshan Lu,* ✉ *rieah@prodigychina.com)* is the latest five-star addition to Shanghai's hotel scene. Rooms start at US$200, but discounts as low as US$90 are often available. The gym and sports facilities are some of the best in Shanghai.

Its sister hotel, the *Regal Shanghai East Asia (Map 8; Fùháo Dōngyà Jiǔdiàn;* ☎ *6426 6888, fax 6426 5888, 666 Tianyaoqiao Lu)* has one less star but is cheaper. Rack rates start at US$160, discounted down to US$80. The hotel has, shall we say, an interesting location; it's built into the western side of Shanghai Stadium. Some rooms actually face into the stadium so check if there's a rock concert planned during your stay!

The *Hilton Hotel (Map 6; Jìng'ān Xīěrdùn Fàndiàn;* ☎ *6248 0000, fax 6248 3848, 250 Huashan Lu)* has rooms starting

at US$230, but it was offering 50% discounts. Facilities include a health club, an indoor swimming pool, and tennis and squash courts. Reservations can be made online at www.hilton.com.

The *Huating Hotel (Map 8; Huátíng Bīnguǎn;* ☎ *6439 1000, fax 6255 0830, 1200 Caoxi Beilu)* was once the Sheraton and, in 1987, was the first 'modern' hotel to appear in Shanghai. It has since been completely handed over to local management but the facilities remain. Singles/doubles start at US$215/235, both discounted to US$108.

Likewise, what used to be the Holiday Inn is now known as the *Crowne-Plaza Shanghai (Map 6; Yínxīng Huángguān Jiǔàn,* ☎ *6280 8888, fax 6280 3353, 388 Panyu Lu).* Singles/doubles start at US$210/230 but both rooms were discounted to US$88 during winter.

At the other end of town near the Bund, the *Sofitel Hyland Hotel (Map 5; Hǎilún Bīnguǎn;* ☎ *6351 5888, fax 6351 4088, 505 Nanjing Donglu)* has singles/doubles starting at US$150/170, with up to 40% discount, breakfast included. It's right in the centre of the Nanjing Donlu shopping frenzy.

Hotel Grand Nation (Map 5; Nánsīyà Dàjiǔdiàn; ☎ *6350 0000, 719 Nanjing Donglu)* is a beautiful hotel in a good location but competition is too stiff not to offer discounts. Standard rooms start at US$130.

The *Jianguo Hotel (Map 8; Jiànguó Bīnguǎn;* ☎ *6439 9299, fax 6439 9714, 439 Caoxi Beilu)* is in a decent location near Xujiahui. Rooms start at Y650.

JC Mandarin (Map 4; Shànghǎi Jǐnwénhúa Dàjiǔdiàn; ☎ *6279 1888, fax 6279 1822,* ✉ *manadin.sjm@meritus-hotels.com, 1225 Nanjing Xilu)* is a five-star hotel located across from the Portman Ritz-Carlton on Nanjing Xilu. Rates are listed at US$210/230 for singles/doubles but quickly folded to US$136/146. Facilities include tennis and squash courts and an indoor pool. It has a Web site at www.jcmandarin.com.

The *Holiday Inn (Map 8; Shànghǎi Guǎngchǎng Chángchéng Jiàrì Jiǔdiàn;* ☎ *6353 8008, fax 6354 3018, 285 Tianmu Xilu & 585 Hengfeng Lu,* ✉ *hidtsha@public8 .sta.net.cn),* near the train station, consists of two wings: In the Plaza Wing rooms start at US$90, discounted down to Y458, and in the Great Wall Wing, rooms start at US$80, discounted down to Y388.

The *Shanghai Hotel* (Map 6; *Shànghǎi Bīnguǎn;* ☎ 6248 0088, fax 6248 1056, 505 Wulumuqi Beilu) offers doubles for Y558 to Y988. It has a good location and is popular with Chinese groups.

Central Hotel (Map 5; *Wángbǎohé Dàjiǔdiàn;* ☎ 5396 5000, fax 5396 5188, 555 Jiujiang Lu) is a new hotel in an excellent location, built by the group that owns the Wangbaohe Restaurant. Rates start at US$160 but in reality go for US$60. The *Jing'an Hotel* (Map 6; *Jìngān Bīnguǎn;* ☎ 6248 1888, fax 6248 2657, 370 Huashan Lu) has singles/doubles in the four-star main building costing US$150/180. Rooms in the west building are cheaper at US$75 but lack charm. Try for a 30% discount.

Hotel Equatorial (Map 6; *Guìdū Jiǔdiàn,* ☎ 6248 1688, fax 1773/4033, 65 Yan'an Xilu, ✉ info@sha.equatorial.com) is a four-star monster near the Hilton. Standard rooms cost Y907, discounted down to Y680, and there are often special packages.

The *Ocean Hotel* (Map 5; *Yuǎnyáng Bīnguǎn;* ☎ 6545 8888, fax 6545 8993, 1171 Dongdaming Lu) has rooms starting at US$110, discounted down to $77. The revolving restaurant on the 28th floor has good views of the Bund and Huangpu. There's also a 24-hour cafe and good Chinese and Japanese restaurants. The only downside is the inconvenient location.

Hongqiao

There's a cluster of hotels in Hongqiao aimed at expats and businesspeople working in the area. The zone is close to Hongqiao airport but a long way from Pudong airport.

The elegant five-star *Westin Taipingyang* (Map 9; *Wēisītīng Tàipíngyáng;* ☎ 6275 8888, fax 6275 5420, 5 Zunyi Nanlu, ✉ westin@uninet.com.cn) is one of the best hotels in Shanghai. Standard singles/doubles are US$210/240, but it was offering bargain rates that slashed room rates by more than 50%. The facilities and decor are excellent. Look out for the great automatic piano in the

lobby. For reservations try the hotel's Web site at www.westin.com or call 1-800-WESTIN-1 in the US or Canada.

The *Marriott* group is to open two hotels in Shanghai in the coming years. The first is on Hongqiao Lu (☎ 6237 6000), near the airport. The second is in the heart of Nanjing Lu at the Tomorrow Square. Expect both to be top end.

The *Cypress Hotel* (Map 3; *Lóngbǎi Fàndiàn;* ☎ 6268 8868, fax 6268 1878, 2419 Hongqiao Lu, ✉ cypress@stn.sh.cn) has a pleasant garden, a health club with a driving range, tennis and squash courts and an indoor pool. Prices run at US$160, discounted down to $98, including breakfast. The *Galaxy Hotel* (Map 9; *Yínhé Bīnguǎn;* ☎ 6275 5888, fax 6275 0039, 888 Zhongshan Xilu) is a four-star place popular with Japanese and Korean groups. It offers rates of US$160, discounted down to US$96.

The *Rainbow Hotel* (Map 9; *Hóngqiáo Bīnguǎn;* ☎ 6275 3388, fax 6275 3736, 2000 Yan'an Beilu) has rooms for US$150, discounted down to US$90, and offers an indoor swimming pool and a gym.

Hongqiao State Guest House (Map 9; *Hóngqiáo Yíng Bīnguǎn;* ☎ 6219 8855, fax 6275 3903, 1591 Hongqiao Lu) has a garden setting and villa-style rooms that were previously reserved for government bigwigs but are now open to all. Rates start at US$100 and facilities include a gym and an outdoor pool.

Hotel Nikko Longbai (Map 3; *Shànghǎi Rìháng Lóngbǎi Fàndiàn;* ☎ 6268 9111, fax 6268 9333, 2451 Hongqiao Lu) is near Hongqiao airport and provides a free shuttle bus to the city centre. Rack rates for singles/doubles are US$160/220, offered at US$80/95 in low season.

Aiming at business and convention travellers, the *Shanghai Worldfield Convention Hotel* (Map 3; *Shànghǎi Shìbó Huìyì Dàjiǔdiàn;* ☎ 6270 3388, fax 6270 4554, 2106 Hongqiao Lu, ✉ conventh@public.sta .net.cn) has rooms at US$170 that are steeply discounted down to Y588 when there are no conventions.

Xijiao State Guest House (Map 9; *Xījiāo Bīnguǎn;* ☎ 6219 8800, fax 6433 6641,

1921 Hongqiao Lu) is a quiet, sleepy place with some of Shanghai's most spacious gardens. The hotel sees relatively few foreign visitors (though Queen Elizabeth II and Japanese Emperor Akihite have both stayed here) and is a great place to escape from the city. Rooms cost US$120 but were discounted down to Y600. Facilities include a health club with tennis and squash courts.

Yangtze New World (Map 9; Yángzijiāng Dàjiǔdiàn; ☎ *6275 0000, fax 6275 0750, 2099 Yan'an Xilu,* ✉ *Yangtze@prodigycn. com)* has rooms at Y1550, heavily discounted down to Y664, or Y588 on the weekend.

Pudong

The newest and brightest star on the Shanghai hotel horizon has to be the *Grand Hyatt (Map 5; Jīnmaò Kāiyuè Dàjiudiàn;* ☎ *5830 3338, fax 5830 8838).* It starts on the 54th floor of the Jinmao Tower in Pudong and goes up another 33 stories; everywhere from the hair salon to the bathtubs has stunning views. Described as 'contemporary

---

World's Highest Bubble Bath

The Grand Hyatt is the highest hotel above ground level in the world (not the world's tallest hotel – that goes to a hotel in Dubai), and so begins an endless line of pointless superlatives – the highest gym above ground level, the world's highest mini-bar etc. The hotel also boasts the world's longest laundry chute (420 vertical m) and an impressive 61 elevators, which shoot high rollers up into the air at 9m/second. The interior atrium is the world's tallest at an impressive 33 stories, and only starts on the 55th floor. It's hard not to believe that the post office on the 88th floor wasn't put there deliberately to make it the world's highest.

To ensure the building's stability in Pudong's boggy soil the building rests on 429 steel pipes rammed 65m into the ground. Still, in case of a freak typhoon you'll need to hold on to your coffee; the pinnacle is designed to swing a stomach-churning 75m.

Art Deco with Chinese touches', the hotel is very much design-led and has endless attention to detail – from the original art on the walls to the custom-made glassware. The rooms are packed with hi-tech gadgets such as TV Internet access, fog-free mirrors, three-jet showers and sensor reading lamps. Doubles start at US$300, which drops as low as US$148 in winter. For business travellers, the Regency Club offers meeting rooms, separate check-in, free breakfast, tea and snacks, all for an extra US$20. The hotel's Web site is at www.shanghai.hyatt.com.

The *Pudong Shangrila (Map 5; Pǔdōng Xiānggélīlā Dàjiǔdiàn;* ☎ *6882 6888, fax 6882 0160, 33 Fucheng Lu)* recently received a five-star rating. Tasteful standard singles and doubles start at US$220 and US$240, with seasonal discounts of up to 40%.

The *New Asia Tomson Hotel (Map 3; Shànghǎi Xīnyà Tāngchén Dàjiǔdiàn;* ☎ *5831 8888, fax 5831 7777, 777 Zhangyang Lu,* ✉ *nathsha@prodigychina .com)*, a little farther east in the heart of Pudong, near the Nextage department store, is another five-star pad, this time with more of a European feel. Singles/doubles start at US$180/210 but rooms were available for as low as US$88. Facilities include a rooftop tennis court.

The *Shanghai International Convention Centre Hotel (Map 5; Shànghǎi Guójí Huìyì Zhōngxīn Dàjiǔdiàn;* ☎ *5879 2727, fax 5887 9707, 2727 Binjiang Dadao)* is instantly recognisable for its gaudy glass globes dumped on the east bank of the Huangpu. Rooms start at US$180 for a garden view, or US$220 for a view of the Bund, though discounted rates were around US$108/128. Facilities include a 9th-floor swimming pool and health club.

The *Hotel Nikko Pudong (Map 3; Zhōngyóu Rìháng Dàjiǔdiàn;* ☎ *6875 8888, fax 6875 8688, 969 Dongfang Lu,* ✉ *hnps bzct@public6.sta.net.cn)* is part of the Japanese chain, with rates at US$150, discounted to as low as US$65. Facilities include an indoor swimming pool, and several Japanese and Korean restaurants.

The *Holiday Inn Pudong (Map 3; Pǔdōng Jiàrì Jiǔdiàn;* ☎ *5830 6666, fax 5830 5555, 899 Dongfang Lu,* ✉ *hipudong sha@poboxes.com)* has a fitness centre and an outdoor swimming pool. Room rates are US$160, discounted down to Y588.

LONG-TERM RENTALS

There are several distinct types of longer-term accommodation in Shanghai. One thing common to all is the need to register with the local PSB.

The cheapest way to stay in Shanghai is to share a flat or rent local accommodation from a Chinese landlord. Classified ads in *That's* magazine and others often advertise apartments or flat-shares. The main difficulty here is that foreigners are only allowed to stay in certain accommodation. Housing is divided by the PSB into *waixiao,* indicating that the property may be legally bought and rented by anyone, or *neixiao,* which is reserved for domestic use. Most accommodation outside of Shanghai's expat apartment blocks is neixiao. It's unusual for anybody to pay much attention if you stay in a neixiao apartment, but you will need to state your address when you go to register with the PSB. (Some bypass this by never registering but you will have a problem extending your visa without registration.) One by-product of this regulation is that while the average monthly rent for Chinese in Shanghai is around Y2 per sq metre, foreigners will be lucky to get by with any apartment less than US$400 per month.

Most expat residents who work in Shanghai rent a serviced apartment. These run the gamut from towering apartment blocks in the centre of town to villa-style communities out in Pudong and Gubei, where you can forget that you were ever in China. Most serviced apartments offer hotel-style facilities such as a clubroom, a gym, and a maid service. Shanghai currently has a glut of these blocks and prices have been falling in the last couple of years. In general, rents vary from US$1000 to US$5000 per month for a two-bedroom apartment. The *Shanghai Property Portfolio,* a free magazine published occasionally

by Ismay, has a useful overview of available serviced apartments.

It is even possible to stay in an old-style Shanghai house. Though the idea of a Tudor house in a secluded French Concession backstreet sounds fine, what you gain in style you often lose in suspect electricity and plumbing, poor heating and a continual need for renovations. You won't save any money by choosing an old house, either. Locals have cottoned on that foreigners like the older houses and most rents run from US$1000 to US$3000 per month.

If you want to actually buy a place you definitely need a property agent (see Property Agents later in this chapter) to help you through the legal minefield. Foreigners can indeed purchase detached houses in Shanghai but are not yet allowed to buy semi-detached houses or apartments.

Property Agents

Whether choosing one of Shanghai's historic homes or selecting an expat community, it is advisable to seek the aid of a knowledgeable property agent. Most cater to a wide range of budgets. Some take a month's rent as commission, while others take a fee from the landlord. Most deal in 12-month, and sometimes six-month rentals, but not normally less than this. The following are some reputable companies, though you'll find dozens more in local listings magazines.

Colliers Jardine (☎ 6279 8677, 1376 Nanjing Xilu, Suite 563 East Tower. Run by Emily Pang and Tess Johnston, this is an excellent source for information on historic and interesting places.

Dragon Realty (☎ 6294 5752) House 3, Tianping Lu, Lane 71. This represents old and new properties for all budget concerns. It will also renovate as to the landlord/tenant specifications.

PA Property Consultants (☎ 6445 0289, 6474 5932). This caters to those on a much larger budget. It provides good service through English-speaking agents and has an excellent property database.

Phoenix Realty (☎ 6437 9891) 47 Yongfu Lu, Room 308–310.

Shanghai Home Search (☎ 6246 0997) 123 Yanping Lu. This is a good source for those on a somewhat limited budget.

Places to Eat

FOOD

Shanghai offers a dazzling array of food and provides an opportunity for cuisine exploration that should be seized with both chopsticks. Stylish dining is one area where Shanghai leaves Beijing in the dust.

Eating out in Shanghai is about more than just the food. It is a social lubricant, a time when families get together and a major pastime of Shanghai's chic. While friends in the West go out for a beer, the Shanghainese will opt for a meal punctuated with numerous shots of rice wine. One method of saying 'How are you?' (nǐ chīfàn le méiyǒu?) translates literally as 'Have you eaten yet?'.

Even if you are a regular at your local Chinese restaurant back home you won't necessarily find yourself at home with Chinese cuisine in China. You'll find no fortune cookies or chop suey in Shanghai and only the occasional prawn cracker.

Most top-end Chinese restaurants have some kind of English menu but even these don't include the more interesting dishes. Try out the language section at the back of this book or, even better, go with Chinese friends and let them order. In general it is always better to eat Chinese food in a group as you'll get a better variety of dishes. Restaurants often have set meals for a table of 10, which is especially useful if you have to hold a banquet for some bigwig. Chinese habitually over order. Most Chinese eat early, at 6 or 7 pm, but lots of trendy late-night Shanghainese eateries buzz 24 hours.

If you are on a tight budget, it's worth knowing that some of Shanghai's most famous restaurants often have a cheaper, less fancy downstairs option serving snacks and cheaper main dishes. Also check for extra charges like tea and napkins and send these back if you don't want them. Always check the bill carefully, as many restaurants overcharge.

Epicureans will tell you that the key to ordering Chinese dishes is to get a variety and balance of textures, tastes, smells, colours

and even temperatures. Most Chinese will order at least one cold dish, a main dish and a watery soup to finish off. Note that both soup and rice are normally served at the end of a meal as fillers, so if you want them to come first you'll have to tell the waiter.

Shanghai

The cuisine of Shanghai is influenced by neighbouring Zhejiang and Jiangsu styles, and is defined, along with Suzhou and Hangzhou cuisines, as Yangzhou or Huaiyang cuisine. It is generally sweeter and oilier than China's other cuisines.

Unsurprisingly, due to its position as a major port and the head of the Yangzi delta (the 'land of fish and rice') Shanghai cuisine features a lot of fish and seafood, especially cod, river eel and shrimp. The word for fish *(yu)* is a homonym for 'plenty' or 'surplus'; fish is a mandatory dish for most banquets and celebrations.

Common Shanghainese fish dishes include *sōngrén yùmǐ* (fish with corn and pine nuts), *guìyú* (steamed mandarin fish), *lúyú* (Songjiang perch), *chāngyú* (pomfret) and *huángyú* (yellow croaker). Fish is usually *qīngzhēng* (steamed) but can be stir-fried, pan-fried or grilled. Both fish and seafood are usually priced by the weight, either 50g or 500g.

Squirrel-shaped mandarin fish is a famous dish from Suzhou. The dish dates from a political assassination during the Warring States dynasty, when a dagger was hidden in the thick sauce until the assassin struck.

Several restaurants specialise in *xiánjī* (cold salty chicken), which tastes better than it sounds. *Zuìjī* (drunken chicken) is so called because it is marinated in Shaoxing rice wine. *Shīzitóu* (lion's head) is actually steamed pork meatballs. A variation on the theme is *xièfěn shī tóuzi,* which mixes crab meat with the meatballs. Crab roe dumplings are another Shanghainese luxury. *Bao* (claypot) dishes are braised for a long time in their own casserole dish.

Vegetarian dishes include shredded pressed bean curd, cabbage in cream sauce, *mèn* (braised) bean curd and various types of mushrooms, including *xiānggū báicài* (mushrooms surrounded by baby bok choy). *Hǔpí jiānjiāo* (tiger skin chillies) is a delicious dish of stir-fried green peppers seared in a wok and served in a sweet chilli sauce. Fried pine nuts and sweetcorn is another common Shanghainese dish.

Dazha hairy crabs are a Shanghai speciality between October and December. They are eaten with soy, ginger and vinegar and downed with warm Shaoxing wine. The crab is thought to increases the body's yin, or coldness, and so rice wine is taken lukewarm to add yang. Aficionados say that the best crabs come from Yangcheng Lake and are black with hairy feet. Male and female crabs are supposed to be eaten together. The

crabs are delicious but can be fiddly to eat. The body opens via a little tab on the underside. Don't eat the gills or the stomach.

Hangzhou

Hangzhou food is currently very chic in Shanghai. It's sometimes described as southern food cooked in a northern style and has noticeably less oil than Shanghai cuisine. There's a predominance of fish, shrimp and green vegetables. Longjing shrimp are soaked with Hangzhou's famous longjing tea. West Lake soup is made with water shield, a green plant that grows in West Lake. *Xīhú yú* (sweet-and-sour West Lake fish) is another popular dish.

Another dish to look out for is *dōngpō ròu* (pork slices), which was named after the Song dynasty poet Su Dongpo. Flavoured with Shaoxing wine, and cooked and served in a pot, the pork is often quite fatty.

Another local delicacy, apparently a firm favourite with the Qianlong emperor, is *shāguō yútóu dòufu* (earthenware pot fish-head tofu).

Jiàohuà jī (Beggar's Chicken) is another famous dish. Originally cased in clay and baked in an open fire, the chicken is now baked in a lotus leaf and ends up deliciously crispy.

Cantonese

This is what non-Chinese consider 'Chinese' food, largely because most emigre restaurateurs originate from Guangdong (Canton) or Hong Kong. In Shanghai every hotel worth its salt has at least one blowout Cantonese restaurant to cater to its Hong Kong guests.

Cantonese flavours are generally more subtle than other Chinese styles – almost sweet, and there are almost no spicy dishes. Sweet-and-sour and oyster sauces are common.

Cantonese snacks *dim sum* (*diǎnxīn* in Mandarin) are famous and are the speciality of several of Shanghai's restaurants. Apart from *chasiu* (barbecued pork) dumplings, you'll find spring rolls, ho fun noodles (*héfěn* in Mandarin), *wánzi* (fishballs), *zhōu* (congee) and, of course, the acquired taste of chicken's feet.

Chaozhou

Named after a coastal area in eastern Guangdong, this is similar to Cantonese cuisine and features lots of seafood and squid, but with stronger flavours and richer sauces than Cantonese cuisine. The most famous dishes are abalone, shark's fin, bird's nest, roast suckling pig and soy goose.

Sichuanese & Hunanese

These are the fieriest of all China's cuisines, so take care when ordering. Lethal red chillies, aniseed, peppercorns and *huājiāo* ('flower pepper') are used. Famous dishes include *zhāngchá yāzi* (Camphor smoked duck), *mápō dòufu* (Granny Ma's tofu) and *gōngbǎo jīdīng* (chicken with peanuts).

Snacks

Shanghai has some great snacks (*xiǎo chī* or literally 'little eats') and it's worth trying out as many of them as possible. They are cheap, quick and there's no need to labour through any pesky Chinese menus. What's more, the places to track them down – Shanghai's backstreets – are interesting in themselves.

Look out for *xiǎolóngbāo*, Shanghai's number one favourite dumpling, which is copied everywhere else in China, but is only true to form here. They are wonderful, but there's an art to eating them – they're full of scalding oil and the interior is hotter than McDonald's apple pies. Tradition actually assigns the invention of the dumpling to Nanxiang, a village north of Shanghai city. Dumplings are normally bought by the *long* (steamer basket), though large versions are sold individually for about Y1 each.

Another Shanghai speciality is the *shengjian*, similar to the *bāozi* dumpling but fried in a black pan with a wooden lid on top. Watch out for the scalding oil. Several Shanghainese restaurants serve *luobocibing* (fried onion cakes), which make a good beer snack.

Huǒguō (hotpot) is particularly popular in Shanghai in winter. The pot in question is a huge bowl of bubbling, spicy broth into which you dip various skewered vegetable and meats. One reason for its popularity became clear in 1999 when it was revealed that several hotpot restaurants were adding opium poppies to the stock!

The following is a rundown of the main street snacks you'll find in Shanghai:

Banquets

The banquet is the apex of the Chinese dining experience. Virtually all significant business deals in China are clinched at the banquet table.

Dishes are served in sequence, beginning with cold appetisers and continuing through 10 or more courses. Soup, usually a thin broth to aid digestion, is generally served after the main course.

The idea is to serve or order far more than everyone can eat. Empty bowls imply a stingy host. Rice is considered a cheap filler and rarely appears at a banquet – don't ask for it, as this would imply that the snacks and main courses are insufficient, causing embarrassment to the host.

Never drink alone. Imbibing is conducted via toasts, which will usually commence with a general toast by the host, followed by the main guest reply toast and then settle down to frequent toasts to individuals. A toast is conducted by raising your glass in both hands in the direction of the toastee and crying out *gānbēi*, literally 'dry the glass'. Chinese do not clink glasses. Drain your glass in one hit. It is not unusual for everyone to end up very drunk, though at very formal banquets this is frowned upon.

Don't be late for a formal banquet; it's considered extremely rude. The banquet ends when the food and toasts end – the Chinese don't linger after the meal. You may find yourself being applauded when you enter a large banquet. It is polite to applaud back.

There is no such thing as everyone chipping in to pay the bill – one person (the host) settles the account with the restaurant. Even in the very rare case where the cost is going to be split, this is never done in front of the restaurant staff – to pass money to your host in front of others would cause a massive loss of face.

Shuǐjiǎo Chinese ravioli, stuffed with meat, spring onion and greens. Sometimes served by the bowl in a soup, sometimes dry by the weight (250g or half a *jin* is normally enough). Locals mix *làjiāo* (chilli), *cù* (vinegar) and *jiàngyóu* (soy sauce) in a little bowl according to taste and dip the ravioli in. Watch out – vinegar and soy sauce look almost identical! The slippery buggers can be tricky to eat with chopsticks. Don't wear white as you'll get sprayed in soy whenever you drop them in the bowl. *Shuǐjiǎo* are often created by family mini factories – one stretches the pastry, another makes the filling and a third spoons the filling into the pastry, finishing with a little twist.

Zhēngjiǎo A steamed version of a shuǐjiǎo.

Guōtiē Like a shuǐjiǎo but fried in oil.

Mántou Steamed dumplings without filling or taste (and also Chinese slang for a woman's breasts!).

Húndun Known in the West as wonton soup, these are small savoury ravioli served by the bowl.

Niúròu miàn Beef noodles in a soup.

Jīdàn miàn Noodles with egg.

Dàpái miàn Beef noodles with a rib or bone.

Jiānbǐng An egg-and-spring onion omelette made to order on a black hotplate and served folded up with chilli sauce.

Chǎomiàn Fried noodles or 'chow mein', not as popular as in the West. There is no such thing as 'chop suey' in China.

Chǎofàn Fried rice.

Qìguō An earthenware pot with a hole in the centre, the soupy contents of which are heated by steam coming up the hole.

Shāguō A stewed casserole cooked in an earthenware pot.

Shāokǎo An upturned skillet on which you can fry your own meat or vegetables.

Other street snacks include *chóu* (stinky) tofu, fried tofu, tea eggs (soaked in soy sauce), tofu soaked in soy sauce, and baked sweet potatoes, which can be bought by the weight.

Keep an eye open for Thousand Year Eggs – duck eggs that are covered in straw and stored underground for six months (the traditional recipe has them soaked in horses' urine before burial!). The yolk becomes green and the white becomes jelly. More interesting snacks available at markets include chicken's feet, pigs' ears, pigs' trotters and even pigs' faces.

Desserts & Sweets

The Chinese do not generally eat dessert, but fruit is considered to be an appropriate end to a good meal. Western influence has added ice cream to the menu in some upmarket establishments, but in general sweet stuff is consumed as snacks and is seldom available in restaurants.

One exception to the rule is caramelised fruits, such as *bāsī píngguǒ* (apple), *bāsī xiāngjiāo* (banana) and even *bāsī tǔdòu* (potato), which you can find in a few restaurants. Other sweeties include *tángyuán* (small, sweet, glutinous balls, traditionally from Ningbo, filled with sugar or bean paste), *bābaófàn* (a sweet, sticky rice pudding known as Eight Treasure Rice), and various types of steamed buns filled with sweet bean paste.

Bīngtáng fulu (toffee crab apples) and strawberries on a stick are a popular winter treat. Roasted chestnuts are popular over winter and sell for Y10 to Y13 a jin. *Dànta* (egg tarts) are also popular among Shanghainese. Shanghai's bakeries stock a wide range of Western cakes, various types of cakes stuffed with bean or date paste, and gummy glutinous balls covered in sesame seeds.

Several shops at the Yuyuan Gardens have been selling pear syrup sweets since 1894 but these are generally not to foreigners' tastes.

Fruit

Shanghai's fruit stalls are well stocked from produce brought from all over the country. November is the best season.

The best fruits are *yòuzi* (pomelos), Fuji apples, pears from Anhui, imported kiwis and bananas from southern China. Mandarins are particularly cheap. Strawberries roll into town around January. Entrepreneurs at the Yuyuan Gardens sell *gānzhezhī* (fresh sugar cane juice) and *hāmǐguā* (slices of Hami melon) on a stick.

DRINKS
Nonalcoholic Drinks

All of the world's major soft drink producers have plants in Shanghai. Coca-Cola set up its first factory in Shanghai in 1927. Taiwanese imports include cold coffee in a can and bottles of iced tea.

Hot tea is normally drunk before or after a meal. There's a wide range of teas available; including *lüchá* (green tea), *mòlihuā* (jasmine), *júhuā chá* (chrysanthemum), longjing, oolong and *hóng chá* (black tea). In traditional restaurants you will be served tea poured out of a foot-long spout.

Excellent ground coffee and even coffee beans are available everywhere – unusual for China – but they are pricey.

Alcoholic Drinks

The most famous domestic brand of beer is Qingdao, originally a German brew, famed because of the mineral water used in brewing. The cheapest local brand is Reeb (*Lìbō*).

Foreign beers have hit China in a big way and Budweiser (*Bǎiwēi*) is on its way to dominating China as it does the US. The German beer Becks (*Bèikè*) has a brewery in China, but though it is very cheap (Y3 per bottle in the supermarket), standards are well below those of the European version. The Japanese beers Suntory and Kirin, and Denmark's Carlsberg, all have breweries in Shanghai. Foreign bars have a selection of Bitburger, Guinness, Kilkenny, Coopers and Steinlager, mostly on tap.

Shaoxing rice wine from south of Shanghai is one of many kinds of *huángjiǔ*. It is traditionally served warm, in a tube.

PLACES TO EAT – BUDGET

Places to eat in the budget range means you can fill up (and usually drink tea) for under Y40. Some of the fancier restaurants serve good-value budget lunch specials.

Breakfast

A typical Chinese breakfast includes pickled vegetables, *yóutiáo* (fried breadsticks) and rice porridge, all washed down with a bowl of *dòujiāng* or *dòunǎi* (soybean milk). If you can't face this there are several cafes where you can get Western breakfasts and every mid-range or top-end hotel does a breakfast buffet.

U & I (Map 5; *Yàlā Cāntīng;* ☎ 6393 5300, 108 Daming Lu) serves OK Western breakfasts and snacks like club sandwiches and salads and is useful if you are staying at the nearby Pujiang Hotel.

At the other end of town, *Keven Café (Map 6; Kǎwén Kāfēi;* ☎ 6433 5564, 525 Hengshan Lu)* serves reasonably priced breakfasts all day, as well as soups and sandwiches, for a hair under Y50. Drinks will double the bill.

Croissant de France (Map 5; Kèsòng) is a good place for a quick breakfast. You can get a freshly baked croissant and coffee for Y15. There's a branch on Jiangxi Zhonglu, near Nanjing Donglu, and another at the corner of Sichuan Nanlu and Jinling Donglu, a block from the Bund.

Sole Coffee (Map 6; Suǒliè Kāfēi; ☎ 6473 1374, 4 Hengshan Lu)* is in a good location and serves set Japanese, French and American breakfasts (with fresh waffles) for Y30 to Y35. Coffee starts at Y25; decaffeinated coffee is Y45. There's a smaller branch at Donghu Lu, just off Huaihai Zhonglu.

For top-end brunches see the Hotel Restaurants section later in this chapter.

Chinese Snacks, Noodles & Dumplings

The Yuyuan Gardens & Bazaar has some excellent snack food. Ask for xiǎolóngbāo (see Snacks earlier in this chapter). Certain stalls are famed for a particular snack, and these inevitably have long queues snaking from the counters, such as the *Nanxiang Steamed Bun Restaurant (Map 5; Nánxiáng Mántoúdiàn)*, where you can sit upstairs and enjoy great views.

These snacks are available in the big-name Yuyuan restaurants such as the *Old Shanghai Restaurant (Map 7; Shànghǎi Lǎo Fàndiàn)*, established in 1875, and the *Green Wave Gallery (Map 5; Lǜbōlàng Jiǔlóu;* ☎ 6328 0602)*, but these places tend to charge extortionate amounts for food that is only marginally better than the stuff served downstairs by street vendors. There's one advantage: they have English menus.

Nanjing Donglu is not what it used to be when it comes to restaurants, and many of the old establishments have moved. **Shendacheng** *(Map 5; Shēndàchéng)* still clings to the corner of Zhejiang Zhonglu and Nanjing Donglu and serves up Shanghai snacks like spring rolls and bean congee.

Wuyue Renjia *(Map 6; Wùyuè Rénjiā; No 10, Lane 706, Huaihai Zhonglu)*, hidden down a backstreet off Huaihai Zhonglu, serves up cheap bowls of Suzhou-style noodles for Y10 to Y15 in a very civilised 'old Cathay' atmosphere. There's no English menu but you can't really go wrong here. You can choose between *tāng* (soupy) or *bān* (dry) noodles; in either case the flavouring comes on a side plate. The *shēng chǎo yúpiàn miàn* comes with tasty fried fish. There are several other branches across town, including another hidden down a backstreet at 595 Nanjing Xilu (Map 4).

Wujing Tang *(Map 8; Wǔjiātàng)* is a Taiwanese chain that serves up good beef, vegetable or seafood noodles for around Y20, and has a wide range of fruit juices. The pleasant environment, classical Chinese music and English menu make it a pleasant choice. There are branches in Metro City and Grand Gateway, both in Xujiahui.

Ajisen Ramen, or *1000 Taste Noodles* *(Map 6; Wèiqiān Lāmiàn;* ☎ *6372 5547, 518 Huaihai Lu)*, has very tasty Japanese noodles (Y12 to Y20) served in great wooden bowls, and set meals for Y23. It also serves side dishes such as salads, shellfish and pickled vegetables. It's a bustling place with good service. There's another branch at Grand Gateway in Xujiahui.

Bi Feng Tang *(Map 4; Bìfēngtáng;* ☎ *6279 0738, 1333 Nanjing Xilu)* is an incredibly popular place that serves cheap dim sum snacks for between Y5 and Y15, as well as coffee for Y10 and Budweiser for Y11. The Nanjing Xilu branch, across from the Shanghai Centre, has an English menu and plenty of outdoor seating when the weather is good. Other popular branches are at 1 Dapu Lu *(Map 6;* ☎ *5396 1328)* and the 24-hour 175 Changle Lu *(Map 6;* ☎ *6467 0628)*.

Mxc *(Map 6; Màixiāngcūn; 30 Sinan Lu)* is a dirt-cheap place selling noodles, rice combos and almost anything else, all in a pleasant environment.

Taiwan Xiaochi *(Map 6; Táiwān Xiǎochī)* is a pleasant but basic snack bar on Changle Lu. Mark your order on (Chinese-only) paper menus. There are noodle and rice combos, and its speciality is egg soup.

Also worth trying is **Haoshiji** *(Map 5; Hǎoshíjiā Kuàicāndiàn)*, a bare-bones snack bar, handy if you are staying in the Pujiang Hotel, that serves *shengjian* (fried dumplings) and excellent-value *gàijiāofàn* (Chinese dish-with-rice combos) for less than Y10.

Food Courts

Food courts can be found on the upper or basement level of most department stores. They don't offer *haute cuisine* but they do provide an opportunity to sample a range of food without having to navigate a Chinese menu; just point at the dim sum, noodles, curry dishes, teppanyaki or drinks. Make sure the hot dishes are steaming or prepared fresh for you.

Food Junction *(Map 8; Dàshídai)* at Xujiahui's Metro City *(Měiluóchéng)* is one of the best 'point-and-pays', with endless varieties of Chinese food, teppanyaki, crepes, fruit, pots of tea, ice cream and a branch of **Sumo Sushi**. Also nearby are **Pizza Hut**, **KFC** and **Wujing Tang**.

Over in Pudong, **Food Court Live** *(Map 5)* is in the basement next to the Jinmao Tower, serving the hordes headed up to the top-floor viewing platform. Chinese fast-food stalls specialise in claypot dishes, Hainan chicken, Cantonese barbecue, wok and noodle dishes, and set meals, all for less than Y20.

Fast Food

Fast-food outlets are everywhere in genuine and counterfeit form. Besides the usual **KFC** *(Kěndéjī)*, **Pizza Hut** *(Bìshèngkè)* and 23 branches of **McDonald's** *(Màidāngláo)*, there are also numerous local variations featuring both Western and Chinese fast food. McDonald's is considerably cheaper here than in the West and there's always a promotion going on. Pizza Hut costs around Y65 for a 12-inch pizza and Y28 for a decent salad cart.

There are two Chinese chains called **Yonghe;** one with a logo that's part Colonel Sanders, part Chairman Mao, and the other with a small child as its logo. Both serve up Chinese snacks and noodles 24 hours a day.

Mos Burger (Mòshī Hánbǎo) is a Japanese chain offering Teppanyaki burgers downstairs and noodles upstairs. There are branches in the Yuyuan Bazaar, on the corner of Huaihai Zhonglu and Shaanxi Nanlu, and at dozens of other places across town.

Pizza Italia (Yìdàlì Bǐsā) is the best-value pizza in town, with a 12-inch pizza weighing in at only Y40, or Y10 per slice. The ovens are specially imported from Italy. There are branches in Gubei (Map 9; ☎ 6209 4720, C6 Rotterdam Garden, 18 Shuicheng Nanlu); in Xujiahui (Map 8; ☎ 6447 3568, 131B Hongqiao Lu) (next to the Grand Gateway); and (Map 6; ☎ 6473 9994, 1111 Huaihai Zhonglu) on the corner of Fenyang Lu. It also offers a limited free delivery service.

Melrose Pizza (Map 6; Měiluósī; ☎ 6431 9802, 845 Hengshan Lu) has free delivery, is open until 2 am and gives a 50% discount after midnight for those with the late-night munchies. The Pudong branch (Map 3; ☎ 5835 7856) is next to the New Asia Tomson Hotel.

Yellow Submarine (Map 6; Huángse Qián Shuǐ Tǐng; ☎ 6415 1666, 911 Julu Lu), recognisable by its Beatles logo, serves up a wide range of excellent pizzas and subs and will deliver to your door for free until midnight. A 10-inch pizza with unlimited toppings costs Y54; a six-inch torpedo costs Y22. There are also branches out in the wilds of Pudong (☎ 5843 1113) and Gubei (☎ 6401 2774).

Shanghai has also been blessed with the opening of a **Delifrance** (Map 7; ☎ 5382 5171, 381 Huaihai Zhonglu) bakery and coffee shop, located in Central Plaza beside the Huangpi Lu metro station. It has coffee/lunch and coffee/cake specials for less than Y30.

Food Streets

For all kinds of restaurants at all kinds of budgets, Shanghai has several streets devoted

almost exclusively to the art of feeding your face. **Zhapu Lu** (Map 5) is close to the Pujiang Hotel and has dozens of restaurants. Even if you don't eat there, check out the great aquarium at the **Wangchao Seafood Restaurant** at No 324.

Huanghe Lu (Map 5), behind the Park Hotel and just off Nanjing Donglu, is another busy street, though restaurant touts can be pushy here.

Yunnan Lu (Map 5) houses some interesting specialty restaurants. Gigantic **Xiao Shaoxing,** at No 75, specialises in cold boiled chicken, while **Xiao Jinling** at No 28, specialises in salted duck. You can also get xiǎolóngbāo, Beijing duck and Uyghur kebabs at various other outlets along the street. **Chang'an Dumpling House** (Map 5; Chángān Jiǎozi Lóu), at No 2, specialises in gourmet dumplings that are as much art as food. The downstairs canteen offers cheap snacks.

A less famous collection of cheap restaurants can be found just off Nanjing Xilu at **Wujiang Lu Snack Food Street** (Map 4). There's nothing special here but there are lots of cheap (Chinese menu only) places.

There's also a growing collection of restaurants in Pudong's Lujiazui, near the Oriental Pearl Tower, which is slated to grow into a complete entertainment complex.

Grand Gateway (Map 8) has a food street of sorts, which includes branches of **Häagen-Dazs, Wujing Tang, Ajisen Ramen, Pizza Hut**, and the very tasty **Kyros Kebab**. The street spills over next door into a huge plaza of restaurants called the Hongji Free Plaza.

There's another bunch of restaurants on the 5th floor of the Grand Gateway, including **Pakim's**, which serves Indonesian fast food, **San Francisco Vietnamese Noodles**, offering fried or soupy pho noodles and snacks, **Yunnan Gourmet** and **Dome Diner**, a retro Hard Rock clone with cheap pasta, pizza and burgers for around Y50, and plenty of desserts.

Chinese

Like everything else in Shanghai, the restaurant industry has witnessed an upheaval over the last five years. Keep your eyes open for the new restaurants that are springing up with increasing frequency. The side streets around town all feature small restaurants serving cheap, local food, though you'll need the Chinese menu reader at the back of the book to make sense of the menus.

If you are staying at the Pujiang Hotel there are several Chinese restaurants nearby, though some have special English menus at higher prices than the Chinese menu. The *restaurant* in the Pujiang Hotel is surprisingly cheap, with dishes like fried noodles for around Y12. Beer is cheaper here than in the next-door bar.

Wangzhexiang Restaurant (Map 5; Wángzhěxiāng Jiǔlóu; 86 Daming Lu) is a friendly, family-style restaurant near the Pujiang, with an English menu.

For good, reasonably priced Chinese food, *Yang's Kitchen (Map 6; Yángjiā Chúfáng; ☎ 6431 3028, 9 Hengshan Lu, Lane 3)* can't be beaten. The *níngméngmì jiānruǎnjī* (lemon chicken) for Y22 is delicious and the *ròumò qiéguā jiābǐng* (stewed eggplant with pork mince), which you roll up in little pancakes, is out of this world. It's down a small lane just off Hengshan Lu.

Bai's Restaurant (Map 6; Báijiā Cānshì; ☎ 6437 6915, No 12, Lane 189, Wanping Lu), hidden down another backstreet off Hengshan Lu, is a small, clean, family-style restaurant with tasty Shanghainese food and an English menu. The *hǔpí jiānjiāo* (tiger skin chillies) is mild and sweet and there's plenty of affordable delicacies like *cháozhou tóngbái xiè* (baked crab, onion and green pepper). Most dishes are priced between Y15 and Y25.

One of the most enduring private Chinese restaurants from the 1980s, the reliable *Grape Restaurant (Map 6; Pútaó Yuán; ☎ 6472 0486, 55 Xinle Lu)* still packs in the crowds in its bright premises beside the old Orthodox church by Xiangyang Lu. Most dishes run between Y15 and Y25. Try the delicious *yóutiáo chǎoniúròu* (dough sticks with beef).

Farther down Xinle Lu, *Henry (Map 6; Hēnglì Cāntīng; ☎ 6473 3448, 8 Xinle Lu)* also serves Shanghai-style food in a minimalist retro 1930s atmosphere. The decor is probably better than the food, but it's still good and the service is excellent. Main dishes run from Y28 to Y38, vegetable dishes from Y18 to Y28. There are also cheap snacks, noodles and desserts at around Y10. The name comes from Rue Paul Henry, the former French name of Xinle Lu.

Yuan Yuan (Map 6; Yuányuán Fàndiàn; 195 Chengde Lu), near Jing'an Temple, is a typical home-style Chinese restaurant, like thousands of others in the city, except that for some reason it's got an English menu. It's cheap, tasty and worth a stop if you are in the neighbourhood.

For Yunnanese cuisine try *Shanghai Drugstore (Map 6; Shànghǎi Júshù Dào Shífǔ; ☎ 6256 5321)*, which serves up endless varieties of *guòqiáomǐ* (Across-the-Bridge-Noodles) and several interesting dishes incorporating Yunnan's famous ham. Dishes run from Y10 to Y35 and the menu is in Chinese only.

Yunnan Gourmet (Map 8; Yúnnán Měishíyuán; ☎ 6407 6031), on the 5th floor of the Grand Gateway, also serves Across-the-Bridge-Noodles, with as many as 25 ingredients. It also serves rice dishes and spring rolls, all for less than Y30.

Gaoli (Map 6; Gāolì Jiǔjiā; ☎ 6431 5236, No 1, Lane 181, Wujing Lu) is a cheap hole-in-the-wall Korean barbecue place that's popular with local students.

Uyghur & Middle Eastern

Most of Shanghai's Muslim restaurants are run by Uyghurs, Central Asians from the Xinjiang region of western China. A tasty alternative to the seafood and sweetness of Shanghainese cuisine, Xinjiang dishes consist of lots of mutton (though chicken and beef dishes are available), peppers, potatoes, spices, and delicious *nan* (flat bread). Shanghai's other main Muslim food is that of the Hui, represented in Shanghai by Lanzhou-style noodles.

A good reason to try a Uyghur restaurant is to savour the conspicuously non–Han Chinese atmosphere. Recordings of swirling Central Asian lute music complement the Arabic calligraphy on the walls.

eakfast in Shanghai: fried bread.

Bamboo baskets of Shanghai dumplings.

nch on the go in the Old Town.

Shanghai produce: colourful freshwater lobsters.

Beijing ducks, hanging around waiting for sale.

Dazzling variety of teas at a local tea market.

A street vendor prepares spicy omelettes.

The ubiquitous rice.

Beautiful waves of leaf-wrapped rice parcels.

Fish on display at a Shanghai market.

Sizzling wok of traditional Shanghai dumpling

Central Asian green tea is drunk out of a *piala* (bowl), not a glass.

The main Uyghur restaurant ghetto is Zhejiang Zhonglu, between Guangdong Lu and Yan'an Donglu. There's little point in giving names, since all call themselves the 'Xinjiang Restaurant', or *Xinjiang Mussulman Ashkanas* in Uyghur. Try *shashlyk* (shish kebabs), *suoman* (delicious fried noodle squares) or *laghman* (long noodles). Vegetarians should ask for *goshtsiz* (without meat).

Two recommended places are the tiny hole-in-the-wall *Xinjiang Restaurant (Map 5)*, at No 81, and the larger, cleaner *Xinjiang Restaurant* (also known as the *Ali Restaurant*) *(Map 5)*, at No 57. The latter has a wider range of dishes.

For a completely different ambience (think world music and warm decor, not pictures of Mecca and lamb carcasses hanging on the walls) and higher prices, try *Ali YY's (Map 6; ☎ 6415 4191, 98 Dongping Lu)*. It has an English menu and you can see the noodles being made through the glass-fronted kitchen. Upstairs is pricier, with Middle Eastern set menus (see Places to Eat – Top End).

Vegetarian

Vegetarianism became something of a snobbish fad in Shanghai at one time; it was linked to Taoist and Buddhist groups, then to the underworld, and vegetarian food surfaced on the tables of restaurants as creations shaped like flowers or animals. Today Shanghai's monasteries all have good vegetarian restaurants.

Gongdelin (Map 4; Gōngdélín Shūshíchù; ☎ 6327 0218, 445 Nanjing Xilu) has been open since 1922 and is probably Shanghai's most famous vegetarian restaurant. All the food is designed to resemble meat, and is convincingly prepared. The food and atmosphere are well worth exploring, even if you are not a vegetarian. Dishes range from Y16 to Y32, but the English menu is poor. Upstairs is more traditional and pricier.

The *Juelin Restaurant (Map 5; Juélín Shūshíchù; ☎ 6326 0115, 250 Jinling* *Donglu)* is another famous vegetarian restaurant. Most dishes run from Y16 to Y22. Lunch is served from 11 am to 1.30 pm, and dinner from 5 to 7.30 pm only, so get there early.

The *Longhua Temple (Map 3)* serves up cheap 100% vegetarian dishes at lunch time. The restaurant in the adjoining Longhua Hotel serves upscale variants at around Y20 to Y28 per dish.

The *Jade Buddha Temple Vegetarian Restaurant (Map 4; Yùfósì Sùzhāi; ☎ 6266 3668, 999 Jiangning Lu)* is a bit fancier than other temple eateries and waitresses may pressure you to overorder. Fake meat dishes and mushroom dishes like *sānsè cǎogū* are washed down with fruity *sanpao* tea (Y5). The menu is in Chinese only; if in doubt, set meals for two run to Y88.

If you're visiting the *Jing'an Temple (Map 6)*, you can also have a basic vegetarian lunch there.

PLACES TO EAT – MID-RANGE

It's tough to gauge Shanghai's mid-range eateries. While some of the mid-range restaurants listed tickle the top end, some of the top-end restaurants serve lunch specials that bring them down to mid-range. The following will generally leave your wallet about Y100 lighter, though some serve budget lunch specials.

Western

Kathleen's (Map 6; Kǎishènglín; ☎ 6445 6634, 207 Maoming Lu) serves large portions of American-style comfort food (burgers, cheesecake, burritos) at reasonable prices. Check out the excellent chicken pesto baguette (Y45) and the weekend brunch for around Y48, including a bottomless cup of coffee, from 11 am.

Always Café (Map 6; ☎ 6247 8333, 1528 Nanjing Xilu) has an excellent-value set lunch special for Y20 that runs from 11.30 am to 5 pm, and then a happy hour from 5 to 8 pm in a warm and cosy atmosphere. Choose from fish and chips, cheeseburger, club sandwich, or spaghetti, with tea or coffee included. The varied dinner menu features chef salads, quiche lorraine and tacos for around Y50 – and don't forget the apple pie (Y38).

Sunshine Cafe *(Map 6; Shēnshēn Yángguāng Kāfēitīng;* ☎ *6473 5996, 1428 Huaihai Zhonglu)* is a friendly place that serves sandwiches, burgers and a few Asian specialities for Y30 and up.

Shanghai Sally's *(Map 6; Shànghǎi Gù* ☎ *6358 0738, 4 Xiang Shan Lu)* serves up British pub grub, and is the place to head for if you are craving bacon rolls, bangers and mash, or fisherman's pie. It also offers specials like doner kebab, and meals can be washed down by a pint of warm Boddingtons. Most dishes are around Y70.

The bar-cum-restaurant ***Badlands*** *(Map 6;* ☎ *6466 7788, 895 Julu Lu)* is an old favourite for good-value nachos, tacos and burritos. Main dishes run between Y50 and Y75; top it off with a cold Corona for an extra Y35.

For a raucous and wonderfully kitsch night of sequin suits, tight pants and ridiculous sombreros, look no further than ***JJ Mariachi*** *(Map 6)*. Free-flowing tequila and a live mariachi band from Guadalajara ensure that the crowd gets going every Friday and Saturday night. Set lunch/dinners cost Y68/98.

For a more sedate atmosphere and French cuisine, ***Le Garçon Chinois*** *(Map 6; Shànghǎi Lè Jiāěrsōng;* ☎ *6431 3005, Alley 3, 9 Hengshan Lu)* is a nicely renovated house and yard tucked in the lane on the way to Yang's Kitchen. The cakes baked on the premises are especially good, and are best consumed with coffee (Y20), while browsing through English mags in the garden. Lunch specials include filled croissants (Y30) and pasta and pizza selections (Y50 to Y70).

Bon Ami Café *(Map 6;* ☎ *6280 8399, 380 Xing Guo Lu)* is a beautiful little place with decadent desserts and speciality coffees. It has a large range of tempting menu items including some good vegetarian options; expats agree it's worth the price. An upstairs bar was recently added to pull a nighttime crowd.

For standard pasta dishes, ***Pasta Fresca Da Salvatore*** *(Map 6;* ☎ *6473 0772)* has a number of outlets in Shanghai, but the one at 4 Hengshan Lu is conveniently located by the metro. Most dishes are around Y60.

For more cheap, no-frills Italian, ***Gino's Café*** *(Map 8; Grand Gateway; Map 5; 66 Nanjing Donglu; Map 8; 33 Caoxi Beilu; 918 Huaihai Zhonglu, Parkson; No 12, Lane 22, Xianxia Lu, Hongqiao; 268 Shuicheng Nanlu, Gubei)* features lunch specials of chicken, pasta or pizza, with cappuccino.

In Pudong the Australian-themed ***Roxy Music Bar & Grill*** *(Map 3;* ☎ *5831 2234, 904 Dongfang Lu)*, open from 3 pm to 1 am, is one of the few alternatives to Pudong hotel restaurants. Kangaroo burgers are listed at Y65, along with nachos, salads and daily specials.

Shanghainese

Stylish ***1221*** *(Map 6;* ☎ *6213 2441, 1221 Yan'an Xilu)* is a favourite among many expats. Meat dishes cost around Y28 to Y38, and the plentiful eel, shrimp and squid dishes are around twice this. The crispy duck (Y48) is excellent and the pan-fried sticky rice and sweet bean paste (from the dim sum menu) makes a good dessert. It's also worth ordering the eight-fragrance tea just to watch it served spectacularly out of two-foot long spouts. The service is excellent.

Baoluo *(Map 6; Bǎouō Jiǔlóu;* ☎ *5403 7239, 271 Fumin Lu)* is an amazingly busy place that's open 24 hours a day and is always packed. It's a good place to get a feel for Shanghai's exciting energy. Expect to queue to get a table. Try the excellent *rùishì niúpái* (Swiss steak), *géli shizitou* (lion's head with clams) or *shī tóuzi* (mandarin fish). There's no English menu.

The Gap *(Map 6; Jǐntíng Jiǔjiā;* ☎ *6433 9028, 127 Maoming Nanlu)* has a warm and inviting environment and good Shanghainese food. Main dishes come at around Y40 to Y60. There are branches at *(Map 4; Westgate Mall, 1038 Nanjing Xilu; Map 6; 4 Hengshan Lu; Map 8; 960 Caoxi Beilu; Map 9; 8 Zunyi Nanlu, Hongqiao)*.

Folk Restaurant *(Map 9; Xiānqiángfáng;* ☎ *6295 1717, 1468 Hongqiao Lu)* is worth a visit for its beautiful atmosphere. It's housed in a Tudor-style building stuffed full of Chinese antiques, but the food is nothing special. Standard Shanghainese dishes run from Y28 to Y50 and there's a hefty English menu made of bamboo.

Merrylin (Map 6; *Měilíngé;* ☎ 6466 6363, 1 Wulumuqi Nanlu) is an easy choice for Shanghainese food. It's in a convenient location near Hengshan Lu's bars and has an English menu that's not heavy on the wallet (mains run from Y25 to Y35). The food can take a while to arrive, so pace yourself.

Shanghai has a host of famous local restaurants, many of which date back to the last century.

Meilongzhen (Map 4; *Méilóngzhèn Jiǔjiā;* ☎ 6253 5353, No 22, Lane 1081, Nanjing Xilu) has been churning out food since the 1930s. The restaurant is in a fantastic old building that was once Communist Party headquarters and the various rooms are bedecked in Chinese woodcarvings and huge lamps. The house speciality is Meilongzhen special chicken, though the menu is also heavy on fish, seafood and the occasional snake, mixing Sichuanese, Huaiyang and Shanghainese tastes. Most dishes are around Y30 to Y50; higher for seafood.

Shenji Liang Tang (*Shénjì Liangtāng*) is a popular place famous for its soups. The Beijing duck is said to be good too. There's no English menu but there are pictures of the dishes so you can see exactly what you are getting. There are many branches around town, the two most useful of which are *(Map 6;* ☎ *6466 8777, 755 Huaihai Zhonglu)* in the back of the Hualian Commercial Store, and *(Map 6;* ☎ *5306 5777, 41 Sinan Lu).*

Wang Baohe Restaurant (Map 5; *Wáng Bǎohé Jiǔjiā;* ☎ 6320 7609, 603 Fuzhou Lu) is a 250-year-old restaurant specialising in crab dishes, from dumplings to whole dazha hairy crabs, all washed down with their own special Shaoxing-style wine.

Out in Pudong, one of your best bets for decent Shanghainese cuisine is **Lulu Restaurant** (Map 5; *Lūlū Jiǔjiā;* ☎ 5882 6679, 66 Lujiazui Lu), on the 2nd floor of the China Merchants' Building. All your Shanghainese favourites are here, including *xièfěn shīzi tóu* (crab and pork meatballs) for Y15 each. Prices range from around

Y30 for meat dishes to Y70 for the more interesting dishes.

Other Chinese

Xinghua Lou (Map 5; *Xìnghuā Lóu;* ☎ 6355 3777, 343 Fuzhou Lu) has been pumping out quality Cantonese dishes and dim sum since the reign of Xianfeng. There's something for everyone here, with a bakery selling savoury dumplings, a snack bar serving light meals for around Y10 and the upper-floor restaurant serving up reasonably priced Cantonese food for Y20 to 40 per dish. There's an English menu for everything except dim sum.

Xinya (Map 5; *Xīnyǎ Cháguǎn*) is a huge Cantonese restaurant dating from 1927, now adjoining the Grand Nation Hotel at 719 Nanjing Donglu. The 2nd floor serves dim sum during the day, while other floors serve a la carte Cantonese cuisine.

Xian Yue Hien (Map 6; *Shēn'aoxuān Jiǔlóu;* ☎ 6251 1166, 849 Huashan Lu) has a great setting in the Ding Xing garden, which was originally built for the concubine of a Qing dynasty mandarin and is now reserved for retired Communist Party cadres. There's an English menu (just about) and Shanghainese and Cantonese main dishes range between Y20 and Y40. The real draw is the dim sum, served on the lawn on summer mornings and afternoons.

Dishui Dong (Map 6; *Dīshuǐdòng Càiguǎn;* ☎ 6253 2689, 2nd floor, 56 Maoming Nanlu) is popular for its spicy Hunanese cuisine. So popular in fact that you really have to book. The waitresses are dressed up in Hunanese blue cloth and there's even the odd Mao-inspired dish. Try one of the claypot dishes. Prices are around Y40 per dish and there's an English menu (though, as ever, the Chinese one offers more range).

Quanjude (Map 6; *Quánjùdé;* ☎ 6433 7286, 786 Huaihai Zhonglu) is a branch of the famous Beijing duck restaurant, offering more than 100 dishes made from every conceivable part of the duck's anatomy. The big draw of course is the Beijing duck, served with pancakes and *hoi sin* sauce, and finally in a soup, for Y168. You can choose your own duck by marking it with a honey pen if you want to pay for that privilege. Fried scorpions with duck liver (Y58) are another speciality. Takeaway duck without all the trimmings costs Y98.

Green Willow Village Restaurant *(Map 4; Lüyáng Jiujia; 763 Nanjing Xilu)*, established in 1936, offers Chuanyang cuisine, a mix of Sichuan and Yangzhou cuisine, with some 'medicinal' dishes (food specifically designed to aid certain ailments, according to Chinese belief) thrown in. Prices vary from Y20 to Y50. There's an English menu but, if you can read it, the Chinese menu has greater variety and a better selection of the cheaper dishes. Regulars recommend the crispy duck.

Jiangnancun *(Map 4; Jiāngnáncūn Jiǔjiā; ☎ 6317 5059, 1033 Chang'an Lu)*, a five-minute walk from the train station on the corner of Chang'an Lu and Tianmu Lu, serves up Hangzhou specialities such as *xīhú cùyú* (sweet-and-sour West Lake fish), water shield soup, and *hángzhōu juànjī* (Hangzhou chicken), which is actually a meatless dish made with bamboo shoots. Most dishes cost Y20 to Y40. The restaurant has an English menu but it's of limited help; look at the pictures of the best dishes stuck up on the wall just inside the entrance.

Zhang Sheng Ji *(Map 6; Zhāngshēngjì; ☎ 6445 5777, 446 Zhaojiabang Lu)* is a huge two-storey place offering a regional mix of Shaoxing, Ningbo and predominantly Hangzhou cuisines. Look for the *tésè* (specialities of the house) page of the Chinese-only menu for dishes such as *zhāngshēngjì lǎoyā bǎo* (Zhang Sheng Ji duck casserole) for Y60. The restaurant is amazingly popular, so make a reservation.

Nanling Restaurant *(Map 6; Nánlíng Jiǔjiā; ☎ 6467 7381, 168 Yueyang Lu)*, in the leafy heart of the French Concession, is very much a hot and noisy Chinese place where locals go to smoke and to consume Y1000 bottles of Remy Martin. Still, it's a good place to go for that Chinese experience and there's an English menu (of sorts). Try the garlic clams (Y28), fish in pine nuts (Y32) or a vodka oyster shot to really get the night going.

Hot Pot King *(Map 6; Láifú Lóu; ☎ 5403 0410, 1066 Huaihai Zhonglu)*, above Planet Shanghai (stairs are in the Shen Shen Bakery), is a steamy place that's a great bet in winter. It has an English menu.

Other Asian

Everyone raves about **Simply Thai** *(Map 6; ☎ 6445 9551, 5C Dongping Lu)* for its delicious, inexpensive dishes. Lunch specials are particularly good value at Y20; prices are more than double at dinner.

Sumo Sushi *(Map 6; Yuánlù Shòusī; ☎ 6466 9419, 29 Dongping Lu; Map 6; ☎ 5306 9136, No 3, Lane 668, Huaihai Zhonglu; Map 8; 106 Tianyueqiao Lu; Map 4; Shimen Yilu metro station)* serves all-you-can-stomach sushi for Y58 from 11 am to 4 pm and 10 pm to 3 am. The food comes around on revolving carousels, so for the best choice sit where the food comes out of the kitchen. The food tastes best with a beer or, better still, warm sake. The chain also goes under the name Ganki Sushi.

Cochin China 1883 *(Map 6; Ōuyuè Niándài; ☎ 6445 6797, 889 Julu Lu)* serves pretty good Vietnamese food, in gorgeous surroundings. Dishes run from Y40 to Y90.

For a bright, friendly atmosphere and Singaporean-style food, try **Frankie's Place** *(Map 6; Fǎlán Jī Cāntíng; ☎ 6247 0886, 118 Changde Lu)*, near the Shanghai Centre on the corner of Nanjing Xilu. Set lunches like fried *kway teow* (broad noodles), Hainanese chicken or *bak kut teh* (pork ribs) cost just Y22, with one drink included. Dinner dishes vary from Y30 to Y50 and a good choice of vegetables is available for around Y15.

Irene's Thai *(Map 4; ☎ 6247 3579, 263 Tongren Lu)* has good Thai food in nice surroundings near the Shanghai Centre. Set lunches, occasional buffets and an early-bird discount from 5.45 to 6.15 pm remain the best value, otherwise expect the bill to head over Y100 per person.

PLACES TO EAT – TOP END

At the top end expect to pay around Y200 per meal and more if you dress it up with drinks and appetisers. If you can't make up your mind, head to Hengshan Lu, where the majority of expat-centric venues are waiting all in a row along with the taxis to take you back home. Many top-end places add on a government tax of 15% and accept credit cards.

Expect several top-end restaurants to open soon in the Xintiandi complex in the French Concession (see the Things to See & Do chapter). On the cards is a restaurant and a bar/restaurant owned by Hong Kong superstar Jackie Chan.

Continental

For the latest trends in international cuisine, Michelle Garnaut has taken her renowned skills from Hong Kong's M on the Fringe to create *M on the Bund (Map 5; ☎ 6350 9988, 20 Guangdong Lu)*, on the 7th floor of the Huaxia Bank. This is probably the top place in town, where the city elite and local foodies schmooze over the modern and eclectic menu. To give you an idea of what you are in for, dishes include oysters warmed with spinach, bacon and hollandaise sauce, and date-and-toffee pudding. There's a magnificent terrace view of the Bund and if you don't feel like dinner, it's worth having a drink at least. There's a happy hour every Friday and Saturday from 5 to 8 pm. M also serves Sunday brunch (Y188 to Y218) and puts on special post-theatre menus for major events. It's also *the* place to come on National Day or Chinese New Year. Expect to blow around Y300 a head here.

50 Hankou Road Bar & Restaurant (Map 5; ☎ 6323 8383, 50 Hankou Lu) serves up hearty Western meals in an eclectic South-East Asian atmosphere. Set four-course dinners run to Y200 and there are good-value set lunches and all-you-can-drink Foster's, Tsingdao or house wine in the evenings for Y100.

If you're looking for fashionable people and food, *Park 97 (Map 6; ☎ 6318 0785, 2 Gaolan Rd)*, at the entrance to Fuxing Park, is the Shanghai incarnation of Hong Kong's 1997 Group. The group also runs a popular Spanish tapas bar called *Lava*. Brunch is served from 11 am to 2 pm Friday to Sunday. Set two/three course lunches cost Y97/127.

Most dinner dishes cost between Y100 and Y150 and there are lots of imported wines.

Ensconced in a house that was once part of the Soong family complex, *Sasha's (Map 6; ☎ 6474 6166, 9 Dongping Lu)* has a great outside barbecue in summer and year-round Sunday brunch with Belgian waffles.

Mandy's (Map 6; ☎ 6474 6628, 7 Hengshan Lu) next door is good for ribs, salmon or lasagne priced between Y85 and Y150.

The draw of *Bourbon Street (Map 6; ☎ 6445 7556, 191 Hengshan Lu)* is New Orleans–style Cajun and Creole specials like jambalaya, gumbo and shrimp, though recently the owners have shifted the emphasis towards club and party nights.

Shanghai has a lot of Italian restaurants. One of the best according to those in the know is *Da Marco (Map 6; ☎ 6210 4495, 103 Zhuanbang Donglu)*, somewhat removed from the former French Concession area proper, in the Golden Bridge Garden complex.

Other Asian

Lan Na Thai (Map 6; Lánnàtàiguó Cāntīng; ☎ 6466 4328, 118 Ruijin Erlu), upstairs from the Face Bar in the Ruijin Guest House, has beautiful decor and great food, making it a favourite for those who can afford the great Thai salads, curries and desserts.

Downstairs, *Hazara (Hāzālā Cāntīng; ☎ 6466 4328)* serves excellent north Indian cuisine in an exotic Middle Eastern-style tent. Main dishes are between Y75 and Y100. With a drink in the bar downstairs, this is a great place to spoil yourself.

Tandoor Indian Restaurant (Map 6; Yìn Dù Cāntīngn; ☎ 6472 5494, 59 Maoming Nanlu), found in the south arcade of the Jinjiang Hotel, features excellent (if a little pricey) food and lovely decor. Tandoori and vegetarian dishes cost around Y60, and it also has a small lunch-time buffet for Y96, which includes one soft drink or beer. It has nice breads baked on the premises and authentic touches like *kheer* (rice pudding) and masala tea (Y38).

Ali YY's (Map 6; ☎ 6415 9448, 9B Dongping Lu) is the place to head for belly dancers, hookah pipes, Lebanese falafel and gold lamé decor. Filling Middle Eastern set dinners featuring hummus, *tabuleh* (salad), *baba ghanoush* (aubergine and tahini), *kubbenee* (potatoes and bulghur wheat), kebabs, Turkish coffee and the like cost Y200 per person, without drinks, but you get to keep the slippers. It's closed on Monday.

There are too many Japanese restaurants in Shanghai to list here, but one of the best is *Ooedo* (Map 6; Dàjiānghù; ☎ 6467 3332, 30 Donghu Lu), which has a delicious all-you-can-eat sushi buffet and other dishes for around Y200.

Wuninosachi (Map 6; Hǎizhīxīn; 402 Shanxi Nanlu), in the French Concession, is another very popular place, largely for its Y150 all-you-can-eat-and-drink sushi-and-sake deals.

American & Pub Grub

Since when are burgers and pub grub at the top end of the price scale? Since they hit Shanghai with imported beers and beef. The following are worth the money if you're craving the heavy stuff.

Paulaner Brauhaus (Map 6; Bǎojiánà Cāntīng; ☎ 6474 5700, 150 Fenyang Lu) brews its own beer and packs crowds in every night of the week, despite the near stratospheric prices. Dinner specials like German sausages and pork knuckle come at Y180 and there are plenty of cheaper snacks like freshly baked pretzels. There's a buffet brunch every Sunday from 11.30 am to 4.30 pm (Y160).

TGIF (Map 6; Xīngqīwǔ Cāntīng; ☎ 6473 4602, 10 Hengshan Lu) serves up predictable steaks and burgers. It has happy hour drink and food specials between 4 and 7 pm.

Hard Rock Café (Map 4; Yìngshí Cāntīng; ☎ 6279 8133, Shanghai Centre, 1376 Nanjing Xilu) does burger or steak combos ranging from Y75 to Y195 with a rock-and-roll theme. Happy hour drink specials run from 3 to 7 pm.

Tony Roma's (Map 4; ☎ 6279 8888, Shanghai Centre, 1376 Nanjing Xilu) is most famous for its fine ribs, which will set you back about Y150. It also serves burgers (Y85) and other grill combos (Y150 to Y170).

O'Malley's (Map 6; Oūmǎlì Cāntīng; ☎ 6474 4533, 42 Taojiang Lu) cooks up Irish stew, rack of veal, steak and chips and can pour a Kilkenny or Guinness for the seriously homesick. Bear in mind that the prices are up to Y170 for a main dish.

Malone's American Café (Map 4; Mǎlóng Měishì Jiǔlóu; ☎ 6289 4830, 257 Tongren Lu) serves hamburgers and Tex-Mex in a sports bar atmosphere. Light meals cost from Y70 to Y100; chicken, ribs or steak push the Y150 to Y200 mark.

Hotel Restaurants

Some of Shanghai's best restaurants are hidden, unsurprisingly, in the big hotels. What is surprising, though, is that some offer very good specials. The local newspaper *Shanghai Star* gives a rundown of current deals. While we were there the Hotel Nikko Pudong had a Y38 dessert buffet and Y48 all-you-can-eat dim sum on weekends. The Rainbow Hotel had an amazing all-you-can-eat-and-drink lunch buffet for Y48 and the Regal East Asia had a good-value set salad-and-soup buffet for Y38. Winter hot-pot Japanese and Chinese buffets are good value at around Y70. The Sofitel has a German buffet every Saturday for Y150, which includes all the micro-brewed German beer that you can pump down your throat.

For good, if somewhat overpriced, generic Chinese food, the *Dragon-Phoenix Hall* (Map 5; ☎ 6321 6888, 20 Nanjing Donglu), on the 8th floor of the Peace Hotel, comes with superb views and unpretentious service.

Blue Heaven Restaurant (Map 6), on the 41st floor of the Jinjiang Tower, has lunch/dinner buffet for Y138/Y260 (plus 15%), and has fine views. It's open from 11.20 am to 2 pm and 6 to 10 pm.

The *Revolving 28* (Map 5) restaurant, at the Ocean Hotel, has perhaps even better views, taking in both Pudong and the Bund. Sichuanese dishes aren't that expensive at Y30 to Y90 and it also sells cheap snacks outside of main meal times.

If it's a view you're after, the Grand Hyatt *(Map 5)* really can't be beaten. 'On 56' is an open-plan collection of four restaurants and a wine bar on the 56th floor.

Cucina has wonderful Italian dishes, breads and pizzas fresh from the oven, and the open-plan kitchen lets you keep an eye on preparation. *The Grill* offers fine imported meats and seafood. The Japanese *Kobachi* features sushi, sashimi and yakitori. The Cantonese restaurant is the flagship and features afternoon dim sum.

The Hyatt's *Grand Café* offers stunning views through its glass walls, and a good-value buffet (Y168), which allows you to choose a main course and have it prepared fresh in the show kitchen. For any of the Hyatt's restaurants reserve a table by the window in advance.

Emerald Garden (Map 9), at the Westin Taipingyang, has an excellent all-you-can-eat weekday dim sum for Y78. On the weekend it's order as you like for Y12 per dish. *Giovanni's (☎ 6275 8888)*, on the 27th floor of the Westin Taipingyang, is widely regarded as the best Italian food in town.

The best Japanese food is available at the Garden Hotel, but it's outrageously expensive. Other good hotel restaurants include *Davinci's* at the Hilton *(Map 6)*, the *Summer Pavilion* at the Portman Ritz-Carlton *(Map 4)* and *Dynasty* and *Chaozhou Garden* at the Yangtze New World Hotel *(Map 9)*.

The latest addition to the hotel dining scene is *Med_00 (☎ 5830 6666)*, in the Holiday Inn Pudong, a designer Mediterranean restaurant serving up a cool mix of Greek, Italian and North African dishes.

For a grand Sunday brunch, the Portman Ritz-Carlton's *Tea Garden (Map 4)* has a Y280 unlimited Moët & Chandon champagne-and-jazz brunch which features lobster, smoked salmon, sushi, imported cheeses, pistachio souffle, Belgian waffles, French pastries... – well, you get the picture. Hours are 11.30 am to 2.30 pm.

Other places for Sunday brunch include M on the Bund, Park 97 and the Sofitel.

TEA & COFFEE HOUSES

Suddenly, Shanghai has become coffee house chic and those watered-down pots of weedy tea that cost next to nothing in the countryside are fetching up to Y40 per pot. A decent cup of coffee is an easy Y30.

More often than not a coffee will double your food bill, though some small back-street Chinese restaurants still serve complimentary tea with the meal. If you're lucky you can find a decent cup of coffee under Y15 and a pot of tea with refills of hot water for under Y12. The only really cheap place to get a hot brew is McDonald's, where a cup of barely bearable coffee or tea costs around Y4.

One of the nicest places for a break is *1931 (Map 6; ☎ 6472 5264, 112 Maoming Lu)*, a small, warm cafe, outfitted with a 1930s theme, serving coffee (Y30), tea, and a range of alcohol. There are set meals for around Y60 that come with soup and fruit and give you a half-price drink, plus good, if somewhat pricey, Shanghainese snacks.

Bonomi Café (Map 5; Bōnuòmǐ Kāfēidiàn; ☎ 6329 7506, Room 226, 12 Zhongshan Dongyilu) is in a great location on the Bund in the former Hong Kong & Shanghai Bank building and has reasonable prices. Branches can be found at the domestic departure lounge of Pudong airport and on the 5th floor of the JJ Dickson Centre' and basement of the Urban Planning Exhibition Hall in Renmin Square.

Old China Hand Reading Room (Map 6; Hànyuán Shūwū; ☎ 6473 2526, 27 Shaoxing Lu) is a bookshop-cum-cafe in the southern part of the French Concession that is popular with expats. It's run by Deke Erh, a local photographer. Coffee is Y30, and the cafe has the cosy feel of a friend's antique parlour, with plenty of old books and magazines to read.

For a hit-and-run caffeine injection try *Espresso Americano (Map 4; Yìměi Kāfēiwū; ☎ 6279 8888, Shanghai Centre, 1376 Nanjing Xilu)*. It's open from 7 am to 10 pm weekdays and 8 am to 9 pm on the weekend. Pricey coffee beans are also for sale here.

Coffee Club (Map 7; ☎ 5382 8370, 8 Jinan Lu) is a chic Singaporean-owned place, popular with expats who live in the nearby Somerset Mansions. Coffee starts at Y30. It also serves hard-to-find decaf and sells coffee beans. Meals such as cheese pork chops, Cajun salmon, and veggie lasagne are just under Y50. There's also a set breakfast: eggs, bacon, juice, and coffee for Y29.

Shanghai Coffee Station (also known as Café de Columbia) *(Shànghǎi Kāfēi Zhàn)*, in the Shaanxi Nanlu and Huangpi Nanlu metro stations, has cheap takeaway Columbian coffee for Y12 and hot tea for Y5.

Starbucks *(Lippo Plaza, 222 Huaihai Zhonglu)*, the granddaddy of American coffee houses, has finally arrived in Shanghai, serving up endless variants of gimmicky mochas, lattes and drinks ending in 'cino'.

There are also a number of Taiwanese-style teahouses around town. One of the most famous is ***Harn Sheh***, which features a cornucopia of bizarre and delicious beverages for around Y30 a pop. Its main branch is called ***Fragrant Camphor*** *(Map 6; Xiāngzhāng Yún; 10 Hengshan Lu)* and is a nice (read expensive) place to relax. There are more happening branches at *(Map 6; 2A Hengshan Lu, 758 Huaihai Lu; Map 8; Grand Gateway)*. The decor is great, as are the smoothies.

A recent addition to Shanghai is ***Ten Ren's*** *(Map 6;* ☎ *5383 3355, 566 Huaihai Zhonglu)* and you can expect dozens more branches to follow. An extensive drink menu includes fruit and milk teas, health and yoghurt smoothies and coffees for Y20 to Y30. Snacks like custards or toast are available for Y15.

Xianzonglin *(Map 6; Xiānzōnglín, 671 Huaihai Lu)* is at various locations and incorporates a fun teahouse/treehouse design with swings for seats (look for the rabbit logo). The place has cheapish drinks (Y16 for most) and specialises in Taiwanese favourites like *zhēnzhū chá* (pearl sago tea) and fruity apple, passionfruit and lemon teas. There are many copycat places around town.

Another chain is the Japanese ***Manabe*** *(Zhēnguō Kāfēi)*, which has dozens of branches around town, including a convenient one in Huating Market and several near the Bund. You can grab a coffee or tea for around Y30, or a hot lunch special for the same price!

If you're going to spend Y40 on a tea, you might as well make an afternoon of it at the ***Grand Café*** at the Grand Hyatt in Pudong, for its all-you-can-manage high tea for Y88.

The ***Donghai Café*** *(Map 5; Dōnghǎi Kāfēiguǎn;* ☎ *6321 1940 at 145 Nanjing Donglu)* is one of the cheaper places for a cup of coffee or pot of tea (Y12) and has a convenient location if you are trekking up and down the Bund or Nanjing Lu. There are also cheap set meals. Upstairs is more comfortable but a little more expensive.

Several nice teahouses cater to the tourist trade around the Yuyuan Gardens. ***Amon's House*** *(Map 7;* ☎ *5382 0416, 452 Fangbang Lu)* is a nice place to stop, as is the ***Old Shanghai Teahouse*** *(Map 7; Lǎo Shànghǎi Cháguǎn;* ☎ *5382 1202, 385 Fangbang Zhonglu)*, which has views of Old St. The latter charges Y35 for tea and snacks or Y25 for a beer and snacks.

At the Yuyuan Gardens, one of the best places to sit and look over the mob below is in the ornate ***Mid-Lake Pavilion Teahouse*** *(Map 5; Húxīntíng)*. A pot of tea and all the hot water you can squeeze inside you costs Y10 to Y15 on the ground floor. Upstairs costs Y25 (jasmine) to Y50 (longjing), which includes some snacks. Window seats get snapped up early, so for a prime seat get there when it opens. The ground floor is open from 1.30 to 5 pm and 6 to 10 pm; the upper floor from 8.30 am to 10 pm.

Yandang Lu *(Map 7)*, running off Huaihai Zhonglu's shopping frenzy, is a pleasant pedestrian street lined with outdoor cafes and live music that is particularly nice in summer.

Other good places for coffee are ***Park 97*** in Fuxing Park and ***Java Jive*** *(Map 9)*, down a side street near the Friendship Shopping Centre in Hongqiao.

If you need something sweeter, ***Häagen-Dazs*** *(Hāgēn Dásī; Map 6; 558 Huaihai Zhonglu; Map 4; Westgate Mall, 1038 Nanjing Xilu; Map 8; Grand Gateway, Xiujiahui)* does a roaring trade in Shanghai, selling amazingly expensive ice cream concoctions.

SELF-CATERING

A rash of 24-hour convenience stores have swept through Shanghai in recent years.

Among the most prevalent are **Lawson** (*Luōsēn*) and **Kedi** (*Kědí*). A step up are the growing number of local supermarkets such as **Hualian, Lianhua, Homegain** (*Jiādélì*) and **Tops** (*Dǐngdǐngxiān*). A large Hualian market can be found on the ground floor of the New Road department store in Xujiahui. Short-term visitors will find most of what they need here, though long-term visitors will want to look elsewhere for things like bread, dairy products, wine and meats.

The former Wellcome supermarket, conveniently located in the Shanghai Centre (*Map 4*) is now called **The Market** and is packed with imported (and expensive) biscuits, chocolates, pasta, cheeses, beverages and other luxuries.

The French chain **Carrefour** (*Jiālèfú*) has branches at Shuisheng Lu in Gubei; the Friendship South store at 7388 Huimin Lu (Lianhua Lu metro) and Jinqiao in Pudong. It's currently the only foreign supermarket that actually turns a profit and on the weekend the place is packed, largely because prices are the same as those in Chinese supermarkets. You can find everything from imported wines to French bread here, daily from 8.30 am to 10 pm.

Jusco (*Map 4*), on the ground floor of the Kerry Everbright Shopping Centre near the train station, has a decent selection of local and imported goods, and an attached bakery and cheap coffee shop. It's not the best but it's near the train station metro stop so you're guaranteed a seat for the ride home.

Another convenient place is the **Park'n'Shop** (*Bǎijiā Chāoshì*) in the basement of the Parkson department store at Huaihai Lu and Shaanxi Nanlu. There's a smaller store in the basement of the Westgate Mall.

The **Friendship Shopping Centre** (*Map 9; Hóngqiáo Yǒuyì Shāngchéng*) in Hongqiao has a good selection of imported goods.

Supermarket City (*Chéngshì Chāoshì*, ☎/fax 6215 0418, home delivery) carries a wide range of imported goods. You can order from its extensive list and it will deliver to your door. Convenient locations are: 8 Jinan Lu; 3211 Hongmei Lu in Hongqiao; and 1233 Zhangyang Lu in Pudong.

Another expat favourite is **Glenmore Deli** (*Map 3; Xīyì Shípǐn Shāngháng*; ☎ 6464 8665, 501 Wuzhong Lu*), tucked down Guyi Lu (the door is disguised in a wild yellow mural). It stocks hard-to-find goodies like Vegemite, sun-dried tomatoes and Australian meats and wines. Open daily from 9 am to 10 pm.

Several hotels have pricey delis and bakeries. The best are at the Hilton, Sofitel, and Westin Taipingyang. The latter, known as the **Bauernstube**, with a little cafe attached, has probably the best cheeses, cakes, bread and meats in Shanghai.

Two of Shanghai's more traditional food stores are **Chang Chun** (*Map 6; Chángchūn Shípǐn Shāngdiàn*) at 615 Huaihai, which sells (and grinds) the city's cheapest coffee beans, and **Shanghai No 1 Provisions Store** (*Map 5; Shànghǎi Dìyī Shípǐn Shāngdiàn*), at 720 Nanjing Donglu.

All China Native Products and Specialty Foods (*Map 6; Quánguótǔ Tèchǎn Shípǐn Gōngsī; 451 Huahai Lu*) stocks more than 5000 speciality foods from around China.

Entertainment

Shanghai is emerging as the most spiritually polluted city in China. All the old evils (and a few new ones) are creeping back, with a vengeance. Over the last couple of years there's been an explosion of nightlife options, offering everything from the incredibly sleazy to the marginally chic. None of it comes cheaply, however. A night on the town in Shanghai is now comparable to a night out in Hong Kong or Taipei.

Shanghai maintains a spirited rivalry with Beijing for the title of China's most cultured city. It has attracted some big names in the last few years. Shanghai's fabulous new Grand Theatre has hosted Jose Carreras, Britain's Royal Opera and the Royal Ballet. The 1999 Shanghai International Festival of Arts featured a variety of performances, from *La Traviata* and the Kirov Ballet to Tibetan opera and Japanese pop. This annual festival, held in November in conjunction with the Shanghai Art Fair and Asia Music Festival, forms one of the highlights of Shanghai's cultural calendar.

Add to this a small but thriving club scene and a never-ending series of locally organised events (anything from Mardi Gras parties to booze cruises on the Huangpu River) and you end up with the nation's most exciting entertainment scene. Shanghai reveals a hedonism that most people never dreamed existed in communist China.

Tickets for all of Shanghai's cultural events can be purchased at the Shanghai Cultural Information and Booking Centre (Map 4; ☎ 6217 2426), at 272 Fengxian Lu, behind Westgate Mall. It often has tickets when other places have sold out. The office has a good Chinese-language Web site at www.culture.sh.cn. It also carries a monthly English-language *Calendar of Performances in Shanghai*, though you can find the same information in the local press.

PUBS & BARS

There's a lot to choose from among the bar and club scene in Shanghai, and new places keep cropping up as older places close down. *That's* magazine keeps its finger on the pulse of Shanghai's nightlife, so check for the hot spots, which come and go according to Shanghai's notoriously fickle crowd.

One thing stays the same, however; drinks at most of the popular bars in Shanghai are expensive, at around Y35 for a bottle of beer or Y40 for a draught. So if you're looking to save money, down a few stiff ones at the local corner stall before venturing into bars, or order drinks with your meal – alcohol in restaurants is usually cheaper than in bars. Most places have a happy hour from around 5 to 8 pm.

Different areas of the city peak at staggered times: Hengshan Lu's restaurants and bars are busy early in the evening until midnight; Maoming Nanlu is busiest from midnight until around 2 am. Many head for a club like YY's (see Discos & Clubs later in this chapter) in the wee hours, while the hard core finish off a late night at Julu Lu around 4 or 5 am. If you can pull an all-nighter it's interesting to see the city's late-night side.

Hengshan Lu (Map 6)

O'Malley's (Oūmǎlì Cāntīng; ☎ 6474 4533, 42 Taojiang Lu) raised the standards of beer drinking considerably when it introduced draught Guinness and Kilkenny beers to Shanghai residents. It still remains one of the most popular expat places to hang out, either on the large lawn in good weather, or the typical old-world pub atmosphere inside. There's live Irish music every night from around 8.30 to 11.30 pm, and plenty of U2 and Cranberries on the stereo at other times. It's not cheap, though, at Y60 for a pint of Guinness. O'Malley's sister pub in Pudong is Dublin Exchange (see later in this chapter).

Beni's Bar (Bèiní Kāfēiwū; ☎ 6433 5964, 705 Yongjia Lu), at the southern end of the Hengshan strip, is less expat-oriented than the rest of Hengshan Lu and feels more like a local bar. Beer is cheap at Y15.

Another good-value place is the nearby **Hello Bar** (*Hālü Bā;* ☎ 6433 0779, *237 Hengshan Lu*), with beer for Y15 to Y20, plus happy hours from 2 to 8 pm, half-price drinks for students, and free coffee refills.

Cosy, clubby **Velvet Underground** (☎ 6472 3090, *608 Jianguo Xilu*) hosts club nights on Friday and some of the best quiz nights for the expat faithful. There's a definite British twist going on here, with occasional 'lads' nights', plenty of Newcastle Brown and Strongbow cider and a sharp sense of humour running through the place. Happy hour gets you two for one, at around Y30 for a bottled beer, more for draught. It's closed on Monday.

Maoming Lu (Map 6)

This street has become a night-time magnet. During the week the place is a quiet mix of bars, cafes and restaurants, but every weekend the bars turn into clubs and crowds spill out into the streets. See the Discos/Clubs section for details of late-night dancing options. Places come and go every six months, so expect things to be different, though more often than not the locations remain the same.

Judy's Too (☎ 6548 1001, 6437 1417, *176 Maoming Lu*) has been going for ages and is still one of Shanghai's most popular places. Sunday is movie night; Tuesday there's live music from 10 pm; Wednesday is salsa and ladies' night from 9 pm; and Thursday is '80s night. On the weekend the place goes mad. Beers cost around Y35.

Dennis Bar (*Háomíng Jiŭba;* ☎ 6473 2849, *141 Maoming Nanlu*) is another good-value place that has undergone several reincarnations, including a revolutionary vodka bar. For now it's quiet and cosy, with cheap food and drink and good lunchtime specials.

In a different vein altogether is the **Jurassic Pub** (☎ 6258 3758, *8 Maoming Nanlu*), a dinosaur theme bar, complete with an over-arching Brontosaurus skeleton, live squawking parrots, and dinosaur-skull urinals in the men's bathroom. The upstairs restaurant grills salmon, ribs and teppanyaki at top-end prices.

Julu Lu (Map 6)

Prostitution is illegal in China, therefore there are no prostitutes in Shanghai, right? But if there were anything close you'd find them on Julu Lu, so watch out who you schmooze with. Located near the Hilton, the seedy and the upmarket happily coexist here. It's quite remarkable that the whole street hasn't been closed down. Aside from the sleaze, Julu Lu's strip of bars is also the haunt of the late-night crowd; it gets going well after midnight and continues until dawn.

Manhattan Bar (☎ 6247 7787, *905 Julu Lu*) is the golden oldie of late-night venues and is a popular retreat after DKD or YY's. Just around the corner on Huashan Lu is the **Old Manhattan Bar**, the first expat pub in Shanghai and still pulling in the Hilton overflow.

Badlands (☎ 6466 7788, *895 Julu Lu*) is a great little place to drift away into margarita-land. As well as margaritas, it serves cold Corona (Y35), two-for-one tequila on weekends after 9 pm, and plenty of nachos and burritos to line the gut. There's also an eclectic jukebox.

Goodfellas (☎ 6467 0775, *907 Julu Lu*) and **Woodstock Bar** (☎ 6466 7788, *893 Julu Lu*), the latter a 1960s-style tie-dye hang-out, continue the bar crawl into a cluster of bars that come and go. Just dig around for what's new on the Lu.

Just around the corner at 322 Huashan Lu is **Raise the Red Lantern** (☎ 6247 1025), a slick bar with plenty of music, Internet access, and friendly staff.

Nanjing Xilu (Map 4)

A more sedate mainstream and business-types bar scene can be found on Nanjing, catering to the expat crowd at the Shanghai Centre.

Long Bar (☎ 6279 8268, *1376 Nanjing Xi Lu*), in the Shanghai Centre, is popular with expat businessmen. It has draught Guinness and Kilkenny (Y60 a pint), plenty of specials (everyday 50% off a selected menu item) and happy hours weekdays from 5 to 8 pm and on the weekend from 3 to 8 pm. The bar is named after the bar of the former British Club, supposedly the longest bar in the world in the 1930s.

The *Hard Rock Café* (*Yìngshí Cāntīng*; ☎ 6279 8133) outside the Shanghai Centre is for those lacking imagination. It offers all the usuals – buffalo wings, BBQ ribs and BLT sandwiches – with a backdrop of live bands and music memorabilia.

Close by, *Malone's American Café* (*Mǎlóng Měishì Jiǔlóu*; ☎ 6247 2400, 257 Tongren Lu) is popular with the bearded and bellied in search of beer, burgers and breakfast. It also has pool tables. Happy hour runs from 5 to 8 pm.

Other Areas

Shanghai Sally's (*Map 6; Shànghǎi Gùxiāng*; ☎ 5382 0738, 4 Xiangshan Lu) is one of the oldest expat bars in town, imitating a British pub with darts and pool competitions, DJs and draught Boddingtons.

Time Passage (*Map 6; Zuótiān Jīntiān Míngtiān*; ☎ 6240 2588, No 138, Lane 1038, Huashan Lu) is the only place in Shanghai apart from the Pujiang Hotel that has a backpacker feel. Drinks and food start at Y15, and there's a selection of books and plenty of interesting things on the walls to look at.

Dublin Exchange (*Map 5; ☎ 6841 2052, 101 Yincheng Donglu*) has the same owners and drinks as O'Malley's across the river. The location in Pudong's Senmao International Building, with its leather chairs and posh decor, shows that the focus is on the business crowd; the place doesn't even bother opening on the weekend. The food is upmarket European. It's open weekdays from 11 am to midnight. To finish the week, it has a happy hour on Friday from 6 to 10 pm.

Tequila Mama (*Map 6; ☎ 6433 5086, 24A Ruijin Lu*) is a laid-back underground bar popular with foreign students. It offers cheap drink deals and a fine mix of reggae and African music among the more predictable tunes.

Hip Hangouts

Face Bar (*Map 6; ☎ 6466 4328, 118 Ruijin Erlu*) has lovely decor, with lots of antique Chinese furniture, and garden seating in summer. Prices aren't cheap at Y60 for a pint of Boddingtons, Y40 to Y60 for cocktails, and Y40 for coffee, but there's a daily happy hour between 5.30 and 7.30 pm with two-for-one drinks. There's also a games room.

Park 97 (*Map 6; ☎ 6318 0785, 2 Gaolan Rd*) is another chic place for a drink, and it's always full of interesting people. Added attractions include a tapas bar, Sunday brunch specials and the best Bloody Mary in Shanghai.

For the cigar-and-martini set, try *Goya* (*Map 6; ☎ 6280 1256, 359 Xinhua Lu*). Try a chocolate martini (Y45) in this seductive little hideaway near the Crowne Plaza Hotel. Look out for the teeny sign and then congratulate yourself on being part of the in crowd.

Francophiles should make a beeline for *Le Bouchon* (*Map 6; ☎ 6225 7088, 1455 Wuding Xilu*), a tasty island of brie, homemade foie gras and red wine in the middle of nowhere in north-west Shanghai. Another wine bar closer to the centre is *Bonne Santé* (*Map 7; ☎ 6384 2906, 8 Jinan Lu*), at the base of the Somerset Residence, which has monthly wine tastings.

Microbreweries

Three bars in Shanghai brew their own beer. *Fest Brew House* (*Map 5; Fēisītè Píjiǔfáng*; ☎ 6321 8034, 11 Hankou Lu) is a warm, pleasant place down near the Bund. Home-brewed beer costs Y28/38/70 for a third/half/one litre. The place also serves simple Western and Chinese snacks.

A few blocks up Nanjing Lu, you can also enjoy good beer at the *Hyland 505 Brauhaus* in the Sofitel Hyland Hotel.

The *Paulaner Brauhaus* (*Map 6; Bǎojiánà Cāntīng*; ☎ 6474 5700, 150 Fenyang Lu*) is the grand master of the Shanghai microbreweries, set in a glitzy three-storey, Munich-style beer hall with stained glass borrowed from German churches. The Chinese staff are all decked out in ill-fitting lederhosen, making it all a bit surreal, but it's very popular with well-heeled Chinese and the nightly bands get the place buzzing. Lager and dark wheat beer, brewed according to original 16th-century recipes, cost from Y50 for a small glass to Y95 for a litre.

Hotel Bars

Top of the World (Map 8; ☎ 6426 6888, *Tianyaoqiao Lu, Regal Shanghai East Asia*) is a sports bar perched in the roof of Shanghai Stadium, with a great view of the stadium. It has English sport on the TV, pool tables, and a daily happy hour from 5 to 8 pm and all day Sunday. There's a Y300 cover charge when events are staged in the stadium below.

The *Grand Hyatt (Map 5)* in Pudong has some of the city's most elegant bars. These places make a great splurge for special occasions and for the extra few kuai you'll feel like you're in heaven. *Cloud 9*, on the 87th floor, gets you as high as you can legally get in a Shanghai bar, featuring superlative views and excellent Asian tapas. It's open weekday evenings and during the day on the weekend. The *Patio Bar* (also a cafe), on the 56th floor, has equally stunning internal views of the hotel's breathtaking 33-storey atrium. The *Piano Bar*, on the 53rd floor, is more sedate and decadent, with suede walls, cosy sofas, opium beds (for drinking, not smoking) and 1930s jazz classics on the piano. It serves up whisky and cigars. Next door, the more austere *Bar Twist* serves martinis to the younger set.

The Penthouse Bar (Map 6), on the top floor of the Hilton, has a pleasant atmosphere, live music and, on a clear day, nice views. Beers start at Y47, spirits at Y57, and there's a happy hour from 6 to 8 pm.

DISCOS & CLUBS

Shanghai is beginning to attract some top-notch DJs from abroad and there are a lot of popular dance venues and even the occasional rave. Smaller clubs have parties with cheap drinks and specials every couple of weeks; look out for fliers and adverts in local magazines. Things can be quiet during the week but the music is often more interesting at these times.

Things get going after midnight in the basement at *YY's (Map 6;* ☎ *6431 2668,* *125 Nanchang Lu)*. Owner Kenny has made a few changes to the club recently but it remains a popular weekend joint. During the day, or to catch your breath, you can enjoy a drink in the tasteful bar upstairs. Thursday night is drum-and-bass night.

A bar on weekdays, *Judy's Too (Map 6;* ☎ *6473 1417, 176 Maoming Nanlu)* becomes insanely crowded on the weekend, when it often gets people literally dancing in the street.

DKD (Map 6; ☎ *6473 7988, 172 Maoming Nanlu)* rips out harder-edged and more interesting dance tracks against stainless-steel decor. This is another place that gets going after midnight.

The newest arrival on the Shanghai club scene is *Babylon (Map 6;* ☎ *6445 2330, 180 Maoming Nanlu)*, near the flower market, which plays a mix of acid jazz, R&B and popular dance hits. There's a popular breakfast buffet at 5 am for the hard core.

Q's (Map 6; ☎ *6415 3188, 166 Maoming Nanlu)* has great student parties on Friday night, with a mix of techno and Latino music and lots of drink specials. Last time we saw the manager he was hanging up coats while serving drinks and playing harmonica on top of the bar. At other times it's a lot more sedate. Anyone with *any* student ID gets Y15 drinks. Upstairs are four pool tables (see Activities in the Things to See & Do chapter). You can order from Kathleen's across the road (see the Places to Eat chapter) and they'll bring the food over to you.

Velvet Underground (Map 6; ☎ *6472 3090, 608 Jianguo Xilu)* is a mix of pub and club with kick-ass club nights and more relaxed quiz nights.

Two larger places popular with local clubbers are *Rojam Disco (Map 7;* ☎ *6390 7181, 4th floor, Hong Kong Plaza, 283 Huaihai Zhonglu)*, which charges from Y40 to Y60 (less for women) and *Real Love (Map 6; Zhēn Ài;* ☎ *6473 3182, 10 Hengshan Lu)*, Shanghai's busiest disco at the time of writing; the Y50 cover charge on the weekend includes one drink.

Galaxy Disco (Map 9; ☎ *6275 0999, 888 Zhongshan Xilu)*, in the Galaxy Hotel in Hongqiao, is popular with students, who get free entry and half-price drinks on the weekend.

For a change of pace (and beat), *Tropicana (Map 5; ☎ 6329 2472, 261 Sichuan Lu, corner of Hankou Lu)* is a salsa club with a fantastic location in a former bank/gas planning commission, just a sidestep from the Bund. The live Cuban dance music, *cuba libres* and *mohitos* put you right into 1930s Havana. The joint gets steamy on the weekend after 10 pm but go midweek at around 8 pm if you want tango or salsa lessons. Sunday is tango night and everyone takes a break on Tuesday. At the time of writing there was no cover charge and Caribbean food was being introduced.

Pu-J's (Map 5; ☎ 5049 1234 ext 8731) is a chic club out in Pudong, part of, but not in the Grand Hyatt, on the 3rd floor of the adjoining podium building. The club has two music venues, one of which features Shanghai's famous jazz vocalist Coco, cigars, wine and a decadent atmosphere. The other has live bands from the USA and elsewhere, and a dance floor. In between is a chic tapas bar. A cover charge of Y100 on the weekend gets you into both places and includes one standard drink, which come at around Y40 each. It's open to 2 am on the weekend; dress up.

Down in Xujiahui, on the 6th floor of the Grand Gateway, is a new club called *Heat (Map 8; Mèili; ☎ 5451 0002)*. It hadn't quite got going at the time of research but it promises international DJs and a cutting-edge sound system. Next door, in the same mall, is *Fire (Map 8; Huǒyàn)*, which has a bar, restaurant and live bands.

Near the Bund, *New York New York (Map 5; ☎ 6321 6097, 146 Huqiu Lu)* has faded somewhat since the heady days of the mid-1990s, but it's still worth a look; it's located in an old French movie theatre and is open from 8.30 pm to 2 am.

GAY & LESBIAN VENUES

Shanghai has a few venues that cater to gay patrons, but as elsewhere in China, it's wise to be discreet. *Eddy's Focus (Map 5; ☎ 5049 3058, 2 Century Blvd)* is a glitzy place patronised by a mix of young professionals,

expats and Asians from neighbouring countries. It's on the 6th floor of the Jinmao Podium in Pudong.

The *101 Bar (Map 6; 98 Xinle Lu)* is a discreet place which had recently opened at the time of writing. *80% (Map 5; ☎ 6329 6979)* recently opened in the stylish basement of the Metropole Hotel though may move again soon.

For the latest venues look for the cryptic comments in local listings magazines.

ROCK & FOLK

Shanghai has a lamentable live music scene. Although the Asian Music Festival brings Chinese bands into Shanghai each November, most bars feature cover bands, carrying on a tradition that once again dates from the 1930s.

There are occasional gigs in the Shanghai Stadium, but these are mostly sappy crooners or plastic pop stars. Once in a while decent bands arrive from Beijing and even the occasional foreign megastar like Whitney Houston flies through on an Asian tour. Check *That's* to see who's playing.

M-Box (Map 6; Yīnyuè Hé; ☎ 6445 9344, 1376 Nanjing Xilu) has an unlikely location on the 3rd floor of the business-like Peregrine Tower, but is one of the few venues for live bands offering anything from cover tunes to acid jazz.

O'Malley's (see Pubs & Bars earlier in this chapter) has live Irish music nightly from 9 to 11.30 pm.

JAZZ & BLUES

Shanghai has a long tradition of jazz, dating from the 1920s when Russian and Philippine bands jammed together in the French Concession. In November 1999 Shanghai hosted an International Jazz Festival, featuring artists like David Sanchez, as part of the 1st International Festival of Arts. With any luck, it will become an annual event.

The *Peace Hotel* bar features a famous, ancient six-man jazz band that has been strumming since time immemorial, but it's debatable whether it's worth the Y42 cover charge (plus pricey drinks). There's plenty of nostalgic covers such as 'Summertime', 'Moon River' and the like.

One of the best bars for live jazz is the *Cotton Club (Map 6; Miánhuā Jùlèbù;* ☎ *6437 7110, 1428 Huaihai Lu),* a comfortable, unassuming place that features blues bands on Friday and Saturday night from around 10 pm and more laid-back jazz the rest of the week. Tuesday is open-mike night and on Monday the place is quiet as a mouse.

George V (Map 6; Qiáo Zhì Wǔshì; ☎ *6466 7878, 1 Wulumuqi Nanlu),* just by the US Consulate, has live jazz and blues during the week and more raucous bands playing on the weekend.

Hot Chocolate (Map 6; Qiǎokèlì Juéshì Yīnyuè Chúfáng; ☎ *6466 8585, 21 Dongping Lu),* just off Hengshan Lu, is a new bar that's been trying to bring in jazz singers from abroad, though to little effect so far.

The *Blues and Jazz Garden Bar (Map 3;* ☎ *6268 8868, ext 85, 2419 Hongqiao Lu),* in a fine setting at the Cypress Hotel near the old Sassoon House, has live music Friday and Saturday night, but it's a long way to go unless you are staying in Hongqiao.

A few hotels such as the Portman and Hilton have rather tame jazz in the early evenings. Shanghai's most famous jazz singer, Coco, performs nightly at *Pu J's* over in Pudong (see Discos & Clubs earlier in this chapter). There's a cover charge of Y100.

CLASSICAL MUSIC

Along with Beijing, Shanghai is one of the great cultural centres of China. The Shanghai Symphony Orchestra (conductor Chen Xieyang), Shanghai Broadcast Symphony Orchestra and Shanghai Philharmonic Orchestra regularly perform classical music. For traditional Chinese music, look out for the Shanghai Traditional Chinese Music Ensemble. The *Shanghai Star* lists weekly music events.

Check what's playing at the *Shanghai Grand Theatre (Map 5; Shànghǎi Dàjùyuàn;* ☎ *6372 8701, 300 Renmin Dadao)* in Renmin Square. It's Shanghai's premiere venue for national and international opera, ballet, music and drama. Ticket prices generally range from Y100 to Y500.

The Web site at www.shgtheatre.com lists upcoming events.

Shanghai Centre Theatre (Map 4; Shànghǎi Shāngchéng Jùyuàn; ☎ *6279 8663, 1376 Nanjing Xilu)* is another place to look for big-name music and drama, as well as excellent acrobatics (see later in this chapter).

Shanghai Concert Hall (Map 5; Shànghǎi Yīnyuè Tīng; ☎ *6386 9153, 523 Yan'an Donglu),* across from the Shanghai Museum, hosts smaller-scale (and cheaper) concerts by local and international musicians, particularly soloists. The theatre normally posts a bilingual program outside its ticket office.

Chamber music is also played every Friday night at 8 pm at the San Diego Hall of the *Jing'an Hotel (Map 6;* ☎ *6248 1888 ext 687, 370 Huashan Lu),* next to the Hilton Hotel. Tickets are a steal at Y20.

The Conservatory of Music (Map 6; Yīnyuè Xuéyuàn; ☎ *6437 2577, 20 Fenyang Lu),* off Huaihai Zhonglu, holds classical music performances on Sunday evenings at 7 pm during term time. Tickets are cheap and the performers are often the stars of the future.

THEATRE

The Shanghai Opera House, Shanghai Ballet Troupe and Shanghai Theatre Academy all present traditional Chinese drama and opera and interpretations of Western opera, ballet and theatre.

Shanghai Grand Theatre and Shanghai Centre Theatre (see Classical Music earlier in this chapter) are the premiere venues, though several smaller theatres hold interesting performances, normally in Chinese only.

Shanghai Drama Arts Centre (Map 6; Shànghǎi Huàjù Yìshù Zhōngxīn; ☎ *6433 5133, 201 Anfu Lu)* is a good place to look for interesting Chinese drama. If the production is a wipe-out, take consolation in the nice old villa-style buildings of the complex.

Shanghai Theatre Academy (Map 6; Shànghǎi Xìjù Xuéyuàn; ☎ *6248 2920, 630 Huashan Lu)* often stages interesting plays in its Experimental Theatre.

ENTERTAINMENT

The *Lyceum Theatre (Map 6; Lánxin Dàjùyuàn; ☎ 6256 4631, 57 Maoming Nanlu)*, completed in 1930, is one of the oldest in Shanghai and once housed the British-run Shanghai Amateur Dramatic Society. Now all manner of acts perform here, including drama, magic, dance, movies and acrobatics (see later in this chapter).

The *Majestic Theatre (Map 4; Měiqí Dàjùyuàn; ☎ 6258 6493, 66 Jiangning Lu)* is another venue for local drama productions, as well as occasional ballet.

Another minor stage is the *Yunfeng Theatre (Map 4; Yúnfēng Jùchǎng; ☎ 6253 3669, 1700 Beijing Xilu)*, near the Jing'an Temple, which stages occasional Chinese-oriented musicals and drama.

OPERA
Chinese Opera
Unfortunately, Beijing and local operas are almost exclusively performed in Chinese and are therefore inaccessible to most foreigners. There are, however, several local opera troupes such as the Shanghai Local Opera School and the Shanghai Peking Opera House, which are worth a look, if only for the spectacle and costumes.

Yifu Theatre (Map 5; Yìfǔ Wǔtái; ☎ 6351 4668, 6322 5294, 701 Fuzhou Lu), formerly the Tianchan Stage, a block east of Renmin Square, is recognisable by the huge opera mask above the entrance. The theatre presents a popular program of local operas, farce, Yue opera and Beijing opera, as well as touring operas from Anhui and Fujian. A standing Beijing opera performs every Saturday and Sunday at 1.30 pm.

Larger venues like the Shanghai Grand Theatre occasionally stage high-profile Chinese operas such as the amazingly popular *Dream of the Red Mansions*.

Western Opera
In recent years Shanghai Grand Theatre has hosted Jose Carreras and productions of *Aida* and *La Traviata*.

Tickets range from Y100 to Y500 and local restaurants often host special post-theatre dinners.

BALLET
The Shanghai Grand Theatre's main hall has seen the State Kremlin Ballet and Britain's Royal Ballet. The Majestic has smaller performances, as well as folk dances from all over China.

CINEMAS
Beijing allows 10 foreign (read Hollywood) movies per year, to be increased to 20 with China's entry into the World Trade Organization (WTO). The Shanghai International Film Festival is held every two years in the city, though Cannes doesn't need to worry about the competition.

Foreign movies are generally dubbed into Chinese but there are exceptions: It always pays to call ahead and double-check the language being screened. Tickets are usually Y20, sometimes Y30 for blockbusters such as *Star Wars*. Cinemas that show Western movies in the original language and Chinese movies with English subtitles include the following:

Golden Cinema Haixing (Map 6; ☎ 6418 7034) 4th floor, Haixing Plaza, 1 Ruijin Nanlu Web site: www.hotcinema.com
Studio City (Map 4; ☎ 6218 2173) 10th floor, Westgate Mall, 1038 Nanjing Xilu
Shanghai Film Art Centre (Map 6; ☎ 6280 4088) 160 Xinhua Lu. This is the main venue for the Shanghai International Film Festival.
Yonglegong (Paradise) Cinema (Map 6; ☎ 6431 2961) 308 Anfu Lu
Golden Cinema Friendship (Map 2; ☎ 6412 0260) 5th floor, Friendship South Shopping Mall, 7388 Huimin Lu. Located out in the southern suburbs but conveniently close to the Lianhua stop on the No 1 metro line.

Some of the bars, such as *Velvet Underground* (Monday night 9 pm) and *Judy's Too* (Sunday night) also show films. *Yang's* (see the Places to Eat chapter) shows classic movies from the 1950s every Sunday night at 10 pm. The film is free and the beers are only Y10. For film schedules phone the bars or look in listings magazines like *That's*.

The *Alliance Française* (see Cultural Centres in Facts for the Visitor) shows French films (in French) on Friday at around 6.30 pm for Y5. The *German Consulate*

CHRIS MELLOR

e bridge to the Yuyuan Gardens teahouse with a srtiking dragon cover for New Years Eve 2000.

BRADLEY MAYHEW

e Jade Buddha Temple, home to two jade buddhas brought to Shanghai from Myanmar (Burma).

CHRIS MELLOR

A Bund newspaper vendor.

CHRIS MELLOR

Cyclists, hawkers and walkers jostle for space.

CHRIS MELLOR

Cafes reminiscent of the French Concession er

BRADLEY MAYHEW

Airing linen in the Old Town.

BRADLEY MAYHEW

The cut-throat world of the abacus trade.

MARIE CAMBON

An antique vendor catches up with the news.

(☎ 6433 6953, 181 Yongfu Lu) shows films in German every Wednesday at 7 pm.

There are plans to build two **IMAX** cinemas in Shanghai, the first on Xizang Lu, near Renmin Square, as part of a 10-screen multiplex cinema, the other in Pudong's planned ScienceLand.

Otherwise, most expats and Chinese invest in a VCD (video CD) player, which offers a far wider choice of films at a fraction of the price (VCDs cost about Y12 each to buy). Don't count on packing your weight's worth of pirate VCDs back to your home country, however. They will be confiscated if discovered.

The chain store Maya rents out videos and VCDs. Its flagship store at 306 Nanchang Lu is open 24 hours; there is also a branch in Grand Gateway at Xujiahui.

ACROBATICS

Chinese acrobatic troupes are among the best in the world, and Shanghai is a good place to see a performance.

The **Shanghai Acrobatics Troupe** (Shànghǎi Zájì Tuán) has performances at the Shanghai Centre (Map 4; ☎ 6279 8663, 6279 8600) most nights at 7.30 pm. Tickets sell for Y30, Y45 and Y60. The ticket office at the entrance to the Shanghai Centre sells tickets for this troupe, as well as other acrobatics, from 9 am to 8 pm. Buy tickets a couple of days in advance.

Shanghai Circus World (Map 3; Shànghǎi Mǎxìchéng; ☎ 6652 2395, 2266 Gonghexin Lu) has a variety of performances at its impressive hall in the far north of town. Stars include a Uyghur tightrope walker and, unfortunately, a performing panda named Ying Ying. Shows start at 7.30 pm; tickets cost Y50, Y80, Y100, Y150 and Y280.

Regular acrobatic and magic shows can also be seen at the **Lyceum Theatre** (see Theatre earlier in this chapter).

ENTERTAINMENT CENTRES

Many of the city's major shopping centres offer a whole range of diversions, from cafes and restaurants to entertainment complexes. These can prove a godsend if you

Acrobatics

Circus acrobatics (tèjì biǎoyǎn) go back 2000 years in China. Effects are obtained using simple props such as sticks, plates, eggs and chairs. Apart from the acrobatics, there's magic, vaudeville, drama, clowning, music, conjuring, dance and mime thrown in to complete a performance. Happily it's an art that actually gained from the communist takeover and did not suffer during the Cultural Revolution. Performers used to have the status of gypsies, but now its 'people's art'.

Acts vary from troupe to troupe. Some traditional acts haven't changed over the centuries, while others have incorporated roller skates and motorcycles. A couple of time-proven acts that are hard to follow include 'balancing in pairs', with one man balanced upside down on the head of another mimicking every movement of the partner below, (even drinking a glass of water!) and hoop-jumping, in which four hoops are stacked on top of each other and the human chunk of rubber going through the top hoop may do a back-flip with a simultaneous body twist.

The 'Peacock Displaying its Feathers' involves an array of people balanced on one bicycle. According to the Guinness Book of Records, a Shanghai troupe holds the record at 13 people, though apparently a Wuhan troupe has balanced 14.

The 'Pagoda of Bowls' is a balancing act where the performer, usually a woman, does everything with her torso except tie it in knots, all the while casually balancing a stack of porcelain bowls on foot, head or both – and perhaps also balancing on a partner.

have kids (or others) who start to yawn and roll their eyes as soon as you step into a shop.

Xujiahui (Map 8) boasts several entertainment centres and promises more to come. The basement of **Metro City** (exit 9 of the Xujiahui station) has Sega machines, air hockey and pool tables.

Atlantic Health Entertainment City (Map 6) at the New Road department store has bowling, an Internet cafe, ballroom dancing and video arcades.

Bridge St (*Qiáowàiqiáo*), across the insanely busy intersection (duck into the metro underground and come up at exit 12), on the 5th and 6th floors of Grand Gateway, is a new Canadian venture which currently offers the city's widest range of hi-tech toys. Attractions include an interactive mini-golf course, a 3-D cinema, laser tag and more virtual reality simulators than NASA.

A tired but well-equipped entertainment centre near the train station in the same building as the **Y Wellness Club** (*Map 4*) has bowling, archery, table tennis, billiards and arcade games. Archery costs from Y30 to Y60 for 30 arrows. The building is next to the Hanzhong Lu metro station.

Most department stores have Japanese-style video arcades, but the best are at **D-Mall** (*Map 5*) under Renmin Square, **Pacific** (*Map 8*) at Xujiahui and **Hong Kong Plaza** (*Map 7*) on Huaihai Lu. Most games cost around Y2 to Y3 for a (very short) game.

For more traditional entertainment, check out **Great World** (*Map 5; Dà Shìjiè;* ☎ 6374 6703, 6326 3760, 1 Xizang Nanlu). This wedding-cake building near Renmin Square was once the famous and salacious Great World of pre-1949 Shanghai (see the Things to See & Do chapter). There's a potpourri of performances available on different stages, including: Shaoxing opera; nationalities' song and dance; acrobatics; comedy sketches; films; magic; a Guinness World Records display; distorting mirrors; and a teahouse. Performances go on all day and peter out after 8 pm.

THEME PARKS

Jinjiang Amusement Park (*Map 2; Jǐnjiāng Lèyuán;* ☎ 6436 4956, 201 Hongmei Lu), near Minhang Metro station, has roller coasters and rides. Entry costs Y40 and includes five rides. There's also a water park.

Oceanworld (*Map 8; Hǎiyáng Shìjiè*) is in the east side of Shanghai Stadium. It's open weekdays 1 to 9 pm and on the weekend from 10 am to 9 pm. Entry is Y40/50 on weekdays/the weekend.

Aquaria 21 (*Map 3; Dàyáng Hǎidǐ Shìjiè, Chángfēng Hǎiyáng Shìjiè,* ☎ 5281 8888, 451 Daduhe Lu) in Changfeng Park, Gate No 4, is a New Zealand built and managed aquarium park. The park follows the course of a river down from Peru into Amazonian jungle and the sea. There are also films and water-life touching tanks, providing loads of fun for children. If the sharks look a bit weeny it's due to nervous import restrictions on the length of live sharks. Entry costs Y80 for adults and Y60 for kids. The entrance is off Daduhe Lu. A neighbouring water-slide park and boating opportunities on Yinchu Lake mean that families can make a nice day of it.

Dino Beach (*Rèdài Fēngbào;* ☎ 6478 3333, 78 Xinzheng Lu), in Minghang District, has a beach, a wave pool and water slides. Cost is Y40 during the week or Y60 on the weekend. It's open during summer only.

Outside the City

American Dream Park (*Měiguó Mènghuàn Lèyuán*), 30 minutes' drive north-west of the city centre, is a Disney-style clone, right down to its Main St, with lots of fun rides. Entry is Y100. Take sightseeing bus No 6B from Shanghai Stadium.

Jinjiang Waterworld (*Jǐnjiāng Piāoliú Shìjiè*), 30km outside of Shanghai in Sheshan, is an excellent collection of water slides that is open in summer (July and August) only. Entry is Y40.

Shanghai Science Land, in Pudong's Huamu district, is a huge theme park due to open in 2001. Planned attractions include lots of interactive educational rides and an IMAX cinema.

Shanghai Wild Animal Park (*Map 2; Shànghǎi Yěshēng Dòngwùyuán;* ☎ 5803 6000) in Sanzao village, near Nanhui in Pudong, is a safari park where you can drive through open enclosures packed with lions, giraffes and the like. The park gained notoriety in 1999 when a park worker was mauled to death when he left his vehicle. Entry is Y70 for adults, Y35 for kids. Get there on the sightseeing bus No 2.

Nearby *Global Paradise* is a park with miniature versions of all the world's major sites.

For more details on sightseeing buses to these and other attractions outside Shanghai city see the Excursions chapter.

SPECTATOR SPORTS

Shanghai Stadium seats 80,000 spectators for major sports events (football is the most popular) and occasional soft rock concerts. Manchester United played Shanghai's Shenhua football team here in July 1999. Tickets range from Y20 to Y100, depending on the event. The best views of the ground come from the Top of the World sports bar (see Pubs & Bars earlier in this chapter), though a cover charge of around Y300 is introduced whenever there is an event.

Shanghai Shenhua, coached by a Yugoslavian manager, is the city's top team and local matches are played in the Hongkou Stadium (Map 3) in north Shanghai. Fans can visit the club gift shop on Xizang Nanlu, just off Nanjing Lu near the No 1 Department Store.

If tennis is your thing, the annual *Shanghai Open* attracts many top tennis players (Michael Chang is a local favourite). Shanghai's local basketball team is the Shanghai Sharks, led by star player Yao Ming (all seven-foot five-inches of him).

One of Shanghai's top sporting events is the *Shanghai International Marathon,* which dodges traffic every November. The marathon starts and finishes at Shanghai Stadium.

Shopping

Shanghai is well known among Chinese as *the* place to shop in China. Ever since the 1930s the city has held the cream of China's department stores and today Shanghai is fast rivalling Hong Kong as a shopper's heaven. Bring some extra spending money; you'll need it.

SHOPPING TIPS

In the larger shops colour-coded price tags have appeared, to make spending money easier. Blue tags signify fixed prices, yellow tags are on clearance items and red tags mean that the price is negotiable. While prices in the whole of Shanghai are supposed to be standardised, it never hurts to ask for a discount. Most shops in the shopping districts in this chapter are open from 10 am to 9 pm, though government-run stores often close at 6 pm. Yuyuan Bazaar and Dongtai Lu Antique Market are both best early in the day.

In most shops, after you've selected an item the salesclerk will write a ticket and then send you to the cashier, who will collect your money and then send you right back to the salesperson, who will have your items bagged. It rarely happens that the wrong item ends up in the bag, but you should always check.

Haggling

In the markets, haggling over prices is all part of the shopping experience. In fact many vendors are genuinely upset when shoppers refuse to partake in the haggling game.

The most common method of haggling is for the vendor to display the price on a calculator, hand the calculator to you, you punch in 25 to 30% of the asked price, the vendor shakes his head and emits a cry like you just insulted his mother, comes down a little, passes the calculator back to you and so on until the price comes down about 50%. At Huating Market you may have to pay around 60% of the asked price, while vendors at the Dongtai Lu Antique Market

and Yuyuan Bazaar will often drop as low as 30%. A lot of vendors have learned to say 'final price', but this is rarely true.

Another method for the less patient is to offer around 35 to 40% of the asking price and when it is refused, smile, shrug and walk away to a nearby stall selling exactly the same thing. Nine times out of 10 the vendor will chase you down and agree to your price, but you could walk away empty-handed.

A few key points to remember will keep haggling from turning into arguing. First of all, try to get the vendor alone; saving face is of utmost importance in China and if you have an audience you'll never get the price you are seeking. If people gather around, bow out and go back later.

Secondly, try to smile throughout the entire process. Smiling will keep the negotiations light even if you can't come to an agreement. Rolling your eyes in disgust, shaking your head and getting angry are sure ways to ruin the deal and to jack up the price for the next customer.

Finally, remember that Y10 is just over US$1 and probably worth it if you are truly taken with the item. If negotiating in pidgin Chinese, be very careful of similar-sounding numbers, like 14 *(shísì)* and 40 *(sìshí),* and 108 *(yìbǎilíngbā)* and 180 *(yìbǎibā),* as these offer great potential for misunderstanding, deliberate or otherwise.

Ultimately, you only get ripped off if you end up buying something you didn't really want in the first place.

Refunds & Exchanges

Most department stores will exchange items with a receipt and some will even offer cash back if they don't have the right size or if the item was defective. Smaller boutiques are more likely to exchange for other merchandise from the store. As a rule, outdoor markets such as Huating Market have an 'every sale is final' clause. To save yourself a headache, make sure you scrutinise the item carefully and try on clothing before buying. Also make sure you have a legible receipt, and write the salesperson's name on it as well as the name and address of the shop, or get a business card.

Shipping & Customs

Most of the reputable dealerships will take care of insurance, customs and shipping for larger items, though find out first exactly what the dealer covers. Separate charges may materialise for handling, packaging, customs duty, and quarantine, driving the shipping charges above the price of the item! Also consider how much it will cost to get the goods from the shipping port to your home. Dealers should also provide the proper receipts and paperwork for antiques being hand-carried out, though customs officers rarely check tourists' hand baggage these days.

Technically, nothing over 200 years old can be taken out of China, but few antiques in Shanghai are really this old. If you are buying a reproduction, make sure the dealer provides paperwork stating that it is *not* an antique. Even the smaller market vendors should issue some kind of written receipt. Keep the receipts along with the business card of the dealer, just in case.

Shipping clothing, curios and household items on your own is generally not a problem and China Post has an excellent packing system for airmailing light items.

WHAT TO BUY & WHERE

All Chinese products and popular souvenirs eventually find their way to Shanghai, and the city is rapidly beginning to resemble one giant shopping centre. The following is a rundown of some of Shanghai's best buys.

Souvenirs

Souvenirs are sparsely spotted inside department stores, expensive hotel lobbies and small boutiques, but die-hard shoppers should head to Yuyuan Bazaar (Map 5), which has literally been established to sell souvenirs.

If you can't stand crowds or if you are hopeless at haggling, the government-run Friendship Store (Map 5), at 40 Beijing Donglu, and Shanghai Arts and Crafts Shopping Centre (Map 5), at 190 Nanjing Xilu, are great places to browse at your leisure. Prices are reasonable and give you an idea of ballpark figures if you plan to haggle elsewhere. The Friendship Store has a good bookshop, carpets, antiques, and some nice shadow puppets, as well as a money exchange open until 9.30 pm.

For more expensive but high-quality souvenirs try the Shanghai Museum Art Store (Map 5), attached to the Shanghai Museum. It offers some variety from the same old tourist hash.

Several side streets are making way for small boutiques selling unique ethnic items. At 108 Changshu Lu look for Passepartout (Map 6), Arabian Nights next door, and Made in Heaven, a few doors down. These shops sell 'Silk Road' and Tibetan handicrafts.

On the corner of Maoming Nanlu and Jinxian Lu, Mandarava (Map 6) sells kilims and crafts from Afghanistan, Iran and Pakistan. It's open from 11 am to 9 pm. Across the street, at 45 Maoming Nanlu, Wangpo Catering is a souvenir/wedding caterer with some fascinating items among the kitsch.

If you are an arts supporter, the Shanghai Arts & Crafts Research Institute (Map 6), at 79 Fenyang Lu, has studios dedicated to paper-cutting, lantern making, lacquer work, and embroidery. It also has some antiques for sale, as well as particularly nice cloisonné vases. The beautiful building alone is worth the trip. The institute takes major credit cards and handles shipping. It's open daily from 8.30 am to 5.30 pm, but try to avoid lunch hours.

The Shanghai Arts and Crafts Trading Corporation at the Shanghai Exhibition Centre (Map 6), 1000 Yan'an Zhonglu, can go on your list if you need some fairly tacky made-for-tourist souvenirs such as plastic 'Tibetan' necklaces or stuffed panda bears. Though the corporation collects handicrafts from all over China, the good items like carpets and embroidery are hopelessly overpriced.

Duolun Lu Cultural Street (Map 3), off Sichuan Beilu in the north of town, has a nice collection of curio and specialist shops, offering offbeat gems such as collectable revolutionary comic books, Tibetan 'zee' stones and antique radios.

Antiques & Curios

Seekers of curios are warned that many of those to be found in the Chinese city are excellent imitations of the authentic article.

All About Shanghai; A Standard Guidebook, 1934

Most antique shops are listed as selling 'antiques and curios' as antiques are not as abundant as the dealers would like us to believe and a curio can be somebody's ashtray bought yesterday at the Hualian department store. Antique usually refers to items at least 50 years old; in Shanghai the majority of goods have been leached from the countryside, artificially antiqued, refurbished and sold at astoundingly high prices. Until recently antiques were required to have a red wax seal affixed; though customs seem to have loosened on this, you may still see antiques with globs of wax stuck to them.

There are a number of stalls at Yuyuan Bazaar selling ceramics, 'antique' posters, pocket watches, paintings and a host of other collectables. Haggle hard as it's all overpriced – if you wander around you will see the same stuff at a variety of prices, which means that a lot of it is fake. However if you like the look of something and can get a fair price for it, buy it for what it is and not as an antique.

Some larger and more distinguished shops have developed in Yuyuan Bazaar. The basement of the Huabao Building, in the centre of the bazaar, has a selection of antiques with extortionate prices. Fuyou Antiques Market (Map 7), at 459 Fangbang Zhonglu, has a permanent market on the 1st and 2nd floors, but it really gets going on Sunday when sellers from the countryside fill up all four floors. Its range is better, but again, there's a lot of rubbish so you need a shrewd eye if you don't want to pay too much over the odds.

A more interesting venue is Dongtai Lu Antique Market (Map 7), a block west of Xizang Nanlu; the market covers both Dongtai Lu and Liuhe Lu. Here you'll find various antique stalls selling some interesting items among the Mao memorabilia. Larger antique shops are tucked behind the stalls. Prices fold to half almost immediately, so bargain hard. Once again, buy what you like and not what the dealer wants you to believe you are buying. Only about 5% of the items sold here qualify as antique.

There is a small group of curio shops at 340 Huashan Lu; the Shanghai Yingzhen Corporation (Map 6) sells reproductions of ancient Chinese art including the Xi'an terracotta warriors.

The Lyceum Jewellery and Antique Store (Map 6), on Changle Lu off Maoming Nanlu, has a whole lot of junk and occasionally some very nice pieces, if you have the time to look.

The Shanghai Antique & Curio Store (Map 5), at 218 Guangdong Lu, is a government-run shop that takes up a full block and has very interesting smaller items. Chong Shin Old Arts & Crafts Store (Map 6), at 1297 Huihai Zhonglu, is a dusty little shop good for quiet browsing. The small Zhenjianzhai Antique Shop (Map 6) at 98 Wuyuan Lu has so many curios strewn about it's hard to tell what's for sale; it makes for great discovery though.

Antique Furniture Serious antique collectors should check out the following reputable locations. Most items sold at these places are large furniture pieces, polished up and costly, but you are ensured a certificate of authenticity, they accept credit cards and they handle shipping and customs. Some dealers will charge separately for handling, packaging, customs duty, and quarantine, which including shipping, costs about US$70 to US$140 per cubic metre. Some dealers charge for shipping only, but the rest of the charges may have been compensated for in the higher price of the furniture. If you are buying a houseful it may save money to pay the one-time fees separately and buy the lower-priced furniture. Take your calculator and get the totals before you decide to buy. As always, get a receipt and business card upon purchase. Most 'antiques' have been refurbished so look carefully to see how much of the piece is original. Hongqiao Lu and Wuzhong Lu (Map 3; south of Hongqiao) are full of warehouses.

Alex's Antique Shop (Map 9; ☎ 6242 8734) 1970 Honqgqiao Lu. This shop has a polished showroom and a giant warehouse of things it hasn't gotten around to stripping yet.

Chine Antiques (Map 7; ☎ 6387 41900) 38 Liuhekou Lu, Dongtai Lu Antique Market. This is the glossiest of all and has been in business for over 10 years. It has sister stores in New York and Beijing, and a storehouse at 1660 Hongqiao Lu (Map 9).

GE Tang (Map 7; ☎ 6384 6388) 7 Hu Qing Ping Hwy, Hongqiao. It also has a shop on Liuhekou Lu at Dongtai Lu Antique Market, and is negotiable and friendly.

Kang-Da Antique Furniture Factory (Map 3; ☎ 6459 3154) 1245 Wuzhong Lu. More reproductions than antiques but also more interesting pieces than your average altar table.

Shanghai Sugu Furniture Shop (Map 9; ☎ 6219 9229) 1438 Hongqiao Lu. These pieces have barely had a spit of polish – dusty finds with more character for about 20% less than some other places and open 24 hours. Ask for Miss Lee.

Shanghai Yuanyou Culture & Art Co Ltd (Map 6; ☎ 6248 3469) 340 Huashan Lu. Open 9.30 am to 10 pm, it sells smaller items as well as furniture.

Zhong Zhong Antique Furniture Co (Map 3; ☎ 6406 4066) 28 Hongxu Lu. More pieces under one roof than anyone can take the time for; ask to see all the rooms (about 15!), including the unrestored pieces in the warehouse.

Blue Cloth

Originally produced in Jiangsu, Zhejiang and Guizhou provinces, this blue-and-white cotton cloth is similar to batik, using a starch-resist method and indigo dye bath. As it has become more and more popular, manufacturers have started block-printing bolts of cloth, which are often inferior to the handmade pieces.

Garments made from this highly stylised cloth can be found nearly everywhere, though there are a couple of specialist shops on Maoming Nanlu, between Nanchang Lu and Fuxing Zhonglu. Cloth is also sold at Lokafook Silk & Woollen Store (Map 5), at 257 Nanjing Donglu. Yuyuan Bazaar sells purses, dresses, shirts and shoes at highly negotiable prices.

For the real thing, check out the Chinese Printed Blue Nankeen Exhibition Hall (Map 6; Zhōngguó Lányìn Huābù Guǎn), at No 24, Lane 637, Changle Lu, which is open daily from 9 am to 4.30 pm. Follow the blue signs and white arrows through a maze of courtyards until you see the cloth drying in the yard. This museum/shop, started by Madam Kubo Mase, displays the starch-resist method and sells items made by hand from the cloth right down to the buttons. It has been in business for 20 years, takes pride in quality, and does not give discounts.

Calligraphy

Fuzhou Lu is the best place in Shanghai to find the 'four treasures' of Chinese calligraphy (brush, paper, ink and ink stone), as well as calligraphy paper, greeting cards and stationery. Duoyunxuan art shop (Map 5), on Nanjing Donglu, also has an excellent selection of art supplies, books, and calligraphy.

Calligraphy artists can be found at Yuyuan Bazaar and the Shanghai Arts & Crafts Research Institute (see Souvenirs earlier in this chapter). You can also find decent-priced calligraphy at the Friendship Store on Beijing Lu.

Chops

Used for thousands of years in China as a form of identification, chops remain an important tool to validate documents and to bind legal contracts. It doesn't hurt to have one made if you are studying or working in China, and they make excellent gifts.

The place to buy one is, you guessed it, Yuyuan Bazaar, where dealers compete just near the exit of the Yuyuan Gardens. Having a name or insignia carved into the chop takes a mere five minutes and should be included in the price, not charged additionally. Give your carver plenty of time to do a good job, however, and make sure yours uses an electronic carving tool if you don't want the carving too crude. A nice 1.5 sq cm chop with initials should be no more than Y50. Try to get an ink pad thrown in.

Embroidery

Eastern China is famous for its *gu* and *su* embroidery (see the Arts section in the Facts about Shanghai chapter). Very fine embroidery is rare today but you may still find some pleasing pieces; check for fine filament and invisible needle marks.

There are some nice framed embroidery pieces at Douyunxuan art shop, on Nanjing Donglu, and there are several shops at Dongtai Lu Antique Market that specialise in 'antique' pieces collected from the countryside. A small shop at 100 Yangdang called Chun Shang Embroidery (Map 6), near Fuxing Park, has a few nice framed pieces. These shops also sell tiny embroidered shoes for bound feet.

Jade

In ancient China jade was considered the most valuable of stones, more important than gold for its durability and lustre. Drinking powdered jade was supposed to bring immortality, and jade symbols were given as noble favour.

Nephrite, or soft jade *(ruǎnyù)*, exported from Xinjiang, is known as true jade and has an oily sheen. Jadeite *(yìngyù)* is the harder, glassier stone, originally imported from Burma around the 18th century. Both stones come in green, white, yellow, red, blue, black and grey. Pure white, green with gold flecks and pale white with green veins are the most prized stones. Each piece is designed depending on the colour, lustre and grain inherent in the stone.

Jade is sold in every tourist shop and market in Shanghai, but to learn more about the carving process try the Shanghai Jade Carving Factory (Map 8; ☎ 6436 2660), at 33 Caobao Lu. Jade artisans can also be found at the Shanghai Arts and Crafts Research Institute (see Souvenirs earlier in this chapter).

Silk

Laokafook Silk & Woollen Store (Map 5), at 257 Nanjing Donglu, and Jinguan Silk and Woollen store (Map 5), at 373 Nanjing Donglu, both sell good-value silk brocade for Y63 per metre. The Silk King (see Chinese Dresses later in this chapter) sells brocade for Y68 per metre.

If you are heading to Suzhou you can pick up some excellent silk there (see the Excursions chapter).

Tea & Teapots

The dark-coloured Yixing ware is the most valued of all teapots in China. Prices range from Y10 for mass-produced pots on bargain tables at Yuyuan Bazaar, to Y20,000 in exclusive teashops. Check for a snug-fitting lid, and, if you can, a non-drip spout. If the teapot trade fascinates you, visit the Sihai Teapot Museum (Map 6), at 322 Xingguo Lu, and view 1000 teapots representing 5000 years of teapot history, for a pricey Y10. You can also check out the excellent teapots designed and made by Xu Sihai.

The exclusive Shanghai Huangshan Tea Co (Map 6), at 853 Huaihai Zhonglu, or one of the many branches of Ten Fu's (there's one opposite the Song Qingling residence on Huaihai Zhonglu) sells mid-priced, novelty teapots (some change colour when hot) as well as packaged teas.

Cheng Yu Xin Tea Store, at 53 Zhejiang Lu, was established more than 160 years ago and is one of the oldest tea stores in China. It sells wild tea from Anhui, free of pesticides and chemicals, for upwards of Y200 per gram. Shanghai Zhejiang Tea Store (Map 5), at 333 Fujian Zhonglu, sells Longjiang tea, reputedly the best green tea, which has a strong aroma and pure taste. The Centre of Tea from Home and Abroad (Map 5), at 137 Daming Lu near the Pujiang Hotel, sells more than 1000 different local and imported teas. A cheaper and more accessible place for Chinese tea is Shanghai No 1 Provisions Store (Map 5), at 720 Nanjing Donglu.

Paper-cuts

Mounted paper-cuts can be found at their most expensive in hotel souvenir shops, or cheapest (a pack of 10, unmounted, for Y10, though the quality is rough) at the Foreign Languages Bookstore (Map 5) on Fuzhou Lu. Displays of paper-cutting techniques ranging from the shopper's profile to elaborate detailed animals can be found at Yuyuan Bazaar stalls and inside Yuyuan Gardens. Prices vary wildly depending on quality. Also visit the paper-cutting studio at the Shanghai Arts and Crafts Research Institute (see Souvenirs earlier in this chapter).

Porcelain

The best place to find decent porcelain is the Shanghai Museum. The shop there sells imitations of the pieces on display in the Zande Lou Ceramics Gallery; the imitations are fine specimens and far superior to the mediocre pieces you see in the tourist shops. However, be prepared to pay a hefty whack.

Jingdezhen Porcelain Artware (Map 4), on the corner of Nanjing Xilu and Shanxi Lu, sells traditional and modern porcelain. It also has a centre in the north-western suburbs, accessible by sightseeing bus No 6B from Shanghai Stadium. Credit cards are accepted and it can handle shipping.

Guohua Chinaware (Map 5), at 550 Nanjing Donglu, has three floors of decent porcelain and a few other souvenirs. The 3rd-floor exhibit includes some fine porcelain toilets!

Computers & Electronics

Due to high import tariffs there are few computer bargains to be had in Shanghai. Prices are similar to those in America and warranties are practically unheard of. If you need to buy a computer, stick with a familiar brand and ask the dealer if it comes with an international warranty, or any warranty at all. Also check if the port is adaptable to the voltage in your home country.

If you need computer accessories or software head to Xujiahui's Metro City (Map 8) or, directly behind, Pacific Computer Square (Tàipíngyáng Diànnǎosì; no English sign). Also try Shanghai Computer Square (Map 5), at 221 Henan Zhonglu, for software and office supplies, or Cybermart (Map 7; Hong Kong Plaza), at 282 Huaihai Zhonglu, for hi-tech brand-name computers and gadgets.

Clothing & Shoes

Shanghai has become inundated with brands from Hong Kong, Japan, America and Europe, and therefore sizing appears to be random – it is highly recommended that you try on anything before you buy it. On the plus side, most prices are moderate to low. Well-known brands include Esprit, Nike, Ralph Lauren, Versace, Bally, Anne Klein, and Benetton. If you are small you will undoubtedly find bargains in some of the Chinese department stores. Huating Market is a haggler's paradise.

Children's clothes are plentiful in department stores; New Hualian Commercial Building (Map 6), on Huaihai Lu, and the 4th floor of the Grand Gateway are particularly good.

Shoes are difficult to find in larger sizes and your best bet is to buy familiar brands at Westgate Mall, Grand Gateway, Isetan, Pacific and Central Plaza (see Shopping Districts later in this chapter). Shanxi Nanlu, north of Huaihai Lu, is packed with small Chinese shoe stores and good prices.

Chinese Dresses Qipaos, the beautiful Chinese-style dresses, also known as cheongsam, started as a Manchurian dress, gained popularity during the Manchu Qing dynasty and later the swinging 1930s, and are now back in fashion. Qipaos are plentiful at Yuyuan Bazaar and prices are negotiable; the cheapest shelf price that we saw (Y240) was at the Huamao Hotel near Hongqiao airport (see Airport Accommodation in the Getting Around chapter), so haggle with that in mind. Most department stores have small collections of qipaos for around Y900.

For gorgeous, unique and sometimes more expensive styles there are several small boutiques on Changle Lu, between Maoming Lu and Shanxi Lu; many of these shops will also custom-tailor. The Gesaiqing Studio (Map 9), at 17 Xianxia Lu, across from the Friendship Shopping Centre in Hongqiao, does beautiful tailoring, ranging from Y680 to Y780 per qipao. There are branches at 209 Changle Lu and 72 Maoming Lu. Wangpo Catering, on Maoming Lu, is popular for tailoring wedding qipaos.

Silk King (Map 4), at 819 Nanjing Xilu, (Map 5) 66 Nanjing Donglu, and (Map 6)

1226 Huaihai Zhonglu, custom-tailors qi-paos for around Y400 plus the price of the brocade; Y68 per metre (count on about 4m). If custom-tailoring expect a three- to 10-day wait, at least two fittings and a fee of around Y600 to Y1200, including the fabric.

Also popular, and increasingly chic in Shanghai, is the *mián'ǎo* (padded jacket). The jackets known as 'Chairman Mao' jackets in the West are known in China as *zhōngshān zhuāng* ('Sun Yatsen' jackets). Also look out for *dùdōu*, skimpy silk halter tops that are really Chinese negligees, going fast in department stores and the D-Mall under Renmin Square.

Designer Chen Jin Rong displays some vintage Chinese clothing and can create custom designs for you. Her shop, Bu Yi Fang (Map 6), is at 77 Yandang Lu.

The Shanghai Drama Costume & Accessories Shop (Map 5; Xìjú Fúzhuāng Yòngpǐn Chǎng), at 181 Henan Zhonglu, is the place to get fake beards and platform stage shoes. For very reasonable prices this opera shop also has nice silk pyjamas, embroidered bags and heavily embroidered robes.

Glasses

Shanghai has long been famous for its optical shops and it is possible to get glasses made here much more cheaply than at home. America's Eyes have branches all over town, including Xujiahui's Grand Gateway, Metro City, at 1002 Huaihai Zhonglu (next to Xiangyang Park) and several branches on Nanjing Donglu. The staff can grind a pair of lenses in a few hours, following a prescription, your glasses, or an on-the-spot eye test. Different specials are featured every month.

Household Items

If you are setting up home in Shanghai, household appliances, crockery, bedding, and furniture can be found in most department stores, as well as a few speciality shops at the west end of Huaihai Zhonglu. Carrefour (see Self-Catering in the Places to Eat chapter) also sells cheap household items with a money-back guarantee. The Swedish company IKEA (Map 8), south-east of Shanghai Stadium at 585 Longhua Lu, has fashionable and useful items for the home. The Friendship Shopping Centre in Hongqiao has an expat-centric collection of household goods. Rumour has it that American giant Wal-Mart is coming to Shanghai.

The House & Garden Superstore (Map 8), 198 Caoxi Lu, is a huge warehouse of landscaping supplies, furniture and do-it-yourself supplies. Yude Lu, north-east of the Huating Hotel, is a street of home furnishing warehouses. Home Mart, at 7388 Huimin Lu, Lianhua metro station, is a giant hardware store.

There is a concentration of interior design and bathroom shops on Jinling Donglu (Map 5).

Music

If you're after Western music you won't be spoiled for choice, so if you are staying for a while you are better off bringing favourites from home or buying in Hong Kong. Shanghai can be a good place to stock up on Chinese music though. Domestic tapes are cheap at Y7; imported classical music CDs sell for around Y130. Hustlers sell (illegal) pirated music CDs outside Huating Market for around Y8 but you should be careful here and never buy in bulk – you can never quite be sure what you are getting. Before buying, ask the shop to test the tape or CD on its stereo.

Shanghai Music Store (Map 5), at 365 Xizang Zhonglu just off Nanjing Lu, has a typical selection of Mariah Carey and Celine Dion, plus Chinese tapes for less than US$1.

The Foreign Languages Bookstore (Map 5) often plays nice Chinese music, tending towards the New Age end of the spectrum, and will play CDs for you to sample.

China National Publications Import & Export Co (Map 4; ☎ 6215 0555), at 555 Wuding Lu, is Shanghai's oldest CD shop. It's a bit out of the way but it has one of the city's best collections of imported classical music and will order anything you want.

The Friendship Shopping Centre in Hongqiao (Map 9) sells a decent range of imported CDs and a few tapes, though they are at Western prices.

China produces lovely musical instruments, such as the *èrhú* (vertical fiddle), *pípa* (lute) and *gǔzhēng* (zither). For both Chinese and Western musical instruments try the various shops on Fenyang Lu, catering to students attending the Conservatory of Music. Other places include the Shanghai Musical Instrument Factory Store (Map 5), at 114 Nanjing Donglu, or the 5th floor of Shanghai No 1 Department Store. Stalls at Yuyuan Bazaar sell *xūn* (traditional egg-shaped wood instruments).

Photographic Supplies

Shanghai is one of the few places in China where slide film is readily available. Slide film (ASA100) costs around Y45 for 36 exposures; slide developing costs around Y45 (24 exp) and Y60 (36 exp) and takes 24 hours.

Shanghai's foremost photographic supplies shop is Guan Long Camera Shop (Map 5), at 190 Nanjing Donglu, where you can get all kinds of film and processing and almost any camera accessory you could ask for. There's another branch at 227 Jinling Donglu, just west of Henan Lu.

New Ray Photo Making Ltd (Map 6; ☎ 6433 0101), at 1650 Huaihai Zhonglu near the Shanghai Library, offers an excellent slide processing service at slightly lower rates than Guan Long.

Sporting Goods & Outdoor Gear

Some department stores, sporting goods stores and Huating Market sell backpacks and sleeping bags, though you'll have to search a bit to find good hiking boots.

Weald Outfitter (Map 7; ☎ 6372 4180), at 22 Chongqing Nanlu, has a good but spartan collection of tents, packs, climbing and outdoor gear including Teva sandals and Timberland boots.

Whitewave Outdoor Gear (Map 6; ☎ 6437 3461), at 247 Wulumuqi Zhonglu, sells backpacks, tents, sleeping bags and other camping gear. Almost all are Chinese-made but not bad quality. It also apparently rents gear for local trips. Nextage, in Pudong, also has a small selection of tents and camping supplies.

Ozark (Map 6; ☎ 6226 6825) at 1 Jiangsu Lu in the north-west of town, sells its own brand of rucksacks, Gore-Tex jackets and climbing accessories.

For tennis rackets and sports gear try Sport City, on the 5th floor of the Westgate Mall at 1038 Nanjing Xilu, or in the basement of the Grand Gateway at Xujiahui. The 7th floor of the Shanghai No 1 Department Store is also devoted to sports.

Toiletries

For foreign-brand over-the-counter medicines or toiletries, try Watson's *(Qūchénshì)* in the Shanghai Centre (Map 4), the Kerry Everbright Centre (Map 4), and at 787 Huaihai Zhonglu (Map 6). For contact lens solution and the like try one of the many branches of America's Eyes (see Glasses earlier in this chapter).

SHOPPING DISTRICTS

Shanghai is catching up with commercial centres like Hong Kong, but it still has a long way to go. The traditional shopping streets were always Nanjing Lu and Huaihai Lu, but now it seems almost every side street is full of boutiques and shops. If wandering aimlessly for miles poking in to every boutique is your shopping style then stick to Nanjing and Huaihai, where you will find Western, Japanese and Chinese clothing boutiques jammed between the major department stores. If you shop purely out of necessity, the department stores listed in this chapter carry nearly everything, including the items sold in the jammed boutiques.

Huaihai Lu (Maps 7 & 8)

This is definitely *the* shopping street in Shanghai. Shops begin on the corner of Changshu Lu (Changshu Lu metro station). Here Maison Mode (Map 6) houses your major wallet drainers – Bally, Prada, Cartier, Gucci – or carry on 100m and find designer copycats at Huating Market for peanuts.

Huaihai Lu peaks near the Time Plaza and peters out around Songshan Lu, though towers are bursting through the ground at an alarming rate and more department stores are destined to appear. Don't forget to peek down the side streets. Yangdang Lu has some nice small boutiques and outdoor cafes. Shaanxi Nanlu, Maoming Nanlu Lu and Changshu Lu are also worth a browse.

There are too many department stores on Huaihai to mention but the following are worth a look; almost all have a food court and arcade on the top floor and the upper floors often have bargain tables.

Hong Kong Plaza (Map 7) has an arcade in the basement, Rojam disco on the top floor and great Columbian coffee at Café City, as well as a sparse selection of boutiques.

Isetan (Map 6) is six floors of great brand-name shopping; there's an arcade on the 5th floor, and Pucci's Café on the 4th floor.

JJ Dickson Centre (Map 6) is a little north of Huaihai at 400 Changle Lu. It houses imported, upmarket and very expensive men's and ladies' fashions.

New Hualian Commercial Building (Map 6) is the place to go for kids. Brands like Cherokee, Sesame Street and Pooh, as well as Lego and Silverlit, are spread out over three floors. It's also a good place to get school supplies.

Parkson (Map 6; Bǎishèng Gòuwù Zhōngxīn) houses some mid-priced foreign (Nike, Elle, Esprit, Revlon) and upscale Chinese brands. The basement has a well-stocked supermarket with foreign goodies and access to Shanxi metro station. The ground floor has an ATM.

Printemps (Map 6) is an elegant and elite department store dropping names like Finity and Anne Klein. The top floor, nestled in a wine bar, is reserved for Givency and Christian Lacroix and there's also the Champs Elysees Café.

Shui On Plaza and Central Plaza (Map 7) connect by a sky bridge. Shui On is a pleasant department store where you can find everything from baby strollers to air-conditioners, as well as foreign and upscale Asian brand-name clothing. Bargain close outs are usually on the sixth floor. Central Plaza has a Delifrance, with great breakfast and lunch specials, a DHL, and hair and nail salons. The basement connects to the Huangpi Nanlu metro station.

Huating Market (Map 6)

Just off Huaihai, Huating Market is famous for its bargains, but beware: These are fakes, folks. Some are so obviously fake that they carry three different designer labels on one garment! Others may have been samples by the manufacturer but never

made it to the big world – even the vendors don't know the difference. Despite the misleading labels, some items are decent quality in their own right. Check every zip and snap and try the rub test to make sure the dye doesn't rub off onto your fingers – we once had a friend leave a streak of blue while swishing down the ski slopes. Finally, make sure clothing fits; there are no return policies here, and remember to haggle hard. However, if an item proves to be truly defective you can state your case at a little office down alley No 71 in the market.

Nanjing Lu (Maps 5 & 7)

Nanjing Lu has been known for centuries as China's golden mile. In the 1920s the department stores Sincere, Wing On, Sun Sun and Da Sun featured imported goods from Paris, London and New York. Once supreme, it's now looking a bit frayed and has slipped a few notches compared with the emerging luxury option of Huaihai Lu and other shopping areas. However, Nanjing Lu still attracts millions of tourists with offers of imported brands, eateries, and traditional Chinese shops.

Nanjing shops stretch for about 5km from the Bund to Chengdu Lu, though there are several sparse areas. Mercifully, a pedestrian strip has been established from Xizang Lu, just east of Renmin Park, to Henan Lu, allowing shoppers to browse without the hassles of traffic, or ride a toy train for Y2 from one end of the strip to the other. Most shops on Nanjing Lu are Chinese department stores, with a few foreign brands throw in, and a good hunt can lead to some bargains. The Hualian department store (formerly No 10, and before that Wing On), at 635 Nanjing Donglu, and the No 1 Department Store, at 830 Nanjing Donglu, are fascinating places to browse if you can stand the crowds. The No 1 Department Store averages 150,000 shoppers a day and holds 12 levels of merchandise. The 5th floor has gifts and souvenirs.

Favourite among expats, the Westgate Mall (Map 4; Méilóngzhèn Guǎngchǎng), attached to another branch of Isetan, is a far trek west of Renmin Park, or a Y10 taxi

SHOPPING

ride. Nearby are branches of Benetton and Esprit.

Yuyuan Bazaar (Map 5)

Though it wasn't originally set up as a shopping district, Yuyuan Bazaar has become exactly that. All souvenirs can be found here, along with some alleged antiques and some interesting shops specialising in things like fans, scissors and walking sticks. Others carve chops, paint calligraphy and cut onlookers' profiles from thin sheets of paper. Pearls from Jiangsu's Tai Lake are sold everywhere and can be a good buy if you have a good eye.

Prices are generally tripled, even in the department stores, so if you enjoy haggling you can come home loaded with teapots, silks, pearls, chops, jade, blue cloth, and a few dubious curios.

The adjacent Old Street is lined with specialist tourist shops selling everything ranging from Jinshan folk paintings (Nos 306, 372, 411), old photographs of Shanghai (No 346), woodcuts (No 389), blue cloth (No 440), coins and old money (No 423), and buddhas (No 349). There are also various shops selling temple gods and other accessories that will come in handy when worshipping your ancestors.

D-mall & Hong Kong Shopping Plaza (Map 5)

Located under Renmin Park (access through Renmin Park Station), D-mall and Hong Kong Shopping Plaza (Díměi Gòuwù Zhōngxīn) are a merging maze of boutiques with swanky Japanese, Chinese and Western styles, refreshingly different than the repeats along Nanjing and Huaihai, and with reasonable prices.

Xujiahui (Map 8)

Easily accessible by metro, Xujiahui has six department stores bordering the busy intersection. It is easier to get to the department stores by using the underground metro walkways than to cross the congested streets. The newest and brightest mall is the Grand Gateway (Gǎnghuì Guǎngchǎng; metro exit 12), China's largest mall, with 250 outlets. The basement has a Lianhua supermarket, Maya CD/DVD sales and rentals and a Kodak Imaging Centre. The complex also houses about 30 restaurants and plenty of entertainment options on the 6th floor.

Pacific department store (Tàipíngyáng Bǎihuò; metro exit 13) isn't as flash as the Gateway but it's packed with some very decent brands that are continually on sale. The 8th floor has video games and a food court. The Orient Shopping Centre (metro exit 11) carries Chinese and lesser Western brands and is a good place for household items. The basement supermarket has a great selection of chocolate, ice cream, coffee and alcohol. The Hui Jin Department Store (metro exit 14) is worth a look for sales on Chinese and foreign brand names; the basement has a decent supermarket with some imported items. Shanghai No 6 Department Store (Dìliù Bǎihuò; metro exit 14) is popular with the locals and is usually crowded.

Metro City (metro exit 9) is filled with shops selling electronics, computers, computer accessories, games and software. Also inside is a good arcade and food court, a Pizza Hut and a KFC.

Pudong

As the district hots up, more and more strip malls and department stores are bound to make their debut along Pudong Nanlu and Central Ave (Map 5). At the time of writing the Cai Tai Riverfest Mall (Map 5) was under construction near the Jinmao Tower. Nextage (Map 5; also called Yaohan), Asia's largest department store (only second in size to Macy's in New York), on the corner of Pudong Lu and Zhangyang Lu, offers 150 retail outlets selling from 100,000 sq metres of floor space. The 10-storey monster was originally a joint venture between Japanese Yaohan and Shanghai's No 1 Department Store until Yaohan went bust. Across the street, Times Square sells mostly Chinese labels.

Excursions

When Shanghai's crowds, claustrophobia and concrete begin to grate there are plenty of day and overnight trips to be made outside Shanghai. Hangzhou and Suzhou are two of eastern China's cultural highlights and if you need to get away from it all Putuoshan offers a fine break. Most visitors to Shanghai head further afield to Yunnan and Tibet or flee China for the ease of Thailand.

CITY SIGHTSEEING BUSES

A fleet of green sightseeing buses, based at the east end of Shanghai Stadium, shuttles tourists to most places of interest outside the city centre. The buses are convenient, comfortable and punctual, and are without a doubt the best way to see the sights around Shanghai. There's no need to book a seat – just turn up. For departure information in Chinese call ☎ 6426 5555. Current bus routes are as follows:

No 1A to Songjiang's Square Pagoda (Y10); every 30 minutes from 7.30 am to 5.30 pm
No 1B to Sheshan (Y10); every 30 minutes from 7.15 am to 4.50 pm
No 2 to Nanhui, via Shanghai Wild Animal Park (Y14); every 15 minutes from 6.15 am to 7.15 pm
No 4 to Qingpu via Shanghai Zoo (Y4), Qushui Park, Zhujiajiao (Y12), Grand View Garden (Y16), and sometimes on to Zhouzhuang; every 30 minutes from 7 am to 3 pm
No 5 to Chongming Dongping Forest Park (Y6)
No 6A to Nanxiang (Y6) and Jiading (Y10); every 40 minutes from 7.30 am to 7 pm
No 6B to Anting, via Jingdezhen Ceramics Gallery (Y2), American Dream Park (Y6); every 30 minutes from 6.30 am to 5.20 pm
No 8 Gongqing Forest Park (Y6)

The bus offers return-trip fares *(tàopiào)* that include entry fees. You don't save much money this way, but it may save some hassle.

AROUND SHANGHAI

The sights listed in this section are in Shanghai Municipality and can be done as day trips. Some sites can even be reached by intrepid bikers, though to really enjoy the trip you may want to transport yourself and your bike part way out of the city in a taxi first.

For details on some of the theme parks surrounding Shanghai see the Entertainment chapter.

Songjiang 松江
Sōngjiāng

Songjiang County, 30km south-west of Shanghai, was thriving when Shanghai was still a dream in an opium trader's eye, though you only get a sense of its antiquity in the timeless backstreets in the west and south-west of town.

The most famous monument is the **Square Pagoda** (Fāng Tǎ), in the south-east of the town. The 48.5m nine-storey tower was built between 1068 and 1077 as part of the Xingshengjiao Temple, which is long gone. During reconstruction in 1975 a brick vault containing a bronze buddha and other relics was discovered under foundations.

The screen wall in front of the pagoda shows a legendary *tan,* a monster of such greed that it tried to drink the sea and ended up killing itself. The Buddhist frieze teaches that desire leads to disaster. Entry to the pretty park is Y5.

Next to the park is the mildly interesting **Songjiang Museum** (Sōngjiāng Bówùguǎn). Entry is Y2 and the museum is closed daily from noon to 1 pm and on Monday.

Other minor attractions in town include the **Xilin Pagoda**, a 30-minute walk away in the west of town, and the **Toroni Sutra Stela**, built in AD 859, which is the oldest Buddhist structure in Shanghai. The tower stands rather incongruously in the Zhongshan Primary School, directly opposite the Songjiang Hotel. You are allowed in to look but be prepared to end up shadowed by a trail of nine-year-olds following you like the Pied Piper.

The **Songjiang Mosque** (Sōngjiāng Qīngzhēnsì), in the west of town, is worth a visit. Built between 1341 to 1367 in the

Chinese style, it's one of the oldest mosques in China. The minaret, the Bangke Tower, stands to the east and the ornate mihrab points the way to Mecca in the west. There are around 300 Muslims in Songjiang and worshippers converge on the mosque every Friday lunch time. Entry is Y5. To get to the mosque head south from the junction of Zhongshan Zhonglu and Renmin Nanlu, and follow a signposted alley leading off to the west.

South of the mosque is the **Zuibaichi**, or Pool of Drunken Bai. The park is built around the villa of the painter Gu Dashen, who built the pool in 1659 in honour of Li Bai (or Li Bo), the famous Tang poet. Bai drowned when he fell drunk into a pond, trying to grasp a reflection of the moon. Entry is Y5.

Getting There & Away

The best way to get to Songjiang is by sightseeing bus No 1A (see City Sightseeing Buses earlier in this chapter). If you don't fancy the walk between sights, cycle rickshaws ferry people around town for a few kuai. It's possible to combine a visit to Songjiang with Sheshan (see later in this chapter) but you'd need to take a taxi to Sheshan (around Y30), before taking the sightseeing bus back to Shanghai.

Sheshan 佘山

Shéshān

Sheshan National Tourist Vacation Area (Shéshān Guójiā Lǚyóu Dùjià Qu) is 30km south-west of Shanghai and is the only part of Shanghai to have anything that even remotely resembles a hill.

The main reason to come out here is to see the Catholic **Sheshan Cathedral**, perched magnificently on the top of the hill. The original Holy Mother Cathedral was built here between 1863 and 1866, and the current Basilica of Notre Dame was completed in 1935. The most interesting way to climb the hill is via the south gate, which takes you up along a Via Dolorosa, past a smaller church (built 1894), a shop selling crucifixes and statues of the Virgin Mary, and several holy shrines. You can also take

a cable car up to the top for Y15 return, or Y8 down.

Sunday is an interesting time to visit, as is May when many local Catholics make pilgrimages here. There's a Y8 entry fee to the hill and Y2 to the church, where photography is not allowed.

Just next to the church is the **Jesuit observatory** (Tiānéntái), built in 1900, which you can look around for Y6. Its modern counterpart stands to the west. China's latest hi-tech earthquake monitoring system in the East China Sea was named after the observatory. On the east side of the hill is the 20m, seven-storey **Xiudaozhe Pagoda** (AD 976–984).

On the east hill is the **Forest Park** (Sēnlín Gōngyuán), which has a lookout tower on the top of the hill and an impressive aviary (*bǎiniǎoyuàn*) that holds 10,000 birds. Entry is Y18.

Also in the area is the tacky Europa World Theme Park (Y30) and Jinjiang Waterworld (Y40); the latter has an excellent collection of water slides and is open in summer (July and August) only.

Intrepid explorers can head 8km south-west of Sheshan to Tianmashan and the **Huzhu Pagoda** (Map 2; Hùzhū Tǎ), built in AD 1079 and known as the leaning tower of China. The 19m-high tower started tilting 200 years ago and now has an inclination exceeding the tower at Pisa by 1.5°. There are occasional minibuses from Sheshan to Tianmashan village, which is at the foot of the hill. A better option is to take a taxi (Y20) or a motorcycle taxi (Y10).

Sightseeing bus No 1B heads to Sheshan regularly from Shanghai (see City Sightseeing Buses earlier in this chapter), as do private minibuses (Y6). If you want to combine a visit to Sheshan with Songjiang, head to Sheshan first as it's easier to catch a bus on to Songjiang than vice versa. A taxi to/from Shanghai costs around Y70 one way.

Sun Island 太阳岛

Tàiyáng Dǎo

This tourist resort (☎ 5983 0888), about 45km south-west of Shanghai on an island in the Maohe River, has a whole range of summer activities including an open-air

EXCURSIONS

swimming pool, yachting, tennis, horse riding, boat trips and an 18-hole golf course. Tickets costs Y60 in summer, Y30 in winter, plus an additional charge for most activities.

Shuttle buses go to the island frequently from the bus station at the intersection of Zhongshan Nanlu and Caoxi Lu, across from the Huating Hotel.

Jiading 嘉定
Jiàdìng

Jiading is a laid-back town surrounded by a canal, about 20km north-west of Shanghai. Together with Nanxiang, the town makes for a pleasant day excursion, especially if you pack a picnic for one of the parks.

Sightseeing bus No 6A drops passengers at the **Dragon Meeting Pond** (Huìlóng Tán), a peaceful garden built in 1588 and named after the five streams that feed into the central pool. Entry is Y5.

Exit out of the west gate to get to the **Confucius Temple** (Wén Miào), built in 1219. On the way you'll pass 72 carved lions, representing the 72 outstanding disciples of Confucius. The temple houses the **Jiading County Museum**, which exhibits the history of the county as well as some local bamboo carving. The Confucius Temple is open daily from 8 to 11.30 am, and 1.30 to 4.30 pm.

A five-minute walk north of the temple along Nan Dajie takes you to the seven-storey **Fahua Pagoda**, and the interesting cobbled and canalled heart of the town. There are several enticing shops and places to eat around the pagoda.

Five minutes' walk north-east along the canal on Dong Dajie takes you to the enchanting **Garden of Autumn Clouds** (Qiūxiápǔ), one of the finest gardens around Shanghai (entry Y8). Nearby, across the canal, is a huge produce market.

On the way back to Shanghai, sightseeing bus No 6 passes through the town of Nanxiang, where (if you are not gardened out) you can stop off at the large **Garden of Ancient Splendour** (Gǔyì Yuán), which was built between 1522 and 1566, and then rebuilt in 1746.

Zhujiajiao
Zhūjiājiǎo 朱家角

This town, on the road to Dianshan Lake and Zhouzhuang, has a lovely historic centre of ancient houses. The main sight is the 72m-long **Fangseng Bridge**, built in 1571 and rebuilt in 1814, with five arches spanning the Caogang River. Sightseeing bus No 4 can drop you there.

Dianshan Lake & Grand View Garden 淀山湖、大观园
Diànshān Hú & Dàguān Yuán

Dianshan Lake, covering a water surface of 6300 hectares, supplies much of Shanghai's freshwater fish. In summer a water-sports centre and yacht club operate on the northeast side of the lake, near Shanghai Country Club.

The major draw for Chinese tourists (but probably of less interest to foreigners) is the **Grand View Garden**, a mock-up of scenes and buildings from the famous Chinese classic novel *Hongloumeng (Dream of the Red Mansions)*. Entry is Y40.

Across the road is the **Minorities Cultural Village** (Y30), which has a few replicas of Thai-style pagodas and Dong drum towers. Entry to both parks, as well as the nearby Qingyun Pagoda, costs Y60. The area has beautiful plum blossom in March and April.

Sightseeing bus No 4 runs to the Grand View Garden, passing en route the pretty Guanwang Temple, with its impressive lake-shore location.

ZHOUZHUANG 周庄
Zhōuzhuāng

Set in the countryside 38km south-east of Suzhou, Zhouzhuang offers a step back in time into what is touted as the first water town of China. Established more than 900 years ago, Zhouzhuang boasts 14 bridges and a vast number of buildings (more than 60%) from the Yuan, Ming and Qing dynasties. Unfortunately, Zhouzhuang has been given the Chinese tourism make-over and from the swarms of rickshaw drivers to the lines of restaurants and souvenir stalls which now dominate the centre of the Old Town, little rings true. The town is *extremely* popular with Chinese tourists, though surprisingly untouched by those from abroad.

Despite the crowds, a day in Zhouzhuang is worthwhile. The cobbled lanes, arched bridges and canals of the Old Town are superbly picturesque, confirmed by the many painters seated alongside the canals. The best bet is to head off the main streets, to where many of the locals continue to go about their day, sitting on their steps, making lace or fishing in the canals with cormorants.

Orientation

The bus station was recently moved 2km north-east of the Old Town, doubtless in an attempt to boost the flagging rickshaw trade. It's an easy 20-minute walk over the bridge into town, or take a rickshaw (Y4). To find the Old Town continue to the Zhouzhuang Travel Service, head east on Quangong Lu and take the first right onto Quanfu Lu. Maps are available everywhere for Y2.5.

Things to See

Entrance to the **Old Town** of Zhouzhuang is through the Ancient Memorial Archway. South of the archway, Zhouzhuang's narrow cobbled alleys are entirely pedestrianised. Within the Old Town are 10 sights including temples, gardens and the former homes of officers from the Qing and Ming dynasties, many of which are still inhabited by artisans and workers.

The **Hall of Shen's Residence** (Shēn Tīng) is considered to be the best of these houses, containing seven courtyards and more than 100 rooms, each connected to a main hall. Inside, wood carvers and weavers are hard at work. South of here, the Hall of Zhang's Residence dates back more than 500 years and was home to a local officer. This house has six courtyards and more than 70 rooms. Running through the residence is the Ruojing River.

At the southern end of town, **Quanfu Temple** (Quánfú Sì) contains 21 gold buddhas plus a large bronze buddha measuring more than 5m high. The temple is surrounded by pagodas and courtyard buildings, extending into **Nanhu Garden** (Nánhú Yuán). This garden was built for Zhang

Jiying, a literary man of the Jin dynasty, and consists of bridges crisscrossing over the water.

The **Zhouzhuang Museum** (Zhōuzhuāng Bówùguǎn) is home to nearly 1000 artefacts, including a number from the local fishing and artisan industries.

All of the sights are visited on one ticket (Y60), which is available at the entrance to any of the sights. All sights close at 5 pm. Almost all of the signs and captions within the sights are in Chinese only.

For a **boat tour** of the canal, head south of the Double Bridge on Nan Shijie in the south-west of town. Half-hour trips cost Y40 to Y60 per boat, holding six to eight people.

Note the imposing **Quanfu Pagoda** (Quánfú Tǎ) just north of the Old Town. The pagoda was built in 1987 to hide the water tower, in preparation for the tourism boom promoted by the provincial government. The campaign seems to have been an enormous success, with Zhouzhuang recently declared an International Heritage Site by the United Nations.

Places to Stay

Zhouzhuang can easily be visited on a day trip from Shanghai or as a stopover en route to Suzhou.

The *Fountaineblean Double Bridge Holiday Inn* (Fèndānshān Qiáodùjià Chuēn, ☎ 721 1549) has shabby doubles for Y200 but the location in the Old Town, with a view of the water, more than makes up for it. To find the hotel, head south on Nan Shijie and take the first left after the Hall of Shen's Residence.

Just north of the bus station is the upmarket *Yunhai Holiday Villa* (Yúnhǎi Dùjiàcūn, ☎ 721 1977, 5 Daqiao Lu). Standard rooms start at a reasonable Y220, with villas ranging from Y350 to Y1800.

Places to Eat

In the central area of the Old Town every other building is a restaurant and your best bet is to take your time and look for one with nice ambience and views. Check the prices first as many cater to Chinese tour groups at astronomical prices. For reasonable prices and outdoor seating try the southern end of Nan Shijie and Nan Hujie, on either side of the canal between Longxing and Baoen Bridges. You can also find cheap eats in the small *restaurants* between Zhenfeng and Puqing Bridges, at the western end of town. An area just north of the Double Bridge has several open-air *teahouses*.

Shopping

A number of local specialities are available in Zhouzhuang, including woven goods, wood carvings, sweets, lace and Yixing teapots. Of particular notice are the locally harvested freshwater pearls. These are available at extremely reasonable prices, in every form, from traditional jewellery to animal and pagoda shapes and even face powder.

Getting There & Away

Sightseeing bus No 4 leaves at 7 and 9 am and 12.10 and 2 pm for Zhouzhuang from the west entrance of Shanghai Stadium (see City Sightseeing Buses earlier in this chapter). Buses return from Zhouzhuang at 9 am and 12.50, 2.30 and 4.30 pm. An all-inclusive return fare and entry ticket (Y98) is not a bad idea as it saves you money; if you don't have this return ticket you may not be able to just take the bus back to Shanghai. Sightseeing buses depart and arrive from Shenjiang Hotel.

Slower local buses depart from Shanghai daily from the Hutai Lu bus station at 9.30 am and 1 pm. Public buses arrive and depart in Zhouzhuang from the bus station, about 2km east of town. The last bus from Zhouzhuang leaves around 4 pm. Buses returning to Shanghai occasionally arrive at the bus station at 80 Gongxing Lu, near Shanghai's old train station. Bus No 65 from the Bund passes nearby. In the event that there are no buses to Shanghai you may have to take a minibus to Qingpu and change.

Six buses run daily from about 7 am to 4.30 pm between Zhouzhuang and Suzhou's north terminal.

You can also take speedboat trips from Zhouzhuang and Tongli for Y180 (for the boat).

SUZHOU

Sūzhōu 苏州

Jiangsu's most famous attraction, Suzhou (population about 600,000) is a famed silk production centre and a celebrated retreat brimming with gardens and canals. However, this hasn't done anything to hold back the gathering tide of urban renewal. Unfortunately, much of the city's charm is being swept away by new road, housing and hotel developments. Nevertheless, a wander through the charming gardens and what remains of its cobbled alleys makes a visit to Suzhou worthwhile.

History

Dating back some 2500 years, Suzhou is one of the oldest towns in the Yangzi Basin. With the completion of the Grand Canal in the Sui dynasty, Suzhou found itself strategically located on a major trading route, and the city's fortunes and size grew rapidly.

Suzhou flourished as a centre of shipping and grain storage, bustling with merchants and artisans. By the 12th century the town had attained its present dimensions.

The city walls, a rectangle enclosed by moats, were pierced by six gates (north, south, two in the east and two in the west). Crisscrossing the city were six canals running north to south and 14 canals running east to west. Although the walls have largely disappeared and a fair proportion of the canals have been plugged, central Suzhou retains some of its 'Renaissance' character.

A legend was spun about Suzhou through tales of beautiful women with mellifluous voices, and through the famous proverb 'In heaven there is paradise, on earth Suzhou and Hangzhou'. The story picks up when Marco Polo arrived in 1276. He added the adjectives 'great' and 'noble', though he reserved his finer epithets for Hangzhou.

By the 14th century Suzhou had established itself as China's leading silk producer. Aristocrats, pleasure-seekers, famous scholars, actors and painters were attracted to the city, constructing villas and garden retreats for themselves.

At the height of Suzhou's development in the 16th century, the gardens, large and small, numbered more than 100. The town's tourist formula – 'Garden City, Venice of the East' – is a medieval mix of woodblock guilds and embroidery societies, whitewashed housing, cobbled streets, tree-lined avenues and canals.

The wretched workers of the silk sweatshops, protesting against paltry wages and the injustices of the contract hire system, were staging violent strikes even in the 15th century, and the landlords shifted. In 1860, Taiping troops took the town without a blow. In 1896, Suzhou was opened to foreign trade, with Japanese and other international concessions. During WWII it was occupied by the Japanese and then by the Kuomintang. Suzhou escaped relatively unscathed from the ravages of the Cultural Revolution.

Information

China International Travel Service (CITS, Zhōngguó Guójì Lǚxíngshè; ☎ 522 2223) is in a separate building to the right as you enter the Suzhou Hotel compound. There is a second CITS at the train station and a third in the east wing of the Nanling Hotel complex that handles international air tickets.

The Bank of China is at 490 Renmin Lu, but the major tourist hotels also have foreign-exchange counters.

North Temple 北寺塔
Běisì Tǎ

The North Temple has the tallest pagoda south of the Yangzi – at nine storeys it dominates the northern end of Renmin Lu. You can climb it for a fine aerial view of the town and the farmland beyond, where tea, rice and wheat are grown. The factory chimneys, the new pagodas of Suzhou, loom on the outskirts, as does the haze and smoke they create.

The temple complex goes back 1700 years and was originally a residence. The pagoda has been burnt, built and rebuilt. Made of wood, it dates from the 17th century. Off to the side is Nanmu Hall, which was rebuilt during the Ming dynasty, with some of its features imported from elsewhere. There is a teahouse with a small garden out the back.

The temple is open from 8 am to 5.30 pm; entry is Y7.

Suzhou Museum 苏州博物馆
Sūzhōu Bówùguǎn

Found east of the Humble Administrator's Garden (see later in this section), this museum was once the residence of a Taiping leader, Li Xiucheng.

The museum offers some interesting old maps, including those of the Grand Canal, Suzhou, and heaven and earth. It also houses Qing dynasty steles forbidding workers' strikes, and relics unearthed or rescued from various sites around the Suzhou district and relics such as funerary objects, porcelain bowls and bronze swords. There are no English captions.

Opening hours are from 8.30 am to 4 pm; entry is Y5.

Suzhou Silk Museum
苏州丝绸博物馆
Sūzhōu Sīchóu Bówùguǎn

Highly recommended by many, this museum houses a number of fascinating exhibitions that provide a thorough history of Suzhou's silk industry over the past 4000 years. Exhibits include a section on old looms and weaving techniques and a room with live silkworms in various stages of life. A second building displays clothing made of silk from the early 1900s. Many of the captions and explanations are in both Chinese and English.

The museum is open from 9 am to 5 pm; entry is Y7.

Temple of Mystery 玄妙观
Xuánmiào Guàn

The heart of what was once Suzhou Bazaar is the Taoist Temple of Mystery. It was founded during the Jin dynasty in the 3rd century and laid out between AD 275 and 279, with additions during Song times.

From the Qing dynasty onwards, the bazaar fanned out from the temple, with tradespeople and travelling performers using the grounds. The enormous Sanqing Hall, supported by 60 pillars and capped by a double roof with upturned eaves, dates

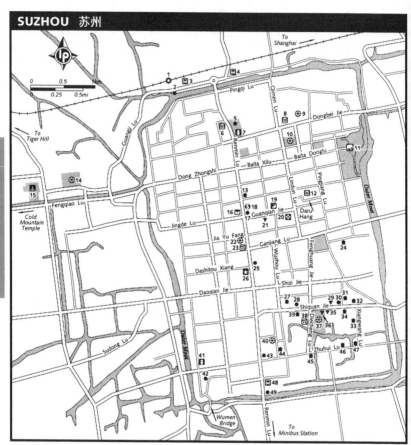

SUZHOU 苏州

To Shanghai

To Tiger Hill

Pingqi Lu

Qimen Lu

Dongbei Jie

Guangji Lu

Rennin Lu

Dong Zhongshi

Baita Xilu

Baita Donglu

Lindun Lu

Pingjiang Lu

Outer Moat

Cold Mountain Temple

Fengqiao Lu

Jingde Lu

Jia Yu Fang

Ganjiang Jie

Guanqian Jie

Daru Hang

Wuzhou Lu

Fenghuang Jie

Dashitou Xiang

Daoqian Jie

Shizi Jie

Shiquan Jie

Diecheng Lu

Xiangwang Lu

Zhuhui Lu

Sudong Lu

Outer Moat

Rennin Lu

Wumen Bridge

To Minibus Station

from 1181. It was burnt and seriously damaged in the 19th century. During the Cultural Revolution, the Red Guards squatted here, and it was later transformed into a library. Today the temple is surrounded by a street market and Suzhou's main shopping district, Guanqian Jie.

The temple is open from 9 am to 6pm; entry is Y10.

Museum of Opera & Theatre
Xìqǔ Bówùguǎn 戏曲博物馆

In the old city of Suzhou, this small museum is worth visiting for the surrounding area of small cobblestone lanes lined with stalls selling vegetables and inexpensive snacks. The museum houses a moveable stage, old musical instruments, costumes and photos of famous performers. From Linden Lu go east on Daru Hang. At the end of the road go right, then take the first left.

Humble Administrator's Garden
Zhuózhèng Yuán 拙政园

Many consider this to be one of Suzhou's best gardens, second only to the Garden of the Master of the Nets (see later in this chapter).

SUZHOU

PLACES TO STAY

13 Overseas Chinese Hotel
华侨大酒店

24 Gloria Plaza Hotel
凯莱大酒店

27 Nanlin Hotel
南林饭店

31 Ying Feng Hotel
迎凤宾馆

32 Dongwu Guesthouse
东吴饭店

33 Gusu Hotel
姑苏饭店

34 Suzhou Hotel; CITS
苏州饭店;
中国国际旅行社

39 Nanyan Guesthouse
南园宾馆

44 Canglang Hotel
沧浪宾馆

45 Pan Gate
友谊宾馆

46 Bamboo Grove Hotel
竹辉宾馆

47 Xiangwang Hotel
相王宾馆

PLACES TO EAT

21 Songhelou Restaurant
松鹤楼

29 Authentic Chinese Dumpling House
洋洋水饺馆

35 Laodakeyi Restaurant
老大可以

36 Yongtte Soya-Bean Milk Shop
永和豆浆

OTHER

1 Train Station; CITS
火车站;
中国国际旅行社

2 Boat Tours
游船游览

3 Local Buses
当地汽车

4 Long-Distance Bus Station
南门汽车站

5 Bicycle Rental
租自行车店

6 Suzhou Silk Museum
丝绸博物馆

7 North Temple
北寺塔

8 Suzhou Museum
苏州博物馆

9 Humble Administrator's Garden
拙政园

10 Lion Grove
狮子林

11 Zoo
动物园

12 Museum of Opera & Theatre
戏曲博物馆

14 Garden for Lingering In
留园

15 West Garden Temple
西园寺

16 Post Office
邮局

17 Sūzhōu Shípǐn Dàshà
苏州食品大厦

18 Bank of China
中国银行

19 Temple of Mystery
玄妙观

20 Suzhou Shangsha Department Store
苏州商厦

22 Garden of Harmony
怡园

23 China Telecom Internet
电信网络

25 China Eastern Airlines Booking Office
东方航空售票处

26 PSB
公安局

28 CITS
中国国际旅行社

30 Bicycle Rental
租自行车店

37 Garden of the Master of the Nets
网师园

38 Internet Bar
必胜网吧

40 Blue Wave Pavillion
沧浪亭

41 Ruiguang Pagoda
瑞光塔

42 Pán Mén
盘门

43 Foreign Languages Bookstore
外文书店

48 Long-Distance Bus Station
南门汽车站

49 Grand Canal Boats Ticket Office
轮船站

EXCURSIONS

Dating back to the early 1500s, this garden's five hectares feature streams, ponds, bridges and islands of bamboo. There's also a teahouse and a small museum that explains Chinese landscape-gardening concepts. In the same area are the Suzhou Museum and several silk mills. The garden is open daily from 7.30 am to 5.30 pm; entry is Y30.

Lion Grove
Shīzi Lín 狮子林

Just around the corner from the Humble Administrator's Garden, the one-hectare Lion Grove was constructed in 1350 by the monk Tian Ru and other disciples, as a memorial to their master, Zhi Zheng. The garden has rockeries that evoke the forms of lions. The walls of the labyrinth of tunnels bear calligraphy from famous chisels. It's open daily from 7.30 am to 5.30 pm; entry is Y10.

Garden of Harmony 怡园
Yí Yuán

A small Qing dynasty garden owned by an official called Gu Wenbin, this one is quite young for a Suzhou garden. It has assimilated many of the features of other gardens and blended them into a style of its own. In the east are buildings and courtyards. The western section has pools with coloured pebbles, rockeries, hillocks and pavilions. It's open from 7.30 am to 5.30 pm; entry to the garden is off Renmin Lu and admission is Y4.

Blue Wave Pavilion 沧浪亭
Cānglàng Tí

A bit on the wild side, with winding creeks and luxuriant trees, this is one of the oldest gardens in Suzhou. The buildings date from the 11th century, though they have been rebuilt on numerous occasions since.

Originally the home of a prince, the property passed into the hands of the scholar Su Zimei, who gave it its name. The one-hectare garden attempts to create optical illusions with the scenery both outside and inside – you look from the pool immediately outside to the distant hills. **Enlightened Way Hall** (Míngdào Táng), the largest building, is said to have been a site for delivery of lectures during the Ming Dynasty. Close by, on the other side of Renmin Lu, is the former Confucius Temple.

The garden is open from 7.30 am to 5.30 pm; entry is Y5. The entrance is off Renmin Lu and is signposted as 'Surging Wave' Pavilion.

Garden of the Master of the Nets 网师园
Wǎngshī Yuán

This is the smallest garden in Suzhou – half the size of the Blue Wave Pavilion and one-tenth the size of the Humble Administrator's Garden. It's small and hard to find, but well worth the trouble as it's better than all the others combined.

This garden was laid out in the 12th century, abandoned, then restored in the 18th century as part of the residence of a retired official. According to one story, this official announced that he'd had enough of bureaucracy and would rather be a fisherman. Another explanation of the name is that it was simply near Wangshi Lu.

The eastern part of the garden is the residential area – originally with side rooms for sedan-chair lackeys, guest reception and living quarters. The central part is the main garden. The western part is an inner garden where a courtyard contains the **Spring-Rear Cottage** (Diànchūn Yí), the master's study. This section and the study, with its Ming-style furniture and palace lanterns, was duplicated and unveiled at the Metropolitan Museum of Art in New York in 1981.

A miniature model of the whole garden, using Qingtian jade, Yingde rocks, Anhui paper, Suzhou silk and incorporating the halls, kiosks, ponds, blossoms and rare plants of the original design, was produced especially for a display at the Pompidou Centre in Paris in 1982.

The most striking feature of this garden is its use of space. Despite its size, the scale of the buildings is large, but nothing appears cramped. A section of the buildings is used by a co-operative of woodblock artists who find the peaceful atmosphere congenial to work.

There are two entrances to the garden. The first is off Shiquan Jie, next door to He Soya-Bean Milk Shop. The second is via a narrow alley just west of the Suzhou Hotel. Going east on Shiquan Lu, take a right onto Daichengqiao Lu, then left down the first alley. It's open daily from 7.30 am to 5.30 pm; entry is Y10.

Garden for Lingering In 蠡园
Liú Yuán

Extending over an area of three hectares, the Garden for Lingering In is one of the largest of Suzhou's gardens, noted for its adroit partitioning with building complexes.

It dates from the Ming dynasty and managed to escape destruction during the Taiping Rebellion. A 700m covered walkway connects the major scenic spots, and the windows have carefully selected perspectives. The walkway is inlaid with calligraphy from celebrated masters. The garden has a wealth of potted plants.

Outside **Mandarin Duck Hall** (Yuanyang) is a 6.5m-high Tai Lake piece – it's the final word on rockeries. The garden is about 3km west of the old city walls. Bus No 5 will take you there via bridges that look down on the busy water traffic. Catch the bus on Renmin Lu, near the Bank of China. The garden is open from 7.30 am until 5.30 pm.

West Garden Temple 西园
Xīyuán Sì

Approximately 500m west of the Garden for Lingering In, this temple was built on the site of a garden laid out at the same time as the Garden for Lingering In and then donated to the Buddhist community. The temple was destroyed in the 19th century and entirely rebuilt; it contains some expressive Buddhist statues.

Cold Mountain Temple 寒山寺
Hánshān Sì

One kilometre west of the Garden for Lingering In, this temple was named after the poet-monk Hanshan, who lived in the 7th century. It was repeatedly burnt down and rebuilt, and was once the site of lively local trading in silk, wood and grain. Not far from its saffron walls lies the Grand Canal. Today, the temple holds little of interest except for a stele by poet Zhang Ji immortalising nearby Maple Bridge and the temple bell (since removed to Japan). However, the fine walls and the humpback bridge are worth seeing.

Bus Nos 30 and 31 will take you close to the temple but it's easiest to catch bus No 5 to the Garden for Lingering In and walk the final kilometre west.

Tiger Hill 虎丘山
Hǔqiū Shān

In the far north-west of town, Tiger Hill is extremely popular with Chinese tourists, but less so with those from overseas. The hill itself is artificial, and is the final resting place of He Lu, founding father of Suzhou. He Lu

died in the 6th century BC, and myths have coalesced around him – he is said to have been buried with a collection of 3000 swords and to be guarded by a white tiger.

Built in the 10th century, the leaning **Yunyan Pagoda** (Yúnyán Tǎ) stands atop Tiger Hill. The octagonal seven-storey pagoda is built entirely of brick, an innovation in Chinese architecture at the time. The pagoda began tilting more than 400 years ago, and today the highest point is displaced more than 2m from its original position.

To get to Tiger Hill, take bus No 5 to its terminus. Entry is Y30.

Pan Gate 盘门三景
Pán Mén

In the south-western corner of the city, straddling the outer moat, this stretch of the city wall contains Suzhou's only remaining original city gate. From the top of the gate there are good views of the moat, surrounding houses and **Ruiguang Pagoda** (Ryìguāng Tǎ), a crumbling pagoda that dates from the 3rd century and is reputedly the oldest pagoda in Jiangsu.

Near the southern end of Renmin Lu, cross over the humpbacked Wumen Bridge and follow the ramp down its right side. This will bring you to Nan Men Lu, which you can follow right to the gate. The gate and its surrounding buildings are open from 8 am to 5 pm; entry is Y8.

Boat Tours

By the canal, south of the train station (opposite the soft-seat waiting room), you can hire a boat that will take you along the canal either south to Pan Gate or north to Tiger Hill. If you are with a group the cost is Y30; if you hire a boat alone it's Y150. The trip takes about an hour. Boats depart from the Foreign Travellers Transportation Company Pier (Wàishì Lǚchē Chuán Gōngsī Mǎtóu; ☎ 752 6931).

Places to Stay

Suzhou has very little to offer in the way of cheap accommodation. However, depending on the season, it is often possible to bargain room prices down. Don't be immediately deterred by the posted rates.

Hotel touts outside Suzhou's train station, especially those with pedicabs, can be extremely aggressive. They will offer a ridiculously cheap fare to your destination and then, once you are loaded into their pedicab, claim that the hotel you have chosen has been bulldozed or burnt to the ground. They will then insist on taking you to a hotel of their choice. The problem is that their choice is often not as cheap as they claim or doesn't accept foreigners.

A couple of hours later you may still not have found a place to stay and will be stuck with a large taxi bill.

Places to Stay – Budget

The *Ying Feng Hotel* (*Yíngfēng Bīnguǎn;* ☎ *530 6291*), over a small footbridge opposite the Suzhou Hotel, offers doubles with bath for Y160. Walk through Ying Feng Restaurant to find the hotel. Don't be put off by the hotel's grotty exterior or drab lobby; rooms are clean and quite nice, some looking onto a central garden.

The *Dongwu Guesthouse* (*Dōngwú Fàndiàn*), run by Suzhou University International Cultural Exchange Institute, has clean, air-conditioned singles for Y140 and doubles for Y200, all with shared bath. From Renmin Lu head east down Shiquan Jie; the guesthouse is on the left just past the Suzhou Hotel.

The *Nanlin Hotel* (see Places to Stay – Mid-Range) has very nice doubles with private bath in an older building for Y178. Unfortunately the karaoke bar is also in this building. You can also try the *Friendship Hotel* (see Places to Stay – Mid-Range) which has standard doubles in its older building beginning at Y160.

South of Shiquan Jie, the *Canglang Hotel* (*Cānglàng Bīnguǎn;* ☎ *520 1557, fax 510 3285, 53 Wuqueqiao*) has somewhat unkempt doubles for Y180, triples for Y225 and quads for Y240.

Places to Stay – Mid-Range

Head to the south-eastern corner of town for mid-range accommodation.

The *Xiangwang Hotel* (*Xiāngwáng Bīnguǎn;* ☎ *529 1162, fax 529 1182*) offers standard doubles with bath for Y220 or Y280. The hotel is at the eastern end of Zhuhui Lu, on the corner of Xiangwang Lu. The sign is in Chinese only.

Just north of Guanqian Jie, the *Overseas Chinese Hotel* (*Huáqiáo Dàjiuàn;* ☎ *720 2883, 518 Renmin Lu*) has rather drab standard doubles for Y300.

The Friendship Hotel (*Yǒuyì Bīnguǎn;* ☎ *529 1601, fax 520 6221*) has opened a new building with clean, air-conditioned singles for Y380 and doubles for Y400. The hotel is on Zhuhui Lu, at the intersection with Diachengqiao Lu.

The *Nanlin Hotel* (*Nánlín Fàndiàn;* ☎ *519 6333, fax 519 1028, 20 Gunxiufangshiquan Jie*) has pleasant gardens and caters to foreign tour groups. Doubles in its new building cost Y270 to Y450. The hotel also has upmarket suites from Y600 to Y1200. Enter the hotel complex off Shiquan Lu.

Places to Stay – Top End

The number of top-end hotels in Suzhou is quickly growing, as is the number of mid-range hotels upgrading and charging top-end prices.

Recently reopened after renovations, the *Gusu Hotel* (*Gūsū Fàndiàn;* ☎ *520 0566, fax 519 9727, 5 Xiangwang Lu*) has singles starting at Y380 and doubles for Y480. A 10% service charge is also added.

The *Suzhou Hotel* (*Sūzhōu Fàndiàn;* ☎ *520 4646, fax 520 4015, 115 Shiquan Jie*) is a sprawling place which does a brisk trade in tour groups. Doubles begin at Y450.

Further along Shiquan Jie, the *Nanyuan Guesthouse* (*Nányuán Bīnguǎn;* ☎ *519 7661, fax 519 8806, 249 Shiquan Jie*) is inside a walled garden compound. Doubles with breakfast begin at Y480.

The *Bamboo Grove Hotel* (*Zhúhuī Fàndiàn;* ☎ *520 5601, fax 520 8778*), on Zhuhui Lu, is the pick of Suzhou's top-end accommodation; it has all the facilities you would expect of a five-star hotel. Room rates start at Y590 for a double, including breakfast.

Close to the old city of Suzhou, the upmarket *Gloria Plaza Hotel (Kǎilái Dàjiuàn; ☎ 521 8508, fax 521 8533, 535 Ganjiang Lu)* also has five-star service, with rooms starting at Y765.

Places to Eat

Suzhou is a tourist town, and consequently there is no shortage of places dishing up local and tourist cuisine. Shiquan Jie, between Daichengqiao Lu and Xiangwang Lu, is lined with bars, restaurants and bakeries. Open 24 hours is the *Yong He Soya-Bean Milk Shop, (Yǒnghé Dòujiāng; 167 Shiquan Jie)*, next door to the entrance of the Garden of the Master of the Nets. It serves tasty rice, noodle and soup dishes; for breakfast there is *yóutiáo* (sweet soya-bean milk) and *dòujiāng* (fried bread sticks).

A little further east along Shiquan Jie, try the *Laodakeyi Restaurant (Lǎodàkǐyī; 173 Shiquan Jie)* for fresh seafood straight from the aquarium. Across the street and further east is the *Authentic Chinese Dumpling House (Yángyáng Shuǐjiǎoguǎn)*. With fresh dumplings, snails and veggie dishes for very reasonable prices, it is extremely popular. Share tables with locals and sip tea from a beer glass. Try upstairs for more seating if downstairs is full.

If you're on a tight budget, try the food courts of the ever-growing number of department stores at the southern end of Renmin Lu. You can fill up for Y5 in the food court on the 3rd floor of the *Suzhou Shangsha Department Store (Sūzhō Shāngshà; 57–69 Guanqian Jie)*. Buy food tickets at the entrance, then redeem them by choosing from the wide array of Chinese dishes and desserts, including dumplings, steamed buns, snails and 100-year-old eggs. It's hard to miss this large store, with its ornate tiled roof.

Located half a block north of the Garden of Harmony is *Jia Yu Fang*, a street lined with several fairly upmarket Chinese restaurants.

If money is no object, you might try the *Songhelou Restaurant (Sÿnghèlóu; 141 Guanqian Jie)*, rated as the most famous restaurant in Suzhou: Emperor Qianlong is said to have eaten here. Its large variety of dishes includes squirrel fish, plain steamed prawns, braised eel, pork with pine nuts, butterfly-shaped sea cucumber, watermelon chicken and spicy duck. The waiter may insist that you be parcelled off to the special 'tour bus' cubicle at the back where an English menu awaits. The Songhelou runs from Guanqian Jie to an alley behind, where tour minibuses pull up. Travellers give the restaurant mixed reviews.

Entertainment

Very popular is the nightly performance of dance and song at the Garden of the Master of the Nets. The audience moves from pavilion to pavilion to watch a variety of traditional Chinese performing arts. The show lasts from 7.30 to 10.30 pm and tickets can be bought from CITS for Y60. Alternatively, turn up shortly before the performance and buy your ticket on the spot.

Shopping

Suzhou-style embroidery, calligraphy, paintings, sandalwood fans, writing brushes and silk underclothes are for sale nearly everywhere. For good-quality items at competitive rates, shop along Shiquan Jie, east off Renmin Lu. The street is lined with shops with names like Mysterious Holy Things and Han & Tibetan Shop and selling anything and everything which might fall within these categories.

For silk try the cloth shops on Guanqian Jie; most cloth shops have tailors on hand who can make simple clothing in about three days. Next to the Temple of Mystery there's a night market that sells very reasonably priced silk.

The Suzhou Food Centre (Sūzhōu Shí Píng Dàshà), at 246 Renmin Lu, sells all kinds of local, traditional specialities and teas in bulk.

The newsagent in the Bamboo Grove Hotel has a good selection of foreign books. The Foreign Languages Bookstore, at 44 Renmin Lu just south of Blue Wave Pavilion, also has a small selection of English-language paperbacks.

EXCURSIONS

Getting There & Away

Bus Buses to Suzhou (Y25 to Y29, one hour) leave every hour between 7.15 am and 4.15 pm from the Xujiahui bus station; every 45 minutes or so from Hengfeng bus station, next to Hanzhong Lu metro station; and every hour from the long-distance bus station at Hutai Lu and Zhongshan Beilu, north of Shanghai train station.

Weekend sightseeing buses to Suzhou (Y24) depart at 8 am from the east end of Shanghai Stadium. Buses (Y50) also leave eight times daily from the parking lot directly in front of the domestic arrival hall at Hongqiao airport, arriving in Suzhou near the PSB on Renmin Lu.

Suzhou has three long-distance bus stations. The main one is at the northern end of Renmin Lu, next to the train station, a second is at the southern end of Renmin Lu and a third minibus stand is further south on Renmin Lu. All have onward connections to every major place in the region, including Shanghai and Hangzhou.

Train Suzhou is on the Shanghai-Nanjing railway line so there are many trains; take anything to Nanjing. Prices for a seat run from Y8 to Y21, depending on the train, and the trip takes from one to 1½ hours. From Suzhou there is an equally plentiful number of trains on to Nanjing, 3¼ hours away.

Boat There are boats along the Grand Canal to Hangzhou. It's basically only foreigners and overseas Chinese who use them these days – locals prefer to travel by bus or train.

Boats from Suzhou to Hangzhou depart daily at 5.30 pm and arrive the next morning at 7 am. Officially, you can only purchase tickets at the 'civilisation unit' window at the boat booking office. Prices there are Y190 for a sleeper in a four-berth room or Y280 in a double berth. Ask, however, at your hotel; some hotels will purchase tickets for guests at a much cheaper rate.

Getting Around

Bus The main thoroughfare is Renmin Lu, with the train and main bus stations just off the northern end, and a large boat dock and another long-distance bus station at the southern end.

Bus No 1 runs the length of Renmin Lu and bus No 2 is a kind of around-the-city bus. Bus No 5 is a good bus running from east to west; it can be picked up in either direction on Renmin Lu near the Bank of China or Overseas Chinese Hotel. Bus No 4 runs from Changmen directly east along Baita Lu, turns south and runs past the eastern end of Guanqian Jie and then on to the Suzhou Hotel.

Taxi Taxis and pedicabs congregate outside the main train station, down by the boat dock at the southern end of Renmin Lu, and at Jingmen (Nanxin Bridge) at the western end of Jingde Lu. They also tend to hover around tourist hotels.

Bicycle There are several bicycle rental shops scattered around the city. The one across from the Suzhou Silk Museum offers the best rates, at Y10 per day, however, with only 10 bikes for hire, they disappear quickly. There are two more shops across from the Suzhou Hotel and another next to CITS at the train station, all of which charge between Y15 and Y30 per day, plus deposit.

AROUND SUZHOU
Grand Canal 大运河
Dà Yùnhé

The canal proper cuts to the west and south of Suzhou, within a 10km range of the town. Suburban bus Nos 13, 14, 15 and 16 will get you there. In the north-west, bus No 11 follows the canal for a fair distance, taking you on a tour of the enchanting countryside. Hop off the bus once you find a nice bridge on which you can perch and watch the world of the canal float by. Unfortunately, parking yourself for too long could make you the main tourist attraction.

Precious Belt Bridge 宝带桥
Bǎodài Qiáo

With 53 arches, this is considered to be one of China's best bridges. It straddles the Grand Canal and is a popular spot with fisherfolk. The three central humpbacks of the bridge are larger to allow boats through. The bridge is no longer used for traffic – a modern one has been built alongside it.

Precious Belt Bridge is thought to be a Tang-dynasty construction named after Wang Zhongshu, a local prefect who sold his precious belt to pay for the bridge's construction for the benefit of his people.

The bridge is south-east of Suzhou. You can get there by taxi or a 40-minute bike ride. Head south on Renmin Lu, past the south moat, then left at the TV towers.

Tai Lake 太湖
Tài Hú

The towns around Suzhou provide ample opportunity for a visit to Tai Lake and its surrounding countryside. Lingyanshan (Língyánshān), 15km from Suzhou, is home to an active Buddhist monastery; Tianpingshan (Tiānpíngshān), 18km from Suzhou, is famous for its medicinal spring waters; and Guangfu (Guāngfú), 25km west of Suzhou, borders the lake with an ancient seven-storey pagoda.

A popular destination for expats is the Mercury Marina. This is a private club but the public can rent speedboats, houseboats and rooms at the nearby Taihu Lakeside Villas and the marina makes a nice weekend getaway.

HANGZHOU 杭州
Hángzhōu

For the Chinese, Hangzhou (along with Guilin) is the country's most famous tourist attraction. Indeed, you can book your hotel room from on board the train as you ease into Hangzhou train station, while announcements on the platform welcome you to the 'tourist capital of China'. This is a warning. Droves of tour groups descend on the city during all seasons, peaking on holidays and weekends and resulting in a blight of tacky tourist amenities and costly hotels. But don't despair – even this tourist excess has not diminished the beauty of Hangzhou's West Lake area.

West Lake is a large freshwater lake, bordered on three sides by hills. Its banks and islands are blanketed with small gardens

and temples. The lake gives rise to what must be one of China's oldest tourist blurbs: 'In heaven there is paradise, on earth Suzhou and Hangzhou'.

History

History notes Hangzhou as existing from the start of the Qin dynasty (221 BC). When Marco Polo passed through Hangzhou in the 13th century he described it as one of the finest and most splendid cities in the world.

Other travellers such as Odoric of Pordenone also visited the city (he referred to it as Camsay), returning with tales of the majesty of the place. Although Hangzhou prospered greatly after it was linked with the Grand Canal in 610, it really came into its own after the Song dynasty was overthrown by the invading J•rchen.

The Jurchen were ancestors of the Manchus, who conquered China five centuries later. The Song capital of Kaifeng, along with the emperor and the leaders of the imperial court, was captured by the Jurchen in 1126. The rest of the Song court fled south, finally settling in Hangzhou and establishing it as the capital of the Southern Song dynasty.

China had gone through an economic revolution in the preceding years, producing huge and prosperous cities, an advanced economy and a flourishing inter-regional trade. With the Jurchen invasion, the centre of this revolution was pushed south from the Yellow River Valley to the lower Yangzi Valley and to the coast between the Yangzi River and Guangzhou.

While the north remained in the hands of the invaders (who rapidly became Sinicised), in the south Hangzhou became the hub of the Chinese state. The court, the military, the civil officials and merchants all congregated in Hangzhou, whose population rose from half a million to 1.75 million by 1275. The city's large population and its proximity to the ocean promoted the growth of river and sea trade, and of ship building and other naval industries.

When the Mongols swept into China they established their court at Beijing. Hangzhou, however, retained its status as a prosperous

EXCURSIONS

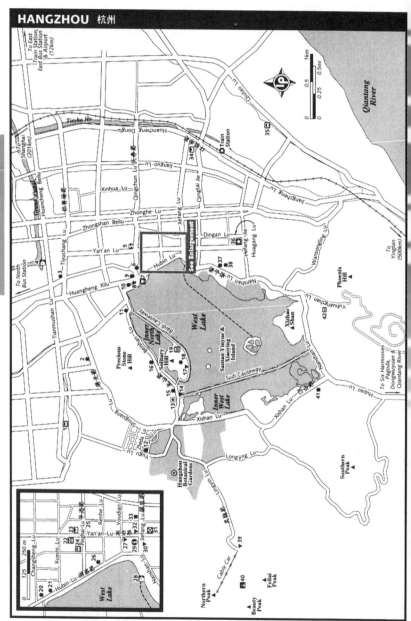

HANGZHOU

PLACES TO STAY

2 Yellow Dragon Hotel
黄龙饭店

6 Haihua Novotel Hotel
海华大酒店

9 Wanghu Hotel
望湖宾馆

12 Foreign Student Dormitory
外国留学生楼

15 Hangzhou Shangri-La Hotel
杭州香格里拉饭店

16 Xinxin Hotel
新新饭店

20 Overseas Chinese Hotel
华侨饭店

26 Xihu Hotel
西湖饭店

33 Xinqiao Hotel
新桥饭店

37 International Art Centre Inn
中国美术学院
国际培训中心

38 China Academy of Art Foreign Student Dormitory
中国美术学院
外事招待所

41 Huagang Hotel
花港饭店

PLACES TO EAT

8 Häagen Dazs
哈根达斯

14 Shanwaishan Restaurant
山外山菜馆

17 Louwailou Restaurant
楼外楼菜馆

27 Roast Duck Restaurant
烤鸭店

30 Croissants de France
可颂坊

32 Mr Pizza
密斯明斯特比萨

39 Tianwaitic Restaurant
天外天菜馆

OTHER

1 West Bus Station
长途汽车西站

3 CAAC
民航售票处

4 Hangzhou Passenger Wharf
客运码头

5 Bank of China
中国银行

7 Casablanca Country Pub
卡萨布兰卡乡村俱乐

10 Foreign Languages Bookstore
外文书店

11 CITS
中国国际旅行社

13 Mausoleum of Generale
岳飞墓

18 Zhongshan Park
中山公园

19 Zhejiang Provincial Museum
浙江省博物馆

21 Paradise Rock
天上人间

22 China Telecom
国际长途电话

23 Post Office
邮局

24 Bus No 308 to Six Harmonies Pagoda
308路车至六和塔

25 Market Street
市场

28 Boats to Santan Yinyue
船至三潭印月

29 Hangzhou Tourist Information Centre
旅游咨询服务中心

31 Jiefang Lu Department Store
解放路百货商店

34 Main Post Office
邮电局

35 South Bus Station
长途汽车南站

36 PSB
公安局

40 Lingyin Temple
灵隐寺

42 China Silk Museum
中国丝绸博物馆

EXCURSIONS

commercial city. It did take a beating in the Taiping Rebellion: in 1861 the Taipings laid siege to the city and captured it, but two years later the imperial armies took it back. These campaigns reduced almost the entire city to ashes, led to the deaths of more than half a million of its residents through disease, starvation and warfare, and finally ended Hangzhou's significance as a commercial and trading centre.

Few monuments survived the devastation, and most of those that did became victims of the Red Guards a 100 years later during the Cultural Revolution. Much of what may be seen in Hangzhou today is of fairly recent construction.

Orientation

Hangzhou is bounded to the south by the Qiantang River and to the west by hills. Between the hills and the urban area is the large West Lake, the region's premier scenic attraction. The eastern shore is the developed touristy district; the western shore is quieter.

Information

CITS (☎ 515 2888) is at 1 Shihan Lu in a charming old building (Wánghú Lóu) near the Wanghu Hotel. It deals mainly with tour groups and is not very useful for the individual traveller, who is better off going to the China Travel Service (CTS, Zhōngguó Lǚxíngshè; ☎ 707 4401, fax 702 0588) beside the Overseas Chinese Hotel.

At the intersection of Yan'an Lu and Jiefang Lu is the Hangzhou Tourist Information Centre, where you can pick up a bilingual map. The centre also offers tours of Hangzhou for Y20.

The Foreign Languages Bookstore, at 34 Hubin Lu, has good maps, including some in English.

The main Bank of China branch is at 140 Yan'an Lu, near Qingchun Lu, and is open daily from 8 am to 6 pm.

Lingyin Temple 灵隐寺
Língyǐn Sì

Lingyin Si, roughly translated as either Temple of Inspired Seclusion or Temple of the Soul's Retreat, is really Hangzhou's main attraction. It was built in AD 326 and, due to war and calamity, has been destroyed and restored no fewer than 16 times.

The present buildings are restorations of Qing dynasty structures. The Hall of the Four Heavenly Guardians at the front of the temple is inscribed with the couplet, 'cloud forest buddhist temple', penned by the Qing emperor Kangxi, who was a frequent visitor to Hangzhou and was inspired on one occasion by the sight of the temple in the mist and trees.

Inside the hall is a statue of the laughing buddha who can 'endure everything unendurable in the world and laugh at every laughable person in the world'.

Behind this hall is the Great Hall, where you'll find the magnificent 20m-high statue of Siddhartha Gautama. This was sculpted from 24 blocks of camphor wood in 1956 and was based on a Tang dynasty original. Behind the giant statue is a startling montage of 150 small figures which charts the journey of 53 children on the road to buddhahood; also represented are Ji Gong, a famous monk who secretly ate meat, and a character known as the 'mad monk'. During

the time of the Five Dynasties about 3000 monks lived here.

The place is normally crawling with tourists. Bus Nos 7, 507 (both from the train station) or 505 (from the zoo) go to the terminal at the foot of the hills west of Hangzhou. Behind the Lingyin Temple is Northern Peak (Běi Gāofēng), which can be scaled via a cable car. From the summit there are sweeping views across the lake and city.

Zhejiang Provincial Museum
Zhèjiāng Shěng Bówùguǎn 浙江省博物馆

This interesting museum is on Solitary Hill Island (Gǔshān), a short walk from the Hangzhou Shangri-La Hotel. Its buildings were part of the holiday palace of Emperor Qianlong in the 18th century.

Most of the museum is concerned with natural history; there's a large whale skeleton (a female *Rhachianectos glaucus cope*) and a dinosaur skeleton.

Mausoleum of General Yue Fei
Yuè Fēi Mù 岳飞墓

During the 12th century, when China was attacked by Jurchen invaders from the north, General Yue Fei (1103–1141) was commander of the Song armies.

Despite his successes against the invaders, he was recalled to the Song court, where he was executed after being deceived by Qin Hui, a treacherous court official. More than 20 years later, in 1163, Song emperor Gao Zong exonerated Yue Fei and had his corpse reburied at the present site.

Iron statues of Qin Hui and his wife, Wang Shi, were traditionally cursed at and spat upon by local tourists, but these days many have to do it surreptitiously, because, as everyone knows in China, spitting is against the law.

The mausoleum of Yue Fei is bounded by a red-brick wall a few minutes' walk west of the Hangzhou Shangri-La Hotel. The monastery was ransacked during the Cultural Revolution, but has since been restored. Inside is a large statue of the general and the words, 'return the mountains and rivers to us', a reference to his patriotism and resistance to the Jurchen.

Six Harmonies Pagoda

Liùhé Tǎ 六和塔

To the south-west of the city stands an enormous rail-and-road bridge which spans the Qiantang River. Close by is the 60m-high octagonal Six Harmonies Pagoda, named after the six codes of Buddhism. The pagoda also served as a lighthouse, and was supposed to have magical power to halt the tidal bore which thundered up the Qiantang River in mid-September every year.

Behind the pagoda is a charming walk through terraces dotted with sculptures, bells, shrines and inscriptions. Take bus No 308 from Yan'an Lu.

West Lake 西湖

Xī Hú

There are 36 lakes in China called West Lake, but this one is by far the most famous. Indeed it is the West Lake on which all other west lakes are modelled.

West Lake is the symbol of Hangzhou, and can make for a pleasant outing, though some of its charm has fallen victim to the plundering of tour groups and tacky facilities. Twilight and evening can be better times to view the lake, especially when it is layered with mist.

West Lake was originally a lagoon adjoining the Qiantang River. In the 8th century the governor of Hangzhou had it dredged; later a dike was built that cut it off from the river completely. The resulting lake is about 3km long and a bit under 3km wide. Two causeways, the Baidi and the Sudi, split the lake into sections.

The causeways each have a number of arched bridges, large enough for small boats and ferries to pass under. The sights – a collection of gardens, bridges and pavilions – are scattered around the lake. Many have literary associations which are lost on most foreigners.

The largest island in the lake is Solitary Hill – the location of the Zhejiang Provincial Museum, the Louwailou Restaurant and **Zhongshan Park** (Zhōngshān Gōngyuán). The Baidi causeway links the island to the mainland.

Most of the other sights are connected with famous people who once lived there – poets, emperors who visited (Hangzhou was very popular with the ruling elite), and Chinese patriots. **Red Carp Pond** (Huāgǎng Guānú) is a chief attraction, home to a few thousand red carp and studded with earthen islets. Hangzhou's botanical gardens even have a sequoia pine presented by Richard Nixon on his 1972 visit.

From **Xiaoying Island** (Xiǎoyíng Zhōu) on the lake you can look over at Santan Yinyue (Sāntán Yìnyuè), a string of three small towers in the water, each of which has five holes that release shafts of candlelight on the night of the moon cake festival in mid-autumn, when the moon is full.

If you want to contemplate the moon from own boat there are a couple of places around the lake where you can hire paddle boats and go for a slow spin. Boats can also be chartered for a lake cruise from the small docks along the eastern side of the lake.

Other Sights

The Hangzhou **zoo** has Manchurian tigers, which are larger than their southern counterparts and are a protected species.

Travellers have recommended the **China Silk Museum** (Zhōngguó Sīchóu Bówùguǎn) on Yuhuangshan Lu. It has good displays of silk samples, and displays on the history and processes of silk production. English-speaking tour guides are available. Entry is Y5 and bus No 31 goes by the museum.

About 60km north of Hangzhou is **Moganshan** (Mògānshān). Pleasantly cool at the height of summer, Moganshan was developed as a resort for Europeans living in Shanghai and Hangzhou during the colonial era. It's well worth visiting and staying in one of the old villas.

To reach Moganshan, take a minibus from the north bus station (Y15, 11½ hours) or take a minibus to Wukang (Y9) and proceed from there. Moganshan has a selection of hotels, with doubles starting at Y250.

Places to Stay – Budget

Fortunately, Hangzhou's hotel prices have dropped slightly from the dizzy heights of the early and mid-1990s but budget accommodation is still hard to come by. It's a good idea to avoid the peak season, weekends and holidays.

The **China Academy of Art Foreign Student Dormitory** (Zhōngguó Měishù Xuéyuàn Wàishì Zhàodàisuǒ, ☎ 702-3415) has a great location on Nanshan Lu. The rooms, Y120 for doubles with air-con and bath, are somewhat dilapidated but the setting more than makes up for that.

The **Foreign Student Dormitory** (Liúxuéshēng Lóu; ☎ 799 6092) at Zhejiang University also has rooms for Y120 per double, but its location isn't as convenient. It's a white, four-storey building down a small lane off Zheda Lu, the main road heading into the university. Bus No 16 takes you there.

The cheapest budget option is the **Xihu Hotel** (Xīhú Fàndiàn; ☎ 706 6933, fax 706 6151, 80 Renhe Lu) has singles/doubles/triples with shared bath and fan for Y80/Y100/120, and air-con (no bath) singles and doubles for Y140 and Y170. Singles and doubles with air-con and bath are Y220 and Y280.

Places to Stay – Mid-Range

The **International Art Centre Inn** (Zhōngguó Měishù Xuéyuàn Guójì Pe'xùn Zhōngxīn; ☎ 571 7070, 220 Nanshan Lu) is beside the entrance to the China Academy of Art. Comfortable doubles are Y380 and larger doubles are Y398. Discounts of up to 30% are available.

The **Huagang Hotel** (Huāgǎng Fàndiàn; ☎ 799 8899, fax 796 2481, 4 Xishan Lu) is set on beautiful grounds on the western side of West Lake. Standard doubles start at Y450, but 50% discounts were being offered at the time of writing.

The **Xinxin Hotel** (Xīnxīn Fàndiàn; ☎ 798 7101, fax 705 3263, 58 Beishan Lu) also has a pleasant, if less serene, location on the north edge of West Lake. Lake-view doubles are Y572 and hillside-view rooms are Y528, but discounts of up to 40% are available.

On the eastern side of the lake, the **Overseas Chinese Hotel** (Huáqiáo Fàndiàn; ☎ 707 4401, fax 707 4978, 15 Hubin Lu) was recently renovated and, while a little overpriced, it is in a convenient location and has good facilities. Doubles start at Y450.

The **Xinqiao Hotel** (Xīnqiáo Fàndiàn; ☎ 707 6688, fax 707 1428, 176 Jiefang Lu) is still within walking distance of West Lake, but is a little uninspired. Singles and doubles start at Y520 and Y590.

Places to Stay – Top End

There's no shortage of top-end hotels in Hangzhou, but the most elegant and romantic place is the **Hangzhou Shangri-La Hotel** (Hángzhōu Xiānggé Lǐlā Fàndiàn; ☎ 707 7951, fax 707 3545, 78 Beishan Lu). Also called the **Hangzhou Hotel** (Hángzhōu Fàndiàn), it's on the northern side of the lake, next to the Mausoleum of General Yue Fei, and surrounded by spacious forested grounds. Doubles here start at Y1600 (plus a 15% service charge). If you can't stay there, at least go there for a drink or a wander around.

The comfortable and efficient **Haihua Novotel Hotel** (Hǎihuá Dàjiuàn; ☎ 721 5888, fax 721 5108, 298 Qingchun Lu) is very good value, with rooms starting at US$85 and lake-view rooms for US$105. The restaurants are excellent and the facilities superb.

The **Wanghu Hotel** (Wànghú Bīnguǎn; ☎ 707 1024, fax 707 1350) is a large hotel nearby with a whole range of rooms, some as cheap as Y350. Standard doubles are Y980.

Another massive place is the **Yellow Dragon Hotel** (Huánglóng Fàndiàn; ☎ 799 8833, fax 799 8090). Starting at US$130, rooms here are overpriced; maybe that's why they are offering 45% discounts. It's also a bit of a hike to the lake.

Both the Hyatt and Radisson are due to open hotels in Hangzhou by 2001.

Places to Eat & Drink

Hangzhou's most famous restaurant is the **Louwailou Restaurant** (Lóuwàilóu Càiguǎn), on Solitary Hill Island right on West Lake. Apart from excellent views of the lake, however, its fame has made the chefs complacent. You're better off trying some of the famous local dishes such as xīhù cùyú

ffic, Suzhou

zhou high-rise urban living .

A winning smile from a Suzhou local at sunset.

e engineering masterpiece of Precious Belt Bridge, Suzhou, straddling the Grand Canal.

JULIET COOMBE

Local street fare in Suzhou.

JULIET COOMBE

The Suzhou basket trade.

JULIET COOMBE

Commuting around the busy streets of Suzhou.

JULIET COOMBE

The sun sets over Huangzhou's magnificent West Lake.

JULIET COOMBE

Suzhou.

(West Lake fish in sweet-and-sour sauce) at other establishments which have better cooks and more reasonable prices. For information on Hangzhou cuisine see the Places to Eat chapter.

Try the **Shanwaishan Restaurant** (Shānwàishān Càiguǎn, ☎ 796 5450), near the Yue Fei Mausoleum or the **Tianwaitian Restaurant** (Tiānwàitiān Càiguǎn, ☎ 798 6621) beside the entrance to the Lingyin Temple.

For Chinese cheap eats, check out **Yan'an Lu**, a street to the east of Hubin Lu. Parallel to Yun'an Lu further east, **Wushan Lu** is a haven for bargain restaurants with snappy service; there are a few popular dumpling restaurants here.

You can order a la carte cheaply at the **Roast Duck Restaurant** (Kǎoyā Diàn) if you can read the Chinese menu. Otherwise ask for kǎoyā (Beijing duck), which costs Y36 for half a duck (enough for two). Downstairs is the cheaper, more down-at-heel option, while upstairs is pricier.

Top-end hotels dish out a wide range of superior cuisine. The **Haihua Novotel Hotel** features a fine Western restaurant in the form of Le Paris. Most of the hotels also have bakeries. There's a **Croissants de France** on Jiefang Lu and an elegant **Häagen Dazs** outlet on Hubin Lu.

Besides the hotels there's a couple of bars on the north-eastern side of West Lake. A rustic place on the lake shore, the **Casablanca Country Pub**, opens at 6 pm and down the road past the Overseas Chinese Hotel there's the **Paradise Rock** pub and restaurant.

You can find **KFC** at various locations, as well as other fast-food outlets like **Mr Pizza** at the corner of Jiefang Lu and Yanan Lu.

Shopping

Hangzhou is well known for its tea, in particular Longjing green tea (grown in the Longjing District, west of West Lake), silk, fans and, of all things, scissors.

Shops around the lake sell all of these, but at high, touristy prices. One of the best places to look, however, is the market street on Wushan Lu in the evenings. Stalls go up

in the early evening and are piled high with a fascinating confusion of collectables. Fake ceramics jostle with Chairman Mao memorabilia, ancient pewter tobacco pipes, silk shirts and pirated CDs. Bargain hard if anything catches your eye.

For silk, try Xinhua Lu, a couple of blocks east of Zhongshan Lu. In the market, make sure you check that the silk (it should feel smooth and soft between your thumb and finger) is genuine and not a polyester clone.

Getting There & Away

Bus Deluxe buses leave for Hangzhou (Y54, two hours) from Shanghai's long-distance bus station at Hutai Lu and Zhongshan Beilu. A sightseeing bus leaves at 7.35 am (Y50) from Shanghai Stadium on the weekends. Buses (Y70) also depart daily from Hongqiao airport's domestic arrivals hall at 10.30 am and 1.30 and 4.30 pm, arriving at Hangzhou's CAAC Hotel.

All three of Hangzhou's long-distance stations are located outside the city. Most buses from Shanghai arrive in the East bus station.

Hangzhou's North bus station on Mogan Lu has deluxe (Y98, five hours) and economy (Y50, seven hours) buses to Nanjing and other points in Jiangsu.

Train Fast trains leave Shanghai train station for Hangzhou at 7.29 am and 2.02, 2.39, 4.58 and 5.42 pm, taking around two hours. Fares cost between Y33 and Y49 depending on the train.

Another convenient way to Hangzhou East train station is from Shanghai's Meilong train station, behind the Hongmei Lu metro stop in Shanghai. Fast trains (Y25, 1¾ hours) depart at 8.22 and 10.16 am and 2.04 and 5.08 pm. Express trains from Hong Kong to Shanghai also stop at Hangzhou every other day.

Some trains arrive and depart from the Hangzhou East train station; check your ticket. At the time of writing, Hangzhou's main station was having a complete overhaul and all trains were being diverted to the absolute chaos of the Hangzhou East train station. This situation should be remedied by the time you read this.

Some of the trains from Hangzhou back to Shanghai continue on to Suzhou.

Boat You can get to both Wuxi and Suzhou by boat up the Grand Canal from Hangzhou. There's one boat daily for Suzhou, leaving at 5.30 pm, and for Wuxi at 6 pm. Both trips take 13 hours. Economy class in a cabin of four people costs Y65. There are also deluxe cabins with four-person beds, at Y88 per bed, and two-person cabins for Y130 per bed. Buy tickets at the wharf just north off Huancheng Beilu.

Travellers have mixed opinions about this trip. On the plus side, it's more romantic to arrive in a place by boat, but keep in mind that most of the journey is in darkness.

Getting Around
Bus Bus No 7 is very useful as it connects the main train station with the major hotel area on the eastern side of the lake. Of course, it doesn't do you much good if your train arrives at the Hangzhou East station; take bus Nos 11 or 31, which will bring you close to the West Lake area. Bus No 15 connects the North and West bus stations to the north-west area of West Lake. Bus No 27 is useful for getting between the eastern and western sides of the lake.

Taxi Metered taxis are ubiquitous. Keep a map handy and watch out for lengthy detours. Prices for taxis depend on the size of the vehicle. Rates are cheap; figure on around Y10 to Y12 from the main train station to Hubin Lu.

Bicycle Bicycle rentals are available in a few places and are the best way to get around. Probably the most convenient place is the outlet beside the Overseas Chinese Hotel. Rentals are Y6 per hour and a deposit of Y300 to Y400 is required. The small kiosk near the Foreign Student Dormitory of the China Academy of Art also rents bikes.

Check out the bikes, especially the brakes, before you take off.

Boat The boating industry on West Lake is the usual throng of boat operators jostling with each other to get you on board; just stand on the eastern shore and they will home in on you. Often the ordeal of bargaining for a private boat can take away some of the charm of the actual ride, but sometimes it's worth the splurge. Larger boats also leave the eastern shore, taking visitors out to the islands for Y16.

PUTUOSHAN 普陀山
Pǔtuóshān
Putuoshan is the China we all dream about and see on postcards and in coffee-table books: temples, pagodas, arched bridges, narrow alleys, fishing boats, artisans and monks. Here you feel miles away from the noise, pollution, concrete-block housing

PUTUOSHAN

PLACES TO STAY
3 Jǐnpíng Mountain Villa
   锦屏山庄
4 Huagung Villa
   华光山庄
8 Xiliu Hotel
   锡麟饭店
9 Xilei
   西来小庄
11 Qianhe Mountain Villa
   千荷山庄
14 Sanshengtang Hotel
   三圣堂饭店

PLACES TO EAT
13 Putuoshan Teahouse
   普陀山茶艺馆
16 Restaurants
   餐厅

OTHER
1 Sauskrit Tidings Cave
   笠轴
2 Fayuchan Temple
   法雨禅寺
5 One Thousand Step Beach
   千步沙

6 One Hundred Step Beach
   百步沙
7 Pujichan Temple
   普济禅寺
10 Bank of China
   中国银行
12 Post Office
   邮电局
15 Passenger Ferry
   Terminal
   轮船码头
17 Boat Ticket Office
   轮船售票处

PUTUOSHAN 普陀山

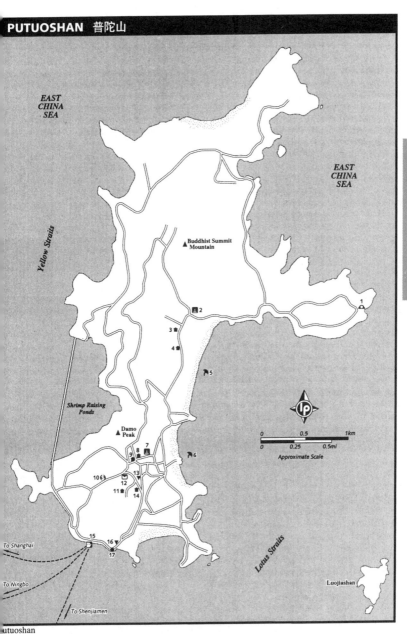

EAST
CHINA
SEA

EAST
CHINA
SEA

Yellow Straits

Buddhist Summit
Mountain

▲2

3

4

5

Shrimp Raising
Ponds

Damo
Peak

8 7

9

6

10

13

12

11 14

0   0.5   1km
0   0.25   0.5mi
Approximate Scale

To Shanghai

15

16

17

To Ningbo

Lotus Straits

To Shenjiamen

Luojiashan

utuoshan

developments, billboards, political slogans and bustle that characterise modern Chinese cities.

The island has a special link with Guanyin, Goddess of Mercy.

The best way to see the island is to amble about from temple to crag and from beach to monastery, rather than rush about in imitation of tour groups. The serenity of the island lies in its unhurriedness, and that is an essential element if you want to enjoy the place to its utmost.

While there is no need to see everything, you can jump aboard one of the numerous minibuses that charge to and fro across the island, stopping at the sights for Y2.50 to Y4.

There's a Y40 entrance fee to the island itself upon arrival, which does not include entry fees to other sights. You can find a post office west of Pujichan Temple and a Bank of China farther west down the road.

Things to See

The two large beaches, **One hundred Step Beach** (Băibùshā) and **One Thousand Step Beach** (Qiānbùshā), on the east of the island, are attractive and largely unspoilt, although you have to pay to get in (Y12). Go at twilight when the ticket office is empty and it's more atmospheric.

Sanskrit Tidings Cave (Fányīn Dòng), on the far-eastern tip of the island, has a temple dedicated to Guanyin perched between two cliffs with a seagull's view of craggy rocks and crashing waves.

The area around the **Pujichan Temple** (Pŭjìchán Sì) is a treat, and from here it is easy to explore the rest of the island. Most of the minibuses go via here.

Places to Stay

It's difficult to provide reliable information on Putuoshan's accommodation as prices vary seasonally and according to demand. There's nothing in the way of budget accommodation, and many hotels do not take foreigners. If you're coming from Shanghai, it may be worthwhile to book accommodation through a travel agency. A barrage of touts meet each ferry and you can always try your luck with them.

The **Xilin Hotel** (Xīlín Fàndiàn; ☎ 609 1303, fax 609 1199) is about 10m to the left of the Pujichan Temple when facing the temple. It has pleasant rooms in a courtyard with doubles starting at Y248. A 20% discount is available on weekdays.

Farther up the road from here, the **Xilei** (Xīlái Xiǎozhuāng; ☎ 609 1812, 609 1023) is a large place with restaurants and shops. The cheapest rooms start at Y468 and they were offering a 30% discount.

The **Jinping Mountain Villa** (Jīnpíng Shānzhuāng, ☎ 609 1500, fax 609 1698) has a nice location near the **Fayuchan Temple** (Făyǔchán Sì), but its cheaper doubles for Y300 are pretty grotty, even with a 30% discount. Nicer rooms with a veranda go for Y480.

Up the road above here is the **Qianhe Mountain Villa** (Qiánhé Shānzhuāng; ☎ 609 1630), a new building with comfortable rooms starting at Y386, but it's often full.

The best and newest hotel in Putuoshan is the immaculate **Huagang Villa** (Huáguāng Shānzhuāng; ☎ 609 2667, fax 609 2537), located near the Fayuchan Temple and the best place to go for a romantic getaway. Standard doubles with sea-view verandas are Y680. Rooms without verandas are Y580 and deluxe singles are Y880. A 40% discount is offered on weekdays.

Places to Eat

Most of the hotel food is both expensive and appalling in Putuoshan, so avoid it and head for the seafood restaurants down near the boat ticket office.

A good place serving Shanghai-style snacks and a variety of teas is the **Putuoshan Teahouse** (Pŭtuóshān Cháyìguǎn) on the south-west side of the pond in front of the Pujichan Temple. It also serves breakfast.

Getting There & Away

Overnight boats to Putuoshan depart Shanghai daily at 6 pm and take 12 hours. Tickets cost Y49 in a dorm, Y120 in a six- to eight-bed cabin, Y163 in a four-bed cabin, or you can have your own twin berth for Y304 or Y348. There is often a second departure or

Friday night to cater for the weekend crowd. It's easy to upgrade once you are on board.

A five-hour rapid ferry service departs daily and costs Y153/Y180 on the lower/upper deck. Buses depart daily at 8 am (and additionally at 10.50 am in the summer) from Shiliupu wharf to take you, in two hours, to either the port of Jinshan or Luchao. The ferry then takes an additional three hours. If there's a rough sea, keep in mind that this can be a difficult trip for those prone to seasickness.

Two boats leave Putuoshan daily at 4 and 5 pm for the return trip to Shanghai.

An airport has been built on the neighbouring island of Zhujiajian, a five-minute boat ride from Putuoshan, but no flights were running there from Shanghai at the time of research.

To Ningbo there are frequent fast ferries (Y51, three hours, with an hour on the boat and two hours by bus) or a slow boat (Y21 to Y52, five hours).

Getting Around

Walking is the most relaxing option if you have time, but if not, minibuses zip from the ferry terminal to the Pujichan Temple (Y3) and from there you can change to other buses going to other sights. It's also pleasant to walk up to **Buddhist Summit Mountain** (Fódīng Shān) from a trail at the Fayuchan Temple. For the less physically inclined there's a cable car for Y25.

Language

MANDARIN

Discounting ethnic minority languages, China has eight major dialect groups: Putonghua (Mandarin), Yue (Cantonese), Wu (Shanghainese), Minbei (Fuzhou), Minnan (Hokkien-Taiwanese), Xiang, Gan and Hakka. These dialects also divide into many more sub-dialects.

The official language of the PRC is actually the Mandarin dialect spoken in Beijing. With the exception of the western and southernmost provinces, most of the population speaks Mandarin, although regional accents can make comprehension difficult.

Writing System

Chinese is often referred to as a language of pictographs. Many of the basic Chinese characters are in fact highly stylised pictures of what they represent, but most Chinese characters (around 90%) are compounds of a 'meaning' element and a 'sound' element.

So just how many Chinese characters are there? It's possible to verify the existence of some 56,000 characters, but the vast majority of these are archaic. It is commonly felt that a well-educated, contemporary Chinese person might know and use between 6000 and 8000 characters. To read a Chinese newspaper you will need to know 2000 to 3000 characters, but 1200 to 1500 would be enough to get the gist.

Pronunciation

Most letters used in Pinyin are pronounced as in English, with the exception of the following:

Vowels

a	as in 'father'
ai	as in 'high'
ao	as the 'ow' in 'cow'
e	as the 'u' in 'fur'
ei	as the 'ei' in 'weigh'
i	as the 'ee' in 'meet' (or as the 'oo' in 'book' after c, ch, r, s, sh, z or zh)
ian	as in 'yen'
ie	as the English word 'yeah'
o	as in 'or'
ou	as the 'oa' in 'boat'
u	as in 'flute'
ui	as in the word 'way'
uo	like a 'w' followed by 'o'
yu	as in the German 'ü' – pucker your lips and try saying 'ee'
ü	as the German 'ü'

Consonants

c	as the 'ts' in 'bits'
ch	as in 'chop', but with the tongue curled back
h	as in 'hay', but articulated from farther back in the throat
q	as the 'ch' in 'cheese'
r	as the 's' in 'pleasure'
sh	as in 'ship', but with the tongue curled back
x	as in 'ship'
z	as the 'dz' in 'suds'
zh	as the 'j' in 'judge' but with the tongue curled back

The only consonants that occur at the end of a syllable are n, ng and r.

In Pinyin, apostrophes are occasionally used to separate syllables in order to prevent ambiguity, eg the word *píng'ān* can be written with an apostrophe after the 'g' to prevent it being pronounced as 'pín'gān'.

Tones

Chinese has a large number of words with the same pronunciation but a different meaning; what distinguishes these 'homophones' is their 'tonal' quality – the raising and lowering of pitch on certain syllables. Mandarin has four tones – high, rising, falling-rising and falling, plus a fifth 'neutral' tone which you can all but ignore.

To illustrate, look at the word *ma* which has four different meanings according to tone:

high	*mā* (mother)
rising	*má* (hemp/numb)
falling-rising	*mǎ* (horse)
falling	*mà* (to scold/to swear)

Gestures

Hand signs are frequently used in China. The 'thumbs-up' sign has a long tradition as an indication of excellence. An alternative way to indicate excellence is to gently pull your earlobe between your thumb and index finger.

The Chinese have a system for counting on their hands. If you can't speak the language, it would be worth your while at least to learn Chinese finger counting (see the illustrations on this page). One of the disadvantages of finger counting is that there are regional differences. The symbol for number 10 is to form a cross with the index fingers, but many Chinese just use a fist.

Phrasebooks

Phrasebooks are invaluable, but it's a better idea to copy out the appropriate phrases in Chinese rather than show someone the book – otherwise they may take it and read every page! Reading place names or street signs isn't difficult since the Chinese name is usually accompanied by the Pinyin form; if

not you'll soon learn lots of characters just by repeated exposure. A small dictionary with English, Pinyin and Chinese characters is also useful for learning a few words.

For a more comprehensive guide to Mandarin, get a copy of the new edition of Lonely Planet's *Mandarin phrasebook*.

Pronouns

I		
	wǒ	我
you		
	nǐ	你
he, she, it		
	tā	他/她/它
we, us		
	wǒmen	我们
you (plural)		
	nǐmen	你们
they, them		
	tāmen	他们

Greetings & Civilities

Hello.		
	Nǐ hǎo.	你好
Goodbye.		
	Zàijiàn.	再见
Thank you.		
	Xièxie.	谢谢
You're welcome.		
	Búkèqi.	不客气
I'm sorry.		
	Duìbùqǐ.	对不起

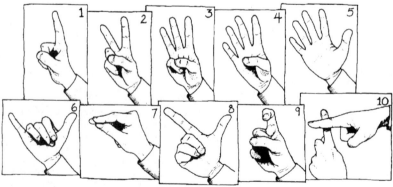

The Chinese system of finger-counting

May I ask your name?
Nín guìxìng? 您贵姓?
My (sur)name is ...
Wǒ xìng ... 我姓...
No. (don't have)
Méi yǒu. 没有
No. (not so)
Búshì. 不是
I'm a foreign student.
Wǒ shì liúxuéshēng. 我是留学生
What's to be done now?
Zěnme bàn? 怎么办?
It doesn't matter.
Méishì. 没事
I want ...
Wǒ yào ... 我要
No, I don't want it.
Búyào. 不要

Where are you from?
Nǐ shì cōng nǎr laíde? 你是从哪儿来的?
I'm from ...
Wǒ shì cōng ... laíde. 我是从 ... 来的
Australia
àodàlìyà 澳大利亚
Canada
jiānádà 加拿大
Denmark
dānmài 丹麦
France
fǎguó 法国
Germany
déguó 德国
Netherlands
hélán 荷兰
New Zealand
xīnxīlán 新西兰
Spain
xībānyá 西班牙
Sweden
ruìdiǎn 瑞典
Switzerland
ruìshì 瑞士
UK
yīngguó 英国
USA
měiguó 美国

Language Difficulties
I understand.
Wǒ tīngdedǒng. 我听得懂
I don't understand.
Wǒ tīngbudǒng. 我听不懂
Do you understand?
Dǒng ma? 懂吗?
Could you speak more slowly please?
Qīng nǐ shuō màn yìdiǎn, hǎo ma?
请你说慢一点, 好吗?

Getting Around
I want to go to ...
Wǒ yào qù ... 我要去 ...
I want to get off.
Wǒ yào xiàchē. 我要下车
luggage
xíngli 行李
left-luggage room
jìcún chù 寄存处
one ticket
yìzhāng piào 一张票
two tickets
liǎngzhāng piào 两张票
What time does it depart?
Jǐdiǎn kāi? 几点开?
What time does it arrive?
Jǐdiǎn dào? 几点到?
How long does the trip take?
Zhècì lǚxíng yào huā duōcháng shíjiān?
这次旅行要花多长时间?
buy a ticket
mǎi piào 买票
refund a ticket
tuì piào 退票
taxi
chūzū chē 出租车
microbus ('bread') taxi
miànbāo chē/ miǎndī 面包车/ 面的
Please use the meter.
Dǎ biǎo. 打表

Air
airport
fēijīchǎng 飞机场

CAAC ticket office
zhōngguó mínháng 中国民航售票处
shòupiào chù
one way ticket
dānchéng piào 单程票
round-trip ticket
láihuí piào 来回票
boarding pass
dēngjì kǎ 登机卡
reconfirm
quèrèn 确认
cancel
qǔxiāo 取消
bonded baggage
cúnzhàn xínglǐ 存栈行李

Bus
bus
gōnggòng qìchē 公共汽车
minibus
xiǎo gōnggòng qìchē 小公共汽车
long-distance bus station
chángtú qìchē zhàn 长途汽车站
When is the first bus?
Tóubān qìchē jǐdiǎn kāi? 头班汽车几点开?
When is the last bus?
Mòbān qìchē jǐdiǎn kāi? 末班汽车几点开?
When is the next bus?
Xià yìbān qìchē jǐdiǎn kāi? 下一班汽车几点开?

Train
train
huǒchē 火车
ticket office
shòupiào chù 售票处
railway station
huǒchē zhàn 火车站
hard-seat
yìngxí, yìngzuò 硬席, 硬座
soft-seat
ruǎnxí, ruǎnzuò 软席, 软座
hard-sleeper
yìngwò 硬卧

soft-sleeper
ruǎnwò 软卧
platform ticket
zhàntái piào 站台票
Which platform?
Dìjǐhào zhàntái? 第几号站台?
upgrade ticket (after boarding)
bǔpiào 补票
subway (underground)
dìtiě 地铁
subway station
dìtiě zhàn 地铁站

Bicycle
bicycle
zìxíngchē 自行车
I want to hire a bicycle.
Wǒ yào zū yíliàng zìxíngchē.
我要租一辆自行车
How much is it per day?
Yìtiān duōshǎo qián? 一天多少钱?
How much is it per hour?
Yíge xiǎoshí duōshǎo qián?
一个小时多少钱?
How much is the deposit?
Yājīn duōshǎo qián?
押金多少钱?

Directions
map
dìtú 地图
Where is the ...?
... zài nǎlǐ? ... 在哪里?
I'm lost.
Wǒ mílùle. 我迷路了
Turn right.
Yòu zhuǎn. 右转
Turn left.
Zuǒ zhuǎn. 左转
Go straight ahead.
Yìzhí zǒu. 一直走
Turn around.
Wàng huí zǒu. 往回走
alley
hútóng 胡同
lane
xiàng 巷
road
lù 路

boulevard
dàdào 大道
section
duàn 段
street
jiē, dàjiē 街，大街
No 21
21 hào 21号

Accommodation
hotel
lǚguǎn 旅馆
tourist hotel
bīnguǎn/fàndiàn/ 宾馆/饭店/
jiǔdiàn 酒店
reception desk
zǒng fúwù tái 总服务台
dormitory
duōrénfáng 多人房
single room
dānrénfáng 单人房
twin room
shuāngrénfáng 双人房
bed
chuángwèi 床位
economy room (no bath)
pǔtōngfáng 普通房
standard room
biāozhǔn fángjiān 标准房间
deluxe suite
háohuá tàofáng 豪华套房
book a whole room
bāofáng 包房
Is there a room vacant?
Yǒu méiyǒu kōng fángjiān?
有没有空房间？
Yes, there is.
Yǒu.
有
No, there isn't.
Méiyǒu.
没有
Can I see the room?
Wǒ néng kànkan fángjiān ma?
我能看看房间吗？

I don't like this room.
Wǒ bù xǐhuan zhèijiān fángjiān.
我不喜欢这间房

Are there any messages for me?
yǒu méiyǒu liú huà?
有没有留话？
May I have a hotel namecard?
yǒu méiyǒu lǚguǎn de míngpiàn?
有没有旅馆的名片？
Could I have these clothes washed,
please?
qíng bǎ zhè xiē yīfú xǐ gānjìng, hǎo ma?
请把这些衣服洗干净，好吗？

Visas & Documents
passport
hùzhào 护照
visa
qiānzhèng 签证
visa extension
yáncháng qiānzhèng 延长签证
Public Security Bureau (PSB)
gōng'ān jú 公安局
Foreign Affairs Branch
wài shì kē 外事科

Money
How much is it?
Dūoshǎo qián? 多少钱？
Is there anything cheaper?
Yǒu piányi 有便宜
yìdiǎn de ma? 一点的吗？
That's too expensive.
Tài guìle. 太贵了
Bank of China
zhōngguó yínháng 中国银行
change money
huàn qián 换钱

Post
post office
yóujú 邮局
letter
xìn 信
envelope
xìnfēng 信封
package
bāoguǒ 包裹
air mail
hángkōng xìn 航空信
surface mail
píngyóu 平邮

stamps
   yóupiào   邮票
postcard
   míngxìnpiàn   明信片
aerogramme
   hángkōng xìnjiàn   航空信件
poste restante
   cúnjú hòulǐnglán   存局候领栏
express mail (EMS)
   yóuzhèng tèkuài
   zhuāndì   邮政特快专递
registered mail
   guà hào   挂号

Telecommunications

telephone
   diànhuà   电话
telephone office
   diànxùn dàlóu   电讯大楼
telephone card
   diànhuà kǎ   电话卡
international call
   guójì diànhuà   国际电话
collect call
   duìfāng fùqián   对方付钱电话
   diànhuà
direct-dial call
   zhíbō diànhuà   直拨电话
fax
   chuánzhēn   传真
computer
   diànnǎo   电脑
email
   diànzǐyóujiàn   电子邮件
(often called 'email')
internet
   yīntè wǎng   因特网
   hùlián wǎng   互联网
(more formal name)
online
   shàng wǎng   上网
Where can I get online?
   Wǒ zài nǎr kěyǐ   我在哪儿
   shàng wǎng?   可以上网？

Toilets

toilet (restroom)
   cèsuǒ   厕所
toilet paper
   wèishēng zhǐ   卫生纸

bathroom (washroom)
   xǐshǒu jiān   洗手间

Health

I'm sick.
   Wǒ shēngbìngle.   我生病了
I'm injured.
   Wǒ shòushāngle.   我受伤了
hospital
   yīyuàn   医院
laxative
   xièyào   泻药
anti-diarrhoea medicine
   zhǐxièyào   止泻药
rehydration salts
   shūwéizhí dīnàfǎ   舒维质低钠
   pàodìng   发泡锭
aspirin
   āsīpǐlín   阿斯匹林
antibiotics
   kàngjùnsù   抗菌素
condom
   bìyùn tào   避孕套
tampon
   wèishēng mián tiáo   卫生棉条
sanitary napkin (Kotex)
   wèishēng mián   卫生棉
sunscreen (UV) lotion
   fáng shài yóu   防晒油
mosquito coils
   wénxiāng   蚊香
mosquito pads
   diàn wénxiāng   电蚊香

Time

What's the time?
   Jǐ diǎn?   几点？
... hour ... minute
   ... diǎn ... fēn   ... 点 ... 分
3.05
   sān diǎn wǔ fēn   3点5分
now
   xiànzài   现在

today
   jīntiān   今天
tomorrow
   míngtiān   明天
day after tomorrow
   hòutiān   后天

three days from now
  dàhòutiān　　大后天

yesterday
  zuótiān　　昨天
Wait a moment.
  Děng yī xià.　　等一下

Numbers

0	*líng*	零
1	*yī, yāo*	一，么
2	*èr, liǎng*	二，两
3	*sān*	三
4	*sì*	四
5	*wǔ*	五
6	*liù*	六
7	*qī*	七
8	*bā*	八
9	*jiǔ*	九
10	*shí*	十
11	*shíyī*	十一
12	*shí'èr*	十二
20	*èrshí*	二十
21	*èrshíyī*	二十一
100	*yìbǎi*	一百
200	*liǎngbǎi*	两百
1000	*yìqiān*	一千
2000	*liǎngqiān*	两千
10,000	*yíwàn*	一万
20,000	*liǎngwàn*	两万
100,000	*shíwàn*	十万
200,000	*èrshíwàn*	二十万

Emergencies

emergency
  jǐnjí qíngkuàng　　紧急情况
hospital emergency room
  jízhěn shì　　急诊室
police
  jǐngchá　　警察
Fire!
  Zhǎohuǒ le!　　着火了！
Help!
  Jiùmìng a!　　救命啊！
Thief!
  Xiǎotōu!　　小偷！
pickpocket
  páshǒu　　扒手
rapist
  qiángjiānfàn　　强奸犯

FOOD
At the Restaurant
I don't want MSG.
  wó bú yào wèijīng　　我不要味精
I'm vegetarian.
  wǒ chī sù　　我吃素
not too spicy
  bú yào tài là　　不要太辣
(cooked) together
  yíkuàir　　一块儿
restaurant
  cāntīng　　餐厅
menu
  cài dān　　菜单
bill (cheque)
  mǎi dān/jiézhàng　　买单/结帐
set meal (no menu)
  tàocān　　套餐
to eat/let's eat
  chī fàn　　吃饭
chopsticks
  kuàizi　　筷子
knife
  dàozi　　刀子
fork
  chāzi　　叉子
spoon
  tiáogēng/tāngchí　　调羹/汤匙

Cooking Methods
steamed
  qīngzhēng　　清蒸
deep fried
  gānjiān　　干煎
pan fried
  gānshāo　　干烧
stir fried
  shēngchǎo　　生炒
grilled
  shāozhì　　烧炙

Rice
steamed white rice
  mǐfàn　　米饭
fried rice with egg
  jīdàn chǎofàn　　鸡蛋炒饭

Soup
egg drop soup
  jīdàn tāng　　鸡蛋汤

hot & sour soup
   suānlà tāng 酸辣汤
three kinds of seafood soup
   sān xiān tāng 三鲜汤
wanton soup
   húndùn tāng 馄饨汤

Vegetables

aubergine (eggplant)
   qiézi 茄子
beans
   hélándòu 荷兰豆
bok choy
   báicài 白菜
brocolli
   gānlán 甘蓝
cauliflower
   càihuā 菜花
four season beans
   sìjìdòu 四季豆
french beans
   biǎndòu 扁豆
snow peas
   wāndòu biǎndòu 豌豆扁豆
lettuce
   shēngcài 生菜
mushroom
   mógu 蘑菇
mushroom
   pínggū 平菇
mushroom
   xiānggū 香菇
potato
   tǔdòu 土豆
pumpkin
   nánguā 南瓜
spinach
   bōcài 菠菜
sweet potato
   yùtou 芋头
taro
   yùtou 芋头
tiger skin chillies
   hǔpíjiānjiāo 虎皮尖椒
tofu
   dòufu 豆腐
tomato
   xīhóngshì 西红柿
wooden ear mushroom
   mùěr 木耳

Vegetable Dishes

beancurd stuffed with ham
   huǒtuǐ dòufu 火腿豆腐
bok choy & mushrooms
   báicài xiān 白菜鲜双菇
   shuānggū
lotus root cakes in sweet & sour sauce
   tángcù ǒubǐng 糖醋藕饼
beancurd with mushrooms
   hēimù'ěr mèn 黑木耳焖豆腐
   dòufu
mushrooms in oyster sauce
   háoyóu xiāngū 蚝油鲜菇
crispy skin beancurd
   cuìpí dòufu 脆皮豆腐
aubergine (eggplant) in ginger sauce
   jiāngzhī qiézi 姜汁茄子
sweetcorn & pinenuts
   sōngrén yùmǐ 松仁玉米

Fish & Seafood

carp
   lǐyú 鲤鱼
eel
   mànyú 鳗鱼
hairtail
   dàiyú 带鱼
lobster
   lóngxiā 龙虾
Mandarin fish
   guìyú 鳜鱼
perch
   lúyú 鲈鱼
pomfret
   chāngyú 鲳鱼
scallop
   shàn bèi 扇贝
sea cucumber
   hǎishēn 海参
shrimp
   xiā 虾
squid
   yóuyú 鱿鱼
yellow croaker
   huángyú 黄鱼

fried shrimp
   yóubào xiārén 油爆虾仁
shrimp in sizzling rice crust
   guōbā xiārén 锅巴虾仁

steamed Mandarin fish
   qīng zhēng guìyú   清蒸鳜鱼
fish slices in wine
   jiǔxiāng yúpiàn   酒香鱼片
Mandarin fish with pinenuts
   sōngzǐ guìyú   松子鳜鱼
dry fried yellow croaker
   gānjiān xiǎo huángyú   干煎小黄鱼
honey smoked carp
   mìzhī xūnyú   蜜汁熏鱼
west lake fish
   xīhú yú   西湖鱼
fish slices in egg white
   fúróng yúpiàn   芙蓉鱼片
fish fillet in tomato sauce
   qiézhī yúkuài   茄汁鱼块
eel soaked in soy sauce
   hóngshāo shànyú   红烧鳝鱼
fried eel
   chǎo huángshàn   炒黄鳝
hot & sour squid
   suānlà yóuyú   酸辣鱿鱼
fish balls
   zhá yúwán   炸鱼丸
lotus flavoured silver carp
   héxiāng báilián   荷香白鲢
hairy crabs
   dàzhá xiè   大闸蟹
fried black carp
   zhá hēi lǐyú   炸黑鲤鱼
braised carp with onion
   cōngsū jìyú   葱酥鲫鱼

Meat

Mandarin style pork ribs
   jīngdū guō páigǔ   京都锅排骨
lionshead meatballs with crab
   xièfěn shīzitóu   蟹粉狮子头
camphor tea duck
   zhāngchá yāzi   樟茶鸭

concubine's chicken
   guìfēi jī   贵妃鸡
crispy chicken
   xiāngsū jī   香酥鸡
crispy suckling pig
   kǎo rǔzhū   烤乳猪
duck with pinenuts
   sōngzǐ yā   松子鸡

soy pork with scallions in pancakes
   jīngcōng ròusī jiá bǐng   京葱肉丝夹饼
curried chicken
   gālí jī   咖喱鸡
sweet & sour spare ribs
   tángcù páigǔ   糖醋排骨
dongpo pork
   dōngpō bèiròu   东坡焙肉
beggar's chicken
   jiào huā jī   叫化鸡
drunken chicken
   zuìjī   醉鸡
snake
   shé ròu   蛇肉

Popular Dishes

spicy chicken with peanuts
   gōngbào jīdīng   宫爆鸡丁
shredded pork & green beans
   biǎndòu ròusī   扁豆肉丝
pork & sizzling rice crust
   guōbā ròupiàn   锅巴肉片
double cooked fatty pork
   huíguō ròu   回锅肉
sweet & sour pork fillets
   tángcù lǐjǐ/ gǔlǎo ròu   糖醋里脊/ 古老肉
pork cooked with soy sauce
   jīngjiāng ròusī   精酱肉丝
'wooden ear' mushrooms & pork
   mùěr ròu   木耳肉
pork & green peppers
   qīngjiāo ròu piàn   青椒肉片
sizzling beef platter
   tiěbǎn niúròu   铁板牛肉
'fish-resembling' meat
   yúxiāng ròusī   鱼香肉丝
egg & tomato
   fānqié chǎodàn   番茄炒蛋
red cooked aubergine
   hóngshāo qiézi   红烧茄子
'fish-resembling' aubergine
   yúxiāng qiézi   鱼香茄子
fried vegetables
   sùchǎo sùcài   素炒素菜
garlic beans
   sùchǎo biǎndòu   素炒扁豆
spicy tofu
   málà dòufu   麻辣豆腐

'homestyle'tofu
jiācháng dòufu 家常豆腐
beef with oyster sauce
háoyóu niúròu 蚝油牛肉
pork & fried onions
yángcōng chǎo 洋葱炒肉片
ròupiàn
ribs
páigǔ 排骨
scallops & kidney
xiānbèi yāohuā 鲜贝腰花
crispy chicken
xiāngsū jī 香酥鸡
chicken & cashews
yāoguǒ jīdīng 腰果鸡丁
lemon chicken
níngméng jī 柠檬鸡
Beijing Duck
běijīng kǎoyā 北京烤鸭

DRINKS

hot
rède 热的
ice cold
bīngde 冰的
water (boiled)
kāi shuǐ 开水
mineral water
kuàng quán shuǐ 矿泉水

tea
chá 茶
coffee
kāfēi 咖啡
milk
niúnǎi 牛奶

coffee creamer
nǎijīng 奶精
soybean milk
dòujiāng 豆浆
fizzy drink (soda)
qìshuǐ 汽水
Coca-Cola
kěkǒu kělè 可口可乐
fruit juice
guǒzhī 果汁
coconut juice
yēzi zhī 椰子汁
mango juice
mángguǒ zhī 芒果汁
orange juice
liǔchéng zhī 柳橙汁
pineapple juice
bōluó zhī 波萝汁
yoghurt
suānnǎi 酸奶
Cheers!
gānbēi 干杯
beer
píjiǔ 啤酒
Chinese spirits
báijiǔ 白酒
red grape wine
hóng pútáo jiǔ 红葡萄酒
rice wine
mǐ jiǔ 米酒
whisky
wēishìjì jiǔ 威士忌酒
white grape wine
bái pútáo jiǔ 白葡萄酒
vodka
fútèjiā jiǔ 伏特加酒

Glossary

arhat – Buddhist, especially a monk who has achieved enlightenment and passes to nirvana at death.

báijiǔ – literally 'white alcohol', a type of face-numbing rice wine served at banquets and get-togethers
Ba Jin – a popular and prolific anarchist writer of the 1930s and 1940s, Li Feigan (his real name) is probably best known for his 1931 novel *Jiā (The Family)*
bāozi – steamed savoury buns with tasty meat filling
běi – north
biéshù – villa
bīnguǎn – tourist hotel
Bodhisattva – one worthy of nirvana but who remains on earth to help others attain enlightenment
bówùguǎn – museum

CAAC – The Civil Aviation Administration of China
cadre – Chinese government bureaucrat
cāntīng – restaurant
CCP – Chinese Communist Party, founded in Shanghai in 1921
cheongsam – (Cantonese) originating in Shanghai, a fashionable tight-fitting Chinese dress with a slit up the side.
chí – lake, pool
Chiang Kaishek – (1887–1975) leader of the Kuomintang, anticommunist and head of the nationalist government from 1928 to 1949
CITS – China International Travel Service; deals with China's foreign tourists
Confucius – (551–479 BC) Legendary scholar who developed the philosophy of Confucianism, which defines codes of conduct and patterns of obedience in society
CTS – China Travel Service; originally set up to handle tourists from Hong Kong, Macau, Taiwan and overseas Chinese
Cultural Revolution – a brutal and devastating purge of the arts, religion and the intelligentsia by Mao's Red Guards and later the PLA from 1966–70

cūn – village
CYTS – China Youth Travel Service

dàdào – boulevard
dàfàndiàn – large hotel
dàjiē – avenue
dàjiǔdiàn – large hotel
dǎo – island
dàqiáo – large bridge
dàshà – hotel, building
dàxué – university
Deng Xiaoping – (1904–97) considered to be the most powerful political figure in China from the late 1970s until his death; Deng's reforms resulted in economic growth, but he also instituted harsh social policies and authorised the military force that resulted in the Tiananmen Incident in Beijing in 1989
dōng – east
dòng – cave
dòngwùyuán – zoo

fàndiàn – a hotel or restaurant
fēng – peak
fēngshuǐ – geomancy, literally 'wind and water', the art of using ancient principles to maximise the flow of *qi* (universal energy)
fó – buddha

Gang of Four – members of a clique, headed by Mao's wife, Jiang Qing, who were blamed for the disastrous Cultural Revolution
gé – pavilion, temple
gōng – palace
gōngyuán – park
Great Leap Forward – failed socioeconomic program that resulted in a devastating famine in the early 1960s
guānxì – advantageous social or business connections
gùjū – house, home, residence

hé – river
hong – (from Cantonese) a company, usually engaged in trade. Often used to refer to

Hong Kong's original trading houses, such as Jardine Matheson
hú – lake
hútòng – a narrow alleyway in Beijing

jiāng – river
jiǎo – one-tenth of a yuán
jiàotáng – church
jiē – street
jié – festival
jìniànguǎn – memorial hall
jiǔdiàn – hotel
jū – residence, home
junk – originally referred to Chinese fishing and war vessels with square sails. Now applies to various types of boating craft

kǎoyādiàn – roast duck restaurant
kuài – colloquial term for the currency, yuan
Kuomintang – Chiang Kaishek's Nationalist Party, the dominant political force after the fall of the Qing dynasty.

Laotzu – a philosopher whose beliefs, inscribed in the slim volume the *Tao Te Ching (The Way & Its Power)*, inspired the birth of Taoism as a religion
Lin Biao – (1907–71) military commander and CCP leader whose roles included Minister of Defence; Lin's death, which came shortly after he plotted to kill Mao Zedong, remains a mystery
lòngtáng – a narrow alleyway in Shanghai
lóu – tower
lù – road
lǚguǎn – hotel
Lu Xun – (1881–1936) acclaimed writer whose works tackled Confucian culture

máo – colloquial term for the jiǎo, 10 of which equal one kuài
Mao Zedong – (1893–1976) leader of the early communist forces, he founded the PRC and was party chairman until his death
mǎtou – dock
mén – gate
Mencius – (372–289 BC) a scholar who raised Confucian ideals into the national consciousness
miào – temple
mù – tomb

name chop – a carved name seal that acts as a signature
nán – south

overseas Chinese – Chinese people who have left China to settle overseas

Pīnyīn – the official system to transliterate Chinese script into roman characters
PLA – People's Liberation Army
Politburo – the 25-member supreme policy-making authority of the CCP
Polo, Marco – Italian merchant who (supposedly) visited China and the Far East in the 13th century
PRC – People's Republic of China
PSB – Public Security Bureau; the arm of the police force set up to deal with foreigners

qiáo – bridge
qīngzhēnsì – mosque

Red Guards – a pro-Mao faction who persecuted rightists during the Cultural Revolution
rénmín – people, people's
Rénmínbì – literally 'people's money', the formal name for the currency of China. Shortened to RMB

shān – mountain
shāngdiàn – shop, store
shěng – province, provincial
shì – city
shìchǎng – market
shìjiè – world
shíkūmén – stone gatehouse
sì – temple, monastery
special municipality – a centrally administered region such as Beijing, Tianjin, Chongqing and Shanghai
Sun Yatsen – (1866–1925) first President of the Republic of China. A revolutionary loved by republicans and communists alike

tǎ – pagoda
tàijíquán – slow motion shadow boxing, a form of exercise. The graceful, flowing exercise that has its roots in China's martial arts. Also known, particularly in the west, as taichi

Taiping Rebellion – A 1.1 million-strong rebellion that attempted to overthrow the Qing dynasty from 1850–64
tíng – pavilion
triads – secret societies. Originally founded to protect Chinese culture from the influence of usurping Manchurians, their modern-day members are little more than gangsters, involved mainly in drug running, gun running, prostitution and protection rackets.

xī – west
xiàn – county

yuán – the Chinese unit of currency, also referred to as RMB; garden

zhāodàisuǒ – basic lodgings, a hotel or guesthouse
zhíwùyuán – botanical gardens
zhōng – middle
Zhou Enlai – an early comrade of Mao's, Zhou exercised the most influence in the day-to-day governing of China following the Cultural Revolution. His death triggered the 1976 Tiananmén Incident in 1976
zǔjū – ancestral home

LONELY PLANET

ON THE ROAD

Travel Guides explore cities, regions and countries, and supply information on transport, restaurants and accommodation, regardless of your budget. They come with reliable, easy-to-use maps, practical advice, cultural and historical facts and a rundown on attractions both on and off the beaten track. There are over 200 titles in this classic series, covering nearly every country in the world.

 Lonely Planet Upgrades extend the shelf lives of existing travel guides by detailing any changes that may affect travel in a region since a book has been published. Upgrades can be downloaded for free from **www.lonelyplanet.com/upgrades**

For travellers with more time than money, **Shoestring** guides offer dependable, first-hand information with hundreds of detailed maps, plus insider tips for stretching money as far as possible. Covering entire continents in most cases, the six-volume shoestring guides have been known as 'backpackers' bibles' for over 25 years.

For the discerning short-term visitor, **Condensed** guides highlight the best a destination has to offer in a full-colour, pocket-sized format designed for quick access. From top sights and walking tours to opinionated reviews of where to eat, stay, shop and have fun.

CitySync lets travellers use their Palm™ or Visor™ handheld computers to guide them through a city with handy tips on transport, history, cultural life, major sights, and shopping and entertainment options. It can also quickly search and sort hundreds of reviews of hotels, restaurants and attractions, and pinpoint their location on scrollable street maps. CitySync can be downloaded from **www.citysync.com**

MAPS & ATLASES

Lonely Planet's **City Maps** feature downtown and metropolitan maps, as well as transit routes and walking tours. The maps come complete with an index of streets, a listing of sights and a plastic coat for extra durability.

Road Atlases are an essential navigation tool for serious travellers. Cross-referenced with the guidebooks, they also feature distance and climate charts and a complete site index.

LONELY PLANET

ESSENTIALS

Read This First books help new travellers to hit the road with confidence. These invaluable predeparture guides give step-by-step advice on preparing for a trip, budgeting, arranging a visa, planning an itinerary and staying safe while still getting off the beaten track.

Healthy Travel pocket guides offer a regional rundown on disease hot spots and practical advice on predeparture health measures, staying well on the road and what to do in emergencies. The guides come with a user-friendly design and helpful diagrams and tables.

Lonely Planet's **Phrasebooks** cover the essential words and phrases travellers may need when they're strangers in a strange land. It comes in a pocket-sized format with colour tabs for quick reference, extensive vocabulary lists, easy-to-follow pronunciation keys and two-way dictionaries.

Lonely Planet's **Travel Journal** is a lightweight but sturdy travel diary for jotting down all those on-the-road observations and significant travel moments. It comes with a handy time zone wheel, world maps and useful travel information.

Lonely Planet's eKno is an all-in-one communication service developed especially for travellers, with low-cost international calls, free email and voicemail so that you can keep in touch while on the road. Check it out on **www.ekno.lonelyplanet.com**

FOOD & RESTAURANT GUIDES

Lonely Planet's **Out to Eat** guides recommend the brightest and best places to eat and drink in top international cities. These gourmet companions are arranged by neighbourhood, packed with dependable maps, garnished with scene-setting photos and served with quirky features.

For people who live to eat, drink and travel, **World Food** guides explore the culinary culture of each country. Entertaining and adventurous, each guide is packed with detail on staples and specialities, regional cuisine and local markets, as well as sumptuous recipes, comprehensive culinary dictionaries and lavish photos good enough to eat.

OUTDOOR GUIDES

For those who believe the best way to see the world is on foot, Lonely Planet's **Walking Guides** detail everything from family strolls to difficult treks, with 'when to go and how to do it' advice supplemented by reliable maps and essential travel information.

Cycling Guides map a destination's best bike tours, long and short, in day-by-day detail. They contain all the information a cyclist needs, including advice on bike maintenance, places to eat and stay, innovative maps with detailed cues to the rides and elevation charts.

The **Watching Wildlife** series is perfect for travellers who want authoritative information but don't want to tote a field guide. Packed with advice on where, when and how to view a region's wildlife, each title features photos of over 300 species and contains engaging comments and insights into local flora and fauna.

With underwater colour photos throughout, **Pisces Books** explore the world's best diving and snorkelling areas. Each book contains listings of diving services and dive resorts, detailed information on depth, visibility and difficulty of dives, and a roundup of the marine life you're likely to see through your mask.

OFF THE ROAD

Journeys, the travel literature series written by renowned travel authors, capture the spirit of a place or illuminate a culture with a journalist's attention to detail and a novelist's flair for words. These are tales to soak up while you're actually on the road or dip into as an at-home armchair indulgence.

The new range of lavishly illustrated **Pictorial** books is just the ticket for both travellers and dreamers. Off-beat tales and vivid photographs bring the adventure of travel to your doorstep long before the journey begins and long after it is over.

The Lonely Planet **Videos** encourage the same independent, tough-minded approach as the guidebooks. Currently airing throughout the world, this award-winning series features innovative footage and an original soundtrack.

Yes, we know, work is tough, so do a little bit of deskside-dreaming with the spiral-bound Lonely Planet **Diary**, the tearaway page-a-day **Day-to-Day Calendar** or any Lonely Planet **Wall Calendar**, filled with great photos from around the world.

TRAVELLERS NETWORK

Lonely Planet online. Lonely Planet's award-winning Web site has insider information on hundreds of destinations from Amsterdam to Zimbabwe, complete with interactive maps and relevant links. The site also offers the latest travel news, recent reports from travellers on the road, guidebook upgrades, a travel links site, an online book buying option and a lively traveller's bulletin board. It can be viewed at www.lonelyplanet.com or AOL keyword: lp.

Planet Talk is a quarterly print newsletter, full of gossip, advice, anecdotes and author articles. It provides an antidote to the being-at-home blues and lets you plan and dream for the next trip. Contact the nearest Lonely Planet office for your free copy.

Comet, the free Lonely Planet newsletter, comes via email once a month. It's loaded with travel news, advice, dispatches from authors, travel competitions and letters from readers. To subscribe, click on the Comet subscription link on the front page of the Web site.

LONELY PLANET

Guides by Region

Lonely Planet is known worldwide for publishing practical, reliable and no-nonsense travel information in our guides and on our Web site. The Lonely Planet list covers just about every accessible part of the world. Currently there are 15 series: travel guides, Shoestring guides, Condensed guides, Phrasebooks, Read This First, Healthy Travel, Walking guides, Cycling guides, Pisces Diving & Snorkeling guides, City Maps, Travel Atlases, Out to Eat, World Food, Journeys travel literature and Pictorials.

AFRICA Africa on a shoestring • Africa – the South • Arabic (Egyptian) phrasebook • Arabic (Moroccan) phrasebook • Cairo • Cape Town • Cape Town city map • Central Africa • East Africa • Egypt • Egypt travel atlas • Ethiopian (Amharic) phrasebook • The Gambia & Senegal • Healthy Travel Africa • Kenya • Kenya travel atlas • Malawi, Mozambique & Zambia • Morocco • North Africa • Read This First Africa • South Africa, Lesotho & Swaziland • South Africa, Lesotho & Swaziland travel atlas • Swahili phrasebook • Tanzania, Zanzibar & Pemba • Trekking in East Africa • Tunisia • West Africa • Zimbabwe, Botswana & Namibia • Zimbabwe, Botswana & Nambia Travel Atlas • World Food Morocco
Travel Literature: The Rainbird: A Central African Journey • Songs to an African Sunset: A Zimbabwean Story • Mali Blues: Traveling to an African Beat

AUSTRALIA & THE PACIFIC Auckland • Australia • Australian phrasebook • Bushwalking in Australia • Bushwalking in Papua New Guinea • Fiji • Fijian phrasebook • Healthy Travel Australia, NZ and the Pacific • Islands of Australia's Great Barrier Reef • Melbourne • Melbourne city map • Micronesia • New Caledonia • New South Wales & the ACT • New Zealand • Northern Territory • Outback Australia • Out to Eat – Melbourne • Out to Eat – Sydney • Papua New Guinea • Pidgin phrasebook • Queensland • Rarotonga & the Cook Islands • Samoa • Solomon Islands • South Australia • South Pacific • South Pacific Languages phrasebook • Sydney • Sydney city map • Sydney Condensed • Tahiti & French Polynesia • Tasmania • Tonga • Tramping in New Zealand • Vanuatu • Victoria • Western Australia
Travel Literature: Islands in the Clouds • Kiwi Tracks: A New Zealand Journey • Sean & David's Long Drive

CENTRAL AMERICA & THE CARIBBEAN Bahamas, Turks & Caicos • Bermuda • Central America on a shoestring • Costa Rica • Cuba • Dominican Republic & Haiti • Eastern Caribbean • Guatemala, Belize & Yucatán: La Ruta Maya • Jamaica • Mexico • Mexico City • Panama • Puerto Rico • Read This First Central & South America • World Food Mexico
Travel Literature: Green Dreams: Travels in Central America

EUROPE Amsterdam • Amsterdam city map • Andalucía • Austria • Baltic States phrasebook • Barcelona • Berlin • Berlin city map • Britain • British phrasebook • Brussels, Bruges & Antwerp • Budapest city map • Canary Islands • Central Europe • Central Europe phrasebook • Corfu & Ionians • Corsica • Crete • Crete Condensed • Croatia • Cyprus • Czech & Slovak Republics • Denmark • Eastern Europe • Eastern Europe phrasebook • Edinburgh • Estonia, Latvia & Lithuania • Europe on a shoestring • Finland • Florence • France • French phrasebook • Germany • German phrasebook • Greece • Greek Islands • Greek phrasebook • Hungary • Iceland, Greenland & the Faroe Islands • Ireland • Italian phrasebook • Italy • Krakow • Lisbon • The Loire • London • London city map • London Condensed • Mediterranean Europe • Mediterranean Europe phrasebook • Munich • Norway • Paris • Paris city map • Paris Condensed • Poland • Portugal • Portugese phrasebook • Portugal travel atlas • Prague • Prague city map • Provence & the Côte d'Azur • Read This First Europe • Romania & Moldova • Rome • Russia, Ukraine & Belarus • Russian phrasebook • Scandinavian & Baltic Europe • Scandinavian Europe phrasebook • Scotland • Slovenia • Spain • Spanish phrasebook • St Petersburg • Sweden • Switzerland • Trekking in Spain • Tuscany • Ukrainian phrasebook • Venice • Vienna • Walking in Britain • Walking in Ireland • Walking in Italy • Walking in Spain • Walking in Switzerland • Western Europe • Western Europe phrasebook • World Food Ireland • World Food Italy • World Food Spain
Travel Literature: The Olive Grove: Travels in Greece

INDIAN SUBCONTINENT Bangladesh • Bengali phrasebook • Bhutan • Delhi • Goa • Hindi & Urdu phrasebook • India • India & Bangladesh travel atlas • Indian Himalaya • Karakoram Highway • Kerala • Mumbai (Bombay) • Nepal • Nepali phrasebook • Pakistan • Rajasthan • Read This First: Asia & India • South India • Sri Lanka • Sri Lanka phrasebook • Tibet • Tibetan phrasebook • Trekking in the Indian Himalaya • Trekking in the Karakoram & Hindukush • Trekking in the Nepal Himalaya
Travel Literature: In Rajasthan • Shopping for Buddhas • The Age Of Kali

LONELY PLANET

Mail Order

Lonely Planet products are distributed worldwide. They are also available by mail order from Lonely Planet, so if you have difficulty finding a title please write to us. North and South American residents should write to 150 Linden St, Oakland CA 94607, USA; European and African residents should write to 10a Spring Place, London, NW5 3BH, UK; and residents of other countries to Locked Bag 1, Footscray, Victoria 3011, Australia.

ISLANDS OF THE INDIAN OCEAN Madagascar & Comoros • Maldives • Mauritius, Réunion & Seychelles

MIDDLE EAST & CENTRAL ASIA Bahrain, Kuwait & Qatar • Central Asia • Central Asia phrasebook • Dubai • Hebrew phrasebook • Iran • Israel & the Palestinian Territories • Israel & the Palestinian Territories travel atlas • Istanbul • Istanbul City Map • Istanbul to Cairo on a shoestring • Jerusalem • Jerusalem City Map • Jordan • Jordan, Syria & Lebanon travel atlas • Lebanon • Middle East • Oman & the United Arab Emirates • Syria • Turkey • Turkey travel atlas • Turkish phrasebook • World Food Turkey • Yemen
Travel Literature: The Gates of Damascus • Kingdom of the Film Stars: Journey into Jordan • Black on Black: Iran Revisited

NORTH AMERICA Alaska • Backpacking in Alaska • Baja California • California & Nevada • California Condensed • Canada • Chicago • Chicago city map • Deep South • Florida • Hawaii • Honolulu • Las Vegas • Los Angeles • Miami • New England • New Orleans • New York City • New York city map • New York Condensed • New York, New Jersey & Pennsylvania • Oahu • Pacific Northwest USA • Puerto Rico • Rocky Mountain • San Francisco • San Francisco city map • Seattle • Southwest USA • Texas • USA • USA phrasebook • Vancouver • Washington, DC & the Capital Region • Washington DC city map
Travel Literature: Drive Thru America

NORTH-EAST ASIA Beijing • Cantonese phrasebook • China • Hong Kong • Hong Kong city map • Hong Kong, Macau & Guangzhou • Japan • Japanese phrasebook • Japanese audio pack • Korea • Korean phrasebook • Kyoto • Mandarin phrasebook • Mongolia • Mongolian phrasebook • Seoul • South-West China • Taiwan • Tokyo
Travel Literature: Lost Japan • In Xanadu

SOUTH AMERICA Argentina, Uruguay & Paraguay • Bolivia • Brazil • Brazilian phrasebook • Buenos Aires • Chile & Easter Island • Chile & Easter Island travel atlas • Colombia • Ecuador & the Galapagos Islands • Healthy Travel Central & South America • Latin American Spanish phrasebook • Peru • Quechua phrasebook • Rio de Janeiro • Rio de Janeiro city map • South America on a shoestring • Trekking in the Patagonian Andes • Venezuela
Travel Literature: Full Circle: A South American Journey

SOUTH-EAST ASIA Bali & Lombok • Bangkok • Bangkok city map • Burmese phrasebook • Cambodia • Hanoi • Healthy Travel Asia & India • Hill Tribes phrasebook • Ho Chi Minh City • Indonesia • Indonesia's Eastern Islands • Indonesian phrasebook • Indonesian audio pack • Jakarta • Java • Laos • Lao phrasebook • Laos travel atlas • Malay phrasebook • Malaysia, Singapore & Brunei • Myanmar (Burma) • Philippines • Pilipino (Tagalog) phrasebook • Read This First Asia & India • Singapore • South-East Asia on a shoestring • South-East Asia phrasebook • Thailand • Thailand's Islands & Beaches • Thailand travel atlas • Thai phrasebook • Thai audio pack • Vietnam • Vietnamese phrasebook • Vietnam travel atlas • World Food Thailand • World Food Vietnam

ALSO AVAILABLE: Antarctica • The Arctic • Brief Encounters: Stories of Love, Sex & Travel • Chasing Rickshaws • Lonely Planet Unpacked • Not the Only Planet: Travel Stories from Science Fiction • Sacred India • Travel with Children • Traveller's Tales

LONELY PLANET

You already know that Lonely Planet produces more than this one guidebook, but you might not be aware of the other products we have on this region. Here is a selection of titles which you may want to check out as well:

Read this First Asia & India
ISBN 1 86450 049 2
US$14.99 • UK£8.99 • 99FF

Healthy Travel Asia & India
ISBN 1 86450 051 4
US$5.95 • UK£3.99 • 39FF

South-West China
ISBN 0 86442 596 1
US$19.95 • UK£12.99 • 160FF

China
ISBN 0 86442 755 7
US$29.99 • UK£17.99 • 199FF

Hong Kong Macau & Guangzhou
ISBN 0 86442 584 8
US$15.95 • UK£9.99 • 120FF

Beijing
ISBN 1 86450 144 8
US$14.99 • UK£8.99 • 109FF

Mandarin phrasebook
ISBN 0 86442 652 6
US$7.95 • UK£4.50 • 50FF

Available wherever books are sold.

Index

Text

Bold indicates maps.

Boxed Text

MAP 1 SHANGHAI AREA 上海

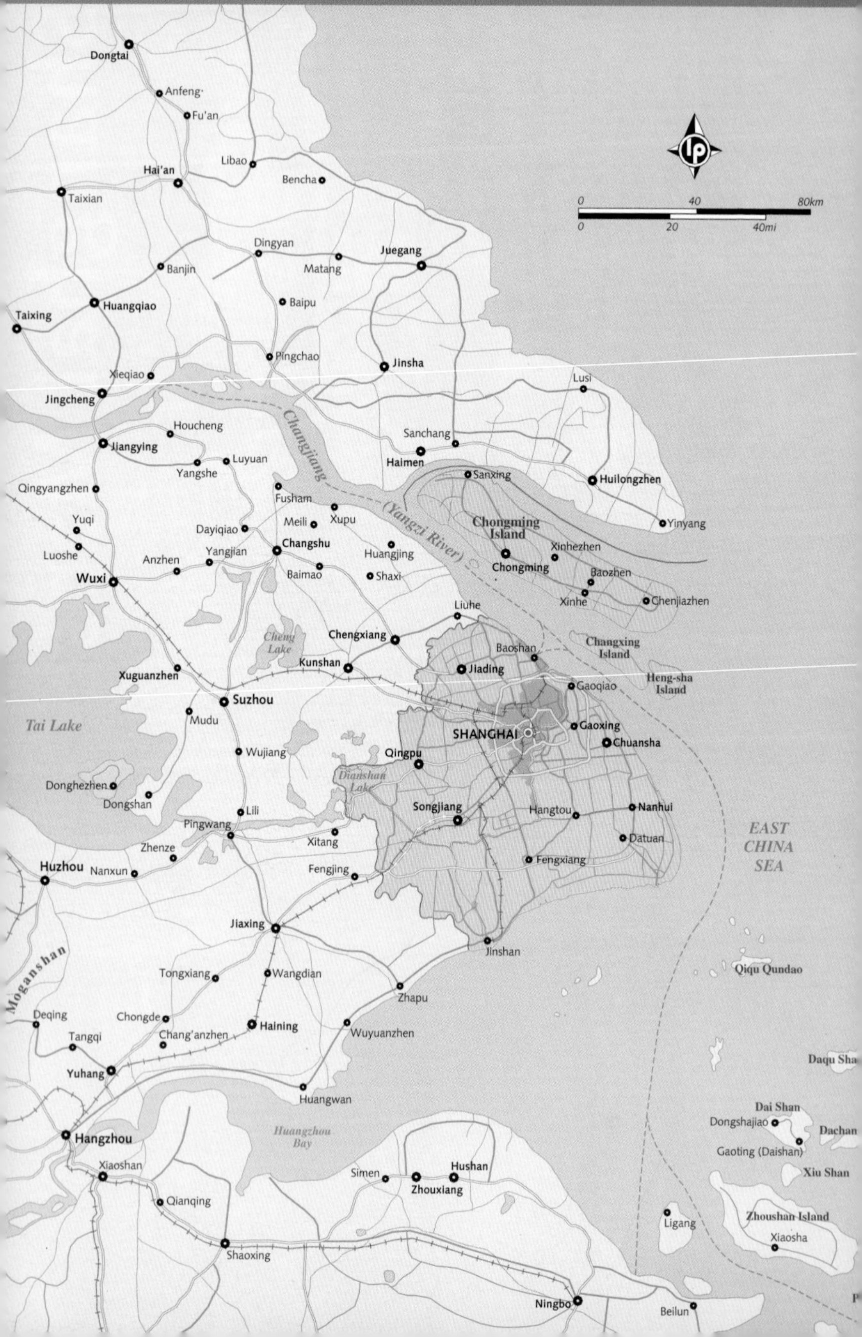

0
40
80km
0
20
40mi
Dongtai
Anfeng
Fu'an
Libao
Hai'an
Bencha
Taixian
Dingyan
Juegang
Matang
Banjin
Baipu
Huangqiao
Taixing
Pingchao
Jinsha
Xieqiao
Jingcheng
Lusi
Houcheng
Changjiang
Sanchang
Jiangying
Haimen
Luyuan
Yangshe
Sanxing
Huilongzhen
Qingyangzhen
Fusham
Xupu
(Yangzi River)
Chongming Island
Yinyang
Yuqi
Meili
Dayiqiao
Changshu
Xinhezhen
Luoshe
Anzhen
Yangjian
Huangjing
Chongming
Baozhen
Wuxi
Baimao
Shaxi
Xinhe
Chenjiazhen
Liuhe
Cheng Lake
Chengxiang
Baoshan
Changxing Island
Kunshan
Jiading
Heng-sha Island
Xuguanzhen
Gaoqiao
Suzhou
Tai Lake
Mudu
Gaoxing
SHANGHAI
Chuansha
Wujiang
Qingpu
Dianshan Lake
Donghezhen
Dongshan
Lili
Songjiang
Hangtou
Nanhui
Pingwang
EAST CHINA SEA
Xitang
Datuan
Zhenze
Fengxiang
Huzhou
Nanxun
Fengjing
Jiaxing
Jinshan
Moganshan
Tongxiang
Wangdian
Qiqu Qundao
Zhapu
Deqing
Chongde
Haining
Chang'anzhen
Wuyuanzhen
Tangqi
Yuhang
Daqu Sha
Huangwan
Dai Shan
Dongshajiao
Dachan
Hangzhou
Huangzhou Bay
Gaoting (Daishan)
Xiaoshan
Hushan
Xiu Shan
Simen
Zhouxiang
Qianqing
Ligang
Zhoushan Island
Xiaosha
Shaoxing
Ningbo
Beilun

Haimen

Sanching

Sanxing

Huilongzhen
(Qidong)

Yujiacun

Yinyang

**Chongming
Island**

Changjiang (Yangzi River)

Chongming

Xinhezhen

Baozhen
Xinhe

Chenjiazhen

JIADING

Baoshan

Jiading

BAOSHAN

**Changxing
Island**

Gaoqiao

American
Dream
Park

Wusong

Gongqing
Forest Park

**Hengsha
Island**

Nanxiang

**SHANGHAI
CITY**

River

Gaoxing

QINGPU

Hongqiao
Airport

**PUDONG
NEW
AREA**

Chuansha

Qingpu

Water Sports
Centre

_Dianshan
Lake_

Zhoujiaji

Sheshan

Jinjiang
Amusement
Park

Golden Cinema
Friendship

Sijing

Pudong
International
Airport

Grand View
Garden

Huzhu Pagoda

MINHANG

NANHUI

Shanghai
Wild
Animal
Park

Nanhui

Sun Island

Songjiang

Chedun

Datuan

SONGJIANG

FENGXIAN

Fengxiang

Nicheng

JINSHAN

_EAST
CHINA
SEA_

Jinshan

0   10   20km
0   5   10mi

To Putuoshan
(80km)

MAP 3 SHANGHAI CITY 上海市中心

Jiangwan Lu

Shuidian Lu
Liuying Lu
T1
T2
Dongtiyuhuo Lu

Dalian Xilu
Hongkou

Xibaoxing Lu
Bellu
Hongkou Park
Dalian Lu
Kongjiang Lu
Jianqpu Lu

ngshan Lu
Linqing Lu
Siping Lu
Heping Park
Zhoujiazui Lu

Zhabel
Zhongxing Lu
Changyang Lu
2
1

Yangpu Bridge

Map 5 Huangpu & Pudong

Tianmu Donglu
T5
Dongdaming Lu
Yangshupu Lu

River

Xizang Bellu
Wusong Lu
Huangpu

Huangpu
Pudong Dadao

M16
Nanjing Donglu
M17
Zhongshan Dong Yilu
M18
Lujiazui Lu
M19
Dongfang Lu
Zhangyang Lu

M12
M3
Yan'an Donglu
Central Ave
36
34 35
M20 (Shiji Dadao)
33
M21

Pudong New Area

Map 7 South East Shanghai

Dongfang Dong Elu
31 32
30
M4
Dongfu Lu
Zhongfu Lu
29
M22

Luwan
Lujiabang Lu
Nanshi
Pudong Nanlu

Xujiahui Lu
Pujian Lu

Luban Lu
Zhongshan Nanlu
M23

Zhongshan Nan Yilu

Central Park

Huangpu River

Pudong Nanlu
Pusan Lu

Chuanyang Canal

0   1   2km
0   0.5   1mi

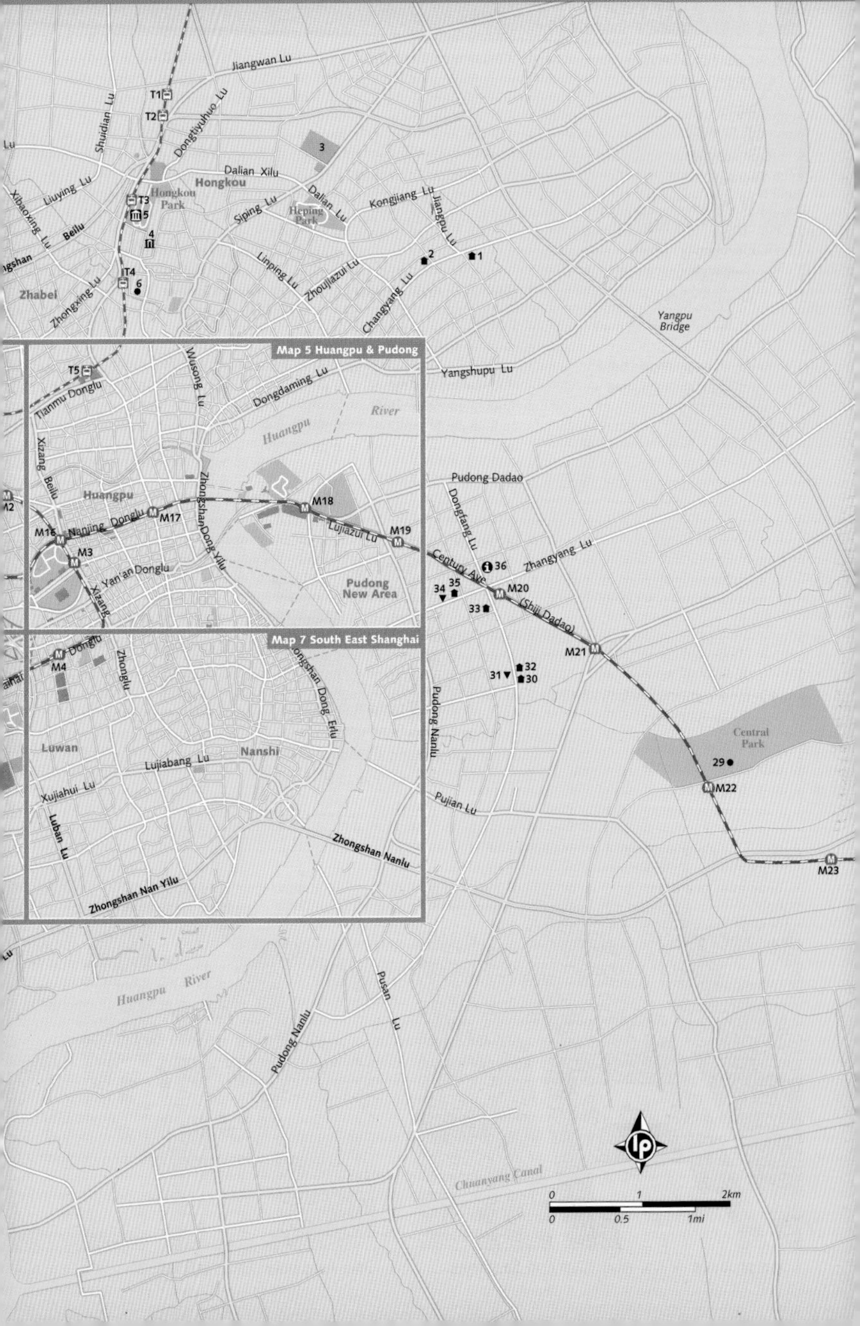

MAP 3 SHANGHAI CITY

PLACES TO STAY

1 Changyang
Hotel
长阳饭店
2 Shizeyuan
Hotel
师泽园宾馆
10 East China Normal
University; The
International Exchange
Service Centre
华东师大；国际交流
服务中心
14 Shanghai Worldfield
Convention Centre &
Hotel
上海光大会展中心
国际大酒店
15 Marriott
16 Zoo Guest
House
动物园招待所
17 Cypress Hotel; Blues &
Jazz Garden Bar
龙柏饭店
18 Hotel Nikko Longbai
日航龙柏大酒店
19 International Airport Hotel;
Bank of China
国际机场宾馆；中国银行
20 Huamao Hotel
华贸宾馆

27 Longhua Hotel;
Longhua Restaurant
龙华宾馆；龙华饭店
30 Hotel Nikko Pudong
上海中油日航大酒店
32 Holiday Inn Pudong
上海浦东假日酒店
33 Purple Mountain
Hotel
紫金山大酒店
35 New Asia Tomson
Hotel
新亚汤臣大酒店

PLACES TO EAT

24 Glenmore Deli
悉谊食品商行
31 Roxy Music Bar & Grill
34 Melrose Pizza
美罗思

OTHER

3 Tongji University;
German Centre
同济大学
4 Former Residence of
Lu Xun
鲁迅故居
5 Lu Xun Museum & Tomb;
Hongkou Stadium;
Masterhand Climbing Club
鲁迅陵；虹口足球场

6 Duolun Lu
Cultural Street
多伦文化名人街
7 Shanghai Circus
World
上海马戏城
8 Long Distance Bus
Station
长途汽车站
9 Jingdezhen Ceramics
Gallery
景德镇陶瓷上海艺术中心
11 Aquaria 21
长风海洋世界
12 Fundazzle; Weicheng
Piantball Centre
翻斗乐；伟成彩弹中心
13 Buckingham Bowling
Centre
21 Kang-Da Antique
Furniture Factory
康达古典家具厂
22 Zhong Zhong Antique
Furniture
中中古典家具商行
23 Shanghai Normal
University
上海师范大学
25 Longhua Hospital
龙华中医
26 Longhua Temple
龙华寺

Local produce: VWs, Audi100s and Santanas.

Bike lane only: bikes still rule Shanghai's roads.

MAP 3 SHANGHAI CITY

28 Longhua Pagoda
龙华塔

29 Huamu Tourism Zone
花木旅游区

36 Tourist Information and
Service Centre
旅游咨询服务中心

METRO STATIONS

M1 Hanzhong Lu
汉中路

M2 Xinzha Lu
新闸路

M3 People's Square
人民广场

M4 Huangpi Nanlu
黄陂南路

M5 Shaanxi Nanlu
陕西南路

M6 Changshu Lu
常熟路

M7 Hengshan Lu
衡山路

M8 Xujiahui
徐家汇

M9 Shanghai
Stadium
上海体育场

M10 Caobao Lu
漕宝路

M11 Xinlonghua
新龙华

M12 Zhongshan Park
中山公园

M13 Jiangsu Lu
江苏路

M14 Jing'an Temple
静安寺

M15 Shimen Yilu
石门一路

M16 Renmin Park
人民公园

M17 Henan Zhonglu
河南中路

M18 Lujiazui
陆家嘴

M19 Dongchang Lu
东昌路

M20 Dongfang Lu
东方路

M21 Yanggao
Nanlu
杨高南路

M22 Central Park
中央公园

M23 Longyang Lu
龙阳路

LIGHTRAIL STATIONS

T1 Wenshui Donglu
汶水东路站

T2 Shangnong
Xincun/Chifeng Lu
赤峰路站

T3 Hongkou
Stadium
虹口足球场站

T4 Baoxing Lu
宝兴路站

T5 Baoshan Lu
宝山路站

T7 Zhongtan Lu
中潭路站

T8 ZhenpingLu/
Zhenhuan Lu
镇坪路站

T9 Caoyang Lu
曹杨路站

T10 Jinshajiang Lu
金沙江路

T11 Changning Lu
长宁路

T12 Yan'an Xilu
延安西路

T13 Hongqiao Lu
虹桥西路

T14 Yishan Lu
宜山路站

T15 Caoxi Lu
漕溪路站

T16 Longcao Lu
龙漕路站

T17 Shilong Lu
石龙路站

T18 Caohejing
漕河泾站

Parking Shanghai-style.

MAP 4 JING'AN 静安

Shiquan Lu

Zhenping Lu/
Zhenhuan Lu
镇坪路站

Panjiawa

Guangxin Lu

Zhongshan Beilu

中山北路

Moganshan Lu

1

Aomen Lu

Yichang Lu

Shanxi Beilu

Putuo Park
普陀公园

Xikang Lu

Aomen Lu

Putuo Lu

Changshou Lu 常熟

Changde Lu

Shanxi

Jianqingbao Lu

Changhua Lu

Beilu

Dongxin Lu

LP

Xinhui Lu

11
12

近宁路

Shanxi Beilu

0   250   500m

0   250   500yds

Xinhui Lu

Anyuan Lu

Guangfu Xilu

Changshou Lu 常熟路

Haifang Lu

Wuning Lu

武宁路

Changping Lu

Jiaozhou Lu

Changde Lu

Kangding Lu

Jing'a

Kuyao Lu

Yanping Lu

Kanding Lu

Wanhun He

Xinzha Lu 新闸路

Wanhangdou Lu

万航渡路

Wuding Xilu

Jiaozhou Lu

Ch

47

Zhongxing Lu

Hutai Lu

Zhonghua Xilu

Jiatong Lu

Zhongxing Lu

Shanghai
Train Station

Shanghai Train
Station
上海火车站

Yongxing Lu

Gongho Xilu

Datong Lu

Hengfeng Lu

2

3

4

8

5

7

6

9

Tianmu Xilu 排挂课秤

Tianmu Zhonglu

10

Wusong

Wuzhen Lu

Datong Lu

Jinyuan Lu

13

14

Hanzhong Lu
汉中路

15

River

Changping Lu

Daguan Lu

Xinzha
Lu
新闸路

Xinzhao Lu

Chengdu Beilu 成都北路

Huangpu

16

Xinzha Lu

Shanghaiguan Lu

Wuding Lu

17

Shimen Erlu 石门二路

Beijing Xilu 北京西路

Fengyang Lu

18

Xinzha Lu 新闸路

19

20

21 22

Shimen
Yilu
石门一路

Nanjing Xilu 南京西路

28 29

23

24

25

26

27

30

31

32

35

34

Shimen Yilu 石门一路

33

Weihai Lu

Nanyang Lu

41

Beijing Xilu 北京西路

36

38 37

45

42 43

40

39

Tongren Lu

Shaanxi Lu

Maoming Beilu

Taixing Lu

46

44

MAP 4 JING'AN

PLACES TO STAY

2 Longmen Hotel; Train
  Booking Office
  龙门宾馆；火车票预售处
5 East China Hotel
  上海华东大酒店
8 Holiday Inn
  上海广场长城假日酒家
10 Zhao'an Hotel
  兆安饭店
15 Liang'an Hotel
  良安饭店
24 Jingtai Hotel
  京泰大酒店
39 JC Mandarin
  锦伦文华大酒店
42 Portman Ritz-Carlton;
  Summer Pavillion; Tea
  Garden
  波特曼-丽斯卡尔顿酒店

PLACES TO EAT

9 Jiangnancun
  江南村酒家
11 Jade Buddha Temple
  Vegetarian Restaurant
  玉佛寺素菜餐厅
23 Sumo Sushi
  缘禄寿司
26 Green Willow Village
  Restaurant
  绿杨村酒家
27 Wujiang Lu Snack Food
  Street
  吴江小吃街
28 Restaurant Street
  美食街
30 Wuyue Renjia; Wushu
  Centre
  吴越人家；武术中心
31 Gongdelin
  功德林

34 Meilongzhen
  梅龙镇酒家
44 Bi Feng Tang
  避风塘
46 Malone's American Café;
  Irene's Thai
  马龙美式酒楼

OTHER

1 Disc Kart
  迪士卡赛车馆
3 Post Office
  邮局
4 Air Ticket Booking Office
  售票处
6 Bus to Pudong Airport
  至浦东机场的公共汽车
7 Kerry Everbright Shopping
  Centre; Jusco Supermarket
  嘉里不夜城
  佳世客购物中心
12 Jade Buddha Temple
  玉佛寺
13 Hengfeng Lu Bus Station
  恒丰路客运站
14 Wellness Club;
  Entertainment
  Centre
  健身俱乐部；娱乐中心
16 Jiangning Lu Market
  江宁路综合市场
17 Calm Wave
  青波康俱乐部
18 China National
  Publications Import &
  Export Co
  中国图书进出口上海公司
19 Former Ohel Rachel
  Synagogue
  犹太教堂
20 Shanghai Airlines
  上海航空

21 Majestic Theatre
  美琪大戏院
22 Shanghai Cultural
  Information and
  Booking Centre
  上海文化信息票务中心
25 Silk King; Alphagraphics;
  Yew Wah International
  Education Centre
  真丝商厦
  Yew Wah国际教育中心
29 Nanjing Xilu Stones and
  Curios Market
  南京西路奇石古玩市场
32 Tomorrow Square;
  JW Marriott Hotel
  明天广场
33 China Northwest
  Airlines
  中国西北航空
35 Westgate Mall; Park 'n'
  Shop; FASCO; Isetan;
  Studio City; The Gap
  梅陇镇广场；百佳超市；
  伊势丹；环艺电影城；
36 CITIC Square
  中信泰富广场
37 Post Office
  邮局
38 Jingdezhen Porcelain
  Artware
  景德镇艺术瓷器
40 Plaza 66
  (under construction)
41 CITS
  中国国际旅行社
43 Shanghai Centre
  上海中心
45 Gold's Gym
  金太阳健身中心
47 Yunfeng Theatre
  云峰剧场

BRADLEY MAYHEW

Detail of a socialist realist sculpture in Huangpu Park.

HILARY ADELE SMITH

Breathtaking balance of Shanghai's acrobats.

BRADLEY MAYHEW

Farcical fun at Shanghai's Great World.

BRADLEY MAYHEW

Avalokitshvara Boddhisttva at the Jade Buddha Temple.

MAP 5 - HUANGPU & PUDONG 黄浦、浦东

5

Huiwu Lu

Baoshan Lu 宝山路
宝山路站
North Railway Station

Wujing Lu

Hailing Lu

Wusong Lu 吴淞路

Zhapu Lu

Kunshan Lu 6 ✚

7 ■

8 ■

Tianmu Donglu 天目东路

Anqing Lu

Huaxing Lu

Shanxi Beilu

Kang'le Lu

Zhejiang Beilu

Hailing Lu

Sichuan Beilu 四川北路

9

Wuchang Lu

Changzhi Lu

Jinyuan Lu

Xinjiang Lu 新疆路

Fujian Beilu

Tangqu Lu

Henan Beilu

河南北路

Tiantong Lu

10 ■

Tiantong Lu

11 ⊟

15

Bei Suzhou Lu

12 ■ 14

🖥 13

Xitang Beilu 西藏北路

Qufu Lu

Tiantong Lu

Nan Suzhou Lu

Yuanmingyuan Lu

37 ●

Garden Bridge

Finish Bund Walk

36 🏛 Huangpu Park 黄浦公

Xitang Zhonglu 西藏中路

Xiamen Lu

Huangpu

Beijing Donglu 北京东路

Fujian Zhonglu

Henan Zhonglu 河南中路

Ningbo Lu

Tianjin Lu

38 ●

39 ■

41 ● 🖥 40

Xinzha Lu 新闸路

北京西路

Guizhou Lu

79 ●

80 ■

Zhejiang Zhonglu 浙江中路

Henan Zhonglu

Henan Zhonglu 河南中路 Ⓜ

58 ●
河南中路 Ⓜ
55 ●

48 ● 47 42 ●
46 43
49 ▼ 50 ▼

54 ●

53 ▼

45 ●

Beijing Xilu

88 ●

81 ●
82 ●
84 ● 85
86 ●
87 ●

89 ●

78 🏛

72 71
67 ●
74 ●

63 ●
59 ●
66 ●
62 ● 60
64 ●
68 ●
70 ● 69
65 ●

57 ●
Jiujiang Lu
56 ●

61 ●

Hankou Lu

52 ●

51 ● 44

110 ●

109 ●

111 ●
112 ▼

Zhongshan Dong Yilu 中山东一路

Sichuan Nanlu

Nanjing Donglu 南京东路

75 ●

73 ●

104 ●

77 ●
76
85

103 🏛
102 ●

105 ●
107 ●

106 ●
108 ●

113 ●

Start Bund Walk

Renmin Park
人民公园

Renmin Park
人民公园

People's Square
人民广场

96 ●

97 ●
99 ▼
98 ●

101 ●

100 ▼

114 ●
119 ●

118 ●

123 🏛

120 ●

90 🏛

91 ●
93 ● 94 ●
92 ●

95 ●

129 🏛
人民广场
Renmin Square

128 ● 127
126 ●

124 ●

125 ▼

121 ●

122 ●

Renmin Lu 人民路

Start Walk

Sanjiao Park

Wusheng Lu

130 ●

131 ●

132 ■

Huaihai Donglu 淮海东路

Jinling Donglu

Ninghai Donglu

Yan'an Donglu 延安东路

Fuyou Lu

133 🖥

134 ●

135 ●

136 ●

137 ●

138 ●
139 ●

Zhong

Joins Map 4

Joins Map 7

Wuhou Lu

Tangshan Lu

Shangqiu Lu

Dongchangzhi Lu

Changyang Lu

Dantu Lu

Gongping Lu

Lintong Lu

Yangshupu Lu

东大名路

Dongdaming Lu

4

3

2

1

Daming Lu 大名路

21

Huangu River

22

Jimo Lu

Changyi Lu

Pudong Park
浦东公园

35

34

33

Pedestrian Tunnel

32

Beihutang Lu

23

Liujiazui Park

陆家咀公园

Pudong Nanlu

Pudong Dadao 浦东大道

浦东大道

29

Liujiazui Lu
陆家嘴

31

Liujiazui Lu

M

24

Tiandu Lu

Qixia Lu

Dongchang Lu
东昌路

M

Pudong Nanlu

28

27

25

Zhonghyang Dadao 中央天道

中央天道

30

Riverside Park

26

Yan'an Donglu
Tunnel

Huayuanshiqiao Lu

Lanmidu Lu

Haixin Lu

Dongting Lu

Rushan Lu

Laoshan Xilu

6

Dingchang Lu

Ferry

145

Zhongshan Dong Erlu 中山东一线

Lujadu Lu

**Pudong
New Area**

144

Yangshou Lu

Ferry

Qixin Lu

Yangliang Lu

Zhennan Zhilu

146

147

MAP 5 HUANGPU & PUDONG

PLACES TO STAY

2 Ocean Hotel;
Revolving 28;
Donghong Hotel
远洋宾馆；东虹大酒店

4 Shanghai E-Best Hotel
上海一百假日酒店

7 Pacific Luck Hotel
金富运大酒店

10 New Asia Hotel
新亚饭店

12 Shanghai Mansions
上海大厦

14 Pujiang Hotel
浦焦店

19 Seagull Hotel
海鸥饭店

27 Grand Hyatt; Jinmao
Tower; Cucina; The Grill;
Kobachi
上海金茂凯悦大酒店
金茂大厦

30 Pudong Shangrila
浦东香格里拉大酒店

34 Shanghai International
Convention Centre &
Hotel
上海国际会议中心大酒店

42 Peace Hotel; Citibank;
Bank of China ATM;
Dragon-Phoenix Hall
和平饭店；花旗银行
中国银行；龙凤厅

43 Peace Palace Hotel
和平汇中饭店

58 Nanjing Hotel
南京饭店

64 Sofitel Hyland Hotel;
Hyland 505 Brauhaus
海仑饭店

65 Central Hotel
王宝和饭店

70 Seventh Heaven
Hotel
七重天宾馆

71 Changshenjiang Hotel
春申江宾馆

75 Hotel Grand Nation;
Xinya
南新雅大酒店

76 Yangtze Hotel
杨子饭店

79 Shanghai Railway Hotel
上海铁道宾馆

81 New World Hotel
(under construction)
新世界大酒店（在建）

85 Pacific Hotel
金门大酒店

87 The Park Hotel
国际饭店

102 Wugong Hotel
吴宫大酒店

109 Metropole Hotel; 80%
新城饭店；百分之八十

124 Dafang Hotel
大方饭店

132 YMCA Hotel; Gym; Train
Ticket Office; Post Office
青年会宾馆；健身房；
火车票预售处；邮局

PLACES TO EAT

9 Zhapu Lu
Food Street
乍浦路美食街

15 Wangzhexiang
Restaurant
王者香

16 U & I
亚拉餐厅

17 Haoshiji
好食家

24 Lulu Restaurant
鹭鹭酒家

28 Food Court Live; Pu-J's
食府；浦劲

29 Restaurant Plaza
陆家嘴美食城

45 50 Hankou Road Bar &
Restaurant
汉口路50号

46 Manabe Café
真锅咖啡

48 Gino's; CITS; Silk King
季诺意大利休闲餐厅
中国旅行社；真丝商厦

50 Donghai Café;
Zhongyang Market
东海咖啡馆；中央商场

53 Croissant de France
可颂

84 Pizza Hut; McDonald's
必胜客；麦当劳

88 Huanghe Lu
Food Street
黄河路美食街

98 Wang Baohe
Restaurant
王宝和

99 McDonald's
麦当劳

100 Xinjiang
Restaurants
新疆饭店

105 Xinghua Lou
杏花楼

112 M on the Bund
米氏西餐厅

114 Manabe Café
真锅咖啡

119 Croissant de France
可颂

125 Juelin Restaurant
觉林素菜馆

126 Yunnan Lu Food Street
云南路美食街

127 Chang'an Dumpling
House
长安饺子楼

135 Snack Bars
小吃店

136 Songyuelou Vegetarian
Restaurant
松月楼

139 Nanxiang Steamed Bun
Restaurant
南翔馒头

142 Green Wave Gallery
绿波廊

OTHER

1 Ohel Moishe Synagogue
(former)
摩西会堂

3 Gongpinglu Wharf
公平路码头

5 Shanghai First People's
Hospital
上海市第一人民医院

MAP 5 HUANGPU & PUDONG

6 PSB
公安局
8 Alliance Française
法国文化协会
11 International Post Office
国际邮局
13 Russian Consulate
俄罗斯领事馆
18 The Centre of Tea From
Home and Abroad
中外名茶总汇
20 MACH Mandarin
Consulting; American Club
汉通咨询; 美国俱乐部
21 International Passenger
Terminal
国际客运码头
22 Ferry
轮渡站
23 Senmao International
Building; Dublin Exchange
森贸国际大厦
25 Site of World Finance
Tower
世界金融中心
26 Yibo Gallery
艺博画廊
31 Cai Tai Riverfest Mall
正大广场
32 Oriental Pearl Tower;
Shanghai Municipal
History Museum
东方明珠广播电视塔;
上海市历史博物馆
33 Pedestrian Tunnel
Entrance
隧道行人入口
35 Boat Dock
码头
36 Bund Historical
Museum
外滩历史博物馆
37 New York New York
38 Railway Booking
Office
火车票预售
39 Friendship Store
友谊商店
40 Pedestrian Tunnel
Entrance
隧道行人入口

41 Bank of China
(main branch)
中国银行
44 Fest Brew House
菲斯特啤酒坊
47 Telecom Office
长途电信
49 Shanghai Musical
Instrument Factory
Store
上海乐器厂商店
51 Tropicana
52 Church of the Holy Trinity
三一圣堂
54 Guan Long Camera Shop
冠龙照相材料商店
55 Laokafook Silk & Woolen
Store
老介福绸布店
56 Physical Ladies Club
舍适堡女子健身美容中心
57 Jinguan Silk & Woolen
Store
金光绸缎呢绒商店
59 Duoyunxuan
朵云轩
60 Landmark
上海置地广场
61 Cambodian Consulate
柬埔寨王国领事馆
62 Museum of Ancient
Chinese Sex Culture
中国古代性文化展览
63 Cai Tong De
蔡同德堂
66 Shanghai Zhejiang Tea
Store
上海浙江茶叶
67 Guohua Chinaware;
McDonald's; KFC
国华瓷器; 麦当劳;
肯德基家乡鸡
68 Century Square
世纪广场
69 Tourist Information and
Service Centre
旅游咨询服务中心
72 Shanghai No.1
Dispensary; Shendacheng
第一医药商店;
沈大成点心店

73 Hualian Department
Store
华联商厦
74 Shanghai No 1
Department Store
上海第一食品商店
77 Mu'en Church; Shanghai
Spring International Travel
Service
沐恩堂; 春秋国际旅行社
78 One Department Store
上海第一百货商店
80 New Shanghai Metropolis
Flower Market
大都市鲜花港
82 New World
新世界百货
83 Shanghai Music
Store
上海音乐图书公司
86 Novel Plaza; Air France
永新广场; 法国航空
89 Shanghai Arts and Crafts
Shopping Centre
上海工艺美术商店
90 Shanghai Art
Museum
上海美术博物馆
91 Shanghai Grand Theatre;
Grand Theatre Tours
Office
上海大剧院画廊
92 Jiangyin Lu Bird & Flower
Market
江阴路市场
93 Central Plaza; Austrian
Airlines; Swissair; Canadian
Airlines International.
奥地利航空; 瑞士航空;
加拿大航空
94 Shanghai Grand
Theatre
上海大剧院
95 Shanghai Government
Building
上海市人民政府
96 Shanghai Urban Planning
Exhibition Hall; Bonomi
Café
上海城市规划展示部;
波诺米咖啡厅

MAP 5 HUANGPU & PUDONG

ERIC L. WHEATER

Man on a bench in Shanghai, a witness to the city's history and metamorphosis.

Bird fanciers discuss the finer points of their feathered friends.

A street scene outside the Yuyuan Gardens.

MAP 6 FRENCH CONCESSION 法租界

Joins Map 4

1

2

Wuting Xilu

Lu

3

4 M Jing Ten

静安

Jing Par

静安公

34

Yuyuan Lu 愚园路

Nanjing Xilu

33 32

M
Jiangsu Lu
江苏路

35

Wulumuqi Beilu

F
W

Dong Zhu'anbang

42

44

37

36

41

46

Zhengjing Lu

38

39 Huashan Lu 华山路

43

47

48

Yan'an Xilu 延安西路

40

Jiangsu Lu 江苏路

Amxi Lu

Lixi Lu

Changle Lu

0 250 500m
0 250 500yds

Wuyi Lu

134 Anfu Lu

132

129 Wuy

Zhaohua Lu

136

130

Ding Xiang
Garden
丁香花园

131

135

133

137

Fuxing Xilu 复兴西路

128

143

144

146

138

145

14

Pingwu Lu

Wukang Lu

141

140

142

Finish
Walk

Faiyu Lu

139

Xingfu Lu

168

169

171

Niugiao Bang

Huashan Lu 华山路

Xinguo Lu

Huaihai Zhonglu 淮海中路

Yongfu Lu

172 173

174

177

Wulong Lu

Hengshan Lu
衡山路

175

Fahuazhen Lu

176

178

Wenping Lu

Xinhua Lu

179

Hengshan Lu

186

190

180

181

Kangping Lu

Yuqing Lu

185 189

187 188

Huaihai Xilu

Tianping Lu

Gao'an Lu

182

Huaihai Xilu

183

184

Da Pu Qiao

Xiangyang Park

Start Walk

Shaanxi Nanlu

Fuxing Park 复兴公园

Changshu Lu 常熟路

Xujiahui Lu 徐家汇路

French Concession Walk 1 ⋯⋯⋯⋯
French Concession Walk 2 ⋯⋯⋯⋯

MAP 6 FRENCH CONCESSION

PLACES TO STAY

22 Jinjiang Tower; Blue Heaven Restaurant
新锦江大酒店

24 Jinjiang Hotel; FASCO
锦江饭店;

28 Garden Hotel
花园酒店

33 Hotel Equatorial; Air Macau
上海贵都酒店; 澳门航空

41 Shanghai Hotel; Shanghai Huating Overseas Tourist Company
上海宾馆

42 Jing'an Hotel
静安宾馆

44 Hilton Hotel; Lufthansa Airlines; Davinci's
上海静安希尔顿酒店;
德国汉莎航空

59 Donghu Hotel
东湖宾馆

60 Donghu Hotel (New)
东湖宾馆（新楼）

78 Jinchen Hotel; Watson's
金晨大酒店; 屈臣氏

106 Ruijin Hotel; Face Bar; Lan Na Thai; Hazara
瑞金宾馆; 兰纳泰;
哈扎拉

117 Conservatory of Music Guest House; The Conservatory of Music
外宾招待所;
上海音乐学院

138 Xingguo Hotel
兴国宾馆

164 Taiyuan Villa
太原别墅

179 Crowne-Plaza Shanghai
上海银星皇冠酒店

185 Hengshan Hotel
衡山宾馆

186 Regal International East Asia Hotel; International Tennis Centre
东亚富豪国际大酒店;
国际网球中心

188 Jiangong Jinjiang Hotel
建工锦江大酒店

PLACES TO EAT

5 Yuan Yuan
元元餐厅

6 Always Café
奥维斯

7 Manabe
真锅咖啡

8 Frankie's Place
法兰奇餐厅

17 Shanghai Drugstore
上海桂树岛食府

19 Dishui Dong
滴水洞饭店

23 Bi Feng Tang
避风塘

29 Taiwan Xiaochi
台湾小吃

37 Da Marco

49 Yellow Submarine
黄色潜水艇

51 Badlands

53 Cochin China 1883
欧越年代

56 Baoluo
保罗酒楼

61 Planet Shanghai; Hot Pot King
上海星咖啡屋;
来福楼

62 Pizza Italia
意大利比萨

63 Ooedo
大江户

64 Grape Restaurant
葡萄园酒家

66 Henry
亨利餐厅

67 Mos Burger
莫师

70 1931

73 The Gap
锦亭

74 Tandoor Indian Rest.; JJ Mariachi; Bookshop
印度餐厅; 书店

75 Quanjude
全聚德烤鸭店

82 Wuyue Renjia
吴越人家

83 Shenji Liang Tang
沈记靓汤

85 Mxc
麦香村

88 Sumo Sushi; Planet Café
缘禄寿司

92 Ten Ren's
吃茶趣

93 Häagen Dazs
哈根达斯

95 Ajisen Ramen
味千日本拉面

100 Park 97; ShangART
香格纳画廊

103 Shenji Liang Tang
沈记靓汤

112 Kathleen's
凯圣琳

116 Wuninosachi
海之幸

120 Manabe
真锅咖啡

122 KFC
肯德基家乡鸡

131 Gaoli
高丽餐厅

135 Xian Yue Hien
申粤轩

137 1221

148 Merrylin
美琳阁

149 Sumo Sushi
缘禄寿司

153 Sasha's; Mandy's

154 Simply Thai

155 Ali YY's

156 Paulaner Brauhaus
宝莱纳餐厅

159 Bi Feng Tang
避风塘

162 Zhang Sheng Ji
张生记

166 Nanling Restaurant
南伶酒家

MAP 6 FRENCH CONCESSION

167 Yang's Kitchen; Le Garcon Chinois
杨家厨房
168 TGIF
美国星期五餐厅
169 The Gap Café
锦亭
171 Pasta Fresca Da Salvatore; Sole Coffee
索列咖啡
173 Bourbon St
177 Bon Ami Café
184 Melrose Pizza
美罗思
189 Bai's Restaurant
白家餐厅
190 Keven Café
凯文咖啡

OTHER

1 Ozark; Ozark Climbing Centre
奥索卡；攀岩中心
2 Le Bouchon
3 Jing'an Temple
静安寺
4 Tourist Information and Service Centre
旅游咨询服务中心
9 Kerry Centre; Kerry Gym
嘉里中心
10 Copy General
西技图文
11 Shanghai Exhibition Centre
上海展览馆
12 Shanghai China Travel Service (SCTS)
上海中国旅行社
13 Moller House
14 Jurassic Pub
恐龙世界
15 Christ the King Church
君王天主堂
16 Wangpo Catering
18 Mandarava
曼陀罗
20 Lyceum Theatre
兰馨大戏院

21 Lyceum Jewellery and Antique Store
兰馨珠宝文物商行
25 Jinjiang Sightseeing Bus Stop
锦江旅游车站
26 JJ Dickson Centre
锦江迪生
27 J Gallery; Shanghai Jinjiang Tours
杰画廊；锦江旅游
30 Black Apple Gallery
黑苹果画廊
31 Snap Printing
时浪印刷
32 Old Manhattan Bar
34 Children's Palace
上年宫
35 China Eastern Airlines
中国东方航空
36 Huadong Hospital
华东医院外宾门诊
38 Shanghai Theatre Academy
上海戏剧学院
39 Air China
中国国际航空
40 Huashan Hospital; Pharmacy
华山医院；药房
43 Shanghai Yuanyou Culture & Art Co Ltd; Shanghai Yingzhen Corporation
上海缘友文化艺术品；上海寅峥工艺精品
45 Cai Yuanpei's Former Residence
蔡元培旧居
46 Raise the Red Lantern
大红灯笼
47 British Council
英国文化教育处
48 Passepartout; Made in Heaven; Arabian Nights
七俗八土
50 Manhattan Bar
曼哈顿

52 Woodstock Bar; Goodfella's
54 Chinese Printed Blue Nankeen Exhibition Hall
中国蓝印花布馆
55 Stanney Gallery
史丹妮艺术空间
57 Shanghai Ko Sei Dental Clinic
厚诚医院
58 101 Bar
101酒吧
65 Russian Orthodox Mission Church
俄国东正教堂
68 Parkson Department Store; Park 'n Shop; Gino's; Metro Station
百盛购物中心；百佳超市；季诺意大利休闲餐厅
69 Printemps
上海巴黎春天百货
71 Dennis Bar
豪名酒吧
72 Cathay Theatre (Guotai Cinema)
国泰电影院
76 Shanghai Huangshan Tea Co.
上海黄 讲杆豆
77 YY's
79 Tequila Mama
巴哈马村庄
80 New Hualian Commercial Building
上海新华联大厦
81 Harn Sheh
寒舍泡沫红茶坊
84 St Nicholas Church
86 Xianzonglin
仙踪林
87 Bank of China
中国银行
89 Post Office
邮局
90 Chang Chun (Luwan) Tobacco
长春食品商店

MAP 6 FRENCH CONCESSION

91 Shanghai Jewish Studies
Centre
犹太研究中心
94 Tourist Information and
Service Centre
旅游咨询服务中心
96 All China Native Products
and Specialty Foods
全国土特产食品公司
97 Isetan
伊势丹
98 Bu Yi Fang Tailors
布衣坊
99 Chun Shang Embroidery
春上艺品
101 Shanghai Sally's
上海故乡餐厅
102 Sun Yatsen's Former
Residence
孙中山故居
104 Zhou's Enlai's Former
Residence
中共代表团驻沪办事处
旧址
105 Ruijin Hospital
瑞金医院
107 Babisong Gallery
巴比松画廊
108 Thumbpoint and
Kangning Massage
Centres of Blind
Persons
大拇指盲人穴位指压按摩
109 Q's
110 JAL
日本航空
111 DKD
113 Judy's Too
114 Babylon
115 Cultural Square
Flower Market
花市地
118 Bank of China
中国银行
119 Silk King
真丝商厦
121 Chong Shin Old Arts &
Crafts Store
创新旧工艺市场
123 Huating Market
华亭路市场

124 Maison Mode
美美百货公司
125 M-Box
音乐盒
126 Post Office
邮局
127 Qihua Tower
启华大楼
128 Cotton Club;
Sunshine Café
棉花俱乐部;
申申阳光咖啡厅
129 Zhenjianzhai Antique
Shop
甄鉴斋古玩商店
130 Whitewave
Outdoor Gear
白浪户外用品商店
132 Shanghai Drama Arts
Centre
上海话剧中心
133 Eastlink Gallery
东廊艺术
134 Yonglegong (Paradise)
Cinema
永乐宫电影院
136 Time Passage
昨天今天明天
139 Sihai Teapot Museum
四孩壶具博物馆
140 New Ray Photo
Making Ltd
新之光摄影图片制作公司
141 German Consulate
德国领事馆
142 Shanghai Library
上海图书馆
143 Australian Consulate
澳大利亚领事馆
144 Singapore Consulate
新加坡领事馆
145 US Consulate
美国领事馆
146 O'Malley's
欧玛莉餐厅
147 George V
乔治五世
150 Hot Chocolate
巧克力爵音乐厨房
151 Shanghai CYTS
中国青年旅行社

152 Harn Sheh
寒舍泡沫红茶坊
157 Shanghai Arts and Crafts
Reserach Institute
上海工艺美术研究所
158 Old China Hand
Reading Room
汉源书屋
160 Golden Cinema Haixing;
McDonald's; Tops; Xinxin
Snooker Club
嘉华海兴影城; 麦当劳;
顶顶鲜; 新新桌球房
161 Museum of Public Security
上海公安博物馆
163 YMCA Bike Shop
(Wolf's Bicycle Club)
青年车行
165 Shanghai Chinese
Painting Institute
上海中国画院
170 Community Church
国际礼拜堂
172 Fragrant Camphor;
Real Love Disco
香樟园; 真爱
174 Hello Bar
哈鲁吧
175 Beni's Bar
贝尼咖啡屋
176 Song Qingling's Former
Residence
宋庆龄故居
178 Body Tech Gym
180 Goya
181 Shanghai Film Art Centre
上海影城
182 Jiaotong University; Gofly
交通大学
183 New Road Department
Store; Atlantic Health
Entertainment City
新路达百货; 大西洋保健
娱乐城
187 Giant Bikes
捷安特自行车
191 Velvet Underground
192 Shanghai Medical
University Children's
Hospital
上海医大儿童医院

A podium-perched policeman.

Shanghai is one of China's busiest ports.

The road layout near Nanpu Bridge.

Roads on top of roads at a busy intersection.

MAP 7 SOUTH EAST SHANGHAI 上海东南区

Joins Map 5

Jinling   Zhonglu

11
14   12
Huaihai Donglu
13
15   Start   Huaihai
19 18   Walk   Park
16   淮海公园
Huangpi   Start
21 17   Walk
20   黄陂南路

Start Walk

10 9   Dajing Lu   8
7
6 5 4
2   Zhon

Qinglian Jie

Fangbang

Fuxing Dong

31

Xicangqiao Jie
Zhuangjia
Jingxiu Lu   Jie

Menghua Jie

32
33
Wenmiao Lu

Peng'ai Lu

Taicang Lu
25   26
Chongde Lu   28   30
29

22   24
Xinye Lu   23
Zizhong Lu

Danshui Lu
Madang Lu
Huangpi Nanlu

Jinan Lu

Jian Lu

Xizang Nanlu 西藏南路

Renmin Lu 人民路

Jinsi Fang

Zhonghua Lu 中华路

Shangwen

34

Daji Lu

Xilin Lu

Dajing Jie

Jianguo Lu

Fuxing Zhonglu

Hefei Lu

Luwan

Dalin Lu

Jianguo Donglu

Yongnian Lu

Lujiabang Lu 陆家浜路

Liyuan Lu

Zhaozhou Lu 制造局路

Shunchang Lu

Xujiahui Lu 徐家汇路

Xiexu Lu

Jumen Lu

Huining Lu

Xietu Donglu

Nandan Lu

Mengzi Lu

Liyuan Lu

Mengzi Xilu

Baduan Lu

Nanlangbang Lu

Xinchaozhou Lu

Quxi Lu

Xietu Lu

Zhizao Lu 制造局路

Xilingjiazhai Lu

35

Zhongshan Nanlu

Zhongshan Nan Yilu

中山南一路

Tiedao Lu

Zhongshan Nan Yilu 中山南一路

Gaoxiong Lu

Joins Map 6

Joins Map 5

▼1

Dongfeng Jie

东路

Zhonghua Lu

Wakulangjie Jie

Guangqi Nanlu

Baidu Lu

Xundao Jie

Miezhu Lu

Maojia Lu

Zixia Lu

Weima Lu

Wangjiamatou Lu

Dongjiadu Lu 董家渡路

Nanshi

Nancang Jie

Duojia Lu

Lujiabang Lu

Zhongshan Nanlu 中山南路

River

Huangu

Dapu Dongjiu

Haichao Lu

Guohuo Lu

Yangjiang Lu

Fuhai Lu

Caojiadu Lu

Weifang Xilu

Pudian Lu

Jiaobaidu Nanjie

Tangqiao Xinlu

Tangqiao Lu

Pujian Lu

Pudong Nanlu 府家路

37 🏛

38 Nanpu Bridge

ish lk

🏛36

500m
250
0

500yds
250
0

39

Tangnan Lu

Jiaonan Lu

Nanmatou Lu

Sanliqiao Lu

Pudong New Area

Bangpongyuan Lu

Old Town Walking Tour ┄┄┄┄┄

Yinan Lu

MAP 7 SE SHANGHAI

PLACES TO EAT

1 Chenyonghe Inn
沈永和
4 Restaurants
饭店
6 Old Shanghai Restaurant
老上海饭店
13 Cafes
咖啡馆
25 Coffee Club, City
Supermarket
香啡阁；上海城市超市
32 Kong Yi Ji Jiujia
孔乙己酒家

OTHER

2 Old Shanghai Teahouse
老上海茶馆
3 Teahouse
茶馆
5 Amon's House
宝立书屋
7 Fuyou Antiques Market
福佑工艺品市场
8 Dajing Lu Produce Market
大境路市场
9 Dajingge
大镜阁
10 Wulong Teahouse
乌龙茶艺
11 Shanghai Square;
Dragon Air
上海广场；港龙航空

12 Times Square
上海时代广场
14 Lippo Plaza; Starbucks
力宝广场
15 Bank of China;
Hong Kong Plaza;
Cybermart
中国银行；香港广场；
赛博数码广场
16 Hong Kong Plaza;
Rojam Disco
香港广场；罗杰娱乐宫
17 Pacific Plaza
太平洋百货
18 CYTS; Shanghai CITS
中国青年旅行社；
中国国际旅行社
19 Hong Kong New World
Tower
香港新世界大厦
20 Shui On Plaza; Citigym
瑞安广场
21 Shanghai Central Plaza;
Delifrance; icafe
中环超市；德意法兰斯
22 Weald Outfitter
旷野户外用品专门店
23 Xintiandi
心天地
24 Site of the 1st National
Congress of Communist
Party
中共一大会址纪念馆

26 Bonne Santè
27 Shuguang Hospital
曙光医院
28 Dongtai Lu Antique
Market; Chine
Antiques
东台路古商品市场
29 GE Tang
集艺堂古玩有限公司
30 Flower, Bird, Fish and
Insect Market
万商花鸟鱼虫市场
31 Xiaotaoyuan
Mosque
小桃园清真寺
33 Confucian Temple
文庙
34 Baiyun Taoist
Temple
白云观
35 Shanghai Dental
Medical Centre 9th
People's Hospital
上海口腔医疗中心
（第九人民医院）
36 Museum of Folk Art
上海民间收藏品陈列馆
37 Bus Terminal
汽车站
38 Ferry
轮渡站
39 Ferry
轮渡站

HILARY ADELE SMITH

A child playing on the train journey from Nanjing to Shanghai.

Watching the world go by on the streets of Shanghai.

Dancing on the Bund in front of a statue of Chen Yi, the first mayor of post-1949 Shanghai.

MAP 8 XUJIAHUI & SHANGHAI STADIUM 徐家汇, 上海体育场

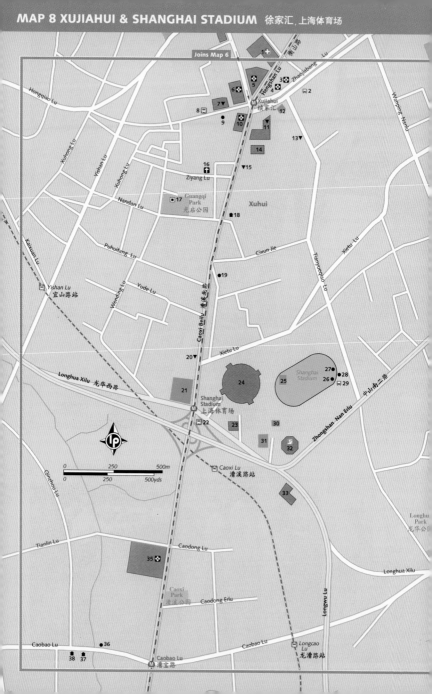

Joins Map 6

Hongqiao Lu

Xujiahui 徐家汇

Xuhong Lu
Yishan Lu
Xuhong Lu

Ziyang Lu

Nandan Lu

Guangqi Park 光启公园

Xuhui

Puhuitang Lu

Keiwan Lu

Yishan Lu 宜山路站

Wendıng Lu

Yude Lu

Cixun Jie

Caoxi Beilu 漕溪北路

Tianyuqiao Lu

Xietu Lu

Xietu Lu

Longhua Xilu 龙华西路

Shanghai Stadium

Shanghai Stadium 上海体育场

Zhongshan Nan Erlu 中山南二路

Shanghai Stadium

Qinzhou Lu

| 0 | 250 | 500m |
| 0 | 250 | 500yds |

Caoxi Lu 漕溪路站

Longhu Park 龙华公园

Tianlin Lu

Caodong Lu

Longhua Xilu

Caoxi Park 漕溪公园

Longwu Lu

Caodong Erlu

Caobao Lu

Caobao Lu

Caobao Lu

Caobao Lu 漕宝路站

Longcao Lu 龙漕路站

MAP 8 XUJIAHUI & SHANGHAI STADIUM

PLACES TO STAY

12 West Asia Hotel
西亚大酒店

18 Jianguo Hotel
建国宾馆

21 Huating Hotel
华亭宾馆

25 Regal Shanghai East Asia;
Topform Health Club;
Top of the World
富豪东亚酒店;
顶级健身中心;
东亚酒廊

30 Sports Hotel
运动员之家

31 Olympic Hotel
奥林匹克俱乐部

37 Huaxia Hotel
华夏宾馆

38 Shanghai Everbright
Convention and
Exhibition Centre
上海光大会展中心
国际大酒店

PLACES TO EAT

7 Hongji Free Plaza;
Pizza Italia
意大利比萨

11 Metro City; Pizza Hut;
Wujing Tang; Food
Junction
美罗城; 必胜客;
伍京堂; 大食代

13 Sumo Sushi
缘禄寿司

15 Gino's Café
季诺意大利休闲餐厅

20 The Gap
锦亭

OTHER

1 New Pioneer International
Medical Centre;
International Peace
Maternity Hospital
新峰医疗中心;
国际妇幼保健院

2 Bus to Pudong Airport
至浦东飞机场的公共汽车

3 Hui Jin Department Store;
KFC
汇金广场; 肯德基家乡鸡

4 Shanghai No 6
Department Store
上海六百

5 Pacific Department Store
太平洋百货商场

6 Grand Gateway; Heat;
Fire; Bridge St
港汇广场

8 Xujiahui Bus Station
徐家汇客运站

9 Foreign Languages Book
Store
外文书店

10 Orient Shopping
Centre
东方商厦

14 Pacific Computer
Square
太平洋电脑市场

16 St Ignatius Cathedral
徐家汇天主教堂

17 Tomb of Xu Guangqi
光启公园

19 Shanghai Film
Studio
上海电影制片厂

22 Bus Station
客运站

23 Tennis Courts
网球场

24 Shanghai Gymnasium
上海体育馆

26 SSC Carting
上海八万人赛车俱乐部

27 Ocean World
海洋世界

28 Pool Hall
撞球馆

29 Shanghai Sightseeing
Tour Buses
上海旅游集散中心

32 Shanghai Swimming
Pool
上海游泳馆

33 Ikea
宜家家具

34 Martyrs
Memorial
龙华寺

35 House & Garden
Superstore
好饰家超级购物广场

36 Shanghai Jade Carving
Factory
玉雕与地毯厂

The dazzling neon lights of Nanjing Lu attracting shoppers, diners, dancers and drinkers.

CHRIS MELLOR

MAP 9 HONGQIAO & GUBEI 虹桥、古北

Institute of Foreign Trade

Xianxia Lu

仙霞路

Ziyun Lu

延安西路

Honggu Lu

Gubei Lu 古北路

Zunyi Lu

China Textil Univers

Zhenshan Xilu 中山西路

16

17

15

18

14

Yan'an Xilu 延安西路

12

13

Yan'an Xilu

6

5

4

3

2

1

8

10

11

9

Shanghai Garden
上海花园

Anshun Lu

Hongqiao Lu 虹桥路

21

22

20 19

28

27

26

29

23

31

25

24

30

Shuicheng Lu

Yan'an Xilu 延安西路

Hongmei Lu

Hongqiao Lu 虹桥路

Gubei

32

33

0   250   500m
0   250   500yds

CHRIS MELLOR

The dome of the Hong Kong & Shanghai Bank.

PHILIP GAME

Customs House clocktower lights up the Bund.

MAP 9 HONGQIAO & GUBEI

PLACES TO STAY
1 Galaxy Hotel;
 Galaxy Disco
 银河宾馆；
 银河娱乐中心
2 Rainbow Hotel;
 Asiana; Bank of China
 虹桥宾馆；韩业航空
12 Westin Taipingyang;
 Emerald Garden;
 Giovanni's
 上海威斯汀
13 Yangtze New World;
 Korean Air; Dynasty;
 Chaozhou Garden
 上海扬子江大酒店；
 大韩航空
21 Hongqiao State Guest
 House
 虹桥迎宾馆
30 Xijiao State Guest
 House
 西郊宾馆

PLACES TO EAT
5 Gino's Café;
 Pasta Fresca Salvatore;
 Java Jive
 季诺意大利休闲餐厅
7 The Gap
 锦亭
20 Folk Restaurant
 鲜墙房
24 Pizza Italia
 意大利比萨

OTHER
3 Gesaiqing Studio
4 Royal Nepal
 Airlines

6 Friendship Shopping
 Centre
 虹桥友谊商城
8 Shartex Plaza;
 Nonggongshang
 Air Travel Service;
 Alphagraphics
 协泰中心；农工商国龙
 航空服务合作公司
9 Fanguzi Art
 Gallery
 梵谷子画廊
10 Maxdo Centre
 (under construction)
 万都中心（在建）
11 Sun Plaza; Dutch
 Consulate-General;
 Swiss Consulate
 太阳广场；荷兰领事馆；
 瑞士领事馆
14 International Trade
 Centre; Danish
 Consulate; South
 Korean Consulate;
 Indian Consulate;
 DHL; Post Office
 上海国际贸易中心；
 丹麦领事馆；大韩
 民国驻上海领事馆
 印度领事馆；
 中外运敦豪国际航空
 快件公司；
 邮局
15 Intex Shanghai
 上海国际展览中心
16 New Century Plaza;
 Drs Anderson &
 Partners
 新世纪广场；
 上海晏打臣公济诊疗所

17 Japanese Consulate-
 General
 日本领事馆
18 Shanghai Expo/
 Shanghaimart
 上海世贸展馆
19 Shanghai Suqu
 Furniture Shop
 述古硬木家具商行
22 Liu Haisu Art Gallery;
 Chine Antiques
 刘海粟美术馆；
 刘海粟美术馆家具
 经营部
23 Gubei Shopping
 Centre; Carrefour;
 Gino's; McDonald's
 古北购物中心；
 家乐福；季诺；麦当劳
25 Gubei Gym Club
 古北健身俱乐部
26 SB7 Bookstore
 外文书店
27 Elegant Art Gallery
 小雅画廊
28 Xianxia Tennis Centre
 仙霞网球中心
29 Gubei Flower & Bird
 Market
 古北花鸟市场
31 Alex's Antique Shop
 亦心缘古典家具
32 World Link
 瑞新国际医疗中心
33 International
 Cemetery; Song
 Qingling's Mausoleum
 万国公墓；宋庆龄陵园
34 Mandarin Centre;
 Fudan University
 复旦大学汉语中心

The opulent buildings of the Bund illuminated at night.

CHRIS MELLOR

MAP LEGEND

CITY ROUTES

Freeway .... Freeway
Highway .... Primary Road
Road .... Secondary Road
Street .... Street
Lane .... Lane
.... On/Off Ramp

.... Unsealed Road
.... One Way Street
.... Pedestrian Street
.... Stepped Street
.... Tunnel
.... Footbridge

REGIONAL ROUTES

.... Tollway, Freeway
.... Primary Road
.... Secondary Road
.... Minor Road

BOUNDARIES

.... International
.... State
.... Disputed
.... Fortified Wall

HYDROGRAPHY

.... River, Creek
.... Canal
.... Lake

.... Dry Lake; Salt Lake
.... Spring; Rapids
.... Waterfalls

TRANSPORT ROUTES & STATIONS

.... Shinkansen Railway
.... Local Railway
.... Underground Rlwy
.... Subway, Station
.... Lightrail Tram

.... Cable Car, Chairlift
.... Ferry
.... Walking Trail
.... Walking Tour
.... Path

AREA FEATURES

.... Building
.... Park, Gardens

.... Market
.... Sports Ground

.... Beach
.... Cemetery

.... Campus
.... Hotel

POPULATION SYMBOLS

✪ **CAPITAL** .... National Capital
◉ **CAPITAL** .... Provincial Capital

● City .... City
● **Town** .... Town

● Village .... Village
.... Urban Area

MAP SYMBOLS

■ .... Place to Stay
▼ .... Place to Eat
● .... Point of Interest

✈ .... Airport
❸ .... Bank
▣ .... Bus Terminal
❸ .... Castle
▣ .... Chalet
✚❶ .... Church
🚲 .... Cycling

◉ .... Golf Course
✚ .... Hospital
▣ .... Internet Cafe
※ .... Lookout
▲ .... Monument
▥ .... Museum
◙ .... National Park

▥ .... Onsen, Sento
▣ .... Pagoda
▣ .... Parking
✚ .... Police Station
▭ .... Post Office
▣ .... Pub or Bar
▣ .... Ruins

▥ .... Shinto Shrine
▣ ..... Shopping Centre
▣ .... Telephone
▲ ▣ ... Temple, Buddhist
▣ .... Tomb
❶ ... Tourist Information
▥ .... Zoo

Note: not all symbols displayed above appear in this book

LONELY PLANET OFFICES

Australia
Locked Bag 1, Footscray, Victoria 3011
☎ 03 9689 4666 fax 03 9689 6833
email: talk2us@lonelyplanet.com.au

USA
150 Linden St, Oakland, CA 94607
☎ 510 893 8555 TOLL FREE: 800 275 8555
fax 510 893 8572
email: info@lonelyplanet.com

UK
10a Spring Place, London NW5 3BH
☎ 020 7428 4800 fax 020 7428 4828
email: go@lonelyplanet.co.uk

France
1 rue du Dahomey, 75011 Paris
☎ 01 55 25 33 00 fax 01 55 25 33 01
email: bip@lonelyplanet.fr
www.lonelyplanet.fr

World Wide Web: www.lonelyplanet.com *or* AOL keyword: lp
Lonely Planet Images: lpi@lonelyplanet.com.au